*LEAVING THE GAY PLACE*

*Jess and Betty Jo Hay Series*

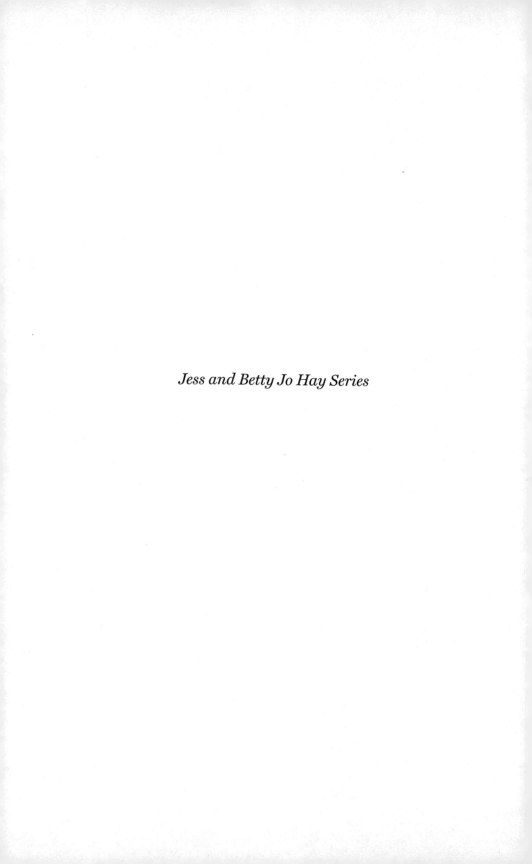

*Also by Tracy Daugherty*

NONFICTION

*Let Us Build Us a City* (2017)
*The Last Love Song: A Biography of Joan Didion* (2015)
*Just One Catch: A Biography of Joseph Heller* (2011)
*Hiding Man: A Biography of Donald Barthelme* (2009)
*Five Shades of Shadow* (2003)

FICTION

*American Originals: Novellas and Stories* (2016)
*The Empire of the Dead: Stories* (2014)
*One Day the Wind Changed: Stories* (2010)
*Late in the Standoff: Stories* (2005)
*Axeman's Jazz: A Novel* (2003)
*It Takes a Worried Man: Stories* (2002)
*The Boy Orator: A Novel* (1999)
*The Woman in the Oil Field: Stories* (1996)
*What Falls Away: A Novel* (1996)
*Desire Provoked: A Novel* (1987)

Tracy
Daugherty

# LEAVING THE GAY PLACE

## Billy Lee Brammer and the Great Society

University of Texas Press
AUSTIN

Printed in the United States of America
First edition, 2018



♾ The paper used in this book meets the minimum requirements of ANSI/NISO Z39.48-1992 (R1997) (Permanence of Paper).

LIBRARY OF CONGRESS CATALOGING-IN-PUBLICATION DATA

Names: Daugherty, Tracy, author.
Title: Leaving the Gay Place : Billy Lee Brammer and the Great Society / Tracy Daugherty.
Description: First edition. | Austin : University of Texas Press, 2018. | Includes bibliographical references and index.
Identifiers: LCCN 2017045676
ISBN 978-1-4773-1635-1 (cloth : alk. paper)
ISBN 978-1-4773-1636-8 (library e-book)
ISBN 978-1-4773-1637-5 (non-library e-book)
Subjects: LCSH: Brammer, Billy Lee. | Authors, American—20th century—Biography. | United States—Officials and employees—Biography.
Classification: LCC PS3552.R282 L43 2018 | DDC 813/.54—dc23
LC record available at https://lccn.loc.gov/2017045676

doi:10.7560/316351

*For Sidney, Shelby, and Willie,*
*and for my road buddy, David Turkel*

# *CONTENTS*

PROLOGUE

# *NEW FRONTIERS*

For two days, Dallas police officers had failed to keep the hallways clear or to provide a proper context for the interrogation of Lee Harvey Oswald. "Despite the desperate gravity of the situation, police security of the building was obviously extremely lax," recalled the FBI agent James B. Hosty, one of the interrogators. During a ten-hour stretch, from the afternoon of Friday, November 22, until early the following morning, Captain Will Fritz hoped to question Oswald without Hosty or anyone else present in his small office on the third floor of the municipal building. One-on-one with the prisoner, he might develop a conversational rhythm that would put the man at ease, but the clamor of reporters outside the office door thwarted any attempt at fruitful dialogue. As the Warren Commission later concluded, the "tumultuous atmosphere throughout the third floor made it difficult for the interrogators to gain Oswald's confidence and to encourage him to be truthful. As [Dallas Police] Chief [Jesse] Curry has recognized in his testimony, 'we were violating every principle of interrogation.'"

When Hosty arrived at the municipal building, less than two hours after Oswald had been transported to the headquarters of the Dallas Police Department, dozens of camera crews, television newsmen, and print reporters thronged the hall, jostling and shouting. Flashbulbs popped.

Microphones screeched. The Dallas district attorney, Henry M. Wade, estimated that early in the evening of November 22 as many as three hundred reporters jammed the building's third floor. The conditions were not "unlike Grand Central Station at rush hour, maybe like the Yankee Stadium during the World Series," Hosty said. He could not catch the elevator to the third floor because an ABC news crew had parked its heavy camera in it. He took the stairs instead. Recording cables ran crazily down the stairwell and out the building's windows, wrapping the structure in an enormous black web. "Initially no steps were taken to exclude unauthorized persons from the third floor corridor," said the *Warren Commission Report*. Then, for a few frustrating hours, police officers attempted to check press IDs. Any semiofficial card passed muster with them. They didn't have time to make telephone calls to authenticate credentials. Reporters had nearly free rein of the building. "Newsmen wandered into the offices of other bureaus located on the third floor, sat on desks, and used police telephones[;] indeed, one reporter admits hiding a telephone behind a desk so that he would have exclusive access to it if something happened," according to the *Warren Commission Report*.

Even worse, as Steven M. Gillon, a historian of the period, wrote, "anyone could have entered the building . . . and positioned themselves within feet of America's most notorious prisoner since John Wilkes Booth." At least twice, between Friday night and late Saturday evening, photographers and TV technicians recalled seeing a "stubby little guy" cut through the pack of reporters talking up a strip joint. "My name is Jack Ruby," he would say, holding out a business card. "I own the Carousel Club. This card will entitle you to be my guest." "At no point did anyone attempt to stop him or ask him for credentials," wrote Gillon. If someone wanted to harm the prisoner, it would have been a simple matter to fake press identification and pose as a journalist or even, as Ruby did, walk into the place with a knowing swagger.

The danger of an attack on Oswald was compounded by the Dallas Police Department's policy of cooperating openly with the press. Under no circumstances would Chief Curry consider restricting media access, especially given this case's high profile and suspicions, already rampant in the halls, that the cops would naturally want to rough up this kid who had apparently killed the nation's president. The only way to prove that no one was mistreating the prisoner was to let reporters see him often. Three times within the first seven hours of Oswald's capture, officers paraded him through the chattering mob. On one of these excursions, just before eight o'clock on Friday evening, he shouted he was a "patsy."

Security measures threatened to unravel altogether early Sunday morning. Chief Curry announced that Oswald would be transferred to the custody of the Dallas County sheriff. What time? reporters wanted to know. "If you fellows are here by ten a.m. you'll be early enough," Curry answered.

On Sunday morning, hundreds of Dallas citizens gathered on Commerce Street, across the boulevard from the municipal building, awaiting a glimpse of Oswald at the basement exit. Though officers had been instructed not to allow anyone but "identified news media representatives" into the basement, the "police accepted any credentials that appeared authentic," said the *Warren Commission Report*. Anthony Ripley, a reporter for the *Detroit News*, testified that he entered the basement and "was not challenged as to his identity"; James Standard, of the Oklahoma Publishing Company, told the commission he had managed to penetrate the area by exhibiting an old insurance card.

Billy Lee Brammer may or may not have had legitimate press credentials that day. It is certain he carried a credit card issued to him by *Time* magazine two years earlier. He no longer worked for *Time*, but he still charged expenses to the card. *Time*'s accountants either hadn't noticed this or hadn't caught up with him yet. In any case, they hadn't canceled his credit line, and it is possible that the magazine hadn't yet bothered to void his press pass.

But then, in spite of this being a clear turning point in his life, with publishers lining up to call him after the Dallas murders, it is also possible that Billy Lee Brammer wasn't *in* the municipal building on Sunday, November 24, 1963. Rather than deflating his mystique, this uncertainty seems to have enhanced it through the years.

"He used to *tell* people he was in the same building when Oswald was shot," his daughter Sidney said. The historian Steven L. Davis declared, "Brammer . . . was at Dallas city jail . . . where he witnessed Jack Ruby shooting Lee Harvey Oswald." "Oh yeah, I remember him talking about Ruby," said Al Reinert, a friend and former colleague. "Just knowing Billy Lee, he'd try to get there. Dallas was Ground Zero that day, and he was still a functional guy then." But another friend, Hugh Lowe, said, "It would surprise the hell out of me to find out he was part of the working press then. I don't remember hearing anything about Billy Lee doing any serious journalism during that period." Dorothy Browne, Brammer's second ex-wife, does not believe he could have been in the basement. Yet his first ex, Nadine Eckhardt, insisted he was a "trickster" who could well have slipped unnoticed into the chaos that day. "It would be just like him."

The story's drama as well as its uncertain provenance is familiar to anyone who has heard, even in passing, of Billy Lee Brammer. If you know of him at all, you know the Billy Lee Myth. If you don't know of him, it is not adding to his myth to say you may have an incomplete understanding of the dynamics of American culture in the late twentieth century. Billy Lee Brammer embodied those dynamics and was a catalyst for their dissemination.

The Billy Lee Myth begins with a fact: he was once one of the most engaging young novelists in the country, greeted by some critics as the second coming of F. Scott Fitzgerald. "Brammer's is a new and major talent, big in scope, big in its promise of even better things to come," wrote A. C. Spectorsky, a former staffer at the *New Yorker*. "[His work] has impressive sweep . . . it makes many of today's novels seem small, contrived, even mean." Brammer earned the $2,400 Houghton Mifflin Fellowship a year after Philip Roth won it for *Goodbye, Columbus*, and in 1961 he published a novel, *The Gay Place*, that David Halberstam, Willie Morris, and Gore Vidal, among others, considered a far more impressive achievement than Roth's debut. *The Gay Place* was "the best novel about American politics in our time," wrote Morris, and Halberstam called it "a classic . . . [a] stunning, original, intensely human novel inspired by Lyndon Johnson . . . It will be read a hundred years from now."

Johnson, for whom Brammer had worked when Johnson led the US Senate, was the *one* reader the book should not have had, according to the myth, for he was said to be so upset by the comic portrait Brammer had framed of him that he froze Brammer out of the White House and killed the biography Brammer had planned to write about him, destroying his confidence, snuffing his brilliant talent.

That is phase one of the Billy Lee Myth. Phase two claims—again, with some roots in fact—that psychedelia wouldn't have exploded in the American 1960s without Brammer's influence. This part of the story says the San Francisco hippie scene evolved out of a group of Texans transplanted from Austin, among them Brammer's pals Chet Helms and Janis Joplin. Since Brammer, fresh from consorting with Ken Kesey, was single-handedly responsible for turning Austin, Texas, on to LSD, the Summer of Love wouldn't have occurred without him.

In sifting facts from the myth, it is instructive to return to the basement of the Dallas Municipal Building at just after 11:21 a.m. on Sunday, November 24, 1963. Whether or not Billy Lee Brammer actually stood on the spot as NBC news reporter Tom Pettit shouted at the cameras, "He's been shot," in a broadcast carried live across the nation, "Lee Oswald has been shot . . . Pandemonium has broken out," and American history took a murky turn from which it has never completely recovered, Brammer stood at the center of the events. He had known John F. Kennedy; they shared a mistress. He knew the man who had just been sworn in as the new president. For years, he had endured Lyndon Johnson's rages, and he had enjoyed the man's difficult friendship. He knew Jack Ruby. In the days leading up to the Kennedy and Oswald assassinations, Brammer had stayed in the Dallas apartment of a friend who was dating a mobbed-up stripper from Ruby's club. On Friday afternoon, when Oswald fled the Texas School Book Depository after allegedly shooting Kennedy, he briefly returned to the house where he boarded, less than three miles from Brammer's parents' house in Oak Cliff, an area of Dallas that Brammer knew had always been a way station for the disaffected and the lonely. He had known dozens of Lee Oswalds growing up in that damned "jicky" place—"jicky" is what they had called it, meaning *crazy-sad*—and he could have told the interrogators a thing or two when Oswald wasn't talking.

"Billy Lee was always ahead of the game . . . He was cuing the rest of us what to expect," said Gary Cartwright, Brammer's friend and colleague at *Texas Monthly* magazine. In a vastly unsettled period, Brammer's gaze encompassed the whole horizon. He observed, more knowingly than anyone before him, Lyndon Johnson, who was "as personally responsible for American history since 1950 as any other man of his time," in the opinion of Ronnie Dugger, author of the LBJ biography Brammer *might* have written. And then "when the culture came a'callin', he was ready," said Brammer's younger daughter, Shelby. Brammer would become as important to certain segments of the sixties counterculture "as Ginsberg was to the Beats," said Kaye Northcott, a former editor of the *Texas Observer*. "They were both mentors, teaching the impatient how to cope with our imperfect world."

In 1960, as Houghton Mifflin was preparing Brammer's book for publication, one of his editors, Dorothy de Santillana, wrote him to say that "B. L. Brammer" would appear on the cover (eventually, the publisher settled on "William Brammer"). "No one, I repeat no one up here [in Boston] thinks 'Billy Lee' is possible," de Santillana said. "With all respect to your parents who gave it to you with such evident love (it is a very 'loving' name) it has not the strength and authority for a novel which commands respect at the top of its voice."

The names Kennedy, Oswald, and Ruby naturally occur to many of us when we think now of what was possible and what was lost in the last third of the American twentieth century. When we watch an old film clip of John Kennedy's acceptance speech at the 1960 Democratic National Convention, at which Brammer was present, drumming up delegates for Johnson; when we hear Kennedy's words, "We stand today on the edge of a New Frontier—the frontier of the 1960s, the frontier of unknown opportunities and perils, the frontier of unfilled hopes and unfilled threats," we think of Malcolm X and Martin Luther King, of LBJ ("How many kids did you kill today?"), of Robert Kennedy, Ho Chi Minh, Richard Nixon. Of Harper Lee and Gloria Steinem. Abbie Hoffman, John Lennon, Bob Dylan. Many others.

The new frontiers that opened up in the United States in the 1960s were personal as much as political—a familiar truism these days. Countless moments arose or were improvised for freedom from traditional restrictions and for destructive self-indulgences. From our vantage point, the real story of these new frontiers may be told most vividly now by studying the movements and companions of a hard-to-locate man with the improbable name Billy Lee.

PART ONE

# *RURAL ELECTRIFICATION*

# 1.

Folklore hung in the trees of Oak Cliff, on the troubled side of the Trinity River in Dallas. The trouble differed from block to block. In neighborhoods where empty blue Milk of Magnesia bottles topped the branches of sycamores and elms, the trouble was haints, and the lore spoke of healing and fear. "There could be a spell put in trees," Eudora Welty wrote in a story called "Livvie," about a practice common throughout the American South, learned probably from Creole slaves harking back to their West African ancestors. "Bottle trees kept evil spirits from coming into the house," Welty explained. The spirits were drawn to bright colors, the blue and green glass of containers whose slender lips had been slipped over the tips of bare limbs, shining, milky, in moonlight. Once the spirits were caught inside the bottles, they would burn to nothing in the morning sunshine. Wind whistling through the bottles at night bolstered these beliefs, as did the crash of shattering glass—like "cries of outrage," in Welty's evocation—when an Oak Cliff boy, bored on a summer afternoon, cracked the brittle spirit-traps by hurling rocks into the trees.

The spirits' lost companions, scattered body remains, posed other troubles, enflaming the listless boy's imagination. Trouble stories here often started with the river: frequently, oversaturated ground, muddy, smelling of ancient mule dung and bristling with bits of arrowheads, purged human bones in the neglected back acres of the Oak Cliff Cemetery, where, according to neighborhood lore, slaves had been buried before the Civil War.

But at least they had been buried. More recent tales suggested that evanescent figures existing between body and spirit, unable to rest in peace, floated all over Oak Cliff, in the river, in secret watery passageways underground. By the time Billie Lee Brammer was born, on April 21, 1929, Dallas's Ku Klux Klan Number 66, once the largest Klan chapter in the nation, had closed its headquarters. It no longer powerfully influenced city government and local law enforcement, but its narrative still echoed loudly in Oak Cliff, an area southwest of downtown Dallas and across the river from it. There, people "lived in a world defined more by the past than the present, more toward the country than the city, more Southern than Southwest," said Brammer's friend Grover Lewis, another Oak Cliff boy. As Horace McCoy, the first novelist to successfully describe the place, saw it in 1937, "This is an overgrown country town, filled with narrow-minded people, bigots—and they'll resent anybody who makes an effort to change conditions."

Reportedly, throughout the 1930s, the Klan continued to drop black bodies, some tortured, some half alive, halfway to haint, in the Trinity River Bottoms, a series of dirt levees littered with the tar-paper shacks of cotton-picking squatters driven by rural drought into the city. Stories abounded of "old lady seers" who would ask a person grieving for a missing family member to row them out in a boat or canoe to the middle of the river. Into the water they would toss a lost man's shirt. Wherever the shirt stopped floating was where the body would be discovered. The spirit was already dissipating in the evening fog creeping along the levees, toasted by the squatters raising bottles of homemade Choctaw beer.

The squatters had their own lore, a cache of stories about heroes and villains embellished each night under gnarled oaks twisting out of the limestone cliffs that shaded their burlap tents, their cooking pots, the quarries and lagoons they huddled among beside the river, lighted only by nearby oil refineries or dim bulbs attached to paper mill smokestacks. These people had been "coughed up by the dust storms of the 1930s and were among the first generation of Texas boys to grow up without the idea of the American West beckoning them to fortunes untold. By their time, America was 'all took up,'" said Grover Lewis. "The world beyond the horizon was nothing but dust and rumor." They longed to go "on the scout . . . running them old hard roads" like Clyde Barrow and Bonnie Parker, young bank robbers and killers who had nevertheless (according to the lore) come from "decent working families [and who] weren't half as sorry as 'the laws' sent out to chase them"—or as contemptible as "respectable" gangsters like Oak Cliff's Herbert "the Cat" Noble. Along with Benny "the Cowboy" Binion, Noble controlled most of Dallas's gambling interests and paid around $250,000 in bribe money each year to Dallas cops while freely murdering competitors' lackeys and throwing their corpses into the Trinity.

Lewis's grandfather, a "Snopesy little-jackleg-of-all-trades," Lewis recalled, was Bonnie and Clyde's "favorite bootlegger." Every Oak Cliff boy heard lurid stories about neighborhood characters like him. Tales of Bonnie and Clyde's escapades and the lawmen who tracked them—single-minded loners like Will Fritz and Texas Ranger Frank Hamer—were some of the first newspaper pieces Brammer read. He taught himself to read, for the most part, with occasional help from his parents, driven by restlessness, boredom, and an early hunger for stories. By the time he entered elementary school, he was already accomplished enough with language to know that, in Texas, he darn well better spell his name "Billy" rather than "Billie," as his folks had written on his birth certificate.

---

Brammer's father, Herbert Leslie, known to friends and family as H. L. or Les, was born in Missouri in 1893. Kate, Brammer's mother, was born in Texas in 1889 to a family named Coorpender. Brammer always referred to himself as a "menopause baby." As the child of older parents, he was doted on and left alone in almost equal measure. Hence, his frequent boredom.

His half sister Rosa was nearly eighteen when he was born, still living at home but spending most of her days out of the house, working full-time at a Sears, Roebuck store after getting her high school diploma. She was the child of Kate's brief first marriage to a man she never named or spoke about to her family; H. L. was the only father Rosa had ever known. Brammer's brother, Herbert Leslie Junior, had arrived in 1923. To avoid confusion with his father, the family settled on "Jim" as a workable nickname for him. Like his folks, whenever Jim was home he rarely left his baby brother's side, but he was often down the block playing with friends.

Brammer cherished the area folklore, but no figures haunting the ghost stories and crime tales peopled his immediate neighborhood. His parents' house, at 922 South Windomere, was part of a formerly middle-class, now workingman's, enclave, promoted before Oak Cliff's annexation in

1903 as Dallas's ideal suburb. Real estate brochures touted lovely Prairie School bungalows, Victorian and Tudor homes, and provided grandiose descriptions of amenities such as the steam-powered train connecting Oak Cliff to Dallas. It ran on the South's "first elevated railway," claimed the brochures—altogether untrue. And the track was elevated only briefly, when it crossed the river.

South Windomere was flat as a board. The house, a small three-bedroom with a single bath, sat by a vacant lot and a winding little creek, long dry. A large backyard spread behind it, brightened by the azaleas and rosebushes that H. L. tended with such pride. He built a screened-in porch out back, where he kept an extra fridge stocked with soda pop. He was a plain fool for Hydrox and Dr Peppers. He collected petrified wood. The rooms of the house were bracketed with his prize displays, along with Kate's antique furniture and scattered sewing supplies. In the evenings, the couple liked to play bridge with friends once they had put their boy to bed.

The greatest excitement in the neighborhood was to watch for the Oak Farms milk truck making its morning deliveries or to walk with Kate to Johnny Green's Ice House and plop forty cents on the counter for a hundred-pound block of ice to be brought to the house or to go to Elmer's to stare at the ceiling fans shaped like airplane propellers and watch the sparkling Sprite syrup trickling over ice chips in the ICEE machine. Many years later, Brammer recalled with shame how sometimes he and his friends threw rotten tomatoes at black kids they saw on the streets or in the alleys. Occasionally, neighbors gathered turkeys and hay bales in front of the nearby Methodist hospital for fund-raisers to keep the hospital running—such scenes replayed almost weekly when the Depression years threatened to close area clinics and stores. Local parks didn't stay open each day as long as they used to. Some of the public water fountains, both the "Whites" side and the "Coloreds" side, went dry. It was a miracle when the Texas Theatre opened, the first movie salon in Dallas built especially for the talkies, with a Burton organ, a water-cooled ventilation system, and a night-sky tableau on the ceiling featuring projected clouds and winking-light stars. Oak Cliff's universe had expanded, even if most folks' wallets were too thin to transport them there.

H. L. worked as a lineman for the Texas Power and Light Company at a time when vast stretches of rural Texas still lived in the dark. Dallas itself, second only to New York City in its swift embrace of electrical modernization, had not completely adjusted to its bright new path. In the 1880s, when the city made the wholesale switch from gas street lighting to arc lamps, local papers quoted Robert Louis Stevenson's sentiment that this was "nightmare light . . . such lighting should shine forth only on murders and public crime, or along the corridors of lunatic asylums, a horror to heighten horror."

In spite of the insect swarms drawn seasonally to arc lamps, Dallas business leaders believed the community's way forward ran on a line of electric current: "The lightning that [Benjamin] Franklin captured from the thunder clouds and imprisoned in a bottle is now made to order," declared the *Dallas City Directory*. To help convince the public, Mayer's Garden, a downtown saloon and one of the first leading establishments to install electricity, served free beer the night the lights went on. "Dallas must have the best of everything," the *Dallas Times-Herald* editorialized, repeating the city council's conviction that "electricity has superseded gas, as the mowing machine superseded the scythe. That is all there is to the question."

Plenty of skeptics remained. It seemed to some observers that thundershower activity had spiked dangerously in recent years and that it must be due to the copious amounts of electricity generated by dynamos along the river. Linemen were treated as a species apart, with a mixture of fear and awe. During the Trinity River flood of 1908, H. L. first admired the workers he would one day join. An electric plant on Flynn Street took on nine feet of water and stayed shut for nine days. Newspapers ran stories about linemen risking their lives to swim around the plant floor and salvage equipment. Afterward, many of the workers embellished their reputations as supermen by standing near plants' leather machine belts during public tours and absorbing static electricity. They told visitors that lightning coursed through their blood. They shook hands with the tourists, giving them a mild shock. The astonished victims spread tales about human torches roaming the flickering city.

If H. L. didn't have the cocky temperament to project himself as a superman, he nevertheless cut an impressive figure when he left the house in the morning, carrying his gaffs and arrayed in his spud belt, felt hat, and knee braces. His sons and daughter watched him proudly. Brammer grasped early that his father was a major agent of change, waving his wrenches and harnessing the power that brought the world, shouting, into the boy's room through the Crosley radio. As Brammer was learning to speak, his family listened each Sunday evening to *Texans, Let's Talk Texans*, a radio show sponsored by Texas Power and Light and broadcast on WFAA. The program played popular versions of classical music and proselytized the glories of conversion. Like a cripple commanded to walk, the Lone Star State would rise from its rural inertia with a burst of urban energy. "The city is coming to the farm!" the announcer proclaimed. From the turn of the century to the early 1930s, the number of kilowatt-hours generated statewide rose from half a million to nearly three billion. The darkness had been banished. No turning back.

As Brammer grew, voices and music riding hot night currents enticed him more and more. Knowledge filled the air from far away, he told his pals, penetrating people's minds with invisible revelations; every day, men like his dad refined the lines of communication, making more things possible than had ever been dreamed.

"We were ten years old and he knew 'everything,'" said his buddy Marjorie Stallard, whose father also worked for Texas Power and Light. "[He knew] that the poppies in the field across the street were used to make opium . . . that grammar was the most important subject in school . . . that he was going to be a journalist and see exciting things . . . that electricity was going to change farmers' lives."

He also knew from his father's suppertime talk that his father's bosses weren't thrilled when Congress passed the Rural Electrification Act in 1935. They feared that the federal government was trying to control their private business and would force them to build transmission lines in towns and on isolated homesteads, where it was not financially feasible to do so.

In 1938, Billy Lee Brammer first heard the name Lyndon Johnson. He didn't understand all the particulars of his dad's stories, but he sensed that Johnson had done something important. The congressman had interceded directly with President Franklin Roosevelt to get some action in his home district, reportedly telling the president one day in the Oval Office, "Water, water everywhere, not a drop to drink! Power, power everywhere, but not in a home on the banks of these rural rivers!" Exasperated, Roosevelt snapped, "Now, Lyndon, now what in the hell do you want?" Johnson explained that the voters in his district were strong FDR supporters and glad for the Rural Electrification Administration (REA), but they weren't getting the benefits of electricity because Texas Power and Light wouldn't relinquish its monopoly. He regaled Roosevelt with stories of how he and his brother, Sam Houston, had, as kids, toted water from a well far from their mother's house and heated it over a wood fire so their mother could do the wash by the light of a kerosene lantern. Touched, Roosevelt phoned the head of the REA. By the end of the year, Texas's Pedernales Coop had received a substantial REA loan and awarded Johnson's contractor buddy

Herman Brown an $800,000 transmission line contract. Almost overnight, Texas Power and Light moved two hundred men into Central Texas and started building parallel lines. Johnson crowed that farm women could "set aside their corrugated washboards and let their red hot cookstoves cool off while they iron on a hot August afternoon. The farmer who has been dragging water out of a well with a bucket all his life can . . . get himself an electric pump to do the work."

In the midst of the power company's activity, Brammer heard his father mention the "Milk Missionaries," marketing strategists who visited remote farmers to teach them the advantages of linking to the TP&L grid. The farmers, suspicious that these city boys had come to steal their freedom and spread macadam across their big green fields, often greeted the energy representatives with hefty loads of buckshot. Still, the sales campaigns succeeded in making country families dependent on electric coolers, ranges, irons, percolators, batteries, and lighting fixtures. No clearer record of the city's encroachment on the farm exists than the inventory list of an East Texas store that notes "one bird dog" was taken "as a trade-in allowance on a refrigerator sale." The residents of Hood County, southwest of Fort Worth, held a jubilee on November 13, 1936, to "junk [their] oil-burners for electric power." Over two hundred of "every type of kerosene-burning illuminators" had been discarded, according to the local paper; county officials awarded prizes to the "most ancient" lamps relinquished that day.

Families became so swiftly accustomed to modern conveniences that the slightest disruption along a transmission line became a cause for righteous anger: *Fix it pronto! I have laundry to clean! I have a cake in the oven!* The sight of linemen circling a dead pole and waiting cautiously for their work orders incensed citizens eager for their power to return. They wrote letters to the company, deploring the men's laziness. They had no clue how dangerous the wires could be, how much careful planning a repair required. In Texas in the early 1930s, one of every two linemen died on the job.

An article in the *Corsicana Semi-Weekly Light* in January 1947 detailed the kind of work H. L. had been increasingly called on to perform in the previous decade: "Although rough winter weather has cut deeply into a mile-a-day work schedule, the Texas Power and Light Company is prolonging construction of its new 132,000-volt high line from Trinidad to Hillsboro . . . H. L. Brammer of Dallas is construction superintendent [overseeing] 100 crewmen and truckers [and 100 men] engaged in clearing the right-of-way . . . cost of the project is expected to run into six figures."

Often, Brammer witnessed his father's heroics. Marjorie Stallard said her dad and H. L. took the kids with them on several projects. "[We] followed the electric lines and brought new life to rural Texas," she recalled. "The crews became 'family' and there was always drama and comedy and small towns to explore. We were in front row seats and didn't realize it . . . the world we knew would never exist again."

The crew would set up camp, usually near a railroad spur on the edge of a town, pitch tents and unfold army cots, or maybe construct a makeshift bunkhouse from cheap lumber. They would hang pulleys and clamps on steel hooks in the walls beside heavy leather belts. At the end of the week, an armored car would pull off the road and park among the tents. Two men with shotguns would get out to guard a fellow sitting at a table in the field and distributing pay envelopes to the linemen, sixty bucks here, eighty there, always in cash. The men would stash their scratch and suit up again, shouldering lines of copper wire or bags of assembly insulators, round porcelain discs resembling button mushrooms. Sometimes the men carried flashlights in their mouths.

Brammer, small and swarthy, easy in the sun, and naturally athletic, bragged to Marjorie that he could clamber up the poles as quickly as any of these skilled young fellows. As he watched them from the ground, he envied the dizzy tension he imagined they experienced between lightness and gravity, floating and falling. From up there, they could see the horizon in every direction. The skeletal H-frames, stark silver against the shallow blue of the sky, shivered and shook. Wind, whistling through gaps in the steel, razored the men's unshaven faces. It blew cigarettes from their fingers. Between the poles, in a chill breeze, you could almost see the sagging copper lines draw up like fiddle strings.

"You know what T, P, and L stands for?" Brammer would tease Marjorie. "Tug, pull, and lift."

The kids loved to watch the linemen in their off hours practice rope tricks, knots, and hitches (the scaffold, the cat's paw), and bowlines (the three-ring, the Spanish, the double). As part of their work, the men had to learn to throw a rope with such precision over towers and poles that men above them could catch it. This skill was also good for cowpunching; several of the men participated in county fairs in the small towns bound together by the new power lines. "They rodeoed on weekends and 'clum some' during the week," said Marjorie Stallard. She recalled listening to lonesome-cowboy singers warble at fairgrounds, gaunt men with thin guitars; and going with Brammer to the Fourth of July rodeo in Belton,

Texas, to watch "Shirttail Johnny"—a part-time deputy sheriff, part-time calf roper named John Bailey Mellon—herd steers with his cotton shirt whipping up dust all around him.

For both cowboys and linemen, preparation was the key to survival. It didn't always work out. Marjorie recalled watching, with Brammer, a "father/son pair who were climbers and the son got into hot wires and his dad went up and carried his body down."

Brammer told his friend that someday he would write about all this. In addition to the world-changing quality of the work, he was quietly drawn to what another novelist, William Wister Haines, saw as fundamental to the occupation: "Just as sailors disdain what seems to them the uneventful life of the landsman, so do the majority of construction linemen disdain the security and bondage of the permanent job," Haines wrote. "The natures that thrive on the powerful daily narcotic of danger and excitement so intrinsic in line work seem to require also the freedom to travel where the work permits."

So it was always a letdown for Brammer to return with his father to Oak Cliff after a jaunt along the lines. Back to Elmer's to see the ceiling fans go round. Or he could stand outside the Oak Cliff Broom Factory, on the corner of Bishop and Seventh, and watch the blind boys who wove the brooms come and go—their vacant stares reminded him of the dead eyes of the linemen who had been seared by sudden flares. Or he could walk down to the ball field by the river, Steer Stadium, where, said local lore, the first night baseball game in Dallas had been played, just a year after Brammer's birth, a game between the Kansas City Monarchs and the Dallas Black Giants, two teams from the Negro Leagues. Newspaper accounts of the game—pieces Brammer studied years later as he prepared to become a sportswriter—spoke in amazement of the size of the crowd, an estimated seven thousand spirited fans; of the impressive portable lighting equipment illuminating home plate; and of the most stunning vision of all, the thrill of joyous black bodies running free across a big green field.

# 2.

"Once upon a time in the real American West, which might have been anyplace people were uprooted, undefined or emotionally underfed, there was seldom heard a word of any kind. Even now, survivors dwell on that experience . . . remembered for its intolerable loneliness and the absence of all but the most basic human inputs," Brammer wrote in 1973, recalling how arid Oak Cliff had seemed to him as a child before he discovered the "miracle of radio transmission."

"We talked many times about how dependent he was on listening to radio," said his daughter Sidney. "He was absolutely fascinated by the many different things one could hear. He was obsessively familiar with radio preachers, advertisements, politicians, hillbilly and R & B artists, and even western swing fiddlers and Mexican orquestras. Like many bored teenagers, he listened almost *constantly*."

The best part for him, as one of those isolated folks "out there on the wretched edge of Western Civilization," he wrote, was that the ether was "turbulent with the babble and burble and atmospheric hiss of much of the Republic's long suppressed derangements: mental, emotional, musical, or mercantile."

The first radio station west of the Mississippi River to broadcast from its own studio was Dallas's WRR, licensed in 1921. It was stronger than ever during Brammer's teenage years, as were KERA, Oak Cliff's KLIF, and WFAA, airing live music each weekend from the Adolphus Hotel downtown. On these and the bellicose stations located just across the Mexican border from Del Rio, Eagle Pass, and McAllen, anchored there in order to flout the regulations of the Federal Communications Commission and swamp the signals of any station operating on channels within fifty kilocycles of their wavelengths, Brammer heard imprecations to the spirit: "But stop right there, hallelujah brothers, for I'm bringing you the message that will unseat Satan!"; balm for the body: "A man is as old as his glands. All energy is sex energy . . . Who wants to be made young again?"; and political theory from the likes of the anti-Semitic Charles Coughlin, once an FDR supporter but now a social reformer passionately certain that Jewish bankers were colluding to conquer the world.

From the radio, Brammer got the news: a Mexican man in Oak Cliff, crazed from smoking marijuana, had knifed five innocent victims, all white; President Roosevelt had visited the State Fair, proclaiming, "I salute the Empire of Texas"—a fair that in 1923 declared a Ku Klux Klan Day and celebrated it with large parades; and by the way, did listeners know that Dallas's first presidential visit ended with an assassination threat in 1843, when Sam Houston, president of the Republic of Texas, arrived to smoke a peace pipe with the leaders of the Kiowas and Comanches? The tribal chiefs suspected Houston planned to poison their tobacco, and so backed out of the summit.

From the radio, Brammer learned American entrepreneurial techniques, otherwise known as hucksterism—order now, a year's supply of diet pills, absolutely harmless, guaranteed to trim those troublesome thighs—from XER, a 75,000-watt station in Villa Acuña—"Mexico's radio outlaw . . . bootlegger of the air"—a man named Doc Brinkley, whose professional credentials consisted of a mail-order diploma from the Eclectic Medical University of Kansas City, Missouri, offered listeners a libido-enhancing treatment called "goat gland transplantation." It involved "taking the goat testicle and putting it in the man's testicle," Brinkley explained. "The man is renewed in his physical and mental vigor."

Most of all, from the radio Brammer heard the musical rhythms of the future emerging from the mixed rhythms of the past, the lonesome-cowboy yodels of Dust Bowl Okies combined with complex talking drumbeats imported from West Africa by southern slaves. On WFAA's live-music show *Saturday Night Shindig*, Brammer caught the first widespread airing of Dallas's homegrown African American laments tricked up as a country-and-western song, "The Deep Ellum Blues" (about a traditionally black neighborhood known as Frogtown, a red light district northwest of a Trinity floodplain); the melody had been appropriated and recorded by a hillbilly band called the Shelton Brothers. WFAA also played songs by Marvin Montgomery and Dick Reinhart, who would later join Bob Wills and His Texas Playboys. These players learned blues licks in Deep Ellum clubs and slipped them into their fiddle reels. Such cross-fertilization made the "Texas country tradition" the "bluesiest of the regional variations of country music," says Kevin Pask, a cultural historian. Brammer would witness a full flowering of these seeds in Austin, many years later, at bars like Threadgill's, where Janis Joplin sang folk songs alongside Stetsoned crooners, and in clubs like the Vulcan Gas Company, where some of Texas's first integrated psychedelic rock bands smoothed the way for "Cosmic Cowboys."

In 1938, the year young Brammer became aware of Lyndon Johnson's rural electrification efforts, Johnson gave a passionate radio address, broadcast the length and breadth of Texas, forecasting the war he would later declare on poverty: "Last Christmas, when all over the world people were celebrating the birth of the Christ child, I took a walk here in Austin—a short walk, just a few short blocks from Congress Avenue, and there I found people living in such squalor that Christmas Day was to them just one more day of filth and misery," Johnson said. "[They] were so poor they could not even at night use the electricity that is to be generated by our great river."

He did not mention that because of his attention to REA funding, his friend and campaign donor Herman Brown was reaping federal money for construction projects along the great rivers of Texas, but he *did* declare: "I am unwilling to close my eyes to needless suffering and deprivation . . . a cancerous blight on the whole community . . . the community O. Henry gave the appellation 'The City of the Violet Crown'" (after the year-round purple twilights shading the hills of Austin above the Colorado River). The O. Henry remark indicated that LBJ was already employing literary men to write his speeches for him, despite his lifelong disdain for book people, and it was guaranteed to kindle the sensibility of a budding literary figure like Billy Lee Brammer. Many years later, the opening pages of Brammer's novel featured a poor migrant family huddled within spitting distance of the Capitol in Austin.

Like the goat-gland salesman on the Mexican border, Johnson understood that America's future would be shaped and defined by the electronic airwaves. In 1943, he convinced his wife to invest her family money in a then-sleepy little radio station in Austin, KTBC. At the time, the Federal Communications Commission, which set the rules for broadcasting and broadcasting transfers, was on the verge of being abolished by the federal government. As soon as Lady Bird wrote her $17,500 check for the station, Johnson used his growing political muscle to strengthen the FCC. Almost immediately, KTBC, formerly a sunrise-to-sunset station, received permission to broadcast twenty-four hours a day. It was allowed to move to 590 AM, at an uncluttered end of the radio dial, where it could be picked up in thirty-eight counties across the state. Two years later, the FCC approved the station's request to quintuple its power, which allowed its signal to reach sixty-three counties. Local businessmen grasped that they could curry Johnson's considerable favor by advertising exclusively on KTBC. In time, he parlayed his wife's modest investment into a multimedia empire worth millions of dollars. This was one of the many paradoxes of Lyndon Johnson, one that the Oak Cliff boy listening desperately to the radio for signs of life, *any* life, beyond the one he knew, would never, perhaps, despite his later acuity, quite come to terms with: how such a self-serving man could be genuinely anguished over the plight of poor people who couldn't afford to turn on a light.

---

Whenever Kate or H. L. told Brammer it was time to turn off the radio, he would read. At the age of twelve he taught himself to type on his mother's machine by laboriously copying paragraphs from his brother's Tarzan books and his father's gardening manuals. Grover Lewis didn't know Brammer then, but when they met years later in Austin, he "recognized him at once as another solitary schoolboy who'd stayed home to read, forging out of the common language a voice purely his own," Lewis said.

A few blocks from Brammer's house, the Carnegie Library became a refuge. Gray brick and concrete on the outside, it featured soothing green and cream interiors. Best of all, the basement, where the children's and young readers' books were kept, was so much cooler than the rest of the building in the summertime—the upper floors lacked air-conditioning. The basement windows loomed high above the floor, just at street level outside, letting in slivers of light. After spending a day in the stacks, poring over books, he would pop outside into the sunshine, sip water from the triple-headed bubbling fountain on the street corner (the spigots marked "White Adults," "White Children," and "Colored"), and head for the Tamale

Man's cart. A few pennies would buy a steaming fresh tamale wrapped in newspaper.

A precocious reader, Brammer discovered, early, the hardened clarity of Hemingway's prose, snapping up *For Whom the Bell Tolls* the moment it appeared on the library shelves; he worked his way through the allusive imagery of Virginia Woolf and Nathanael West. But it was Scott Fitzgerald's "softly undulating sentences . . . [that] awakened his urge to write," according to Al Reinert. Brammer was five when Fitzgerald published *Tender is the Night*. Reinert remembered that, thirty-five years after Brammer had first read the novel as a child, "Billy could still quote favorite passages."

An urge to write doesn't automatically translate into the confidence to do so. It wasn't until he had read J. Frank Dobie, one of Texas's first leading men of letters, that he envisioned the possibility of a literary life. Dobie was a professor at the University of Texas in Austin who never precisely fit the institutional mold. He didn't consort comfortably with his colleagues in the English Department; in his view, they spent too much time studying European literature and American writers from New England and the South. Where were the novels and poems of Texas experience, and the scholars *promoting* them, he wanted to know. His colleagues felt he had "too much of the cowboy in him." He proclaimed himself "exiled from [his] own birthright." He assumed directorship of the Texas Folklore Society, an outfit founded years earlier by John Lomax, a collector of cowboy songs, early blues, spirituals, and other folk tunes. To these ballads, and the rich stock of Texana, Dobie added vaquero tales, Native superstitions, and family stories told around campfires on wearying cattle drives. It was this rural lore, collected in books with titles such as *Coffee in the Gourd*, that Brammer read. The stories themselves didn't impress him as much as the revelation that it was possible to chronicle local experience and shape it into lyrical expression. The literary wasn't just *out there* somewhere; it could be anywhere. "It never occurred to me—ever—until I read J. Frank Dobie that I could be a writer," Brammer said. "There simply were no writers in Texas."

Dobie said that folklore must be written as the "original teller should have told it." From this tenet, Brammer understood that the language of one's experience, one's neighborhood, one's region, combined with the elements of craft and style learned from published works of literature, could be forged—like the mix of country and blues—to form a unique voice.

In the mid-1940s, while Brammer was a high school student reading Dobie and Fitzgerald, Dobie got caught in a fight over academic freedom at the University of Texas, a school that "has never been wholly comfortable with the notion of robust speech," in the opinion of Dave Richards, a labor and civil rights lawyer who would become one of Brammer's close friends. The campus battle presaged future troubles for Brammer over issues of free expression, and marked the "first postwar manifestation of liberalism in Texas," said Richards. The liberal movement would consume much of the lives of Brammer and his friends in the coming decades.

Two consecutive, strictly conservative Texas governors, W. Lee "Pappy" O'Daniel and Coke Stevenson, both increasingly upset with New Deal liberalism (and FDR's man on the ground, Congressman Lyndon Johnson), moved to restrict the dissemination of dangerous thinking at the university, a stone's throw from the Capitol. They appointed like-minded men to the school's board of regents, who then, in Dobie's words, "tried to build a Maginot line around the institution to keep ideas out." Regularly, they called for the ouster of "radical" professors. At one point, they reprimanded an instructor who had assigned John Dos Passos's "immoral" trilogy *USA*. They demanded he be fired. The university's president, Homer Rainey, refused to bow to the regents' pressure, so the board fired *him*. Dobie came to Rainey's defense, haranguing the regents as a bunch of "homemade fascists." He was dismissed from the university.

Rainey decided to run for governor, emphasizing free expression in his challenge to the conservative candidate, Beauford Jester, in the Democratic primary. Rainey's campaign exposed a left-right schism within the Texas Democratic Party. Jester, who had once had ties to the KKK, won the contest by tarring Rainey as a "nigger-lover" and a communist.

Brammer followed the primary battle on the radio and in the newspapers. He was too young to articulate a coherent political ideology, but he responded to words—how could a man's character be any good if his talk was sloppy and mean?—and he responded to wit, as in the published political cartoons of men like Bob Eckhardt (who would become Brammer's friend one day as well as the second husband of Brammer's first wife). In one Eckhardt cartoon, lampooning Beauford Jester's wealthy donors, figures representing oil and sulfur steal away with the state of Texas tucked tightly under their arms. Behind them on a table sits a stack of Dos Passos's trilogy, arranged as a public distraction from the *real* immorality of their thievery.

Years later, Brammer structured his political novel as a trilogy of stories. Gore Vidal compared him to John Dos Passos, and in an irony he could not have foreseen as a high school student, a powerful Texas politician did his damnedest to banish the book from sight and to prevent its author from spreading any more ideas.

---

As an adolescent boy in "Cracker Eden"—Grover Lewis's term for Oak Cliff—if you didn't run in the approved social circles, and especially if you weren't a jock, "you were forever defined as being far down the food chain." In the workingmen's districts, "where a lot of [poor] families got blown to smithereens," local sports teams offered shards of glory to talented kids. The "football fraternity tended to be arrogant, bullying swine," Lewis said. Small and spry, Brammer could hold his own with many of the athletes at Greiner middle school and at Sunset High, doing one-armed push-ups all morning in the gym, winning medals for swimming and diving, and chasing pop flies with easy grace in the infield.

The grammar teachers tended to be "stiff old biddies," in Lewis's memory, obsessed with Latin conjugations and sentence diagramming. They believed in homework the way ascetics believed in wearing hair shirts. After school, groups of teens took streetcars to the Skillern's Drugstore on Edgefield for the free shakes offered there along with every one-dollar purchase of school supplies. On weekends, they pooled their allowance and part-time work money to gather at Kelly's Skating Rink or the Pig Stand on Chalk Hill Road, or to hold hands under the false stars of the Texas Theatre. *Gone with the Wind*, *Snow White*, *Mr. Smith Goes to Washington*. The war in Europe was always the leadoff: the kids cheered the newsreels every time a German plane burst into flames on the screen. As the war widened and engulfed America—Brammer was riveted to the radio on December 7, 1941, when President Roosevelt declared a "day of infamy"—weekly routines changed in and around school. Blackout drills, raising blankets over the windows, became a regular part of the daily lesson plan. Students saved and donated aluminum chewing gum wrappers to the conservation effort. They collected nickels and dimes for war bonds: little girls wearing army caps, pleated skirts, and ballet slippers for their after-school dance classes went door-to-door in the old neighborhoods, carrying fat tin cans.

In 1942, Brammer's brother, Jim, got his draft notice. He received flight training at the Air Force Navigation School in San Marcos, near San Antonio, and subsequently trained as part of the 505th Bombardment Group at the Harvard Army Airfield in Nebraska. In November 1944, he and his troop mates shipped out of Seattle on the USS *Sea Star*. They made stops in Pearl Harbor and Eniwetok (a future atomic bomb test site) before heading to Tinian, a flat semitropical island in the Marianas. From there, the bomb group flew several B-29 sorties against the Japanese Empire, destroying military targets, transportation hubs, and industrial sites.

While movie-house newsreels presented overseas military campaigns as unqualified successes and troop morale as unshakable, Brammer knew otherwise from reading his brother's letters. Jim was careful about what he revealed, but it was clear that life in a Pacific Theater Quonset hut was not a night out at the Pig Stand. On a Special Services radio receiver arranged on a stack of empty packing crates in the midst of the squadron's pup tents, the American flyers heard songs from home—"California, Here I Come," "Back Home Again in Indiana"—before Tokyo Rose came on the air and suggested the GIs enjoy the music before being annihilated by the Japanese Royal Navy and the Imperial Air Force.

The international conflict touched Texas when the government established a German prisoner-of-war camp at a railroad spur near the town of Trinity. Newsreel footage of the prisoners goose-stepping as they came off the trains chilled Brammer and his friends. Edward R. Murrow interrupted Bob Hope and *Ellery Queen* on the radio to bring listeners news of the bombardment of London. The Brammer house was sadder without Jim's saxophone playing—before leaving home, he had taken up the instrument in order to emulate his favorite jazz artist, Stan Kenton. Rose continued to be gone most of the time, but even when she came around now, Brammer barely knew her: she had met a new boyfriend, who took her deer hunting almost every weekend, and that was all she would talk about, though clearly she didn't enjoy hunting and Brammer certainly didn't want to hear about it.

He skipped many of his classes at Sunset High School. They bored him. Eventually, he graduated ninety-fourth in a class of ninety-six students. Kate was working as a secretary now to bring in extra money; she and H. L. were too busy to know that their boy was often home alone, listening to the radio, reading, or catching crawdads down at the riverbank. He missed almost an entire semester of his senior year. Boys and girls gathered at his house in the afternoons for petting parties. He would talk older kids into buying beer for the group with money his father had given him without ever asking what he wanted it for. H. L. could never say no to his baby boy, especially after the two older kids had left the house.

When Brammer *did* show up at school, it was to swim, to visit his fellow journalism students, to lay out the latest issue of the *Sunset Stampede*, or to talk to his favorite teacher, Nelson Hutto. Mr. Hutto had gotten his master's degree at Columbia and worked for a while at the *New York Times*. Now he wrote sports stories and pulp fiction. A short fellow with a square jaw and heavy black glasses, he always seemed wary around his students. Brammer recognized a natural affinity with the man: both of them would rather be home writing and reading than spending time at school. Between lessons, Mr. Hutto turned his back on the class and doodled Disney figures on the blackboard, one of Brammer's classmates remembered. From Mr. Hutto, Brammer learned about Horace McCoy, best known for his novel *They Shoot Horses, Don't They?* but important to local writers because he had slipped a vivid fictional portrait of Oak Cliff into his crime novel *No Pockets in a Shroud* (1937). His example reinforced Dobie's conviction that literature, popular, pulp, or otherwise, could be made from Texas experience. Brammer felt a gleeful thrill of recognition when he read, in McCoy's novel, about the "faint sucking noises of the water and the dull traffic noises of the city" or about the smell of the furniture factories in middle-class neighborhoods "when you crossed the viaduct and started down the hill to the reclaimed flatlands."

Despite the wartime economy, which limited the availability of building materials, the local landscape was changing, and it was getting harder to recognize the old and familiar. A real estate developer named Angus Wynne, whose son would become a major rock and roll promoter in Texas, and a pal of Brammer's, was paving the way for strip malls and shopping centers in Oak Cliff, attracting national chain stores to the area. He encouraged local entrepreneurs to invest in an exotic cuisine called Tex-Mex, supporting families who had taken their mothers' recipes out of the small steamy kitchens of shotgun houses and into neighborhood restaurants. The energy behind these developments reflected an optimism that the war would soon end and a period of prosperity and celebration would follow. (In the 1960s, Wynne opened Six Flags over Texas, an amusement park modeled after Disneyland, themed around Texas's wars and turning the state's past into one big roller-coaster ride.)

Brammer was as buoyed by this optimism as any young person, but his euphoria was balanced by spooky undercurrents. His brother, Jim, had been shot down over Iwo Jima. Jim survived: as the plane's navigator, he had made an instantaneous life-or-death decision—do we try to land and risk becoming prisoners of war, or do we ditch? Luckily, he chose to land, and the crew was rescued before the Japanese found them. Jim returned to the States wearing a medal for bravery.

The liberation of the German death camps was cause for cheer, but Brammer could not stop staring in horror at the pictures in the May 7, 1945, issue of *Life* magazine: the living corpses of Buchenwald, the stacks of skeletal bodies, the stark evidence of a complete absence of human spirit.

A month earlier, he could not stop staring at pictures of Franklin Roosevelt, who had shocked the nation by dying in office.

From the radio, Brammer learned that Governor Jester and Lieutenant Governor Allan Shivers, working with a self-proclaimed Christian leader named Vance Muse, had enacted the nation's first right-to-work laws in Texas, attacking labor unions for allowing black and white men to mingle in meetings, against the laws of God and nature. Brammer's political convictions were still inchoate, but the difference in the governor's harsh tone and the tone of Lyndon Johnson's speech about the poor was striking to him. He was more certain than ever that clarity of thought and principle was not just expressed by language, but also embodied by it.

# 3.

"Charming, reckless, crazy Billy": this was Grover Lewis's first (and enduring) impression of Brammer when the men met in the early 1960s; the personality traits he listed were already prominent when Brammer left home in 1947, initially to enroll at the University of Texas in Austin as a journalism major and then, following a round of poor grades, to attend North Texas State Teachers College in Denton, north of Dallas. Brammer was admitted on an athletic scholarship. Immediately, he went to work writing for the *Campus Chat*, the school newspaper, covering sports, reviewing books and local music, and lampooning the gaudy social events of fraternities. A considerable portion of Brammer's charm came from his gently self-deprecating manner. Despite this, and his wavy brown hair and brown eyes, he had trouble getting dates. Servicemen returning from the war, wearing spiffy uniforms and exhibiting an air of youthful world-weariness, wooed and won most of the girls on campus. Brammer tried to distinguish himself by becoming a swimming champ. He strained so hard at the sport that he required a hernia operation in the summer of 1948.

He lived with two roommates just off campus in a tiny prefab apartment. The place was always cluttered with empty beer bottles, bottles of Coke, candy bar wrappers, and overflowing ashtrays after evenings spent with friends listening to Milton Berle's *Texaco Star Theatre* on the radio. In a couple of years, the boys would buy a television set. Berle would move his show to the small screen and become the world's first TV celebrity. More and more in the evenings, the radio sat silent in a dark corner of the apartment.

Denton was a "somnolent backwater," said Grover Lewis, who attended North Texas State a few years after Brammer did, along with another promising young writer, Larry McMurtry. The school was a "kind of gulag operation in the boondocks, a mélange of ugly buildings surrounded by greasy eating joints." Lewis recalled the campus fishpond: the "pool and its canopy of trees was a small, wilting patch of sylvan green the administration had not yet figured out how to pave or put to loftier use." In 1947, the classrooms were already feeling the chilly edge of the approaching tide of McCarthyism. By and large, the tweedy teachers did not encourage intellectual freedom. Rewards were promptly dispensed for rote answers to predictable academic questions. The school was "freighted toward business and education degrees," and "you could be judged violently nonconformist just by liking jazz," Lewis said.

Brammer had arrived on campus attuned to Stan Kenton, from his brother's love of the saxophone (as well as to the bluesman Big Bill Broonzy and the doo-wop singers he had heard on his parents' radio night after night), but it was his "interest in jazz and be-bop at North Texas that was the beginning of his interest in *live* music and musicians as real people one could get to know from your own town, and it was all a part of his growing sophistication and hipness about things in general," said Sidney Brammer. North Texas "had a famously innovative music department"—especially for a "backwater"—"and Ornette Coleman, Dewey Redman, and Jimmy Giuffre were there just before and/or during Bill's time."

His immersion in live music, in addition to the time he spent swimming and diving, weakened his already frail commitment to classroom work. A report card dated June 6, 1948, shows that he flunked a course called "Elementary Math of Finance" (a warning his future wives could have used) and received Ds and C-pluses in everything else, except for a B in a "Bible as literature" course, "The Life and Letters of Paul." His journalistic assignments absorbed his hours. He wrote pieces on Jim Crow, the poll tax, and Joe McCarthy. The editors of the town paper, the *Denton Record-Chronicle*, had noticed his articles in the *Campus Chat* and invited him to join their sports beat, his first professional activity. He sent his clippings home to his mother, who saved them carefully in a box in a closet, next to boxes full of stock certificates—H. L. had begun investing, modestly, in the economic uptick after the war—and memorabilia from her other children. Jim was studying physics at Texas A&M; the atomic bomb, credited with ending the war, had sparked his interest in alternative energies. And Rosa had married a man she met while working as a secretary at the San Marcos air base. Unlike her baby brother, she developed a good business sense and was an expert at tallying finances. Soon, she and her new husband would purchase properties in South Dallas, motels and a service station. He would manage them, and she would keep the books. They bought a small apartment complex in Oak Cliff just a few blocks from the house where Lee Harvey Oswald lived during the last months of his life.

In 1948, the number of clippings Brammer sent his mother nearly tripled. Among other events he covered that year, Lyndon Johnson announced his second run—after an unsuccessful attempt in 1941—for the US Senate, and the *Campus Chat* sent Brammer to profile his North Texas campaign appearance. It was Brammer's most exciting assignment to date. He remembered his father's stories about the young congressman and the Rural Electrification Act. He recalled the radio speech about the poor. He had been intrigued (and appalled) when Johnson, announcing his bid for the Senate seat, said, "At Hiroshima when the first atomic bomb exploded . . . a new era was born—the Atomic Age. The power that ended the world's greatest war within forty-eight hours became ours to use, either to Christianize the world or pulverize it."

"All his life Billy could remember with perfect clarity the first time he saw Lyndon Johnson," Al Reinert said. "Johnson was barnstorming by helicopter that year—he was the first politician to use one":

> [Johnson's] queer new machine came churning in just above the rally, noisy and fascinating, circling many more times than was necessary, Johnson leaning from the window and whooping, gesticulating, waving a big white Stetson, which he sailed out into the crowd as the helicopter abruptly sank to a jarring landing. Johnson emerged almost instantly, grinning broadly, tall and lanky, looking for all the world like Jimmy Stewart, and he strode toward the podium followed by a University of Texas all-American football star whom he curtly instructed to fetch his hat. Then, grasping the microphone with both hands, his legs quivering with nervous energy, he loosed an incredible torrent of promises and platitudes that somewhere included (as Billy recalled it) a brave defense of the Marshall Plan to rebuild Europe.

Reinert believed that "Johnson . . . won a piece of Billy's heart that day and he owned it for the rest of both of their lives."

---

The trick with the Stetson, ordering a big athletic boy to "fetch" it, was perfectly in keeping with Johnson's controlling, insecure personality as well as with the image of the Texas Democratic Party. Brammer grasped this, later, when he researched Johnson's background. The party projected "populist-cowboy conservatism," a codified set of views whose emphasis on fierce independence, loyalty, and tradition was calculated to appeal to patriotic white men, on the ranch and in the city. It was an image captured in performance by the lone hillbilly singer at a county fair and by the Stetson-wearing LBJ in his whirlybird.

To his surprise, Brammer discovered that the Republican Party had always been largely irrelevant in Texas. The Democrats had kept firm control, especially since passing a poll tax in 1903, making it difficult for voters, particularly poor voters, to register unless they planned to vote Democratic. The Republicans, first organized in Texas in 1867 and associated with the abolition of slavery, were predominantly African American in the party's beginning; years of disenfranchisement followed. Former Republican gubernatorial candidate Rentfro B. Creager once said, "What's best for Texas is for every state in the union to have a two-party system and for Texas to be a one-party state. When you have a one-party state, your men stay in [the United States] Congress longer and build up seniority." All battles between conservative and liberal viewpoints played out internally among the Democrats, though in truth, Brammer saw, the few liberals in the group barely got a voice.

Johnson, hovering in the sky above cotton farmers, waving his cowboy hat, wasn't playing a role just to solidify his party's image. "About my background, you might say Lyndon Johnson is a cross between a Baptist preacher and a cowboy," he said. To Ronnie Dugger, who, as the editor of the *Texas Observer*, would shortly employ Brammer to report on Texas politics, LBJ was "a wild Christian, a woman-ridden outlaw, completely mixed from the day of his birth in the slave-owning whites' honor-ridden South, the Indian-fighting range-riders' West, and the state that gloried in itself as if it were still a nation." More immediately, said Bob Sherrill, a Texas newswriter, Johnson was "a trifling, undirected, boozing redneck" as a young man, "no better or worse than most others turned out by the wretched rural Texas schools of the day."

If Johnson seemed destined for politics, in spite of his aimlessness, it was because his father had engaged in public service. "He was trying to better humanity. He didn't have too much to show you for it," Johnson said bitterly years later. Because the elder Johnson let the family down, scoring few political victories, drinking heavily, and losing a lot of money, LBJ came to associate "political idealism with defeat, poverty, and failure," Dugger mused. "[If] you stand by your principles . . . you don't *succeed*," Johnson insisted. Politics is a ruthless game of give-and-take and self-promotion. He drew his strength from his stolid mother, a quietly pragmatic woman. "There is no force that exerts the power over me that [you] do," he wrote her once. Her influence on him remained singular all his life, though their closeness withered; years later, as a US senator, he directed Brammer and others on his staff to write notes to his mother and sign his name to them.

He first moved to Washington, DC, in 1931 as an aide to Texas congressman Dick Kleberg, a first cousin of Bob Eckhardt's. Kleberg called himself a "Boll-Weevil" Democrat, a southern conservative staunchly opposed to desegregation. His work habits were slack, and he became better known as a playboy and cockfighting enthusiast than as a congressman. LBJ took advantage of his laziness and assumed control of his DC office. Setting a killing pace for his staff, a routine Brammer would become all too familiar with, Johnson dictated as many as 320 letters a day. "I'm crazy about my work," he wrote a friend soon after settling in Washington. "Have a Very efficient Stenographer—Jew girl about 28 who was formerly Sec. to several prom. Congressmen . . . All in all I'll have three assistants."

Johnson signed Kleberg's name to the letters he composed, but already he was scheming to advance his career and his political agenda. Earlier, as a student at Texas State Teachers College in San Marcos, he had learned to appreciate the power of written communication, despite his distrust of intellectuals and writers. He edited and wrote for the campus newspaper, shaping the campus in *his* image. Then, working briefly as a teacher of Mexican American students in the poverty-blasted South Texas town of Cotulla, his "dream began of an America . . . where race, religion, language, and color didn't count against you," he said. Though he would never make his father's mistake, draping *principle* like a millstone around his neck, that didn't mean he lacked vision. And it certainly didn't mean he didn't have a plan.

In 1937 he was elected to Congress on a platform of *Roosevelt, Roosevelt, Roosevelt!* His 1941 bid for a Senate seat was thwarted by Governor W. Lee "Pappy" O'Daniel, a one-man circus whose Senate campaign consisted of "the Ten Commandments and the Golden Rule," hundreds of thousands of dollars' worth of radio ads, the hillbilly music of the Light Crust Doughboys, and donations collected in flour barrels from his successful mill business. He would exhort the crowds at his rallies to "Please pass the biscuits, Pappy!" His election was ensured when the Texas beer industry organized to send him to Washington—if he was no longer the governor, he couldn't stop sales of alcohol on Texas army posts. Last-minute votes came pouring in for him, mysteriously, from counties in East and South Texas controlled by unscrupulous political bosses. Johnson staffers knew their man had probably violated federal campaign finance laws, but in the long run, Pappy was a better cheater. "Next time, sit on the ballot boxes," FDR advised Johnson. Johnson swore, "I'll tell you this: if I ever get in another close election, I'm not going to lose it!"

The war stalled his ambitions, but he managed to use the fighting as publicity material in his personal story: as a congressional observer on a B-26, he witnessed some air-to-air combat and was awarded a Silver Star. A Roosevelt aide described the episode as LBJ's "politically essential plunge into the Pacific," which polished his military bona fides and secured his status as an American hero. David Halberstam referred to Johnson's medal as "one of the least deserved but most often displayed Silver Stars in American military history."

Meanwhile, events were stirring in Southeast Asia that would bear somber consequences for Johnson's political career, the US social contract, and Brammer's life in the coming years. In 1945, the Vietnamese nationalist rebel Ho Chi Minh began battling French colonial control of his country. Though America tried to avoid the skirmish, US leaders saw an opportunity to keep Europe secure in the aftermath of the world war. America wanted West Germany to remain economically strong, while the French feared a resurgent German state. In exchange for French support of increased West German steel production, the United States committed $2.3 billion to arm French troops in Indochina. Harry Truman had put his heavy stamp on the as-yet-unrealized Lyndon Johnson presidency.

Johnson's opponent in the 1948 Senate race was a rough old rancher and canny politician, former governor Coke Stevenson. Johnson knew he couldn't authentically out-cowpoke the old fellow, so he took a page from Pappy's playbook and ran a circus campaign, using Lady Bird's Austin radio station to record a series of ads that swamped the airwaves, employing country singers and cheerleaders to appear at his rallies, and hiring a chopper as his primary means of transport. While Stevenson invited photographers to watch him clear brush on his ranch, or snap him driving patiently around the state, using his one-armed nephew as his chauffeur, Johnson was tossing his Stetson from the skies. His biggest fear was that the rotor blades would slice up a couple of kids at a rally and finish his career.

In keeping with his promise not to lose another close election, this time he lined up his own unscrupulous political boss, George Parr of Duval County, who controlled much of South Texas's Mexican American vote through coercion, enticement, and intimidation. At the last minute, ballot box 13 in Alice, Texas, previously uncounted, gave Johnson a statewide margin of eighty-seven votes, propelling him toward the Senate and earning him the nickname "Landslide Lyndon."

"I was beaten by a stuffed ballot box and I can prove it!" Stevenson yelled at reporters. In *High Noon* fashion, he strode, coatless, into Alice one day, headed for the bank where the ballot box rested in a vault. He was accompanied by Texas Ranger Frank Hamer, one of the lawmen who had ambushed Bonnie and Clyde. At the bank entrance, Hamer, flashing the pistol in his holster, frightened Parr's heavily armed guards into stepping aside. No matter. Though a quick glimpse of the voting lists convinced Stevenson and his men that irregularities abounded—names of dead people, duplicated names, penciled-in additions, dozens of signatures all in the same hand—the men were not allowed to copy any information. They could prove nothing later. Eventually, the box 13 mystery ballots disappeared.

---

That the showy politician who had won a piece of Billy Brammer's heart wasn't perfect didn't bother Brammer overmuch. "Billy . . . was not so naïve as to think that politics, especially Texas politics, was as decorous and principled as people were accustomed to pretending," Al Reinert said. "On the contrary Johnson's impressive [box 13] majorities merely underlined the deeper mystery of the man's phenomenal vitality." Brammer kept his eye on the freshman senator. When Governor Beauford Jester died unexpectedly in office in 1949, and Allan Shivers took over, Brammer saw how Johnson courted the conservative "Shivercrats" back home even as he continued to espouse New Deal policies in Washington. Everyone wanted to know where Lyndon *really* stood on the issues. Brammer grasped that Johnson stood for himself, though his outrageous drive suggested he was guided by some profound personal vision. The precise nature of Johnson's contradictions would come to vex Brammer, but contradiction itself he well understood. He had heard it in that very first radio address he had listened to nearly ten years earlier, when Johnson bemoaned the plight of the poor. "A regional rhetoric is more than a way of talking, it has a content," Ronnie Dugger once said. "Southern American experience is embedded in the southern literary rhetoric—nostalgia for gallantry and the splendor of returning cavalry officers; defeat; bitterness; revenge; personal racial guilt; a melancholy. The Western rhetoric, though, is lit up by the new hope and adventure of the frontier, the spirit of conquest, a man's pride in taking a risk, in offhand daring." Like Johnson, Brammer had "received his being" in the "rocky fracture of the great American state that is both South and West." They shared a regional rhetoric and a conviction that in contradiction, politics found its core. Principle or the search for perfection would get you nowhere—lost in the dark thickets of South Texas. It was in the dirt and shame of *acting*, and in honestly examining your acts, that politics found its direction and its opportunities for incrementally bettering the world. Standing in an Oak Cliff alley and throwing rotten tomatoes at black boys to win the approval of your friends, all the while knowing that what you were doing was awful and that you damn well better find a way to avoid this situation in the future: *that* was politics.

---

Brammer's editor at the *Campus Chat* was a quiet boy named Bruce Henderson, from McAllen, on the Texas-Mexico border near the international bridge to Reynosa, where Doc Brinkley sold his goat glands on the air. Before enrolling in school, Henderson had worked as a dust pilot, swooping low in a Piper Cub over the cotton fields and citrus groves of the Rio Grande Valley, spraying crops. Sometimes, in buzzing the fields, he would dip under the electric wires strung by Texas Power and Light. Brammer loved his daredevil flying stories and his descriptions of the lazy palm trees and fertile wet fields of the valley, where the Rio Grande emptied into the Gulf of Mexico. One day, early in 1950, Henderson told Brammer that a friend of his from McAllen, a young woman majoring in art, had enrolled at North Texas State and that Brammer might like to meet her. Henderson knew his pal had just lost a girl he had been dating to an Olympic diver from Dallas. To his friend from McAllen, Henderson described Brammer as "an intellectual *and* an athlete."

Nadine Cannon was a dark-haired beauty, short and petite. When she arrived at North Texas State, she still wore the pink angora sweaters she had adopted as a uniform in high school to match the ideal feminine model presented in Frank Sinatra's song lyrics, but she had cut her hair short, like Ingrid Bergman in *For Whom the Bell Tolls*. She began to buy earrings and Mexican shoes. For a Christmas issue of the school newspaper, Henderson snapped a picture of her wearing a metallic-blue bathing suit and smiling up at a fraternity boy, clearly delighted by the gift of this gorgeous girl.

In her memoir, *Duchess of Palms*, Nadine wrote that her first impression of Brammer, when Henderson introduced them in the *Campus Chat* office, was underwhelming: "[He] looked to me like a Dallas hood, or a pachuco from the Valley. He had a ducktail haircut, blue suede shoes, and a slouchy walk. He wore his collar turned up." Brammer could sit as still as a doll and nothing about him engaged Nadine "until he spoke." Right away, she learned how witty he was, funny and curious—well read and knowledgeable about politics. He tossed off S. J. Perelman zingers. Before they parted that day, she realized, "I had never met anyone like Billy Lee Brammer."

Initially, their meetings always included Henderson. The three of them would get together for Mexican food, to fantasize about living in Europe and sitting in sidewalk cafés. They would make fun of the fraternities and sororities on campus, though all of them had pledged. Eventually, Brammer and Nadine started hanging out at his apartment alone, drinking Pernod or Cointreau and Tom Collins mix, smoking cigarettes, listening to *Bolero*. It was a period when hatred of communists dominated American politics; in 1950, students at North Texas State were forced to pledge a loyalty oath to the United States. The young couple considered themselves too sophisticated for that sort of knee-jerk nonsense—they were ahead of their peers in their awareness of music and art. "We were copacetic," Nadine told me, largely because they both loved to dance. They would attend performances by the North Texas State Laboratory Jazz Band and by R&B bands from Ft. Worth, Deep Ellum, and Houston in clubs in the seedier parts of Denton. "If you look at photos of Bill and Nadine (before North Texas and after) you can see that they both made physical transformations from the general World War Two big band dance couple look to a much more hipster look one would associate with smoky jazz clubs and east coast sophistication," their daughter Sidney said. "Nadine kept cutting her hair very short, Bill lost his jocky look and went for thin ties and khakis instead of letter sweaters and jeans/overalls."

Many years later, Nadine insisted she was a "very straight girl" when she first met Brammer. He was the daring, rebellious one: "Everyone loved

Bill; he was charming, witty, gentle, and nonthreatening . . . Men liked him because he could talk sports and was athletic, intelligent, and naughty. Women liked him because he asked questions about their lives and actually listened when they answered—and because he was naughty," she wrote. But the more Brammer got to know her, the more he learned about her past, and he realized that a "restlessness . . . simmered just under [her] sweet persona: the *picante*." She was "straight" only in projecting a proper middle-class façade in public. Brammer kept trying to loosen her up. "One night he told me that I needed to speak all the words I was avoiding," she recalled. "He said, 'I want you to yell "shit" as loud as you can yell it, so you can understand what I'm telling you.' We drove around the square in Denton, with me hollering 'shit!' as loud as I could."

Nadine decided, "We were just bizarre enough for each other," but her wildness, her fierceness, far exceeded his. Her childhood had been tough. She barely knew her father, a musician named Leslie Wells. Before Nadine was born, he played organ scores for silent films in Oklahoma City. He joined the Orpheum Circuit, a national booking agency for vaudeville shows and movies. In grand old theaters built along the North Canadian River, in plush auditoriums with soft gas lighting, he wore a white tuxedo and raced his fingers across the Wurlitzer's keys. He had the same reckless love of art that Brammer would exhibit. Despite the surface glitz, life was hard; the musicians' union often struck for higher wages. Oklahoma City became known as a difficult place to book shows. Finally, the talkies put prematurely embittered men like Leslie Wells out of business.

His wife, Nadine Ellen Thompson, a theater manager in the city, knew a friend who owned a farm in the Rio Grande Valley. The friend invited the couple to come work the land. Their little girl, named after her mother, was born in a McAllen farmhouse on January 20, 1931. Working in the fields did not suit Leslie Wells. Soon, he became drunk and abusive. His wife left him, taking her kids—Nadine and her older brother, Leslie—and went to work as a waitress in a bar. Nadine's father fled the valley, leaving her only a large black-and-white photograph of him wearing a black tux, seated in front of an organ. She spent hours dreaming over the picture, trying to reconcile the man's warm glamour with the silent anger his name provoked in her mother.

Two Mexican women fed Nadine and her brother while their mother worked at the bar each day. Finally, Nadine's grandmother Rose moved to McAllen from the Texas Panhandle to tend the kids. She was a quiet, powerful woman, proud of her independence. She walked two miles every morning, rain or shine. Nadine admired her steady strength—learned, Rose said, entirely on her own: she had never had any use for men.

Just before Nadine entered first grade, her mother married a gentle forty-year-old bachelor, a policeman named Noah Cannon. Though lacking the glamour of the man in the tux, he radiated comfort and calm. With a pencil-thin mustache, he looked like Clark Gable gone to fat. Nadine loved the stiff blue uniform he put on every morning to go to work, with its shiny cap and silver badge. When she grew a little older, more aware, she would fret whenever he left the house. Once, he had had to kill a prisoner in the front seat of his patrol car when the man went for his gun. Frequently, he had to bust up gang fights between Mexicans and whites in the tiny town of Pharr, where he became the chief of police.

When Nadine reached the cusp of puberty, her brother, always a sullen, disruptive kid, tried to molest her sexually. "[He had] a desire to harm me. He was jealous of my friends, my grades, and my mother's obvious delight [in me] . . . I began to truly hate him," Nadine said. "I escaped his advances only because he was physically small and not very smart." Frightened, ashamed, she didn't tell her mother or Daddy Noah. For a while, she became wary around boys, but she also kept an eye on her mom: ever since remarrying, Big Nadine had done everything she could to please her man, dressing prettily, cooking pork roasts and Parker House rolls on her big kitchen range. Nadine understood that this was a better routine than waitressing in a bar. "Success, I concluded, meant finding the right provider," she said, even if boys were not to be trusted. Her insight grew messier when she experienced her "first sexual feelings watching Gene Autry sing by the campfire." Male bodies could excite as well as frighten: a mighty confusing state of affairs. The Autry movie played at the Queen Theatre, which her mother now managed for extra money. Maybe Nadine's grandma was right—men *weren't* any use, really. They didn't guarantee success.

Still, by the "time I was thirteen, I was boy-crazy, running around with my girlfriends, flirting with the cutest, nicest boys, and feeling insecure about whether or not they liked me," Nadine wrote. "Dicky Harris gave me my first kiss, planting it on my forehead as we danced at the Fox Hole," a recreation hall whose crowning glory was a jukebox featuring "One O'Clock Jump." "When boys started giving me valentines, Christmas gifts, etc., I wondered why . . . I felt unaffected by it until, after noticing the envy of my girlfriends, I realized that my effect on boys was a form of power . . . I learned to juggle the endless stream of men and somehow, in my confused way, I felt I had to be absolutely wonderful for each and all."

Sailors and fliers home from the war, stationed at Moore Field Air Force Base, gave Nadine plenty of attention, though she refused to date them. By the time she got to high school, she and her friends, including Bruce Henderson, would drive regularly to Reynosa to spend long evenings at nightclubs and restaurants, where they could drink zombies, hurricanes—"all kinds of weird stuff," Nadine said—no matter how young they were, and where they would jitterbug and rumba until their high heels broke. In addition to the drinks, the kids could easily—and cheaply—obtain five-milligram tablets of Benzedrine. Promoted, on and off the black market, as antidepressants and weight loss aids, the pills would perk them up and keep them dancing, according to the young war veterans they met in the clubs; the vets had learned of the pills' stimulating effects when the air force dispensed them to bomber pilots flying long runs.

"Always, on the way home from the Monte Carlo Club, someone would have to get out of the car to throw up," Nadine said. "My mother and I had a parrot on the screened porch of our house. My dates would kiss me good night and the parrot would whistle and scare them half to death.

"Guys loved me. I had several boyfriends. One would be for dancing. One would be for something else." In her memoir, she wrote, "I managed to avoid real sex no matter how much tequila I drank, until curiosity and competitiveness with my girlfriends got the best of me. I had my first [encounter] with a boy to whom I was sexually attracted, but it was messy and painful, not what I had expected. I didn't want to go out with him again."

At seventeen, she was "chosen Duchess of Palms by audience applause at the Palace Theater," she wrote. "This meant I was to represent McAllen in the annual Citrus Fiesta, a Valley-wide celebration of the citrus industry. My picture was in the newspapers, and the Chamber of Commerce gave me one hundred dollars for a gown of my choice, which was palm green, of course . . . I loved being Miss Hot Shit."

Soon enough, she realized there was nothing but a downward spiral if she stayed in the valley. Unless she got out, marriage and Parker House rolls were all she could anticipate. She lasted three days in a local business college, a little longer at a nearby junior college, and then, after saving money from a job at a McAllen drugstore, she enrolled at North Texas State.

Bill Brammer was not as traditionally handsome as some of the boys she had danced with in Reynosa, but "his whole effect was very sensual and attractive to women," she said, and he was the first young man to stimulate her mind. Almost immediately, "he seemed to be more certain than I was that [our] union was meant to be," she said. She wasn't convinced until

Easter vacation. She had driven with friends from Denton to McAllen to visit her family. At the end of the week, on the way back to school, she and her buddies were cruising in an open Oldsmobile convertible, speeding, "passing cars on the wrong side of the road, beer cans flying out of the car, when someone said, 'Hey, was that Bill Brammer in that Chevy that just went by?'"

Nadine ordered her friends to turn around. Brammer had stopped by the side of the road. She got out of the car. "What the hell are you doing here?" she asked him.

"Driving you back to school," he said. He had come hundreds of miles just to see her.

Nadine waved good-bye to her friends. He cranked up "Rag Mop" on the radio, and they sped away.

A few days later, on April 20, 1950, about four months after they had met, they eloped to Lewisville, Texas, interrupted a one-legged judge's game of dominoes, and asked him to marry them. Across the street from the judge's house, a Pentecostal revival tent had been erected in a vacant lot. While the couple said their vows, the Holy Rollers chanted and clapped and a loud little boy shouted his spiritual testimony. Brammer was one day shy of twenty-one. Nadine was nineteen. The young lovers didn't really know what they were getting into, she admitted later: "We just wanted to keep having a good time, keep going on with our educations. Do what we were doing." Living together "in sin" wasn't an option in 1950s Denton. Marriage had the practical benefit of keeping Brammer from the draft. It kept Nadine from returning to the valley. "My mother didn't like Bill. She lost five pounds the week I married," she told me. "She really wanted me to marry the mayor's son. But it was my hometown and I just thought, 'Yuck.' I was up for something different."

In her memoir, she wrote of the great ambivalence she felt after consenting to wed: "Call it impulse, intuition . . . whatever it was, our decision to marry was not rational."

To me, sixty-five years later, she said simply, "We were stupid."

---

Back in Denton, Brammer and Nadine found a small apartment and resumed their course work. Somehow, they imagined that his part-time job as a sportswriter for the *Denton-Record Chronicle* would keep them afloat. That first semester, borne by the energy of their optimism and the commitment they had sworn to each other, they both made the dean's list for the first time. Because they were both photogenic, they appeared in a university publication touting the journalism program—"What Makes a Top Newsman?"—Brammer copyediting pages with Nadine gazing over his shoulder.

She fixed tacos almost every night—all she knew how to cook. Between classes and stringing for the paper, Brammer survived on Dr Peppers and candy bars. The pages flying out of his typewriter were smeared with chocolate and x-ed out sentences. "His copy was messy, but it was always good," Nadine said.

She introduced him to Benzedrine tablets. Amphetamines were readily available in American drugstores, sold as diet pills, as was Dexamyl, a combination of an amphetamine and a barbiturate, recommended for mental and emotional distress. In 1947, the American Medical Association had approved amphetamines for weight loss. By 1949, Smith, Kline and French in Philadelphia, among other pharmaceutical laboratories, was manufacturing well over fifty-five million tablets a year and racking up annual sales of over $7.3 million. "Everyone had their stash of diet pills . . . swallowed them with their orange juice," said Jay Milner, who would become a friend of Brammer's:

> On-the-go, up-and-coming executives of all persuasions popped them to keep up with the competition. It wasn't speed; they were only Diet Pills. It was like you were the only one who knew they gave you an edge. Distinguished believers in the Hippocratic oath got ever richer and richer dispensing prescriptions for the little boogers, and there was no warning on the label. Stealing pills from each other's medicine cabinets became a common compulsion. Merely a misdemeanor. It wasn't against the law to buy or sell these pills then. Nobody had mentioned the danger. Flip-outs were blamed on other things—like a fundamental weakness of character. Most people claimed they could take them or leave them. Others found they could not.

Brammer was grateful to Nadine for alerting him to the drugs' amazing effects. "I used [them] to cram for tests—stay up all night and forget everything as soon as I took the exam. But Bill liked [them]. I mean, he really liked [them]," Nadine said. He said the pills helped him with his writing. He could type for hours, nonstop. He wanted to devote more time to his desk, not just for his sports columns but also for his literary ideas. In the last two years, Norman Mailer had published *The Naked and the*

*Dead*, J. D. Salinger had come out with *The Catcher in the Rye*. It was an exciting period for the American novel, and Brammer was eager to test his imagination. He gave Nadine all of Fitzgerald's books to read. She absorbed them with intense concentration. She believed her young husband could become a famous author and support them with his talent.

Visits with Brammer's parents led to the first domestic trouble. She adored H. L. and Kate. Sweet people. Unlike her mother, they were delighted with the marriage. But the degree to which they indulged her husband alarmed her. "His mother would cry when Bill came home because he was her baby boy," she recalled. H. L. refused him nothing. He lent the couple money. He "gave Bill a car that he had used in his work. It was a Chevy in mint condition. Bill could hardly wait to trade it in on something nicer, but more expensive to maintain, a Pontiac of some kind. At the time I didn't have the maturity to question this, so he kept on doing it." Within just a few months, she learned that he "was entirely unable to manage money. He spent foolishly—compulsively. He bought things on credit; life became a constant search for money to pay off what he had already bought." In the next six years, he would purchase nine cars, "everything from a Morris Minor to a Jaguar to a Plymouth station wagon."

Toward the end of 1950, attempting to address Nadine's debt fears, Brammer decided to apply for the Aviation Cadet Training Program. His brother had told him military pay might provide a nice supplement to their future income. It could create a "more pleasant life for us," Brammer told his bride, besides which, "I'm sure I'll be stunning in a uniform. Particularly a hat. I always look good in a hat." His only worry was getting shipped overseas. He didn't think he was cut out for "electronic countermeasures," but, he assured Nadine, "there are also openings in psychological warfare and foreign propaganda—more along my lines." On December 10, he took a physical at Carswell Air Force Base in Ft. Worth. He passed, despite a touch of asthma and the presence of seven cavities in his teeth. Four cavities was the air force's upper limit, but Brammer talked the doctor into fudging the report. By February 7, 1951, he had lost his chance to be considered for Officer Candidate School. He scored 171 points on an exam requiring a minimum of 255. He discarded his dream of flight.

He cast about for other ways to be solvent. The *Caller-Times*, a newspaper in Corpus Christi, on the southern Texas coast, was looking for a sportswriter. He applied for the post and got it. He had helped Nadine pass her reporting courses, and she had gotten him through Spanish. All that remained for him to graduate was to take a correspondence course on the

Bible. He received his diploma in the mail at the small apartment he had found in Corpus Christi.

His boss at the *Caller-Times* was a friendly workaholic named Roy Terrell, who would soon move east to write for Henry Luce's fledgling *Sports Illustrated* magazine. Eventually, he would become its editor and a conduit for Texas writers hankering to work in New York. The story went that Luce, cofounder of *Time*, attended his first baseball game when a friend took him to the World Series between the Yankees and the Brooklyn Dodgers. Luce was the son of missionaries, and he had been raised in China. The cheering crowds astonished him. "What's this all about?" he said to his friend. "It's sports, Henry. Americans love sports," his buddy replied. "Maybe we ought to do something about it," Luce said. Initially, *Sports Illustrated* floundered, covering dreary dog shows, yacht races, and polo. But then a new editor, Andrew Laguerre, brought in a posse of Texas cowboy-scribes. Laguerre was a Frenchman with an instinctive understanding of American populism, and the link between Hollywood westerns and sports narratives. The Texans "had a touch of irony," said the Houston journalist Thomas Fensch. They carried chips on their shoulders, and a "we're-better-at-this-than-anybody-else attitude." Laguerre hired Terrell, Dan Jenkins, and Bud Shrake, the last two from the *Ft. Worth Press*; both eventually became Brammer's great pals. In 1951, at the *Corpus Christi Caller-Times*, under Roy Terrell's guidance, Brammer got a taste of the driving professionalism that would transform the New York magazine world.

It wasn't *all* work in Corpus Christi. Once the deadlines had been met for the day, *Caller-Times* sportswriters and photo editors gathered with Terrell at the Oso Pier, a long wooden walkway at the remote southern end of Ocean Drive, featuring a bait house and a small amusement center. They would drink Schlitz and Falstaff beers and eat boiled crab. They would shoot pool and pick fried shrimp out of paper sacks. It cost twenty-five cents to fish off the edge of the pier with a cane pole, a nickel to cool your throat with a Coke. Brammer would join the group late in the day, perching on Pearl beer crates to drink and tell jokes, to sniff the salt air. It was strictly a boys' club. Sometimes marine science profs from Corpus Christi College or Texas A&I, in nearby Kingsville, would join the journalists. Photographs of the time show young ladies wearing tight white shorts and cotton shirts tied at the midriff mingling with the group, fishing and flirting with the men.

Nadine, kept from these festivities like all the other wives, knew no one in town. She would shop for the same old beef and cheese each day, fix tacos at night, drive out to Padre Island to read in the sun. From the first, she hated Corpus Christi—a blinding impression of too much blue, too much open flatness, too many sun-baked tennis courts. She feared it was a physical manifestation of the landscape of her marriage. Later, she remembered thinking, "What a ghost town."

PART TWO

# *ELECTRONIC NOISE*

# 4.

In Austin, in the summer of 1951, the heavy-honeyed air buzzed with flitting new life drifting lazily over hillocks and streams. Scorpions scurried along oak bark on the banks of the Colorado River. Muddy ravines bearded with hanging willows were thick with the scent of horsehair. Stale, mossy odors rose from sun-baked rocks. Bats lifted from the river in the late afternoon, slicing erratically through the sun's low rays. The fading crimson light shattered into sapphires on the surface of the water, casting yellow triangles onto striated sandstone cliff walls and high into gnarled red cedar limbs. Along the Balcones Fault, the escarpment dividing the Edwards Plateau from the Coastal Plains, the city spread gently—wood and pink granite, glass and ridged metal—among sunflower thickets, chinaberries and sycamores, where the American South met the American West.

The Brammers had moved to Austin at Nadine's insistence, abandoning the salty heat and crab smell of Corpus. They found an apartment on Harris Boulevard, in the center of the city. She hired on as a secretary to the director of the university's architecture school, and he covered sports for the *Austin American-Statesman*. They both enrolled in courses at the University of Texas.

The city's founder, Mirabeau B. Lamar, at one point the president of the

Republic of Texas, was an "impulsive poet," according to A. C. Greene: the place has never lost its distinctive air of having been "founded on beauty . . . alone among Texas cities." Frederick Law Olmstead, traveling through the region in the 1850s, noted Austin's "rolling and picturesque" character, its "agreeable views of distant hills," but was quick to add, "There is a very remarkable number of drinking and gambling shops, but not one book store." O. Henry, the city's first notable scribe, wrote that the first settlers "killed off all the Indians between the [Texas State] lunatic asylum and the river, and laid out Austin. It has been laid out ever since." In the 1890s, he said, the city consisted of "one soap factory, one electric light works, one cemetery, one dam, one racetrack, two beer gardens, one capitol, two city councils, [and] one cocaine factory." In 1951, when the Brammers arrived, little had changed.

Mary Lasswell, a writer living in Austin in the early 1950s, and a fleeting acquaintance of Brammer's, wrote, "Texas is an eternal synthesis of past and present, superimposed one upon the other." Austin, she said, "produces a feeling of being in two places at once. Skyscrapers . . . in one block, and a few blocks away an ancient wooden store with a false front high above it bears the crudely lettered words RAW FURS BOUGHT. The frontier past and the urban present . . . are separated by a very short span of time."

The moonlight towers, 150-foot-tall former arc lights converted to mercury vapor lamps, purchased from the city of Detroit during Austin's 1890s electric boom, still illuminated many streets, giving certain neighborhoods an otherworldly feel of having materialized whole from an earlier century.

Kenneth Threadgill's café on the Old Dallas Highway, still looking like a former Gulf filling station, was another monument to the enduring past. A former bootlegger and a yodeling enthusiast, Threadgill waited in line all night outside the downtown courthouse on December 6, 1933, to receive the first beer license in Travis County after the repeal of Prohibition. By the 1950s, he was hosting hootenannies and sing-alongs of what was beginning to be called folk music. Despite being primarily jazz buffs, the Brammers dropped by from time to time.

And then there was the Scholz Biergarten on San Jacinto Boulevard, sitting nearly in the shadow of the university's football stadium (already a well-established religious shrine). In the nineteenth century, hundreds of families immigrated to Texas from an area of Germany in Saxony and Prussia to pursue religious and political freedom. One of these men, August Scholz, got caught up in the Civil War on the side of the Confederacy. After his service in the war, he purchased an old boardinghouse in Austin for

$2,400 and built a bar and café on top of it. In 1893, following his death, his stepson sold the establishment to the Lemp Brewery, makers of Falstaff Beer; the place was sold again in 1908, this time to a German-language singing club, the Austin Saengerrunde, which ever since has leased the bar and beer garden to a succession of managers. The club built a private bowling alley behind the garden's back wall. Every so often, a thunderous clatter echoed as if from nowhere, startling the outdoor drinkers: God calling the end of time.

Time blurred among the garden's curling elm trees, in pale flakes kicked up from its caliche turf. Old World rituals mixed with modern work schedules. The slow, rural pace of the older patrons (hailing from small towns full of "more Baptists than people," as Bill Moyers once said of his Texas birthplace) clashed with the urban trendsetters' impatience. Eddie Wilson, underage at the time but a regular drinker in the garden nonetheless, said of the prevailing atmosphere of diversity, "We [were] arbiters of manners. See, an ol' boy might call another one a chickenshit motherfuckin' cocksucker or some such and the second ol' boy will think that's ill-mannered and break the other fellow's jaw."

Throughout the early to mid-1950s, Scholz's became the Brammers' favorite watering hole. In *The Gay Place*, Brammer christened it the Dearly Beloved Beer and Garden Party and wrote, "The beer garden was shielded on three sides by [a] low yellow frame structure, a U-shaped Gothicism, scalloped and jigsawed and wonderfully grotesque . . . Record music came from a speaker overhead, somewhere in the trees. The music was turned loud so it could be heard above the noise from a next-door bowling alley . . . The sounds from the bowling alley ruined only the ballads."

State legislators, members of their staffs, newsmen, students and teachers from the university, all gathered in the evening at Scholz's, beneath the nearby Capitol dome and the UT Tower. Outside, canopied by trees, self-proclaimed political liberals—a small bunch of outcasts—huddled at wooden tables over pitchers of beer and baskets of sausage and kraut to commiserate about their invisibility and apparent lack of effect on world affairs. "The soul of the place was found in conversation; something about [it] engendered leisurely discourse," said Brammer's pal Dave Richards, who arrived in Austin in 1954, and whose wife at the time, Ann, would one day become the governor of Texas. "Our politics were pure—we did not win much in the way of elections. Our enemies were gross and obvious . . . As a result, our job was fairly simple, as it required no great sophistication to oppose this old order."

In the fifties, the Scholz regulars had plenty to shout about. "The Lyndon Johnson forces were attempting to wrest the power of the Democratic party from the Allan Shivers forces, the Shivers forces being the conservatives and the Lyndon Johnson forces being the liberals," said Ann Richards. In 1951 and 1952, Shivers particularly incensed liberal Democrats by throwing his support to Dwight Eisenhower and Richard Nixon instead of Adlai Stevenson. Ralph Yarborough, a young lawyer who rather feebly challenged Shivers for the governorship in 1952, said he could not understand the term "Eisenhower Democrat. That's like saying you're a Christian who believes in Mohammed." In the years ahead, many Texas liberals would hook their hopes to Yarborough to beat back the conservative wing and—as Yarborough often promised in speeches—to "put the jam on the lower shelves so that the common people could get their share." The trouble was, a lot of people couldn't stand Yarborough personally. "He's a drag," Brammer said of him. He was arrogant and humorless, quick to blame others when things didn't go his way. Jimmy Banks, a political columnist for the *Dallas Morning News*, wrote, "Most of his old friends, who felt his views had been on the moderate side, believe he was 'pushed' into the extreme liberal camp by his post-war political ambitions simply because it was the liberals who were looking for someone to carry their banner."

And it was hard for many in the Scholz crowd to trust Lyndon Johnson. In 1952 he seemed especially bellicose and outlandish, announcing that if "*any*where in the world—by *any* means, *open or concealed*—communism trespasses upon the soil of the free world, *we should unleash all the power at our command upon the vitals of the Soviet Union*."

Ronnie Dugger said LBJ sounded like a sheriff hoping "for a final shoot-out with Bonnie and Clyde."

The Brammers eagerly joined these discussions in the garden, spending many pleasant evenings under the elms. "There was a real magic in Austin then," Nadine said. "There was lots of excitement and energy, a lot of young people who wanted to try new things—new music, new politics, new ideas—new everything!" The garden became a libertine enclave in a narrow cultural wasteland.

"I thought they were the ideal married couple," said Robert Benton, then a student at UT; he would go on to cowrite the screenplay for *Bonnie and Clyde* and to direct such films as *Kramer vs. Kramer* and *Places in the Heart*. He met the couple through a woman he was dating, a colleague of Brammer's at the newspaper. "They were people you'd make a television series about—he the serious sportswriter, she the beautiful nutcase who always got into mischief. They were terrific. They were what I thought I would have in my life if I was lucky. I'd have the kind of life that Bill had, and I'd be married to the kind of woman Nadine was.

"They were very quick to take advantage of their friends," he added. "They tested my loyalty early and unloaded a Siamese cat on me. We got along very well together."

Benton believed Brammer "wasn't confident in the Texas sense of 'confident,' but he was sure of himself as a writer. He knew he was good. He was active, curious, with a certain kind of real ambition to be taken seriously as a writer, not just as a sports reporter. Nadine wanted to be Zelda—not a bad thing to want to be, and if anybody could have pulled it off, it was Nadine. Bill was really in love with her. She was probably the stronger of the two: always the teenage beauty queen. A great life-spirit. Being with her was like being in a car with someone who's driving twenty miles an hour too fast. It was always hard to get her to be serious. She'd pretend not to be. She'd put on her beauty queen mask."

Men flirted with her—the husbands of her friends—while the pitchers emptied and the leaves drifted lazily onto the red-checked tablecloths. She liked the attention. She encouraged more of it. "This wonderful couple . . . maybe the world opened up for them too quickly and in a way they didn't have the experiences or the resources to handle," Benton said.

Celia Buchan—soon to be the wife of Willie Morris, who would edit *Harper's* in the 1960s—came to know the Brammers in the mid-1950s at Scholz's. Later, she would marry Bob Eckhardt, Nadine's second husband, following Nadine's divorce from him. "We used to joke about creating a wall chart of marriages and liaisons in order to better understand the interplay [of our group], but the task was too daunting," Dave Richards said. "The Texas liberals of that era all seemed to know one another one way or the other."

Celia Morris was one of the first of Brammer's friends to appreciate how powerfully charismatic his steady and generous personality could be. She said, "He could be stiller than anybody I'd ever known, and I trusted him because I felt that he was genuinely curious about who I was. Where other men seemed out to prove something—to win an argument, perhaps, or score points, or feel their own sexual magnetism—Bill simply liked women, and they liked him . . . Although he did not seem personally driven by sex, he had an abiding sense of the havoc it wreaked with our best intentions, and perhaps he was the first person I really cared for who had something close to the tragic sense."

While friends greeted one another ("How are you, you old horse fucker, you"), laughed about the latest jibes they had heard against conservatives on John Henry Faulk's radio show, and shook their heads at Lyndon Johnson's latest pronouncement—"Someday, somewhere, someway, there must be a clear-cut settlement between the forces of freedom and the forces of communism. It is foolish to talk of avoiding war"—they coyly courted one another's spouses, often harmlessly but sometimes risking grave domestic danger. Brammer observed it all in silence, said Celia Morris. He seemed to know something that "I sensed was true but didn't understand." He "just seemed to sit back and watch us all muck up."

---

Brammer's first serious attempts to develop a literary arsenal took place in an introductory literature course at the university taught by Professor Truman Guy Steffan, a Byron scholar whose variorum edition of *Don Juan*, which he would publish in 1957, helped put the University of Texas on the national map in the humanities. The course that Brammer took from him in the fall of 1951 offered readings in short fiction, primarily, supplemented by critical analyses of the stories and creative responses to the readings. Brammer was challenged to think through structure and style while exploring techniques for bringing new life to the page. He kept a notebook full of highlights from class lectures and his own thoughts about fiction. In neat, precise handwriting he wrote of Anthony Cooper's "Portrait of Henry Hastings," "True fiction gives us a complete character analysis *through action* . . . character along with action plus change." After reading O. Henry, Brammer noted, "A trick doesn't make a good story." He preferred Katherine Anne Porter's "complexity." Elsewhere, he mused, "Man craves an activity he can participate [in] as a whole man, not merely as a mind, or body—an activity in which body and mind participate harmoniously."

Steffan asked his students to write two descriptive sketches, one of a person and one of a place. "The principle of suggestion or implication," Brammer jotted in his notebook. "Beware of diction. Use active words. Dominant impression is conveyed by sensory details."

He put these lessons into play in his own stories for the class. A piece entitled "Fight Team!" was indicative of his work level at the time. The story unfolds in a university football stadium on game day and is notable for revealing Brammer's early interest in examining not one character at a time but rather a whole set of social relationships: a modern comedy of manners. The piece has a documentary feel, foregrounding reportage instead of fiction's impulse to inhabit characters. It is clearly based on a sportswriter's close observations. The opening contains strengths and weaknesses that would remain signatures of Brammer's writing:

> It is one o'clock on a Saturday afternoon during the fall, a typical Indian summer day and a little too hot for football. There is already a hum of activity around the stadium. Negro and Mexican boys are setting Coca-Cola boxes along the bottom row of the stands, and under the stadium, the concession stand owners are giving their employees last minute instructions before the crowd begins its invasion . . . Addington Blackstone . . . has his own special seat reserved in front of the press box. Addington is a prominent banker in the town, and he gave $20,000 to the University for the construction of a new statium [*sic*] last year.

Steffan circled the words "typical" and "hum of activity." He said they were trite. In trying to establish a large sphere of action, a broad setting, Brammer could overlook significant details. He relied too much on exposition rather than letting information surface naturally in characters' conversations. On the other hand, the boys' "Coca-cola boxes" were well observed, the banker's name was perfect, and social distinctions between the wealthiest and poorest members of the community were swiftly established.

Brammer wrote to his teacher: "I tried to show that the little Mexican boys"—who find a pack of cigarettes to share beneath the bleachers—"were probably the only happy people after the game." He was not yet confident enough to set in motion a series of actions and follow their consequences; instead, he hoped thematic irony would carry the day. In his mature writing, Brammer would demonstrate a wickedly accurate ear for dialogue, but dialogue is the weakest element in "Fight Team!" He worked hard over the next few years to capture the essence and music of talk.

His concern with the "least of these" among his characters—the poor, the disaffected, the social outcasts—and the frustrations of powerful men would remain central to his vision. His note to Steffan is eloquent in laying out his view of human affairs: "The theme of this project was to show how people will plan on having a good time someplace, but only succeed in being confused, unhappy, and uncomfortable. Because many people come to football games, operas, etc., to see and be seen, and care very little about the event. The event is only a medium of social exchange."

During the school term, he endeavored to sharpen details and shape natural plots springing from character. He wrote fables, historical set pieces, melodramatic monologues, parodies of public speeches. "Keep trying to get a unity of theme," the professor urged him. In return, Brammer asked, "Was the description . . . all right?" or "Do you think it is too vulgar?" In one note to Steffan, he said, "I don't know whether you approve of the style, but it felt pretty good . . . Do you find any social significance? I hope the hell you do. I threw in a little of everything." Attached to another assignment, the complaint: "Well, here I am again with an idea for a story, but no plot. I just can't seem to get a main line of action . . . I was happy as all hell to finish it. I'm just about spent for any more material." To this, Steffan replied, "Just keep your eyes and heart open."

---

"The city lies against and below two short spiny ribs of hill. One of the little rivers runs round and about, and from the hills it is possible to view the city overall and draw therefrom an impression of sweet curving streets and graceful sweeping lawns and the unequivocally happy sound of children always at play," Brammer would write of an unnamed Austin in *The Gay Place*, giving it a Gatsby-like glow. As Larry McMurtry said later, the novel made life in the city in that era sound "more charming and less destructive than it really was." "On brilliant mornings," Brammer rhapsodized, "the white sandstone of the [college] tower and the Capitol's granite dome are joined for an instant, all pink and cream, catching the first light."

The Brammers' ideal marriage, as Robert Benton saw it, was similarly a romantic projection, filled with genuine moments of passion, hope, and excitement, but also rife with restlessness, tensions over money and work. Nadine couldn't abide her husband's spending habits. "He knew every new product that came on the market; we had a Waring blender before anyone else on the block." He would buy her an exquisite set of clothes, and they would spend the next several months trying to pay it off. "I knew we were doing something wrong—we could barely pay for necessities like food and gasoline—but it didn't occur to me to assert myself and tell Bill to control his spending," Nadine said. "Fifties women played passive roles. We looked to men for guidance and expected them to take care of us, and we often felt helpless."

One night, she opened a can of food for the Siamese cat she would later give to Benton. The smell of it made her nauseous. She was listless for days. She suspected a gas leak in the apartment. Then a doctor told her, "There's nothing wrong with a healthy girl like you. You're pregnant."

Brammer was ecstatic. "He always wanted children; I didn't," said Nadine. "My mother empathized with me—she knew I wasn't ready for motherhood. She also knew that Bill was irresponsible."

Shaky and scared, Nadine wanted to be near her mother, so she went to live temporarily with her parents in McAllen. Brammer wrote her weekly, almost daily, letters asking after the new life in her belly and groaning about his loneliness: "Rooter-Pooter [he called her]: Very no good here," "Ate Del's tamales for supper . . . I feel like you do in the mornings [sick] . . . Hope I can wake up to go to school this morn." In fact, he all but stopped going to classes. He ate very little. His mother sent him pecans and fruitcakes. He didn't know what to do with them. Nadine's replies to him reflected her relief at her mother's care as well as her ongoing worries: "I'm strangely bored and yet am enjoying myself at the same time . . . Sorry you're lonesome. I am too—sorta. Wish I could talk to you about getting a job . . . I don't know what our plans are—was just wondering how we're going to pay the bills," "Have you decided anything about the finances?" "All we need is *money*."

He was still scrambling to make ends meet: "Yesterday I discovered that there was nothing between the tubes on our rear tires except a teeney bit of webbing . . . They wouldn't have lasted another trip. Cost $50, but was able to pay five down and pay the rest at five a week. Guess we'll survive."

"I feel not so good about everything," Nadine pressed him. She totted up their monthly expenses. "There will be days I will have to scrounge without good food and I don't think that would be good for me—or YOU. There will be a few doctor bills along too. NO GOOD!!!! . . . There is nothing else. What am I to do? Will come back when my stomach can take the apartment."

Brammer tried to placate her, but his favorite strategy—shopping for her—was the core of the problem. "Got you many kinds of prayzunts," he wrote. "Started to get you a new doucheee bag, but didn't think it would look nice when you unwrapped it." He considered the possibility of moving to McAllen and writing for a local newspaper there. At first, Nadine liked the idea. The long separation began to soften her, and she told him how much she missed him. "Be good to your phallus and hurry [down here]!!!" she wrote. She signed her letters playfully: "Let's do it, Your pregnant whore," "Su 'concubina,'" "Virgin Mary." "My phallus yearns for your wombus," he wrote.

Nadine realized that her time in Denton and Austin had distanced her, temperamentally and politically, from her family and old high school friends. She loved Daddy Noah, but she was appalled by his racist views, clearer than ever: "Went to town yesterday," she wrote Brammer. "It was ghastly—'All them spics spend more money than the white folks.'" Soon, the idea of living permanently in the borderlands no longer appealed to her. She remembered how trapped she had felt as a girl. "I'm glad we aren't moving to this stinking valley," she told her husband.

But just *how* she wanted to live remained an open question. Throughout the separation, particularly early on, Brammer worried about what she might do. "Be happy," he wrote to her. "Don't do nothing to yourself. If you don't want what comes out, I'll take it, and you can flee away."

"In fact, at one point I tried to take some medicine that would make me abort," Nadine said. "Bill called me when I was about to take it."

"Love and nice things," he signed one of his letters to her, "and don't do nothing to yourself or I'll leave you."

# 5.

Shortly after New Year's Day 1952, Nadine wrote to Brammer: "On January 25, our fetus will be 3½ inches long with head, hands, feet, legs, and a mouth that opens. Also, sex will be differentiated, but no bones yet. I am learning, papa, and will inform you when I see you." Then she asked again what they would do about money.

He deflected the money question by telling her he had found an affordable house for them to rent, and if they wanted to buy it eventually, it would cost $8,500, no down payment. The house was near a railroad track. It had a "dirty solid pink" carpet whose "look" nevertheless was "very good," he wrote. The best part was that it had plenty of space for a small family. "You are a genius for finding it," Nadine wrote to him. "Tell me about it. . . . You're no good when you don't give details. But you're a good husband. I love you." They decided to buy.

Seven months later, on August 11 in Austin, their baby girl, Sidney, was born. She was an unusually pretty infant, said Robert Benton, fair skinned and delicate, and Brammer, he said, was besotted with her.

Within weeks, however, Nadine had fled back to her mother in McAllen, taking the baby. Ostensibly, the separation was for a short time only, occasioned by scheduling difficulties and Nadine's need for her mother's help while Brammer balanced classes with press assignments. In reality, she was unhappy with staying home while Brammer worked and studied during the day and went out with friends in the evenings. She no longer felt sick in the mornings, but she was terribly isolated. It upset her that she couldn't return to school—they couldn't afford day care or babysitters. Brammer's spending habits hadn't changed, and his salary from the newspaper remained a meager fifty-six dollars a week.

Nadine's letters to him during this period were chilly and short, written on printed stationery featuring her mother's name, Nadine Cannon (her own name before she married). One weekend, after Brammer had driven down to visit her, she wrote to him: "Thought of you around 1 a.m. when I was feeding Sidney. Presume you didn't have a bloody wreck on the way home. Am staying in bed today . . . there's nothing else to say. You forgot your dirty shorts. I miss you, but think it will do you good to have a vacation from my bitchery. Go to Dallas and go swimming and play for two hours—please. You need it."

Alone in Austin, he was miserable, staying up nights, swallowing pills, doing homework, and typing out his sports assignments. He had to have two molars pulled; his mouth ached, and he struggled to pay the dental bill. Desperate to prove to Nadine that he could provide for her and the child, he resurrected his air force idea: "Pay begins at $335 per month plus about $150 more for you and Syd [*sic*], plus $100 more during a 10 weeks flight training deal. That's a lot of money. Thought I'd look into it. What do you think?" His initiative pleased Nadine. Her letters to him warmed: "Am having little sex dreams of you, so guess it's nearing the time when we can enjoy each other's body—oh good thought!" "Am generating energy to come back to you and feed you sexually and physically. Hope you are still healthy enough to eat."

This time, to aid the success of his application, he wrote to his state representative, Homer Thornberry, as well as to the senator who had won a piece of his heart. He sent a direct appeal to Lyndon Johnson's Washington office, requesting expedited consideration for a position in the air force. "My dear friend," said the reply, "I am glad to know of your interest in active military service . . . and it will be a pleasure for me to get in touch with the authorities here and get some information as to chances for your call to active duty in the near future."

Almost immediately, a major general informed Thornberry there were no "present requirements for additional officers." A few days later, Brammer received a brief letter of regret from Johnson's office: "My dear friend . . . I want you to know I was very glad to inquire into this matter for you and if at some future date I can be of any assistance to you in any way, just let me know."

---

Nadine remained in McAllen. Brammer worked twice as hard as before, hustling newspaper assignments. He convinced his editors that he could cover politics as well as sports. He trolled for legislative gossip at the Forty Acres Club or on the top floor of the Headliners Club, where lobbyists gathered to drink. He attended meetings of the state's Agriculture Commission. "Have been staying out till about three each morning with [friends] bitching about the election," he wrote Nadine. "Heard Adlai speak last night and he is better than any radio comedian—Heard Ike talk today to a bunch of farmers, and he sounded like a high school football player trying to make the debate squad. He wasn't interrupted by applause, either."

On the weekends, stimulated by Benzedrine, Brammer drank late at Scholz's or watched James Mason movies with Benton at the Varsity Theatre on Guadalupe or headed out the Old Dallas Highway to Threadgill's. Threadgill had been a steadfast supporter of Hank Williams. He booked Williams frequently, despite the singer's increasing reputation as an undependable drunk. Williams played his last full show in Austin, at the Skyline Club, on December 19, 1952—though rumors spread among Brammer's press corps pals that the poor sod had been whisked to Brackenridge Hospital following his performance while his baby-blue Cadillac remained parked at the club. It was also rumored that a Dallas bar owner, Jack Ruby, whom Williams had been avoiding because of Ruby's reported mob connections, had finally managed to book the singer a few months prior to his Austin appearance. When Williams passed out cold in the dressing room, Ruby charged customers to see him laid out on the floor. Years later, the singer-songwriter Doug Sahm would tell Brammer he had been present at Williams's Skyline show. He was eleven years old at the time, learning to play a little steel guitar; Williams sat the boy on his bony knee, his breath smelling powerfully of whiskey, and told him to keep practicing. He did, and eventually Brammer was one of Sahm's biggest supporters.

In the early 1950s, Brammer became deeply fascinated by the road life of popular musicians—reminded of the peripatetic lives of his father's lineman buddies. Hard as it would be to move from place to place each day, the freedom from domestic responsibilities appealed to him, and it would be comforting to always have your next paying gig lined up. As he had predicted as a boy, his father's electrical wizardry had helped shape the future: Austin's energy now "wound through its nightclubs," said the writer Barry Shank, "linking power amps and speakers, transistors and tubes into a clashing counterpoint of discordant tonalities played together."

---

For the next year, Nadine shuttled back and forth, carrying Sidney, from Austin to McAllen. Whenever she spent an extended period with her mother, Brammer drove to see her on weekends. In the meantime, he tried to make the house he had bought merrier: "I've got sort of a study fixed up in the spare bedroom with the extra bed, typewriter, table, desk and lamp," he wrote. "It is very nice, and the record schism resounds all over the house. Carpets feel good on my athlete's footus." He lamented the chill in his lonely bed and signed his letters "John the Baptist" or "Copulation."

He remained in debt after frequent dental work and clothing sprees at Reynolds-Penland or Scarborough's over in the "hip" part of town, at Congress and Sixth. To try to compensate, he asked his editors for more and more assignments, taking more and more pills each night as he tried to meet his deadlines. At the end of 1952, he won a *Statesman* press award for "excellence in writing." Just over a year later, the Texas Associated Press singled out the *Austin American-Statesman* for distinguished reporting, citing Brammer's work on the Agriculture Commission as well as a feature on the "exuberant happiness and newfound confidence of the [Texas] Longhorn football team" after an upset victory over an archrival. The feature was notable for the same clear gaze that had animated "Fight Team!" It focused less on game facts than on individual athletes and the relationships among them in the locker room. "He told the story in his usual unusual style, which has become the delight of thousands of *American-Statesman* readers," said the newspaper in announcing the awards.

In fact, the story was mostly fiction. It revealed Brammer's now-accurate ear for speech. One of his colleagues, Anita Howard Wukasch, said to him, "Bill, you weren't even there. How did you know what the boys were saying [in the locker room]?" "They always say the same thing," he answered. "Nobody has accused me of misquoting."

He was becoming increasingly restless writing about sports. Just a stone's throw from his university classes, on Guadalupe Street, known as the Drag, he witnessed remarkable social changes that most reporters were ignoring. A man named Block Smith managed the YMCA on the Drag. Frequently, in the Y's meeting rooms, he hosted interracial student gatherings, infuriating the university's conservative board of regents. He urged members of the journalism faculty to denounce the university's racist policies—from him, some students first heard the word "racism" and inquired about its meaning. Few of the young people knew of Heman Sweatt, an African American man who had sued to be admitted into the UT Law School. The stress of the drawn-out legal process, which reached the US Supreme Court, and the hostility that greeted him on campus caused him to withdraw from school in 1952. Ever since, the university had used his example to argue against fully integrating. When the journalism faculty remained silent about this, Smith muttered, "I'm gonna give you a liver pill so you'll stand up for something."

In the spring of 1954, an organization called the Sons of the Republic, led by the Houston oilman Hugh Roy Cullen (a major benefactor of the University of Houston), invited Senator Joe McCarthy to speak on anticommunism at the San Jacinto Monument, the site of Texas independence. Cullen had called McCarthy the "greatest man in America"; he had been the single largest donor to McCarthy's 1952 reelection campaign. A few years earlier, Cullen had stood at the monument and wondered aloud "if our grandfathers wouldn't decide it was time for another Texas Declaration of Independence," severing the state from America's godless ways. In Austin, Block Smith led a campus demonstration against the "appalling travesty" of McCarthy's visit, but the protest garnered scant press coverage—certainly, it received far less attention than the state legislature's vote in praise of the Wisconsin senator.

In May, the United States Supreme Court ruled unanimously in favor of school desegregation in the case *Brown v. Board of Education*. Hugh Roy Cullen said the court had just "done more to destroy individual freedom than any government action since the founding of this nation." The UT campus newspaper, the *Daily Texan*, hailed the decision, writing, "Negro children . . . will be unacknowledged martyrs for the future equality of their race"; Block Smith organized demonstrations against movie theaters along the Drag to persuade them to open their doors to members of all races; Governor Allan Shivers declared desegregation would be the law in Texas only over his dead body—it was clear that a tumultuous summer lay ahead.

The Brammers' summer ended in tumult and joy when Nadine gave birth to their second baby girl, Shelby—equally as gorgeous as her big sister and just as beloved by her father, Robert Benton said. Nadine recovered from her pregnancy, taking the girls to Deep Eddy Pool near Lake Austin to cool off and play-swim most afternoons. She urged Brammer to find a better-paying job. He enraged her one day when he traded in the couple's

Nash Rambler for a new Plymouth station wagon. He didn't consult her. "I loved that Nash convertible," Nadine said. "I had a little back seat for Sidney. He said we'd have more room for the girls' playpen now, but really, he just thought it would be more comfortable to take long trips in."

Tired of feeling trapped at home, she decided to bring her babies with her whenever she wanted to enjoy a fine evening out. Sidney and Shelby turned white as little ghosts after crawling through the thick caliche under the wooden tables in the beer garden. Other young mothers brought their kids to play beneath the strings of colored lights in the elms. "[Our] children claim they were raised [at Scholz's], which is a slight exaggeration," said Dave Richards. "They did, indeed, spend many a Friday romping around the garden."

"We [became] . . . the Texas equivalent of Jack Kerouac's Beat Generation," Nadine reminisced in her memoir. "We were in love with romance, decadence, politics, and literature. We read competitively . . . [so as] to be witty and sparkling in the most esoteric way." She wanted to be "elusive, quixotic, irresistible to men," Hemingway's Lady Brett. But when her writer-husband pressed her with questions—the better to understand the female point of view, he explained—she felt his "intrusive" interest "verged on voyeurism." He would "set me up in conversations so he could watch me interact with various attractive male friends," she said. "If I met someone at a party and engaged them in conversation, he would quiz me on it when we got home. In current psychological terms, he didn't respect my boundaries."

Whenever the flirting in the garden got too serious, "we lied to ourselves and to each other . . . rationalizing it later with intellectual verbiage," Nadine said. "We couched it in clever repartee and witty put-downs, served with plenty of alcohol."

At a certain point, she recognized that her husband had become "uncomfortable" with the "fun and games." "He saw me enjoying myself, taking care of the girls, swimming every day, and partying on the weekends, and he felt the pressure to bring in more money to stay on par with some of our friends, who were either from wealthy families or were making more money in their jobs."

As ever at Scholz's, political outrage salted the sexual tensions. Everyone derided the cowardly legislators who had ducked the vote praising Joe McCarthy; they couldn't in good conscience support the brute, but not wanting to alienate their constituents, they made themselves scarce by hiding in the men's room. Maury Maverick Sr., a fiery former congressman from San Antonio (the term "political maverick" came from him), labeled them "shit-house liberals." He included his son, Maury Maverick Jr. Given the demagoguery emanating from the governor's office in advance of the 1954 elections, the Scholz liberals knew they had to back bold candidates if they were to have any hope of moving the Democratic Party to the left. Once again they rallied around Ralph Yarborough as he challenged Allan Shivers for the governorship. Yarborough managed to force Shivers into a runoff, at which point the campaigns' dirty tricks exceeded the usual tactics of jamming the opposition's phone lines and towing cars away from polling places. Shivers's supporters sent a well-dressed black man, wearing an expensive gold watch and driving a Cadillac plastered with Yarborough bumper stickers, into East Texas. He would stop at filling stations and yell at the white attendants that he needed a dollar's worth of gas right away. They had damn well better hurry because he was "working for Mr. Yarborough." By swearing that Texas would *never* integrate its schools, by equating desegregation with godless communism, Shivers won the race.

A still-fledgling political reporter, Brammer was learning the media's dirty tricks in an age of rapidly changing technology. While covering storms, mobile units would beat on the sides of their vans with two-by-fours to fake the sound of windblown detritus. It became standard practice for print reporters to pull the plugs of TV cameramen at news conferences so that the papers could get the story first. Many smug newspapermen felt television had no future in the information business, but Brammer knew differently. He had long understood the power of those big black cords. As always, he kept a keen eye on developments in *all* fields. For example, "He underwent a vasectomy after I was born," Shelby Brammer told me. "I . . . find it amazing that he managed to [do that] in the mid-1950s (always on the cutting edge of technology)."

Did any of these new techniques, like his impulsive purchases, really solve his problems? He knew his reporter's salary didn't provide enough support for his family. Silently watching the "fun and games" at Scholz's each night, "he must have felt under a lot of pressure in the marriage . . . not to have another pregnancy," Shelby said. But of course "he couldn't stop Nadine from her exploits . . . and people do what they want to do regardless."

---

Nadine wanted to work. She wanted to stay with her family in McAllen. She wanted to be a responsible mother. She wanted to spend evenings at Scholz's. She did all these things in tandem, or tried to, over the next few months, and she tried to wrest control of the money. She placed her husband on an allowance. "I need some clarification. You have me depositing money every Thursday. Does that mean that I can't start spending my spending money (this week $8) until Thursday?" he wrote to her at one point. "I don't need it now, but it might be a long time between this Thursday and next. How now?"

In Austin, Nadine worked for the editor of the *Austin American-Statesman*, clipping articles for him from Texas newspapers. During her extended stays in McAllen, she wrote only short notes to her husband, while his lengthy letters to her grew more mournful: "I am missing you tonight with tingling scrotum; also our children . . . Television is no good when you can concentrate on it instead of changing diapers . . . My teeth hurt every night . . . [found] a dentist who extracts on the installment plan: easy pull, easy pay." He asked her to hug his kids for him.

And then "Bill walked into my life unbidden," said Ronnie Dugger. "I was too isolated to ask anyone for help and too young to know I needed it."

Dugger had just begun the thankless, some said foolhardy, task of editing a small liberal newspaper in the heart of Texas, from a tiny office on West 24th Street, just off the Drag. He had honed his skills, a few years before, as the editor of the *Daily Texan*—after spending time with Edward Murrow's news team as a student in London and working briefly as a reporter for Lady Bird's radio station in Austin. At the *Texan*, he wrote in favor of civil rights, proposed national health care, called for drunk drivers to be jailed, urged boycotts of barbers near campus who had raised the price of a haircut from eighty-five cents to a dollar, railed against the university for failing to provide students with enough pencil sharpeners or with hot rolls in the cafeterias. His critiques of Lyndon Johnson's lackluster legislative record caught the senator's eye in Washington. The *Daily Texan* was just a student newspaper, but it rankled Johnson that this boy would go after him. He didn't know the meaning of compromise, Johnson grumbled. He was a "kamikaze liberal," a "red hot." The senator told one of his staffers, "If you investigate that boy's bloodline, you'll find a dwarf in there somewhere."

Dugger sat next to Heman Sweatt in the first law class Sweatt attended after winning his discrimination suit against the university. He witnessed the man's bravery and travails. He grieved when Sweatt left school. And then, after the liberals' statewide losses in the 1954 elections, he felt "ashamed of my culture, my countrymen," he said. Allan Shivers had been reelected on a platform of racism, and a right-wing Republican named Bruce Alger had been elected in Dallas to the state's congressional delegation. The Left had lost further ground—not to slick political operatives, but to "platoons of energetic women effectively carr[ying] out a grass-roots campaign, backed by telephone squads and canvassing teams," according to reporters. Dugger considered retreating to a coastal town in Mexico, going to work on a shrimp boat, and writing a novel about migrant laborers.

Meanwhile, the 1954 losses galvanized others—specifically, Frankie Randolph, an heiress to the Kirby lumber fortune in East Texas, wife of a prominent Houston banker, and one of the founders of Houston's Junior League. She had been a strong New Deal supporter and a major financial bulwark of Adlai Stevenson's 1952 presidential campaign. One of her friends believed "Frankie . . . was to Texas what Eleanor Roosevelt was to the United States . . . Her wealth gave her an easy familiarity with men of power, but she cared about working people, the union movement, racial equality, social justice, and peace . . . Earthy, blunt, and honest, she had more independent political power than any woman in Texas history." After the electoral debacle, she agreed to finance and serve as publisher of the *Texas Observer*, a successor to two earlier but erratic liberal publications, the *State Observer* and the *East Texas Democrat*. These ventures had lost a lot of money; a group huddling in Austin's Driskill Hotel in the fall of 1954 to plot the liberals' future strategies feared that by backing the *Observer*, Randolph would waste precious funds best saved for the next campaigns. But she agreed with Bob Eckhardt that pragmatic policies and electable candidates were only part of the story: political initiatives required "panzer troops" to set a social "conscience."

That was where the *Texas Observer* came in. Eckhardt, working as a labor lobbyist in Austin, helped draft legal documents to establish the newspaper. He and Randolph wanted Ronnie Dugger to serve as editor. Randolph liked his "spunk." She offered him a $6,500 annual salary. Dugger agreed to put Mexico on hold and to take the job only if he had full editorial control. He drafted a masthead statement that read: "We will serve no group or party but will hew hard to the truth as we find it and the right as we see it." His creed upset some members of the planning group, who wanted the paper to be nothing more than the Democratic Party's left-wing propaganda organ. One of them said, "If ever a rattlesnake rattled before he struck, Dugger has." Dugger threatened to quit before he began. Eckhardt backed him and provided a political cartoon for the first issue, published on December 13, 1954—a man with a top hat and cane, proclaiming, "I do not agree with anything you say, and I will fight to the death your right to say it." Right away, said the writer Larry L. King, "Dugger dug his talons into Governor Allan Shivers, conservative state legislators, uncaring corporations, fat-cat lobbyists, the reactionary *Dallas Morning News*, LBJ, and any person or institution who failed his high standards of honesty and caring." Eckhardt called the *Observer* a "little star in the murky night of Texas journalism."

Brammer had met Dugger over a pitcher of beer at Scholz's. "He was a relaxed, soft-spoken fellow with much self-deprecation in his manner," said Dugger. "He laughed at more than I laughed at, and in a different way, but I did not notice this at the time."

One evening early in 1955, as Dugger labored late in his basement office with the nearly impossible job of putting out another issue of the *Observer*, Brammer dropped by unexpectedly after his shift at the *American-Statesman*. The men didn't talk much. Brammer watched Dugger "going regularly, unfailingly bump all over the place," he recalled. He recognized the man's "total commitment," how he brought "all his resources and crackling nervous vitality" to his work.

Brammer dropped by on another evening. And another. After a while, his late-night appearances became quiet routines. "Without remarking he would go sit down at the long sidetable, which was always laden with mounds of Texas newspapers, and read and clip them for me," Dugger said. The job of putting out another issue of the *Observer* became a little less impossible.

"He came [to me] because he believed, or he wanted to believe, that things can be reformed, but he came just as much, too, because he wanted to watch, to overhear and to laugh. He was a born spy," Dugger said.

The men could not have been more different on the surface. "If he seemed a bit overmuch in those early days, perhaps my own assessments and receptions weren't even minimally enough," Brammer wrote—a way of saying that Dugger was an intense, often humorless, crusader, whereas Brammer, for all his vast interest in politics, didn't take the game quite so seriously. His time as a reporter in the Capitol cloakrooms and the lobbyists' private bars had taught him that the major players were fallible and all too human and that few solutions to social problems were fully satisfactory or permanent. In moments of busy frustration, Dugger would accuse Brammer of being completely apolitical, but reminiscing to me, years later, he said, "I exempt Billy Lee from my own sets of attitudes and values on people in politics . . . I loved him . . . obviously, coming to me nights when he got off work from the *American-Statesman* and I was alone, then offering to join me in the lowly work of clipping newspapers, and then quitting his downtown job to become my first associate editor, he was acting within his politics and political-societal values."

In his future writing—both in sections of *The Gay Place* and in private notebook jottings—Brammer indicated that he took more seriously betrayal by a friend than a politician's broken promises (which he more or less expected). The intersection of politics and friendship was a major point of interest for him, personally and literarily. This is one explanation for his decision to leave his regular newspaper job, despite the pressure from his wife to fix their finances, in order to join what he called a "provocative but clearly doomed experiment in independent regional journalism." For Dugger, the crusade was all; for Brammer, the venture was more about helping a friend whose principled commitment he admired. "Dugger [gave] far more to the *Observer* than he ever stood to gain," Brammer saw, and he pulled off a "miracle . . . shak[ing] us a little in our Hookworm Belt complacencies," in a place where few politicians tolerated even "an occasional honker of dissent." Dugger's "drives and demon-lusts and continuous manic flights and forced landings," though sometimes "debilitating" to be near, were the source of extraordinary achievement, Brammer said. They were reasons for him to show up night after night to help, jeopardizing domestic ease and a stable career path. The lack of challenge he had felt while writing for the *American-Statesman* was another motivating factor: too much football, too many agricultural subsidies. He told Nadine he had been stimulated by a recent conversation with a group of Houston newsmen. The media market there set much higher standards than the Austin papers: "We are a bunch of dull, dreary hacks here compared with Houston . . . But who wants to live [there]?"

He liked to watch Dugger get "swacked" on his own adrenaline, as if "tossing down straight shot snifters" of the stuff. But more than that: in spite of the superficial differences between them, Brammer recognized a kindred spirit. As a young man, Dugger had sworn to himself he would "rather disappear into oblivion than to give my life over to anything but my own work."

---

Precisely as the *Observer* was hurling its first stones at Goliath, Lyndon Johnson was consolidating his position as the youngest and—given his mastery of the body's arcane rules—the most powerful Senate majority leader in history. Though Johnson consistently denied to his colleagues that he harbored any greater ambitions, Dugger understood that "he was hell-bent on the presidency." In short, this involved making the "[Democratic] party and the nation stop thinking of him as a southerner," explained Robert Caro. Southern conservatives held sway in the Senate; Johnson couldn't afford to lose their support. At the same time, to broaden his power base, he had to persuade northern liberals he was on *their* side. All this he had to accomplish without riling his home-state backers, the oilmen and the Shivercrats, while appearing to be driven solely by principles rather than careerism. Dugger wasted no opportunities in the *Observer* to expose Johnson's machinations. "No one maintains he is not a man of his word—he is; it's just that he doesn't give it when it matters," Dugger would write. Later, he admitted: "I damned Johnson to hell and back."

"Lyndon Johnson loathed what Ronnie wrote about him because it was so on target . . . [He] constantly tried to figure him out so that he could either convert him or compromise him—he failed," Bill Moyers said. "I think LBJ understood that the kind of populism Ronnie espoused was the kind of politician he would have liked to have been if only he could have been elected statewide on those ideas." Reading the *Observer* "was like reading the Old Testament prophets," he recalled, "except that Ronnie didn't wait to hear God's voice in his ear."

Brammer's gentle satirical tone provided a needed counterpoint to Dugger's orations. He kept up the drudge work of pulling pieces of interest from the pile of "rotgut" Texas newspapers on the clipping table. And just as quietly as he had begun appearing night after night, he began to suggest story ideas for future issues. Dugger asked him to write them. Then Dugger offered him the associate editor position—salary unspecified and unstable, depending on the fluctuating circulation numbers.

Brammer didn't resign his post at the *American-Statesman* right away; "to conceal his leftist treachery from his bosses downtown," Dugger said, he signed his pieces "BB" or "WLB." The first one began, "It was two or three weeks before the [governor's] Inauguration, and the city, as some people put it at the time, was 'electric' with excitement. As a matter of fact . . . it was pretty dreary for us." The piece veered into fiction. Brammer claimed Governor Shivers called him accidentally one morning: "That mellifluous voice. It loses none of its rich, crunchy goodness over the wire." It was a "splendid opportunity" to lobby the governor, but he failed to exploit it, he wrote. Still, he carried the "consolation that we had been near greatness, in one way or another, and we had made small talk with someone special."

With this first article, neither reportage nor editorial, he had announced himself as the fool to Dugger's tragic prince.

"To Hell with the Facts" he subtitled his second column: "The State of Texas is in the hands of a terroristic band of soapbox radicals, perverted pinkos and dirty Reds. They control the legislature; they're stacked three deep on the boards; they're rotting in the courts. They stink." He debunked the holy site of the San Jacinto Monument: "They stuck a shaft in the ground at San Jacinto and called it the tallest stone monument in the world . . . [Then] Joe McCarthy came, saw, and re-conquered the battleground." He published a one-act play concerning the US Justice Department's opposition to Texas's leasing of its tidelands for oil drilling. "The scene is a lonely, submerged, oil-rich beach off the Texas coast. Four lonely, submerged, oil-rich figures are visible," the play began. Then the Texas governor—an early, rough sketch of Arthur Fenstemaker in *The Gay Place*—says, "Youah Govahnah went to Illinois. He talked with Ada-lie Stevenson. He asked Ada-lie if he was going to take the tidelands away from ouah schoolchildren if elected president. Ada-lie said yes, he was. How do you like that?"

Issue after dogged issue, Dugger exposed and Brammer mocked. The pressure to include political commentary prevented each Brammer piece from becoming fully realized on its own—not quite story, not quite play, not quite essay. These were opinion pieces gussied up as satires. Brammer wanted to be S. J. Perelman. The *Observer* needed him to be I. F. Stone.

Finally, he left the *American-Statesman* and backed his *Observer* work with his name:

> There is a certain intimidating circumstance concerned with putting words down on paper. The words, if you're sober that day, are liable to fall into sentences and from these may fall an opinion or two.
>
> And then along comes some spoilsport who holds your stuff up to the light and finds it a bit roseate.
>
> All things are relative, though, particularly opinions adjudged as pink.

Looking around at this "hysterical, No-Think" moment in American history, encouraged by Dugger's example, he had girded himself for direct battle with what he termed "our own mid-century Inquisition—[with] everyone [acting] . . . torpid and uncomplaining in the clutch of the Peckerwood and the Ignoranti."

He continued to write satires, but now he also engaged in gumshoe reporting, investigating official abuses, the backroom shenanigans of lobbyists, and Texas's political temperature. Always, he looked for the quirky detail, an image to crystallize the absurd hypocrisies underlying social behaviors. "A Department of Public Safety narcotics agent who admitted he kicked a Latin American service station attendant who was lying on the ground was found not guilty of depriving the attendant of his civil rights," Brammer reported. The narcotics agent, W. F. Hendricks, had forced the service station attendant, Abraham Maldonado Calderon, to strip to his underwear and drop to the ground. "Hendricks said he kicked Calderon 'three or four times on the leg . . . in order to search Calderon . . . not to deprive him of any rights,'" Brammer wrote, noting that Calderon had suffered four broken ribs.

In a profile of a San Antonio police officer suspended for participating in white supremacist activities, Brammer quoted the fellow's lengthy anticommunist diatribe, delivered while the man's little boy came flying through the room shooting a water pistol, shouting, "Communist, Communist, Communist."

In another instance, Brammer coaxed an interview subject to indict himself unwittingly with his own statements. "We've got everything under control here," an East Texas newspaper editor bragged to him. "I led the fight . . . There's not going to be any mixin' of nigger and white children in East Texas for a long, long time." The "fight" he had led was an organized series of physical threats against community members who had asked the local school board to uphold *Brown v. Board of Education.*

In an article on the state treasurer, deliciously named Jesse James, Brammer raised questions about the use of public money and mentioned, in passing, "old Jesse's private sideline, a motel on a nearby lake." And in a piece on the public relations "huckster" Phil Fox, who had helped Allan Shivers smear both Homer Rainey and Ralph Yarborough, Brammer referred to an incident in which Texas House member Barefoot Sanders was denounced as a communist by one of his opponents. On the spot, Sanders challenged the fellow to a fistfight—a scene replayed as high farce in book two of *The Gay Place.*

The May 23, 1955, issue of the *Texas Observer* carried Brammer's short story "The Green Board," about a freshman member of the Texas House. The man had landed "in trouble" with his colleagues for not cozying up to lobbyists. He remembered the innocent days when he had arrived "in the Capitol with a white Stetson, a string tie, and some gaudy cowboy boots with a silhouette of the three counties he represented emblazoned across the front of them." Four months later, the "string ties and Stetsons had disappeared, and so had the $25 a day. And so has my virginity, he thought. He wasn't quite so naïve now. He knew, now, what was going on down here, and he didn't like it much." The story showed a vast improvement over "Fight Team!" After rereading *Tender Is the Night*, Brammer learned to balance scene setting with his characters' interior voices. "The Green Board" predicted the matter and atmosphere of *The Gay Place* as well as the jaundice that would shade Brammer's already dark view of politics. "He had lived pretty high the first month," he wrote. "He'd brought the wife and kids down, and the $700 monthly from the State had seemed like a lot at the time. Now, the family was back home and he had been sending them money. Almost all of his last $350 check had gone that way." If these circumstances echoed his own present affairs—the money woes and frequent separations from Nadine and the girls—the next sentences would stand as a cold prophecy of his future, his embodiment of Fitzgerald's character Dick Diver, eroding spiritually, vanishing little by little: "At first he had lived in a rather sumptuous suite in one of the nicer hotels. Later he switched to a second-rate hostelry, and now he was in a rooming house near the Capitol."

---

"He was a very special person," Nadine would say of him later. "[But] Billy Lee never developed an adult ego state. He was my playmate—we always had fun. As long as he didn't have to be an adult, be responsible, he was so much fun to live with." But now with two little girls, the need for steady income, and the constant attentions of attractive men at places like Scholz's, Nadine was not always fully present, even when she shared Brammer's bed. More often than not, she spent weeks with her mother in McAllen, leaving him in the disorderly, dirty house. To fill his time, he began to rough out a novel about a group of Austin malcontents. He welcomed long nights in the cramped *Observer* office. Perhaps his humorous, self-critical editorial "A Fragile Subject," declaring "sex" the *Observer*'s "missing ingredient . . . whether from sheer ennui or just plain boyish modesty," was a cri de coeur.

The *Observer*'s other missing elements were art and cultural criticism, a paucity that Brammer sought to remedy with a column called "The Texas Mind." In one issue, he profiled the Dallas journalist Paul Crume, a "slightly sad-eyed and ungainly fellow" whose prose has a "glitter to it that distinguishes him from the hundreds of hackers who daily fill the Texas prints." This, in spite of the fact that Crume "has never done what major writers like to call 'major writing,'" Brammer wrote. Clearly, the thrust of his column was to urge Texans toward greater ambitions. He sounded deeply aggrieved when offering reasons why so many talents in the state had failed to deliver on their promise. "Perhaps it is the novel form that intimidates people like Crume," he wrote. "They prefer the essay, but there is no easy avenue to its recognition—particularly when it appears in so short-lived a medium as a daily newspaper."

In few other nonacademic Texas publications of the time were people writing at this level of seriousness about the state's literary prospects. In speaking of the terrors of the novel form, Brammer was of course talking to himself, trying to pluck up his courage.

"Billy was the first genuine, practicing literary man I ever knew," said Willie Morris, then the editor of the *Daily Texan* and a Scholz habitué, quaffing foamy pitchers with Brammer after dispatching his late-night deadlines. "We talked often . . . about the books I should be reading . . . He cared passionately about literature and had confidence in his own writing. [He said] good writing endured beyond the momentary fashions, and to read, read, read." Brammer and Dugger admired the principled stands that Morris took at the *Texan*. He excoriated the governor's support of "interposition"—that is, defiance of *Brown*. And when the UT Board of Regents pressured Morris to stop printing pieces critical of the state's oil-depletion allowance, he ran blank spaces on the page where editorials should have appeared.

The beer garden gave Brammer company when otherwise he faced an empty house; the people there made him feel part of a cause larger than himself—though he had never been, and never would be, a foot soldier for causes. Nadine told her parents she and Brammer considered themselves more liberal than Lyndon Johnson, but not as liberal as the Scholz crowd, Ronnie Dugger, or the rest of the *Observer* team. More to the point, Brammer's piece on Paul Crume revealed directions better suited to his abilities than muckraking, and a restlessness to try them. He admired principled stands, but he was beginning to see that his talent lay in sly observations—leaving the judgments to others. Dugger ran comments from social activists to the effect that "we speak of the [Texas] slums, we shake our heads, and yet how skillful we are in resisting the full truth about ourselves!" In the same issue of the *Observer*, Brammer praised Crume's writing philosophy: "[My] column is not for or against anything. We are the innocent bystander, the one that always gets shot. We have a horror of positive opinions."

Dugger's opinion of Lyndon Johnson was hardening. In preparation for the 1956 elections, and a possible run for the presidency, Johnson was marshaling the rules of the US Senate as his personal tools, using his position as majority leader to give the appearance of empowering colleagues while in fact subordinating their goodwill—and their votes—to his cause. His top administrative assistant, Walter Jenkins, recalled hearing LBJ, behind his closed office door, rehearsing scenarios of conversations with senators, playing both parts—himself cajoling, the other man resisting or agreeing. Johnson would act out the stories' variations until he had locked up the narrative tight, ending always in his favor. To Jenkins, these little dramas were hilarious—like Brammer's satirical one-act in the pages of the *Observer*. But Johnson understood the power of *story*, of shaping an image, of cause and effect.

He told different tales to northerners and southerners in the Senate. He helped Hubert Humphrey and other northern liberals pass a public housing bill while he insisted to his southern colleagues that he agreed with *them*—public housing was "socialism." Off the floor, away from debate, he guided Humphrey in lining up the necessary votes while he convinced the southerners that voting against certain amendments to the bill would weaken its overall effect.

Meanwhile, to secure his home-state support, he maneuvered to place on the Democratic National Committee, as Texas's representative, Lieutenant Governor Ben Ramsey, a "reactionary and racist . . . who presided as the dictator over the Texas Senate to the purring pleasure, protection, and profit of every corporate fat cat in the state, the oilmen most of all," Dugger said. It was imperative that the *Observer* catalogue and oppose every twitch of Lyndon's little finger. But Dugger couldn't raise his associate's ire. Brammer's attention had wandered elsewhere. He had learned that Warner Bros. was set to film *Giant*, the screen adaptation of Edna Ferber's overheated oil novel, in the tiny West Texas town of Marfa, near the Mexican border. The movie would star Rock Hudson, Elizabeth Taylor, and James Dean. Brammer seized on the news of its production as an opportunity to reread Ferber's novel and to pen for the *Observer* another thoughtful overview of Texas's literary promise. Ferber's book was "richly-conceived and rottenly written," he wrote. "Instead of portraying Texans as proud, primitive, super-patriots obsessed with sheer bigness and magnitude, which many of us are, she made us out as oil-rich robber barons and feudal lords, buffoons and mountebanks, which, it is hoped, few of us are." He concluded that the "people who make up the state of mind that is Texas" tended to be more urban than rural now, neither excessively wealthy nor exceedingly poor, but rather middle-class folk often transplanted from other parts of the country. "Miss Ferber failed to sense this," Brammer wrote. "Perhaps the next novelist will."

While Dugger worried that "Americans were about to be trapped in the history that Lyndon Johnson would make," Brammer decided the *Observer* should send a reporter—him—to the film set in Marfa.

"He asked me to go with him—in that damn station wagon he'd traded the Nash for," Nadine said. "I had no interest. I'd *been* to Marfa."

Named for the family servant in *The Brothers Karamazov*, the novel the railway overseer's wife was reading when her train paused in West Texas in 1881, Marfa was situated barely tight against the wind in a sometimes grassy desert sixty miles north of Mexico, near the Dead Horse Mountains and the cone of an ancient volcano. It consisted mostly of cattle ranches and warehouses built as prisoner-of-war barracks during World War II. The first thing Brammer noticed, pulling into town on a sunny June afternoon, was that the "townspeople [hadn't] changed much" under the Hollywood onslaught, but the crew from Burbank had "attempted to dress like Texans." "The women have been wearing such things as denims and stoles and stetsons [*sic*] and four-inch wedgies. One lady was even seen wearing riding pants and a turban," Brammer wrote. He said the men tended toward "khakis and dress shirts and French cuffs" as well as "Jungle Jim 'safari' helmets": "It's something like seeing a mob of zoot-suited drugstore cowboys."

Warner Bros. had leased several "mesquite-studded and stunted ranches" for the movie shoot. "Some miles out from town, south on Highway 67, there looms large on the horizon a macabre structure which should remain for years a curiosity for West Texas cattle and cowpokes. Sticking starkly out of the prairies is a three-storied Victorian mansion, all gingerbread and lightning rods, rococo and utterly inelegant," Brammer reported in the second of two articles on the movie, in the July 4, 1955, issue of the *Observer*. The house was "a sham," he said, "built in California, in prefabricated units, the simulated stone façade being plaster on wood and metal, and shipped to Texas by flatcar": "It's here that the crowds foregather, here and down the road a piece, to watch [director] George Stevens and several hundred slightly parboiled Californians labor in the

Texas sun. It's as if a vast, traveling circus has broken down in the midst of this desolation and set up shop for some kind of performance. There are tents and trucks and trailers and tractors, buses and vintage cars and a great, milling mob of carpenters, technicians, cosmetologists, and even an occasional moom-pitchure star."

The gabbling activity and the equipment reminded him of the Texas Power and Light construction camps he had stayed in as a boy with his father. The two of them had, in fact, camped near here once, on a line project, by an old silver mine that was now the site of a ghost town. He liked the frenetic, temporary feel of movie lots: long black cables strewn across dry hummocks of gravel and sand. He liked the desert's edge-of-the-world atmosphere. But what really caught his fancy was the unintentional surrealism of Hollywood's daily business. Tumbleweeds were too scarce, here, for the director's taste, so the studio had trucked in some from California. If the wind didn't blow on the days the director needed it to, the crew would manufacture gales with blowers. The local range grass wasn't green enough for the cameras, "so the moviemen simply sprayed on a green vegetable dye. It looks real pretty," Brammer wrote.

His "dispatches from Marfa are . . . the most sophisticated writing of any Texas journalist at the time," Steven L. Davis wrote. Brammer focused very little on the larger-than-life celebrities. Elizabeth Taylor was "every bit as pretty as she seems in the movies and bearing up well in the Texas sun, although she seems a bit slim in the shanks, a trifle weak in the pasterns." James Dean seemed at home in the desert: "A kind of fuzzy-cheeked Marlon Brando . . . blend[ing] into the scenery . . . He looks like he's been rolling in it, in fact. He's what you'd call a dusty-colored fellow." Instead, Brammer highlighted the social—implicitly political—differences between West Texas and Hollywood, between the hardworking ranchers and the California mythmakers. The movie's fake mansion was erected "on the Worth Evans ranch," he noted. "Mr. Evans wouldn't even have made it as a bit player in the Ferber novel. He only has 35,000 acres."

By the time he returned to Austin, he was already imagining a novel, or part of one, set on a movie shoot in far West Texas. Earlier in the year, Governor Shivers had made a cameo appearance in a Paramount production called *Lucy Gallant*, starring Jane Wyman. Brammer began to speculate on intersections between politics and Hollywood, candidates, actors, and directors. Eventually, details from his Marfa reporting, such as the fake Victorian mansion, looming on the horizon "like a great landlocked whale," the dyed green grass, and the trucks full of tumbleweeds, would make it into *The Gay Place*. Says one of the characters, explaining how set technicians planned to prepare the tumbleweed scene, "It don't tumble. Even when there's a good wind. It just don't tumble. So they brought out some big blowers—big 'lectric fans—to make the tumbleweed tumble when they shoot the moom pitcher."

Still ecstatic over what he'd seen in the desert, Brammer was not in a particularly receptive mood when an anxious Dugger showed him a lengthy *Newsweek* article calling LBJ "THE TEXAN WHO IS JOLTING WASHINGTON." Dugger hoped to recruit Brammer back into battle. He said he thought "the FBI or 'The Lobby' or some other ubiquitous, indefinable Dark Force of Reaction was engaged in tapping his and my and the *Observer*'s telephone lines," Brammer recalled. "Perhaps they were being tapped—I've always hoped they were. There's been precious little intrigue in my life, and . . . I'm inclined to welcome a really first-rate gang of spies and trenchcoat-flapping saboteurs."

But before the two editors could schedule upcoming assignments or work out their growing differences about the *Observer*'s focus, their world wobbled on its axis. The news came in early July. Lyndon Johnson had suffered a massive heart attack.

# *6.*

In his State of the Union Address to the nation in 1965, Johnson recalled his childhood landscape in Central Texas: "It was once barren . . . The angular hills were covered with scrub cedar and a few live oaks. Little would grow in the harsh caliche soil. And each spring the Pedernales River would flood the valley." He said that a president does not "shape a new and personal vision of America." The "answer" about how to proceed as a leader was to be found in one's birthplace. A president "collects" his vision "from the scattered hopes of the American past."

Following his heart attack in the summer of 1955, and a five-week recovery period in Bethesda Naval Hospital in Maryland, Johnson wanted to gather his scattered hopes in the land of his family, on the ranch he had developed a few miles west of Johnson City, west of the spot where he was born and where his grandfather's log cabin once stood. He told reporters in DC that he was lonesome for the ballads of Hank Williams, that he wanted to shut off radio news broadcasts and rest. He said his illness had taught him the importance of relaxation. The truth was just the reverse: he had dipped into a raging depression, reading the headlines: "Heart Attack Drops Johnson from White House Hopefuls."

At the ranch, he left Machiavelli's *The Prince*, Plato's *Republic*, and other books scattered about the rooms so that visiting reporters would think he was reading. His disdain for books remained as powerful as ever. He instructed his staff to put Strauss waltzes on the record player—which were immediately silenced when the press corps departed for the day. His depression worsened. Lady Bird was beginning to look as gaunt as he was, waiting on him every few minutes.

In mid-August, Brammer asked Dugger whether he could travel to the Johnson ranch to report on the senator's convalescence for the *Observer*. Dugger said sure. The paper needed to know what was happening with the wounded warrior. Brammer drove down from Austin, winding past limestone ranges and hard, cracked earth in the heat, through hills that never quite got hilly. Passing through Johnson City—the smell of brisket, onions, and enchiladas wafting from backyards somewhere behind the courthouse—he imagined nothing much had changed here since before the coming of the electric wires. Drinkers in Red's could sit in the dull pink glow of a flickering Pearl Beer clock, its lighted minute hand visible through an open, slanted doorway; flies could gather on the warm, glowing sign of Groft's Humble Service Station; but other than that, time here might as well have been stored in old molasses jars. It had stopped dead still. Voices full of gravel called "Howdy" to one another across the shadows of vast wooden porches; otherwise, cicadas screamed and horseflies buzzed. In the distance, the Twin Sisters Mountains rippled blue in the heat-thinned air.

Brammer headed west on Highway 290 toward Stonewall. The old Johnson family cemetery stuck its gray monuments up through tall range grass beside the Pedernales. (Eventually, Brammer would learn that one of the first things Johnson did, upon returning to Texas, was to visit the family graves and draw an *X* in the dirt with his shoe tip to mark his *own* resting spot.) The ranch's big white house, almost purple in the oaks' waving shade, came into view. A kidney-shaped swimming pool, just built, threw sunlight diamonds from the surface of its water right back at the sun.

Brammer was one of only a few reporters allowed to talk to the senator that day. This was the first time he had seen the man face-to-face since covering his campaign appearance in North Texas in 1948. It wasn't the same Lyndon. He had lost nearly fifty pounds since suffering the first chest pains, less than two months earlier. He was pale and subdued. *Fragile*. He let his worried mother speak to him sternly, urging him to be more active. ("I would rather face ten of Al Capone's gangsters in a back alley than have to spend one hour alone with that woman," LBJ's press aide, George Reedy, confided to reporters.) Johnson's eyes clouded whenever Lady Bird, immaculately made up and attired in the midst of her constant chores, left the room for a moment: "Where are you, Bird?" "I'm here, I'm here," fluttering like one of the nervous sparrows in the pecan trees outside. Despite obvious irritation, Johnson quietly accepted the "healthy" meals his cook, Zephyr Wright, brought to him, along with a list of the food's calorie, fat, carbohydrate, and protein counts. He would take the list from her strong black hand and thank her for the "love letter."

In a swirl around him, his staff—including Mary Margaret Wiley, a recent University of Texas graduate who had just come aboard as a secretary; Walter Jenkins, a quiet, accommodating man, never far from Johnson's elbow; and the senator's rather rickety younger brother, Sam Houston—scrambled to keep track of the mail. Johnson insisted that every letter from well-wishing strangers be answered immediately, and he dictated personal responses to his colleagues in the Senate ("I have been sitting here on my Ranch looking over the Country in which I was born and just relaxing and enjoying myself thoroughly"). In fact, the constant banging of typewriters made it impossible to relax in the house.

Impressed by Johnson's humble demeanor, his apparent courage, and his desire for normal work to resume, Brammer reported to the *Observer*'s readers, in a piece entitled "Lyndon Comes Home" (August 24, 1955), that Johnson was "kind and obliging" to his visitors. He had lost a shocking amount of weight and appeared to be frail, but he was handling his crisis with quiet dignity. He was a true leader, under whom the "Democratic Congress" had managed "genuine achievements." Although Dugger had been more than ever on the warpath against the mercurial Texas senator, this was the friendliest piece the *Observer* had ever run on Lyndon Johnson.

---

The specifics of how Billy Lee and Nadine Brammer came to work for Johnson remain a bit obscure, in the way formal correspondence skates past daily routine ("My dear friend, I want you to know I was very glad to inquire into this matter for you").

When I interviewed Nadine in the winter of 2014, and again the following spring, her memory of the time was too indistinct to add much to the generalized version in her memoir. Further, the memoir confused important dates. Nadine wrote, "After hearing that LBJ was looking to hire a Texas pressman, Bill talked to someone in his office, and was hired. Soon thereafter, I had an interview with Walter Jenkins, Johnson's right-hand man, and was hired as well." Thirty years before writing the book, she told her friend Al Reinert, "We'd all heard that Lyndon was looking for a house liberal for his staff, someone who was friends with the rest of the young liberal crowd. I think they were all secretly trying for the job. It turned out that Lyndon had read some of Bill's articles and been impressed. So he hired him. Later, he gave me a job, too."

These accounts ignore the complex political wars Johnson was waging as he emerged from the twin hollows of his heart attack and depression; they ignore the degree to which the *Texas Observer* had gotten under his skin; and they ignore Brammer's comings and goings at the ranch during this crucial time.

Brammer published his sympathetic account of Johnson's recovery in late August 1955. A second article about Johnson, who, still at the ranch, was preparing for a triumphant return to national politics, appeared in the *Observer* on October 5. Just over two weeks later, the *Dallas Morning News* surmised that "Lyndon Johnson's relations with Texas labor unions may be helped with the addition to his staff of Bill Brammer, reporter for the liberal weekly, *Texas Observer*, on November 1." On November 2, the *Observer* announced, "Bill Brammer, associate editor of the *Texas Observer* and one of the state's best journalism stylists, became associated with Senator Lyndon Johnson's staff November 1. He and his family will move to Washington in December." Then, on November 18, a brief column in the *Corsicana Semi-Weekly Light* listed Bill Brammer as a member of "the senator's Austin office." The piece said he was organizing a celebratory fund-raising dinner for Johnson in Whitney, Texas, at which Johnson would deliver "one of his first major speeches since his midsummer heart attack."

Between late August and mid-October, Johnson set his sights on Brammer, and Brammer leaped. He did not walk into the senator's office in the state Capitol, résumé in hand. He had chatted with the senator in more relaxed surroundings at the ranch. Though initially the occasions included other news reporters, the men were getting to know each other in circumstances far different from a formal job interview. At some point, Johnson requested a private conversation. Years later, Joseph Califano, a Johnson hire, would describe the man's favorite method of conducting business one-on-one at the ranch. He would invite his guest into the swimming pool, "instinctively and intentionally pick[ing] a depth of the pool where he could stand and [the guest] had to tread water." Califano and Brammer were both short men, a fact that Johnson would not fail to exploit. Johnson would hold forth, "his finger poking my shoulder as though it were punctuating a series of exclamation points," Califano said. The heated pool was new when Brammer first appeared at the ranch.

It was surrounded by piped-in music from speakers lodged in live oaks and equipped with telephones for long-distance conference calls. Johnson used the pool frequently in the summer and fall of 1955, ostensibly as part of his relaxation regimen, but really as a rallying spot for his staff. It is not a stretch to imagine Brammer, a former competitive swimmer, being hired while treading water.

Johnson may have been looking for a "house liberal" to add to his crew, but several options were available to him. They all bore higher profiles than Brammer. The journalist Jan Jarboe Russell wrote that Dan Rather arrived at the ranch one morning. As a reporter then for KTRH radio in Houston, he was not yet the famous man he would become, but he worked in a news market reaching far more people than Brammer did with the *Observer*. But LBJ clashed with him, calling him rude and untrustworthy. First and foremost, Johnson looked for loyalty in the people he let past his gate. Al Reinert speculated that Johnson "welcomed [Billy Lee's] careful perspective and reflective temper, the inward bent of his mind, and he trusted him because he could dominate him, or so it seemed." Nadine said, "We were a couple of snobby, prissy intellectuals, and [Johnson] recognized us right away for what we were. He used to argue with Billy about what a waste of time it was. After a while, you know, he really got to liking Billy. I mean he really liked him."

If Johnson, never a deep reader, was "impressed" by Brammer's writing, it was because Brammer, unlike Dugger, wrote stories about people rather than ideas. He let the details speak for themselves. Johnson, as editor of his college newspaper in San Marcos, had once written, "It seems to be the tendency now to discover in historic characters rather disappointing and unadmirable traits and to reveal these . . . This practice deserves pronounced condemnation. The great have their weaknesses, but for these weaknesses to be magnified and exploited works no good to the reading public. Hero worship is a tremendous force in uplifting and strengthening humanity." Johnson sensed that "Billy understood himself too well to ever look down upon someone else's shortcomings," Reinert said. He also saw in Brammer a gentle storyteller with a capacity for painting Johnson as larger than life—as the conscience-stricken public servant walking through Austin on a cold Christmas evening and worrying about the poor, the way he had presented himself in the radio address that charmed Brammer as a boy.

And this was not just *any* storyteller. This man was Ronnie Dugger's associate editor, his best writer. If LBJ could steal Brammer, it might leave Dugger adrift without a rudder. "At some point" in the fall of 1955, as

Johnson was courting and securing Brammer for his staff, Dugger "received a phone call that Senator Johnson would like to see me, and would I call on him at the ranch at a certain hour on a certain afternoon," Dugger said. "I had never been out there. After wheeling my family's 1948 Chevrolet, which we called the Green Hornet, through the Pedernales River muscling itself shallowly over Johnson's low-water bridge, I pulled up in front of his grand spread and saw that he was swimming in the pool." Johnson pulled himself out of the water, toweled off, and dragged up a couple of pool chairs. "Ronnie, what's the circulation of your paper?" he asked. "Oh, about 6,000," Dugger replied. "Stick with me and we'll make it 60,000," Johnson said. Dugger realized that "he was trying to bribe me." Dugger remained polite as Zephyr Wright brought the men lemonades. The damp plastic of the chaise longue began to stick to his trousers. Finally, he rose and said it had been an honor to meet the senator. He didn't want to overstay his welcome. "Why don't you stay to dinner," Johnson said. "No problem. Bird'll have plenty."

Dugger sat through an awkward meal with the senator, Lady Bird, and Mary Margaret Wiley, whom he had known in high school in San Antonio. Johnson maintained his pressure. As courteously as he could, Dugger tried to explain his understanding of the role of journalism, the importance of the fourth estate's independence from government. Johnson insisted, "No, the thing a smart young reporter does, and should do, is survey the field of candidates, pick the best one, and enter into a deal to help that one win whatever office and prevail in whatever controversy, subordinating his reporting and comment to the interests of the candidate."

After dessert, Dugger tried to escape the ranch as quickly as he could, but Johnson followed him out to the low wire fence. The senator braced his knees against the wire and jutted his face within inches of Dugger's, leaning forward a little more until "my head bent back," Dugger said. He planted his heels in the dirt. Neither man gave ground. Earlier, by the pool, Dugger had asked Johnson "why he, the Senate majority leader, would bother himself about what a weekly paper said about him. Shifting his weight in the chaise lounge . . . he bawled out, 'I don't want people to think I've gone back on my raisin'.'"

It isn't clear whether Johnson already had Brammer in line as a backup if Dugger failed to fold, whether he would have hired Brammer anyway, or whether he turned to Brammer in revenge, as his second-best strategy. In any of these scenarios, it is doubtful that Brammer would have minded much if he thought LBJ saw him as a pawn. Even this early, "[Billy] was fully aware of Johnson's reckless flaws and self-deceptions," Reinert said. And all the evidence, going forward, suggests that Johnson genuinely valued Brammer's temperament and skills.

In any event, Dugger and Brammer experienced very different visits to the ranch that fall, though they received similar blasts of what the staff tagged the "Johnson Treatment": the caterwauling, the crowding of personal space, the body touching, the badgering.

If Johnson had reasons to warm to Brammer, what lured Brammer to LBJ? He had been fascinated with the man since the whirlybird days—for sheer drama, the guy was hard to beat, a folkloric figure. Even Ronnie Dugger could see "he played every part, he left out no emotion; in him one saw one's self and all the others. I think he was everything that is human. The pulsing within him, his energy, his will, daring, guile, and greed for power and money, were altogether phenomenal, a continuous astonishment"—impossible for a literary sensibility to ignore.

Brammer started to know Johnson when he was vulnerable. Shocked by the senator's frailty, impressed by his handling of public affairs in the midst of his crisis, Brammer felt sympathetic. Johnson took note of his *Observer* pieces. At the ranch, Brammer would naturally have caught the flickerings of troubled love and disappointment between Johnson and his brother. In the years ahead, Sam Houston came to love Brammer, and confided in him. Brammer would hear the stories of how LBJ, a prodigious drinker (though he claimed to nip only a little "bourbon and branch water" now and then), disparaged Sam Houston for his alcoholism—like the time Lyndon came reeling off a golf course, snockered, and shook his brother awake. "Yes, by God, I want you to take a damned good look at me, Sam Houston. Open your eyes and look at me. 'Cause I'm drunk, and I want you to see how you look to me, Sam Houston, when you come home drunk." Brammer would learn how Lyndon, as a boy, stood outside saloons, yelling, "Come on home!" while his father got hammered inside with his political cronies. In the fall of 1955, LBJ, helpless at the ranch, feeling like the wreck he had seen his father become, gazed at his broken brother with pity and scorn, as if to say, "Is *this* all I've got left to help me?" Brammer saw it—and he saw that Sam Houston *did* aid his big brother, every chance he got. As his brother knew he would. Robert Caro reported that Sam Houston was responsible for dragging Lyndon out of his depression that fall: he talked an Austin reporter into writing that LBJ's health was no impediment to his seeking the presidency.

On some level, Brammer must have recognized in Lyndon Johnson a similarly impulsive personality with addictive tendencies ("charming, reckless, crazy"). A man with no adult ego state. "I had seen people smoke and drink dinner before," said Bobby Baker, LBJ's Senate aide, but in the months and weeks before the heart attack, Johnson "did it like a man trying to kill himself." In August, as staffers in Washington were packing the private plane with Johnson's things for his convalescence at the ranch, he whispered to one of his secretaries to smuggle a couple of bottles of Cutty Sark on board. "Make sure Lady Bird doesn't know about the booze," he told her.

At the ranch, Brammer watched Johnson play dominoes with his daughters Luci and Lynda. Johnson bragged that after he had arrived back in Texas, Luci threw her arms around his neck one day and said, "Daddy, it sure is nice to have you around the house so much." He said he had missed his little girls while working so hard in the Senate, and it was time, now, to get to know them. Brammer understood this was partly an act for reporters—but he shared the aching realities of a father's separation from his daughters, even if the father's will, or lack thereof, had created the circumstances.

---

On September 24, Johnson's prospects for the presidency improved considerably: Dwight D. Eisenhower had a heart attack while golfing in Colorado. Newspaper editorialists as well as many Washington insiders assumed he would not seek reelection. His health crisis eclipsed Johnson's in the national conversation, and Johnson set about, more concertedly than ever, to project an image of renewed strength and vigor. At least twice a day, he phoned Jim Hagerty, Eisenhower's press secretary, to check on the president's condition and ask whether there was anything he could do. The worse the news, the better he felt about his path to the White House.

He knew he had to maintain his home-base support, which meant quieting the liberal crowd without alienating the Shivercrats. On the other hand, an open alliance with Shivers's segregationist stance would damage him nationally. Texas liberals and conservatives saw that he was playing them against each other; he hoped Brammer could moderate the tone of the disagreements and prove to both sides that—as Harry McPherson, another recent Johnson hire, explained—"political issues were [not] cast in chiaroscuro." This was not a holy war, and yet the passions would not cool; the need to pacify them would largely occasion John F. Kennedy's visit to Texas in 1963.

Johnson also sought to expand and consolidate his control of media outlets. He had failed to co-opt the *Observer*, but he succeeded in persuading advertisers to buy more airtime on KTBC, strengthening the station's connections with the state's business leaders. He purchased another radio station, KANG in Waco, working secretly with the FCC chairman to improve the station's financial future by exploiting FCC rulings not yet made public.

In late September, Johnson invited to the ranch Adlai Stevenson and Sam Rayburn, Speaker of the US House of Representatives and one of Johnson's strongest supporters, for what Brammer called the "Pow Wow on the Pedernales"—a strategy session for the 1956 elections. Johnson had hoped to keep the meeting a secret, but word leaked to the press. When he heard that a posse of reporters planned to show up at the gate, his eruption of anger "could be felt all the way to Austin," said George Reedy. Reedy was afraid that "he was going to bring on another heart attack and die." Sardonically, Johnson remarked to Stevenson and Rayburn, "[The reporters] think that you, Adlai, and you, Mr. Sam, and I are plotting to take over the government while Ike is dying." When the press corps arrived, Johnson charmed the writers and photographers by playing the gracious host, giving them a tour of the ranch, showing off his Herefords, extolling the beauty of the river. Brammer covered the summit for the *Texas Observer*—his last reporting for the paper. He wrote that LBJ "looked fit, very much better than upon his return from Washington." He moved so energetically that Stevenson—the Democrats' presumptive presidential nominee; LBJ had not yet declared his ambitions, even to allies—scrambled to "keep falling in behind the fast-striding Johnson."

Ronnie Dugger could not have been pleased that the *Observer* was following the lead of other Texas newspapers in presenting Johnson's preferred public image.

Brammer's final editorial for the paper, in his role as associate editor, was a satirical commentary on the oil-depletion allowance, "That Old Depleted Feeling." He concluded, "We here at the *Observer* . . . are terribly depleted at the moment. We have lost a good deal of our initial momentum. Our enthusiasm at the onset of this experiment has been dulled by too many speeches, too many scandals, and, perhaps, too many crusades against the oil depletion allowance." These were not joking words. Fighting the good fight had exhausted him. He was fed up playing the underdog. He longed to be "spared the carnage seasonally heaped on Texas liberals," he said.

"Some of our friends gave us a hard time" for decamping to the enemy's compound, Nadine said. Dugger was saddened when Brammer told him he was going to take "what stale enthusiasms remained" in him into Lyndon Johnson's employ, but later, when anyone in the beer garden rebuked Brammer, "I defended my friend," Dugger said. He knew Brammer was not really a political animal. He was "genuinely a literary person[;] he had this special nature and this special way of seeing and being." On a deeper level, Dugger understood that Brammer "wanted a conservative personal life, but did not find it among his . . . Austin friends." Brammer hoped to bring his family together again in a Washington home. He hoped to temper Nadine's Zelda-like desire to be irresistible to other men.

Shortly after hiring Brammer as a press aide, Johnson tapped Nadine to be one of his secretaries. It was a habit with him to hire married couples. "An eight-hour man ain't worth a damn to me," he would say. He expected his employees to work round the clock, and "I don't want some wife at home complainin' that the cornbread's gettin' cold while her husband's doin' something for *me*."

His formal return to the public stage, a calculated demonstration that he was "back in the saddle again," occurred in a high school auditorium in the small Central Texas town of Whitney, following a dinner with local officials and business leaders, arranged with Brammer's aid. Brammer also helped draft Johnson's talking points for the upcoming congressional session, a plan Johnson called "A Program with a Heart," a phrase sure to remind listeners of Johnson's recovery as well as the president's current distress. Of the thirteen points in the program, twelve were pitched at liberals, including a tax revision to benefit low-income groups, a broadening of Social Security, and increased funding for medical research. Tucked mutedly into the middle of all this was LBJ's sop to conservative oilmen: "A natural gas bill that will preserve free enterprise."

On December 11, Brammer flew to DC with the rest of the Johnson entourage. He helped prepare a Capitol Hill press conference and worked the roomful of reporters, spreading perceptions and key phrases that would disseminate LBJ's recovery narrative among the nation's major papers, erasing all doubts about whether he was healthy enough to resume his role as majority leader of the Senate.

Brammer rented a small unfurnished apartment near the Senate Office Building. He would be there only to sleep a few hours each night. He kept the otherwise empty refrigerator stocked with Dr Peppers. He opened a local bank account, but his first check bounced. Nadine stayed in Austin to pack things up, sell the car, and find someone to rent the house. Finally, just after New Year's Day 1956, she trundled Sidney and Shelby onto a "cushy, luxe Brown & Root plane," usually reserved for lobbyists, and flew to Washington. "It didn't look like any plane that I ever saw afterwards," Sidney recalled. "It was furnished like a living room and carpeted and we were served a meal like we were in a restaurant." In years to come, she was disappointed when other airplanes didn't match up. Seven months later, Nadine appeared in a photograph with her husband and two other couples who worked for LBJ, standing behind the senator and Lady Bird on the steps of the US Capitol. The picture accompanied an article in the *Corpus Christi Caller-Times* entitled "They Take Their Wives to Work." Brammer, twenty-six, short-haired and stiff in his suit and tie, looks like a tiny marionette dangling from invisible strings attached to the senator's elbow. Nadine, twenty-four, smiling and demure, wearing a long dark skirt and sweater blouse, gazes at Lady Bird and Johnson as though she were a guest at their wedding. The article called Johnson Washington's "most unusual boss" and hailed his policy of hiring couples as a progressive experiment in fostering "team spirit." "Housewives! Instead of a day-long battle with dust, dirty dishes, laundry, lunches and dinner, would you rather lock the door on all that and go to work with your husband each morning?" wrote the reporter. Lady Bird chimed in: "It's a rare and wonderful opportunity when husband and wife can work together. No one is as interested in a man's business as his own wife. Nothing makes for greater unity and understanding." Asked how she felt about the arrangement, Nadine responded, "I come into the Capitol with Bill every morning and sometimes I don't see daylight again until the next morning. Usually we have a sandwich at our desks for lunch, and it's dark, most evenings, when we leave. But I wouldn't change this for the world. I would rather be at the office with my husband and have a peep-hole view of history than stay home wondering what time he'll arrive." She mentioned nothing about her little girls. Over fifty years later, writing in her memoir, she admitted the portrait of unity was an election-year put-up job. "I was already straying sexually and emotionally, and had had several flings by the time [that] photo on the steps of the Capitol was taken," she said. "In it I look dazed and confused. I was."

# 7.

It was a lamentable room in the old Senate Office Building, so raspy and clattery that you could barely hear yourself think: rows and rows of Robotypers, air pumps hissing, rolls of perforated paper spasmimg forward into what appeared to be an old-fashioned sewing rig attached to an IBM typewriter. The keys pulsed mechanically, guided by hooks and levers responding to the coded air holes in the master roll of paper. An early duplicating machine, it was a "Rube Goldberg–looking thing," Nadine said, designed to produce many copies of a single letter, so constituents at home would believe they had received personal correspondence from their congressman. Nadine was reminded of the player pianos that had replaced men like her father in the grand old movie theaters of the Midwest. Day and night—"Johnson worked all the fucking time," she said—LBJ's staffers minded the machines, three to a person, collecting and stacking the letters, making sure they were neat and pristine, readying them for the senator's signature. The minimum daily quota was one hundred letters per staff person. Under his breath, Brammer had taken to calling Johnson the Big Pumpkin because of the man's large head. He tickled his colleagues, mocking the typical LBJ missive: "My dear friend: I remain your very dear friend. Your friend, Lyndon."

Most of the letters were rote responses to Texans who had written to complain about local issues requiring federal intervention or asking for official favors. These were called "case letters." Johnson also liked to send "warm letters"—kind notes to people he had become aware of in his former congressional district who were having health problems or who were, for some reason, distressed. Early in LBJ's career, Juanita Roberts, one of his secretaries, had begun to organize his files and collect materials for posterity, assuming that his public contributions would one day be of interest to historians. According to Johnson's brother, Brammer had not worked long in Washington before Roberts told him "she regretted to report that most of his letters to constituents—all signed by LBJ, mind you—would not be retained because they had no archival value." Brammer joked about "archivality," and proudly flaunted his failure to meet the standard.

Initially, his duties included writing a weekly newsletter for dissemination to the daily papers in Texas—many of the newsletters emphasized Johnson's courtship of northeastern labor unions, to convince the liberals back home that he was pursuing a progressive agenda. Brammer wrote statements for the *Congressional Record*. He wrote short speeches for the senator. Eventually, at Johnson's request, he began to forge daily chatty notes to the senator's mother so that she would think her son had not forgotten her.

George Reedy believed Johnson hoped Brammer "could get Ronnie Dugger to soften some of his attacks . . . That really worried Johnson, because Johnson at heart very much approved of the Dugger style of operation, but since it was directed against him he could never quite admit it. I think he thought he might get some [help] out of Bill Brammer. Well, he couldn't. Bill was not that kind of a person . . . [he was] a strange man, very much of a loner." But Reedy was impressed with Brammer's keen awareness of detail. "Bill was an extraordinarily acute observer," he said. "You could send Bill through a convention and he would come back and tell you just about what everybody was thinking, mostly because they didn't notice him. He could sit in a room and nobody would be aware of his presence, and he'd listen to everything that was going on and he would record it mentally."

He shared a spacious office, Room 201 in the Senate Office Building, with another staffer, Booth Mooney. (Upon assuming the majority leadership, Johnson had commandeered, without asking anyone, all the office space he wanted—his own room, G-14, was decorated with two chandeliers that had hung in Theodore Roosevelt's White House, and it came with a fireplace that Johnson lighted every afternoon.) Brammer's space had a "crystal chandelier, marble fireplace, leather sofa, [and] an outsized desk that straddled me like some enormous draft animal," he said. It had a "matchless view of such Capitol Hill wonders as Sen[ator] Byrd walking his aged spaniel, Mr. Justice Frankfurter walking himself, [and] a remarkable number of public servants walking hell-bent for the drinking/wenching relief of the Carrol Arms Hotel." Room 201 was located directly beneath Richard Nixon's office. Brammer entertained colleagues by inviting them to come hear the "groan of the vice-presidential plumbing." He got along splendidly with Mooney. Mooney once told him he was convinced that Johnson's election to the Senate in 1948 had been illegal. He said he and his wife had vacationed in Mexico a year after the controversy with the ballot boxes in Alice, Texas. He claimed to have met the man who had burned the fake ballots—this fellow had been spirited away across the border for safekeeping until the story died down.

However LBJ got to the Senate, he was now strictly in control, and he brooked no sloppiness or insubordination from his staff. "I only think about politics eighteen hours a day," Nadine later recalled him saying, and he expected his workers to do the same. He "consume[d] his staff as fuel," said Harry McPherson.

"As a human being he was a miserable person . . . a bully, a sadist, lout, and egotist," George Reedy said. "His lapses from civilized conduct were deliberate and usually intended to subordinate someone else to his will. Were there nothing else to look at save LBJ's personal relationships with other people, it would be merciful to forget him altogether. But there is much more to look at. He may have been a son of a bitch, but he was a colossal son of a bitch."

"Clean up your fucking desk," he might say to one of his assistants while passing through an office. "I hope your mind isn't as empty as that desk." He would rip a sheet of paper from someone's typewriter, read what the person had written, and bellow, "God, you're stupid! You couldn't pour piss out of a boot if the instructions were printed on the heel!" If a secretary watered down his evening scotches, or accidentally poured him a glass of sherry instead, he would yell about being poisoned. On one occasion, dissatisfied with the quality of the drink he had been handed, he hurled the glass and shattered it against the wall. He insisted that his female employees stay within certain weight limits, and if a woman got too chubby, in his view, he would mock her mercilessly. He could be a wicked mimic, imitating the odd gaits in people's walks. To his male employees, he would sometimes brag about the size of his penis—nicknamed "Jumbo"—and on occasion he would force them to sit in the bathroom with him while he emptied his bowels and dictated orders, stressing his overpowering physical presence and humiliating the men. He referred to his male staffers as his "hard-peckered boys."

"Johnson had no concept of order, none whatsoever," Reedy said. "He knew how to handle people as individuals, and if some of those people could bring organizations along with them, well and good. But he would constantly put subordinates in an impossible position in front of *their* subordinates. He would issue contradictory orders and then never even realize that they were contradictory. He was always embarrassing people, making them look very small, in their own eyes at any rate, in front of other people."

On the other hand, one staffer told Robert Caro, "You felt that the world was moving, and Lyndon was going to be one of the movers, and if you worked for him, *you'd* be one of the movers." Willie Morris, traveling to London, stopped in Washington to visit Brammer and found him "enthralled by Johnson—by his complexity and his promise," though in those very early days, Brammer rarely encountered his boss. "He is just about 50 feet away in another office, but [I] never see the Lord of the Manor," he wrote Ronnie Dugger.

Instead, he would sit slumped late at night in the Robotyper room's sterile glare. "Empty Coke bottles, piles of mistyped pages, ashes and pallor," Harry McPherson described it. He recalled the end of one long day: "Bill Brammer's eyes, as he waited for a machine to finish so that he might begin the cycle once more, were large and red. 'Do you love it, Brammer?' I shouted. 'I love it, I love it!' he replied. After a while we switched off the current and went out for a beer."

---

"Washington is hideous," Brammer wrote Dugger in early January 1956 before Nadine and the girls arrived in the city. He was surviving on Butterfingers, warm Jell-O, and amphetamines. The days were cold and misty, gray but for smudges of neon here and there, a bad impressionist painting. A smell of ashes—bus exhaust—lingered over everyone. The tires of hustling taxis hissed on wet pavement. DC was swiftly efficient, cruelly unforgiving. "We [had] been young and liberal in Texas, where to be liberal was to be righteously happy under siege," McPherson said. "We [had entered] the North, where one [needed to] be astute as well as compassionate." Power was a flat pervasive odor as unmistakable as cordite, he said.

"[Bill] was working hard . . . ten to twelve hours a day . . . but had few friends in Washington and not much 'free' time to have a social life," said Glen Wilson, a fellow staffer whose wife, Marie, would sometimes cook for Brammer in their suburban Alexandria home. She worried about how thin he was and how little sleep he got. "He developed this peculiar pattern," Wilson said. "When the regular work day was done at 7 or 8 pm, he would grab a quick sandwich and then go to his small apartment . . . and take a 2 or 3 hour nap. He would then arise about midnight and, fortified with coffee and Dr Pepper . . . write until dawn. He would have another quick nap, get up, shower, and go to work. How he was able to keep up this grueling regime—even though he was still in his 20s—I don't know."

Brammer told Dugger, "I am almost finished with the first draft of M*Y B*O*O*K. Have written about 30,000 words more." This was the manuscript about Austin miscreants, "glib talkers sauntering from episode to episode, headed nowhere skeptically, existential as all get-out," Al Reinert said. Brammer called it *The Heavy-Honeyed Air*. He admitted to Dugger that it lacked focus. He worried as well that he had ingested so much Scott Fitzgerald, "my prose took a turn toward a seedy parody of his style." To counter this tendency, he immersed himself in Saul Bellow, but "the Jewish influence makes my southwest characters talk like Yiddish immigrants."

Dugger read between the lines of Brammer's letters. He knew his friend was serious about writing, but his enthusiasm for the "B*O*O*K" seemed forced, a pallid attempt to cheer himself up. Dugger wrote back, "I am desperately fearful you will become some wispy haunting feather on the night wind." Undaunted, Brammer replied, "I am two chapters short of completing the first draft . . . The hero edits a liberal weekly, but it ain't you . . . You make my brain hurt . . . So . . . you aren't in it, and if that's disappointing, I'm sorry. You shouldn't be so damned inscrutable. (Have you ever known any scrutable women?)"

In the early morning hours, rereading what he had written before the clatter of the Robotypers began in earnest, he worried even more that his characters, based on the Scholz crowd, lacked purpose and interest. Much as he hated Washington, he agreed with McPherson: "It was one thing to sit about the tables of the Scholz Garden in Austin, drinking iced Pearl in schooners, and mock [politicians'] benighted efforts to run the country like a small corporation. It [was] another to confront this city with its mysteries of authority." The complexities of power, the ambiguities of political conflicts, could turn the fiercest convictions into doubt. Brammer wondered what sort of unstable element he could introduce among his existential characters to shake them up a little.

---

"I know every son of a bitch who works for me," Johnson would holler. "I know what he *can* do and what he *can't* do. And if he's not doing what he *should* do, he's either fucking me or fucking the dog. And I'm not paying for his pleasure either way."

As the Senate session crawled forward and campaign season approached, Brammer saw more of the Big Pumpkin in and around the building and on the Senate floor. He marveled at the man's personal contradictions. One minute he would slam a staff member for dressing poorly, a reflection on *him*—"My people aren't sending me to Washington to watch hayseed sprout from my nostrils or onion shoots coming out of my ears. They want someone to represent them they can be proud of, not a country yokel in a dirty shirt with snuff juice dripping off his chin"—and the next minute he would pick grossly at his teeth with a matchbook cover.

Brammer witnessed the rages at his peers. He joked about issuing Purple Hearts. He avoided his boss's tongue-lashings by remaining unobtrusive. If his work was unsatisfactory for any reason, LBJ would simply give him the silent treatment for a few days. Brammer began to keep extra pairs of white shirts in a desk drawer in his office so that he could change throughout the day and stay crisp. He found the abuse bracing, in its way, especially when he saw how Johnson turned it on his Senate colleagues. "LBJ seems to have strangled off (scrotum-wise) all opposition," he wrote Dugger. The man *did* know everyone who worked for him, and that included his fellow senators. He knew their strengths and weaknesses—who the drinkers were, the womanizers; he knew what their constituents needed back home, what they would be willing to trade on the Senate floor to keep their voters happy; he knew just when to dispatch his aide, Bobby Baker, to whisper deals and counterdeals in the cloakroom, to tally support for any given bill. "Johnson is in his element. He is passing bills like crazy . . . and that's what he likes most. Better'n sex, probably," Brammer told Dugger. "I'm continually amazed by [him]. This month, for instance, he is worried sick about electing liberals to the Senate . . . He's trying to raise money for those liberals . . . The conservatives can take care of themselves, their voting records will do it for them. Today he told me since '[Wayne] Morse [of Oregon] has cussed out anybody who ever had more than 40 cents in his pocket,' it's going to take a lot of hard work for all the Democrats to raise enough money in his campaign . . . Control of the Senate is what's at bottom of it, of course, but it's still a good feeling to know he knows the problems of finance."

Brammer *was* trying to call off Dugger's attacks, as Johnson wished him to do, but his letters were genuine expressions of his feelings. He sympathized with Johnson, in spite of the man's outrageous bluster. He noticed how native northeasterners and lifers in the government bureaucracy underestimated his intelligence because he spoke with a "funny" twang. LBJ was quicker and smarter than all of them put together. His sharpness intimidated Brammer. It swatted away, like a big Stetson wave, his confidence in his writing: the characters in his novel were merely clever, without the heft of brains or commitment to any grand cause beyond themselves. Dugger remembered Brammer saying at one point, "either . . . Fitzgerald said of himself or someone said of Fitzgerald that he had a first-rate talent and a fifth-rate intelligence—and of Bill making or implying some self-deprecatory application of the same judgment to himself." He feared he hadn't read widely enough: "Perhaps I'd better start all over again and work up toward Dostoeviesky (and learn to spell his name) . . . Hell, all I ever read was the sports pages," he said.

Brammer's officemate, Booth Mooney, had just published a book about Johnson, *The Lyndon Johnson Story*, essentially a hagiography timed to match the election cycle. "I suggested to [Johnson], after the heart attack, that he let me write a book about him and he said, 'No,' he didn't want to," Mooney said. "But I thought he had come so near dying I did feel that there was something [to] the idea of getting down a record of what he had accomplished." Johnson relented, finally appreciating the book's publicity value. He "was well-pleased . . . when it came out," Mooney said.

Brammer's old colleague at the *American-Statesman*, Anita Wukasch, reviewed the book for the Austin paper. One day she received a response to her review, written on LBJ's stationery and allegedly signed by the senator. "Having the normal amount of human vanity" it began. She hooted. She knew the note had come from Brammer.

He wrote Dugger, "I could write a book on LBJ's time, like Booth Mooney," though LBJ would have considered that "fucking the dog." "My plot, of course, would revolve around the exploits of an associate editor of an independent, liberal, weekly newspaper. The editor will be shown for what he is—an amusing, erratic, half-baked Irish Hamlet. I will permit the editor to get the girl, if that's any consolation. And it probably is."

His wife and daughters finally arrived in the city. Glen and Marie Wilson helped the family find a "funky" old colonial house to rent in Alexandria, seven miles south of DC, on the western bank of the Potomac River. There, Brammer learned, one of the nation's oldest slave markets had shipped African families to New Orleans. John Wilkes Booth's corpse had arrived there for an autopsy aboard a steamer, a few days after Abraham Lincoln's assassination. Glen Wilson said the house's distinguishing feature was its "footed cast iron bath tub." Sidney, almost four, recalled little of the house itself, but she retained vivid memories of the African American woman who tended her and Shelby while their parents worked each day and late into most of the evenings. The woman's name was Ella, and she wore a starched white uniform. She cooked and cleaned, vacuumed and ironed. "She was a large woman who loved listening to the radio and I must have learned a lot of songs hanging out with her all day that I mysteriously knew years later," Sidney said. "Rosemary Clooney, Dinah Washington, Perry Como, Etta James. This woman in white sang along and made us sing, too."

Of course, Sidney's father went out and bought the very latest big-console television. "Someone had given me a coonskin cap because I loved Davy Crockett and I can only assume that I was exposed to Fess Parker and Disney via that TV," Sidney said. "I climbed on furniture with an imaginary rifle like I was tracking."

"Broke as they were," Brammer also bought "a very large and garish 'hi-fi' stereo on which he played albums, listened to a.m., f.m., and even short wave radio," Sidney added. "He and Nadine had a pretty large collection of jazz lps . . . I can remember the ever-present sound of music in the house."

Usually, it was to Ella's singing that Sidney and Shelby went to sleep each night.

Nadine wasn't as enamored of Lyndon Johnson as her husband was. His "lechery was frequently a topic of conversation among the staff," she said. "We didn't have a term for it then, but we do now: sexual harassment." He kept a "meticulously decorated hideaway in the Capitol basement. Everyone, including the Capitol guards, knew that this . . . was where Johnson had his trysts with willing women."

If one of his married female staff members got pregnant—a development he didn't like, since it interfered with her work—he said he hoped the baby was a boy, and in all seriousness, he would offer money if she named the infant "Lyndon."

"LBJ could grope your whole body in a split second: this once happened to me as he 'helped' me get out of the backseat of a car," Nadine said.

"It happened so fast I didn't even have a chance to complain . . . He was so large and his eyes seemed magnified behind those glasses. It was as though he was a great Tasmanian devil . . . pouncing on you before you knew it."

She had experienced a few brief public meetings with him, in Austin and since her arrival in Washington, but he introduced himself to her formally one afternoon at the end of the normal workday. Her desk sat in George Reedy's press office. Her job consisted of clipping newspaper articles for Johnson's daily briefings and compiling his old speeches. He popped into the press room and said, "Honey . . . do you want to come down to mah office for a little birthday party for Mrs. Roosevelt?" Nadine recalled. Eleanor Roosevelt was visiting the Senate Office Building that day.

The majority leader's office was gorgeous, warm in the amber light from the chandeliers and the softly smoldering fire. The walls had been painted a soothing moss green to match the carpeting. "Everyone grew mellow on Scotch . . . and Lyndon made his way around to introduce himself," Nadine said. "Jiggling the change in his pocket constantly, he asked me . . . 'What does your Daddy do?' and 'How do you like your job?' His attention was flattering, his charm and charisma considerable."

After that, whenever he saw her in the halls, he would ask, "When're you and me gonna have a drink?" She would answer, "Why, Bill and I would love to have a drink with you, anytime."

In her memoir, Nadine portrayed Johnson's deference to her as no more or less than he showed any woman, but she may have downplayed his interest. "I think Johnson was . . . very much attracted by Bill's wife, who was a rather spectacular girl," George Reedy said. Harry McPherson agreed: "I think Johnson was taken with Brammer's wife, Nadine, and that probably complicated [Bill's] relationship with him."

She deftly deflected the senator's advances but she relished the "high that [came] from flirting with new, exciting men" on Capitol Hill. She met the reporters that dropped by the office to speak with George Reedy; she "ferried press releases to the Senate Press Gallery" and talked to reporters there. Like the senator, many of them asked her out for drinks. "This was heady stuff for a twenty-five-year-old girl from McAllen," she said. "I felt love for Bill, but I was regretful that I hadn't gotten a degree, and resentful that I was expected to carry the entire domestic load . . . I had never stopped feeling ambivalent about my marriage, and I yearned to be single."

Red-eyed and weary from lack of sleep (Nadine often found her husband nodding over his typewriter early in the mornings), his head ringing with the noise of the Robotypers, Brammer nevertheless recognized his wife's distance from him. His plan to pull the family closer by moving to Washington hadn't worked.

It wasn't long before Nadine began a serious affair with a *Time* reporter, a man named Marshall Berger. He was ten years older than she was, and married. His manner was more refined than that of the Texans she had known. For the magazine, he covered labor issues, the AFL-CIO; in conversation, he could make these topics interesting. "It was intoxicating to sit in the Senate Gallery and flirt across the Senate floor while he was in the Press Gallery covering the goings-on," Nadine said.

The affair was not a secret from Brammer. "Bill was miserable, because he knew I longed for another man and I felt a lot of guilt," Nadine admitted. "In spite of this, Bill, Booth [Mooney] and I had a great time." Brammer bought a Telefunken stereo for his office and turned the room into a kind of salon. He would invite colleagues to come for after-hours drinks and music, and to listen to Nixon flush his toilet upstairs. They would all eat the leftover Texas-shaped cookies that Lady Bird had baked for visiting constituents—usually South Texas farmers seeking exemptions from federal regulations requiring them to treat their migrant workers humanely.

Brammer befriended a new couple in town, Barbara and Marcus Raskin. Eventually, Marcus would go to work for the Kennedy administration, and Barbara would write novels. On evenings when Nadine was nowhere to be found, probably off with her *Time* reporter, Brammer invited the Raskins "to go crawling in the first-floor window of the Senate Office Building," Barbara recalled. He would sneak them into Johnson's office: "We'd tap into the bourbon supply." Then they'd go to Room 201, "put on some records and stay there and cool off, and sleep on the floor and the sofas there." In later years, she could never think of Lyndon Johnson as the president. "To me, he was Billy Brammer's boss."

Brammer met a young writer, a Texas transplant named Larry L. King. They would go out and "drank [themselves] a bunch of dranks," King said. Brammer read King's manuscripts, offering editorial advice. Reluctantly, he would talk about his own novel in progress, which he was revising. He was also getting to know the senator's brother, Sam Houston. They would meet for scotches in the bar of the Carroll Arms Hotel. Sam Houston told Brammer how the teenage Lyndon used to talk him into spending the money he had earned by working in a general store on presents for *Lyndon*.

More and more, LBJ pulled Brammer into his inner circle. "Lyndon perceived Bill's intelligence," Nadine said. "He wanted us over at his house all the time in Washington." Johnson would kid Brammer, calling him "Boy" and striking matches off the stiff lapels of his suits: an Abbott and Costello routine. Brammer became the perfect straight man. Over after-dinner drinks, with an intimate crowd, "Billy Lee would ask Johnson questions and Johnson was the center of attention expanding on this and that, and Billy Lee was always cuing him," Nadine recalled. Brammer would feed Johnson a line, and LBJ would turn his bulk on him and shout, "Who are you?" "A nameless sycophant of no great importance," Brammer answered. Johnson would roar and hold forth some more.

Sometimes on weekends, Johnson and Lady Bird returned to Austin to meet with constituents and do some local politicking. They would bring the Brammers along on the Brown and Root plane. "We'd go out to the ranch . . . Our little girls would play with the Johnson girls, we'd drive around looking at cows, and Bill and Lyndon would talk for hours," Nadine said. The couples would eat "Crazy Tacos" at El Matamoros in town, one of LBJ's favorite spots, where he had courted Bird. He would complain about not being able to smoke anymore since his heart attack, but nothing stopped him from knocking back one salty margarita after another. He offered Brammer fatherly and political advice: "You gotta *give* something to *get* something," "Your judgment is only as good as your information," "Never trust a nary-assed man," "You ain't learning anything when you're talking." Nadine and Lady Bird traded tips on Elizabeth Arden products.

Brammer's old Austin pals shook their heads at how he "waited on [Johnson], rhapsodized over him, toted and fretted and apologized for him," Dugger said. "Billy exhibited all the symptoms of teenage dementia, worse even than usual because it was so obviously heartfelt and he was so smart."

For his part, Brammer felt impatient now with his liberal friends, jumping at every "progressive" bugle blat and refusing to consider both sides of complex issues. Dugger approached him with the possibility of writing something new for the *Observer*, but eventually Brammer decided, "After the lengths to which Ronnie's gone in condemning LBJ, [I] don't think I could write anything for the *Observer* for a long while." He told Nadine, "Sounds shitty, but I like Johnson, and I can't very well lend my name to a paper that calls Johnson a racist and a labor baiter. As much as I respect Ronnie, it's just not true."

Johnson's refusal to sign the Senate's Southern Manifesto, an attempt to reverse *Brown*, didn't satisfy the Texas liberals, who saw his gesture as a ploy to appease them while he worked to pass a natural gas bill that would clear producers of federal regulations. He got the gas bill approved in the Senate, but then two Texas lobbyists, coordinating with Johnson's man, John Connally, were charged with trying to bribe senators to support the bill. President Eisenhower vetoed the legislation. Brammer would remember this incident, combine it with details from a tape-recorded bribe offer a year later in the Texas Capitol, and build a plotline in *The Gay Place* around a bribery scandal.

Johnson secured the endorsement of the AFL-CIO for his run at the presidency, which encouraged the liberals; the Americans for Democratic Action withheld its support because of his "questionable" civil rights record—this heartened the conservatives. He worked with the economist Eliot Janeway in drafting legislation supportive of Israel—Janeway, a New Yorker, could help deliver the powerful northeastern Jewish vote—while assuring his Southern Baptist constituency he would always support strong Christian values. Despite expertly diddling all elements of the electorate, he frequently fell into a paralyzing depression, moaning about his "disability"—the fact that the country would never send a Texan to the White House, no matter *how* qualified he was. He would say he wasn't going to run after all; he would relinquish his seat in the Senate; he would fly back to the Lone Star State and buy another radio station. The next day, he would pump his staff to get their asses back on those Robotypers: More letters! We need more endorsements! It was an utterly schizophrenic performance. He would tell Brammer that politicians were sick ducks, sometimes very, *very* sick. Anyone compelled to get on his hands and knees and beg people to prove their boundless love by voting for him was deserving of compassion and comfort. The illness would pass every four years or so, but in the meantime, great care was needed, even pity. Then Johnson would gently squeeze Brammer's arm and quietly quote the book of Isaiah: "Come, let us reason together."

---

"Shivers charged me with *murder*," Johnson told Ronnie Dugger. The 1956 election season soured quickly. Shivers said he couldn't support Lyndon Johnson for president because LBJ had twisted too far to accommodate liberals. Sam Rayburn pressured Johnson not to broker any deals with the governor—he had never forgiven Shivers for supporting Eisenhower in 1952. A power struggle broke out between the senator and the governor over control of the Texas Democratic Party. In the fray, Shivers made a speech accusing Johnson of ordering a hit on a former deputy sheriff in Alice, Texas, a man named Sam Smithwick, who had threatened to produce the missing ballot box that secured Johnson's Senate seat in 1948. "*Murder*!" Johnson repeated to Dugger—in such a way that Dugger felt he was meant to consider the truth of it. Johnson mocked the charge while planting the information as a frightening possibility, intimidating anyone who might question him. "There was no evidence to prove that Smithwick was murdered," Dugger concluded. Still, this wasn't the last time conspiracy lore would touch Lyndon Johnson. Many times, he would be accused of eliminating his enemies.

His attempts to appoint Lieutenant Governor Ben Ramsey to the Democratic National Committee failed; the *Observer* team flexed its muscles and inserted Frankie Randolph into the powerful role of Texas representative. The state party's internal divisions constantly required Johnson to travel to Texas on feather-smoothing missions—at agricultural laboratories in McAllen, at the naval base in Corpus Christi, at Bergstrom Air Force Base in Austin—and each time he took Brammer with him. "Johnson . . . enjoyed Brammer," Harry McPherson affirmed. "[And] Brammer held Johnson in great affection." Jan Reid, who would meet Brammer in the 1970s, wrote, "On trips home to Texas Bill would accompany LBJ to small towns and watch the senator deliver speeches he had written. In the car he would jabber in staccato rhythms, wired on speed, as Johnson drawled back in volleys, fueled by scotch and his own vast opinion of himself." He told Brammer, "Stick with me, boy, and I'll make you rich."

One day, in a speech to ranchers at the Diamond M Ranch in Abilene, Johnson reminisced fondly about how he had brought electricity to West Texas. Then he veered into a mild rebuke of the men's political inflexibility. "The only way you're going to get [things] done is by joining with people . . . who have the same voting interest and voting with them, and you've got to support them sometimes on some things that make you kind of uncomfortable," he said.

> When they say, "We've got to have a little civil rights bill, we've got to have a little voting rights. Make it possible for people to vote," you know that may stir people up in your area, but you've got to go along with that a little bit. And when they say, "I got to have a little minimum wage increase here for these women that sit in these hot shops and sew all day long"—when those people say, "I've got to have a little of that," you got to

> be sympathetic, you've got to think, "Well, there's my friend and there's somebody that I'm on the same side with when it really counts." And if we stick together, and if we vote together some, we might be able to bring about lower interest rates and that'll make it possible for Grandma to have that new refrigerator.

It was a stunningly gut-honest moment. Brammer wished the Scholz crowd could have witnessed it. His admiration for the man expanded. On another occasion, Johnson told a group of county party volunteers a story about a teacher seeking work in a public school in rural Texas. The school superintendent asked the young man, "What would you teach our students about the world—that it's round or that it's flat?" The fellow replied, "I can teach it either way—how would you *like* me to teach it?" The important thing was that he *taught* it. *Compromise* is not a dirty word, Johnson told first the liberals, then the conservatives. (A version of this story would appear in *The Gay Place*.)

On the plane, Brammer was enraptured, and a little spooked, whenever Johnson went into one of his visionary reveries, cinematically mapping the scenes he would produce as the leader of his country, throngs of poor children, like great schools of fish, moving toward his outstretched arms. And then he would plummet into the next day's mundane chores, all the tiny, pragmatic details needing immediate attention. Finally, he would slump in his seat, exhausted and melancholy. It was as if there were two very different Lyndon Johnsons, and even *he* didn't know how to accommodate them both.

Back in DC, he wasted no time reasserting control over his staff—"Look at George moving his fat ass across the floor," he would say loudly, to anyone in earshot, referring to the overweight George Reedy, perspiring in the Senate Chamber. He would crack the whip on his fellow senators. "Hubert!" He snapped his fingers and Humphrey came running. Brammer always remembered the first time he saw John Kennedy on the Senate floor, laughing and joking with his colleagues and "trying to get some Senate business done before a weekend recess." He tried to cajole Johnson into suspending some rules on his behalf so that he could call his bill to a vote. Johnson barked, "I haven't got time to worry about any of your damn fife and drum and bugle corps up there." He turned and was gone, leaving Kennedy agape.

Johnson had not participated in any of the state primaries—he seemed to think he could wrap up his party's nomination for president at an open convention (though he had not announced his interest in running). Reedy, McPherson, Mooney, and others whispered that their leader, for all his brilliance in the Senate, didn't appear to understand how the national convention really worked. "I think . . . [an] ambivalence about the presidency began to set in," Reedy said. Johnson recognized the challenge a southerner faced in seeking the White House. Perhaps he simply didn't want to risk the humiliation of defeat. "This was Lyndon Baines Johnson versus Lyndon Baines Johnson," Reedy noted.

He became frantic. If anyone tried to thwart his daily business, he would say, "I will gut him till his balls squall and his pecker squeals 'Sweet Betsy from Pike.'" He would run from phone to phone in his office, pausing only long enough to kick off his shoes so that an aide could take them to be polished and then return, slipping them back on Johnson's feet while Johnson continued to yell into the receiver. He insisted his speeches be delivered to him five pages at a time while they were still being drafted in some other office, with line spacings to tell him where to wait for applause, with fourteen-point characters so he could read the text without his glasses. At parties he drank and danced like a dervish.

At one gala affair, in George Brown's pre–Civil War mansion in Middleburg, Virginia, where Johnson had retreated to meet with lobbyists and potential donors, Brammer and Nadine came along at his invitation. Given his edginess, they didn't feel they could say no, though Ella wasn't available that weekend and so they had to bring Sidney and Shelby. Goaded, perhaps, by Johnson's overwhelming anxiety, all the adults got spectacularly drunk. The little girls wandered around the mansion alone. "I got bored and fussy and wanted to go outside to explore the estate," Sidney said. "I was in a purple sock-dress, not warm enough. Bill took me out for a little walk by a lily-pond. He said, 'I'm going to go inside and get another drink. I'll be right back.' I slipped and fell into the ice-covered pond and nearly froze to death, holding onto dead cattails and screaming bloody murder." Inside the house, Brammer thought he heard screaming, but no one else seemed to be bothered by it, so maybe it was only the collective noise of the partiers, or maybe it was the echo of the Robotypers in his head. Finally, he went outside to check. He spotted Sidney grasping at weeds, her head barely above the pond's waterline. He rushed over and pulled her out. Together, they shivered on the flagstones, hugging and crying. Many years later, he told her, "I was never more frightened in my life." He included the incident in book three of *The Gay Place*. When Sidney was older, he said to her, "I meant for the scene to be a turning point for that character, the father."

---

"Am being good but it sure is hard," Nadine wrote in a diary she kept during this period. She described several disturbing dreams of appearing naked in public, of being "very nasty and catty" to her female friends, of being threatened by "hazy" black men. In one terribly realistic nightmare, she watched "Senator Johnson . . . [as he] slumped to the floor. Had three 'hard' heart attacks and died . . . Bill immediately whispered, 'I wonder who I can get a job with now.'"

In a letter to her parents, she mentioned "entertaining the Texas Correspondents in Senator Johnson's suite. The press has been treating Johnson with a bit of bitterness and it takes a little good booz [*sic*] and some kindness every once in a while to get them in line again. It's rather disgusting." The Washington dance was beginning to pall for her; more and more her dreams centered on fights with friends, scenes of abstract violence.

One night she dreamed of opening a closet door in her bedroom and finding an "embryonic-looking sac" moving around in it. A "mother cat" crouching inside the closet nibbled at the sac's gooey skin and "out popped a baby—(mine)? looked exactly like Sidney—a male with big ears . . . Gad, what are we going to do with another baby? (Bill's attitude: indifference)."

---

"It is the 1956 Democratic National Convention [in Chicago], redolent of the randy and bucolic effluvia of stockyards and streetwalkers, senile dementia and barber shop talcum, sippin' whiskey and soda pop," Brammer wrote, in a retrospective piece. "Jack Kennedy and Estes Kefauver materialize [on the convention floor], with separate little entourage armies and something *more*. Both men, it's now apparent, are somehow virtually aswarm with women; a sort of heavenly horny host of nubile admirers, whooping, screeching, clutching, stroking, whispering, whistling, always reaching desperately out—Jesus knows what for?" He noticed Speaker Sam Rayburn standing nearby in his dandruff-dusted suit coat, as still as if he had been "whittled from WPA marble." "Rayburn does not appear remotely interested in anything," Brammer noted, until he spotted the "rosy lips" and "fabulously coiffed" hair of the political groupies. "'Goddam,' he mumbles. 'Ever'body screws!'"

In this overheated atmosphere—a "sort of pageant of promiscuity"—a preview of the reckless Kennedy years and the loosening of the nation's stays in the 1960s, Johnson's southernness, stiff and blustery in public, overly deferential in private, didn't stand a chance. If he had any hope of becoming the party's standard-bearer, it lasted about a minute, Brammer figured. Once again, Adlai Stevenson received the coronation, nominated dramatically by Kennedy. (In the wings, Johnson scoffed at Stevenson, questioning his manhood—he has to "sit down to pee," he would say.) Kefauver, from Tennessee, got the vice presidential nod, Tennessee being more genuinely southern than Texas and therefore more essential to court.

Johnson was bruised. For months now, and for months to come, part of Brammer's job was to keep his boss from plunging into the mopes. The Abbott and Costello routine was always good for that. And at one point Brammer wrote a confidential memo to LBJ, assuring him there "were certain obstacles to overcome in this campaign [season] that a lesser champion of the principles involved would have found insurmountable." He praised Johnson's "standing" and "ability" and asserted, "You are now a whole man in the eyes of the people . . . Too many people in their letters these days are likening you to FDR and his 'fireside chats' for this to be ignored," and insisted that "your heart attack has not slowed you down . . . You [can] still mix it and win votes." "If you [have] lost any friends, they weren't worth keeping," Brammer wrote. "Some conservative friends you thought you had turned out not to be conservative at all—but . . . Dixiecrats, Racists, or Republicans. One would assume all liberals would have supported you. Most of them did. Those who didn't turned out to be not liberals at all—but suicidal-complexed peddlers of unconvention. They don't want to be right; they want to be different."

He concluded: "Your strength, as always, again emerges from a joint mutual admiration society: Classic liberals and classic conservatives who can recognize a man for his abilities and honesty rather than whether he fits the mold of their own partisan views."

In addition to serving as a pep talk for Johnson, the memo laid out what Brammer *hoped* the man would become rather than what he knew the man to be on his worst days.

In due course, Stevenson and Kefauver lost the election to a revitalized Eisenhower and his running mate, Richard Nixon; Allan Shivers was replaced as Texas's governor (torpedoed, in part, by vitriolic LBJ press releases penned by Brammer); and Ralph Yarborough would soon make his way to the US Senate, where he became a constant irritant in Johnson's craw. The "sick ducks" would look ahead to the next onset of their collective illnesses, in 1960.

---

Nadine feared that something was terribly wrong with her: she couldn't quell her longing for this other man. She wanted to be a "straight" wife and mother; on the other hand, it thrilled her to sneak across town and meet her lover in a hotel room. "I had fantasies of leaving Bill," she said. Then "I tried going to a psychologist with the hope that he would 'fix' me and turn me into a 'good wife,' but unbeknownst to me, the psychologist contacted Bill and had a session with *him*." The man's approach was to pressure her, shame her, into accepting her domestic role, no questions asked. "I felt conspired against," she said.

She was also slightly confused—though inspired—by the example of Lady Bird. Here was a devoted mother, but she relished power just as much as her husband did, and she worked constantly. "She took care of [her husband's] business, even while she was waiting for her children at the dentist's office," Nadine said. She did a much better job than LBJ of securing the loyalty and gratitude of the staff. She had a "creative relationship" with the senator "that served to accomplish their mutual goals for money and political power. She had to either compromise and put up with the guy, or leave—so she compromised." The "effective political wife" became a model of behavior attractive to Nadine, but neither her circumstances nor her own character, at this point, aligned to make such a position achievable.

Once the election scramble was over, she drove with Brammer to Manhattan—their first visit to the city. They both hoped a stimulating getaway would restore their bond: *My Fair Lady* on Broadway, hard bop at the brand-new Five Spot Café, where it was rumored that Willem de Kooning, Jack Kerouac, or Allen Ginsberg might show on any given night—names most Americans weren't aware of yet. Nadine loved sitting in a dark corner with her in-the-know husband, whispering, "Is *that* . . .? could *he* be . . .?" When the clubs closed for the evening, nothing remained to distract her from the stark realization that her problems, her children, and a scowling Ella awaited her in Washington.

Upon her return, Marshall Berger told her he was willing to leave his wife for her. They could start over together in Detroit, where *Time* wanted to send him as bureau chief. Car sales had plummeted nationwide—it was a big story, and his coverage of it could be a major career break for him.

She was almost tempted to accept when she learned that Brammer had failed to maintain the payments on the house in Austin. They lost it. She railed at him for racking up debts, for collecting Brooks Brothers suits he didn't need. He tried to win her back with wistful humor. On Sidney's fourth birthday, he made his little girl type gobbledygook on a card, and he provided a brisk translation: "Dear Gary [one of Sidney's playmates]: It is all over with us. I am four years old today and you, alas, are three. I will try my best to remember you. Come up and see me and I will bake a lemon pie. Love, The Next to the Littlest Little Bitchie." When this failed to rouse Nadine, he made a point of telling her that on one of his trips to Texas with the senator, he had had a fling with an Austin girl he met at a party. Clearly, he was trying to snag her attention, to punish her for her own affair. Rather than getting angry, she simply felt sad. Then she discovered she was pregnant.

# 8.

"If you'll name that boy after me, I'll give him a heifer calf and he'll have a whole herd by the time he's twenty-one," Johnson told Nadine.

Before she made her condition public, she had considered an abortion. Brammer knew the child wasn't his, but he told her he wanted to stay married. He would raise the child as his own. He would try to rein in his spending. He would finish his novel and get a fat publishing contract, and they would be okay.

Berger repeated his offer to take Nadine to Detroit, but "in her usual freewheeling style, she was moving on—from him and ultimately Billy Lee," said Shelby Brammer.

When Brammer made another swing south with the senator, Nadine saw an opportunity to ignore his wishes and terminate the pregnancy, but he "arrived home before I could get an abortion," she said. Now, unavoidably, she faced the prospect of being a broke mother of three. She wanted to be near her parents. She wanted not to wake to another cold gray Washington morning. She wanted the sunny, expansive skies of Texas. She talked Brammer into finding a rental house in Austin—Austin would be a much better place to raise the children. Though a long-distance relationship would be hard on them both, he could come to Texas when Congress was in recess and they could work on their marriage, she told him. He found a boxy little two-story place with a screened porch and a big backyard, tucked among rangy oaks on Austin's Enfield Road. He called the neighborhood "Coonass Gothic." To him, the location's best selling point was its late-night radio reception: the Mexican border stations came through crisply in that part of town, along with San Antonio's WOAI, playing Bob Wills round the clock.

Fighting waves of morning sickness, Nadine wrote a polite letter of resignation to LBJ. He told her well, all right, he would *only* allow family considerations to take her away from him. He made her promise to come see him soon. Brammer moved into a dank basement room in the Betty Alden Inn, near the Senate Office Building. He rarely spent time there, preferring to catnap at night in his office.

"How do you like our bizarre house?" he wrote Nadine in April 1957, in care of her neighbors, once she had taken the girls to Austin. "Think the kids will love it. When I get there I must do something about the lights in the huge living room . . . You also better get a mail box up so I can start sending my letters there."

His cheery attempt at domesticity left Nadine cold. She had learned from old friends that while in Austin looking for a house, he attended several wild parties. "Your sojourn here was obviously a real nightmarish, drunken interval," she wrote back. "Am sending your brown shoes [that you forgot]." She was terribly sick in the mornings. Her letters to Brammer complained that her pals were not helping her fix the house as much as they had promised they would. She was overwhelmed with the pregnancy and care of the girls.

"I have no memories of Nadine and Billy Lee being together," Shelby said. "He's in DC and she's fed up." Her first clear memory is of Easter that year—an incident vividly recounted in *The Gay Place*. He came for a visit; one evening, when Nadine and the girls were out of the house, he discovered, in the refrigerator, several dyed eggs. "He [decided] he would hide them all in the backyard, in the deeper growth beyond the swings and the sandpile," he wrote in the novel. "Then he would wait for the children and they would wander outside together and hunt for the eggs. When every one was found they would take turns hiding them all over again. He would stay close to them and they would talk; he would tell them a story, spin out a parable on what it was all about, improvise, make a speech. Surely he could think of *something*—anything—to say to his own lovely children." The following morning, he awoke to Nadine shouting at the girls. They complained that the eggs were gone and that they wanted more. Nadine accused them of eating them all or of burying them somewhere. She refused to go to the store again. Quietly, Brammer suggested, "Perhaps . . . one of those big Easter rabbits came downstairs last night and hid them for the girls. Have they been in the backyard yet?" Sidney and Shelby ran outside, whooping merrily, "Rab-*buts*!" "Sorry," Brammer said sheepishly to Nadine.

Early in the mornings, he would snuggle in bed with the girls to watch television cartoons. "His favorite was *Tom Terrific*," Shelby said. "He was a lot of fun, like a playmate. He liked kids. Maybe it's because he was so much of a kid himself. He'd hang out for a while and then he'd be gone: 'See you next time.' I just assumed that was the way things were."

On another occasion that spring, "he drove up in a black Fiat convertible and the children just went crazy," Nadine said. "I don't know where he got it. It was just to dazzle the children. He was one of these guys who thought one big gesture could make up for lots of neglect. And it sort of worked."

Perhaps he was feeling a little more flush now. At the beginning of the year, Ralph Yarborough entered a special US Senate race to fill a vacant post—Price Daniel had resigned from the Senate after winning the governorship. Yarborough offered Brammer a top press relations spot in his campaign. Johnson learned that his "boy" was about to be lured away. He flew down to the ranch with him, grabbed a bottle of scotch, and drove him in a Jeep into the dusty mesquite-tangled fields, there to apply the Johnson Treatment. Brammer knew that with "favored lady visitors," a "livestock tour" of the ranch was a favorite LBJ tactic. One of Johnson's secretaries told him the senator had once "recklessly wheeled" her about in the Jeep "until, pausing at a pen enclosing a couple of Democratic donkeys, [Johnson] honked his jeep horn and watched with enormous satisfaction as the Jack mounted the Jenny. 'Ain't that somethin'?' he inquired with eye-rolling innuendo. 'They show off that way ever' goddam time!'"

Now Brammer was the one being courted. He didn't need much persuading. Yarborough was the Texas liberals' commander in chief, but Brammer had become disgusted with their inflexibility, and he didn't care for Yarborough personally. Still, he was happy to drink the senator's scotch. Yarborough had offered Brammer a steady salary and an almost unlimited PR budget. Billie Sol Estes, a wheeler-dealer in West Texas agricultural affairs, would help finance radio broadcasts; in the past, he had made his private plane available to Yarborough for statewide campaign appearances. Johnson knew all about Billie Sol, he said. (In just a few years, scandals involving Estes and Bobby Baker would seriously threaten Johnson's political career.) You don't want to get involved with such men, he told Brammer. Stick with me. He offered a $700 raise, "the biggest raise that LBJ has ever given anyone at one time," Nadine wrote to her parents, impressed in spite of her anger at her husband. "Obviously, he thinks a lot of Bill."

But the extra money and the attempts to salvage the marriage didn't ease Brammer's misery. "Life is hideous here [in Washington]," he wrote Nadine. "I am eating nothing but pizza and . . . hamburgers . . . It's just dull here and I hate it . . . Damned lousy weekend in which I walked the streets and wished for you and the girls." Occasionally, he tried to tweak Nadine's jealousy: "[At a party] I got alternately charming, tight, more articulate than usual, drunk, drunker, hideously drunk, ravenous toward all the women, sick in the bathroom, and my sober sweet self again in the course of the evening." The good news: he had time to read and write. Just a few pages in, *Lolita* seemed like a "classic," he said. He said he had written several new pages of his novel: "I am amazing. It is pretty good so far."

On May 24, 1957, Nadine gave birth to a boy. The couple named him Willie, after their friend Willie Morris. Almost immediately, Nadine decided she "needed a break from child-rearing"; she asked Brammer to stay in Austin with the children while she flew to DC to help LBJ with some press matters normally dispatched by her husband. She "passed a pleasant weekend in Johnson's Washington home," along with his secretary Mary Margaret Wiley, she said. "Lady Bird was not there. The Senator tended to business between Scotches and gossiping and trying to get his two young companions to see things his way . . . [We] defended our liberal friends. Lyndon couldn't let it rest." (How could she have named her baby *Willie*? he asked). He ranted about the *Texas Observer*. He bemoaned the fact that his only chance to become president lay in winning northeastern liberals by supporting a civil rights bill, in which case he'd lose the South. He was trapped in an impossible bind. Most accounts of Johnson during this period depict him as morosely depressed, uglier than usual toward his staff after his failed White House bid. But that weekend, he "kept his hands to himself, seeming . . . relaxed," Nadine said. "I felt warmly toward him." Clearly, he relished the company of young women.

Nadine decided she could not, would not, live without an active social life, children or no children. Upon her return to Austin, she hired a young Mexican-Irish live-in nanny to mind the kids. That summer, "I went out with my friends" almost every night, she said. "When Bill was home, we partied together." ("You are invited to an ORGY at 2210 Enfield Road," he addressed one invitation. "The guest list is restricted: girls girls girls! boys boys boys! This will be a really *bad* party"—a line from *Tender is the Night*—"*All* the wrong people are invited.") "When Lyndon was at the ranch, we spent weekends out there, including the children," Nadine said. "Zephyr Wright . . . churned out popovers . . . Lyndon soaked up the attention while Lady Bird saw to it that everyone had a drink and was comfortable." From time to time, Nadine saw Johnson slip upstairs to one of the second-story bedrooms with one young lady or another.

By the end of the summer, Brammer was telling Nadine, only half in jest, "Let's sneak away to Mexico and never come back." She insisted she would stay in Austin—it was the best environment for the kids (though they saw very little of her)—and he had to return to DC and a secure salary. On his brief visits that fall with the children, "he was always snooping into everything I had," Nadine said. "Well, I gave him really good reason to. I started seeing guys, and that was fun, and I just didn't care about Bill anymore, because he had been such a screw-up. I really enjoyed Austin. We were wild and woolly." One weekend, the Headliners Club, where the lobbyists drank, threw a bash. To Brammer's dismay, if not to his surprise, Nadine worked hard to seduce the CBS newsman Eric Sevareid, a visiting guest—"I groupied him," she said. Later, Sevareid would only say he had had a most enjoyable time after the gala, but he needed to go into training before accepting the hospitality of Texans: "It was the most strenuous fun I have had in ages."

Brammer's letters to Nadine that autumn lament the time he missed spending with her and the kids: "It is all mixed up . . . Austin sounds gorgeous . . . would like to have been there for the party [you mentioned]." All he was doing, he said, was writing his book. "People are dull and so am I."

---

The same idealism behind his positive appraisals of LBJ, despite the man's corrosive behavior, informed his view of the literary world. His general cynicism notwithstanding (formed by experience with politics and bureaucratic structures), he sincerely believed a successful novel might solve his financial, and thus his marital, problems. It was worth a shot, anyway. He summoned the gumption to send *The Heavy-Honeyed Air* to James Street, a literary agent with the Harold Matson Company in New York.

Brammer knew the novel's scenes exposed loose narrative ties. But he needed external confirmation—or honest denial of the fact—that he was not wasting his energy.

James Street was the son of a hard-drinking, best-selling writer of southern historical novels, a former Baptist preacher whose down-home stories of boys and dogs had first become popular in the *Saturday Evening Post*. Street recognized, in Brammer, his father's talent for gently evoking place. He was delighted with the quality of the writing. In spite of Brammer's "misgivings that it's uneven and needs some more work," he was willing to test the waters with publishers. About six months later, Robert D. Loomis, a Random House editor, wrote Street that he was "considerably impressed" by Brammer's manuscript, but "the book tries to cover too much . . . the effect is spotty." Don't panic, it is a nice start, Street assured Brammer. He would send the pages to Henry Holt.

Meanwhile, Nadine hounded Brammer with notes for more money each week ("I am really going into the depths of despair about Bill," she wrote her mother), and he stayed busy, twelve hours a day or more, helping Johnson prepare memos and materials for the biggest challenge of his career: a civil rights bill.

Watching Johnson maneuver his way around the Senate floor, slouching, jumping, laughing, scowling, play-punching, bear-hugging his colleagues, talking, slumping silently, calling votes, or delaying them based on *who knew* what nifty calculations, was more entertaining and suspenseful than any story in literature. Always, Johnson's aide, Bobby Baker, trailed the senator, head bent as though it had evolved at the perfect angle for murmuring into LBJ's ear. Brammer knew the civil rights bill was essential to Johnson's presidential aspirations—"[A]ll I ever hear from the liberals is Nigra, Nigra, Nigra," he'd grouse in private conversation. The Republican Party wanted to bring a bill to a vote, forcing Johnson to side with the southerners against it (as he had done with similar legislation in the past). At a time when Klan activity was horribly resurgent in the South, Johnson's "southern" stance would further weaken his moral standing with the public.

Brammer also knew, from listening to Johnson's scotch-fueled monologues at the ranch, that action on civil rights was more than just a political game with the man. He had heard Johnson speak of the brutality of picking cotton—Johnson had done the hard work as a child, under the merciless Texas sun—and he had heard him insist that blacks were "not gonna keep taking the shit we're dishing out." Johnson often told the story of the dangers that Zephyr Wright faced whenever she drove through southern states, with no place to stop to go to the bathroom. She had shared with him harrowing tales, and Brammer could see he was genuinely moved by them. Johnson knew, too, that with "600,000 more [Texas] Negroes voting, I'd be in a much better position. They're citizens; I want them to vote."

No civil rights bill had passed in the US Congress since 1875. To succeed, Johnson would need to talk many senators into voting against their own interests or against their instincts. Working stealthily with the northerners, he convinced them he could shape a bill that would at least "break the virginity" in Congress regarding civil rights legislation; and working stealthily with the southerners, he convinced them that supporting the bill would buy them goodwill with the press while doing nothing substantial to advance the Negro cause. Both of these promises were true—in the end, the legislation was limited to voting rights, and did not attempt to sweepingly outlaw racial discrimination. But it was a first step. At the last minute, before the final vote, the northerners believed they were backing a much stronger bill; the southerners thought a far weaker bill had landed on the table. Both sides felt hornswoggled. And Lyndon Johnson had pulled off a minor miracle. As a side benefit, he had snatched civil rights away from the Republican Party and made the issue a Democratic Party priority.

"LBJ fooled hell out of Eisenhower, and there's serious talk now that Ike might veto the bill just so Democrats can go through the whole civil rights mess again next year," Brammer wrote Nadine. "It's not too bad a bill—as good as anyone can get against the bastard southerners, I'd say—and if Ike feels so strongly about the demerits of it he could have insured its success by saying something about it earlier. He's such an ass hole." It was true that Eisenhower had provided no leadership whatsoever on the issue, which made Johnson's light shine even brighter, in spite of liberals (including Ronnie Dugger) complaining that the bill was too watery to be effective.

"Civil rights bill passed last night," Brammer wrote Nadine on September 10:

> I'm pretty well convinced it is a good one, despite what some of the screaming liberals say . . . spent about an hour after the vote listening to Johnson and Humphrey talk things over (aren't you envious?). Humphrey is a terrific guy and he was full of praise for LBJ getting the bill through without a long, divisive filibuster . . . He said that what impressed him most was the absence of demagoguery and hate stuff from the southerners, and again he credited Johnson. It was a big week

> for Johnson, probably the biggest of the year. He wrote the bill as it now stands, handled all the strategy and got the first civil rights bill through the Senate since Reconstruction . . . So . . . [what does] *Time* magazine [do] . . . a cover story on Dick Russell [the leader of the southern bloc].

If Brammer hoped to get some downtime after the civil rights push, a chance to revise his novel in the daylight hours rather than the pill-stoked late nights, he was disappointed: Johnson drove his staff harder than ever. Nothing worse than resting on one's laurels. Reviewing his manuscript, Brammer recognized that his characters were "all too sophisticated to be moved by tacky melodramas," but he didn't know how to infuse the story with more dramatic energy.

Then the response arrived from Henry Holt: "Brammer has more wit and facility and sophistication, and larger concerns, than any young writer I've seen in some time; I'd like to work with him; but I cannot pretend that 'The Heavy Honeyed Air' is not a rough, spotty, half-formulated novel that needs a lot of work."

# 9.

"They don't mix—art and politics—like Scotch whiskey and Pepsi-Cola they don't mix," Brammer wrote. Yet it was not until he leavened his art with politics—or more accurately, with the dynamics of American political culture—that his fiction breathed, that his clever, aimless characters found direction. When Nadine left Washington to return to Austin, she bid good riddance to a world she thought she had discarded. Politics was for suckers, she told her friends; powerful men were lechers and bullies who surrounded themselves with "asses for aides." Johnson was the worst: "I'm sick of him . . . or his doings," she wrote Ronnie Dugger, "and his weak little people and all the mangled personalities surrounding him."

"Nadine is just a bitter fishwife," Brammer told Dugger. "Pussanully, ah just loves that Lyndon." Especially after watching Johnson shepherd the civil rights bill through the Senate, Brammer was entranced by the minutiae of the political process. It was all the more remarkable to him that anything got done, precisely *because* the personalities involved were so "mangled." Personal weaknesses and political greatness ("Ever'body screws") were intertwined in endlessly fascinating ways—the stuff of great art, of the Greek tragedies, of Shakespeare.

He wasn't sure he would ever get the chance to develop—even on a minor scale—a Shakespearian vision. His agent, James Street, was always full of bad news, he wrote Nadine. *The Heavy-Honeyed Air* met with one rejection after another. It was a "big, grubby manuscript," Brammer admitted. "I am surprised any publisher was interested [even momentarily]. It is pretty bad, though interesting in stretches."

"I think now that it would be a mistake to continue to share it until you have had a chance to incorporate . . . revisions," Street wrote Brammer in mid-January 1958.

Brammer told Nadine it would be damnably tough to discipline himself to stay at the book, but he would try. "People keep feeling sorry for me and asking me to dinner. It is hard to hurt their feelings and say I'd really prefer not to. Have about 60 pages of revision."

He would sneak into Johnson's office at night, pop a Dexamyl, and settle over the bulky typewriter at the senator's solid old desk—Harry Truman's vice president, Alben Barkley, had once used this desk. From time to time, one of the security guards poked his head through the doorway and offered Brammer a can of beer in exchange for forty winks on Johnson's couch. "What grim slobs they all are around here," Brammer wrote Nadine. The senator was the exception: "He made a beautiful speech yesterday to the Democratic Caucus . . . [I] was so inspired."

Inspired enough to consider again a novel about a politician on a movie set, like the one he had seen in Marfa. But what would the story be? Instead, he attempted a few chapters of a novel about a set of twins, and then he sketched a couple of short stories—none of which interested Street. "I am lost," Brammer told his wife.

Throughout 1958 and 1959, in one pill-dependent late-night session after another, Brammer wrestled with his visions and drafts, and worked his way toward essential material. That the drafts of the book were typed amid bursts of impassioned letters to his increasingly estranged wife suggests that like the letters, the book was written to keep his marriage together. "Maybe I'll get the book published; maybe we'll make a lot of money; perhaps they'll take me off to jail," he wrote Nadine.

For her part, "I was having a ball in Austin," Nadine told me when I interviewed her in Shelby's house in the winter of 2014. "It was so much fun, and I just didn't care about Bill anymore. I was done with him." She laughed. "I blew him away."

Shelby told me later, "That evening, Nadine sat at the kitchen table, quietly looking through old photographs of Bill. After you left that day, she cried a little."

---

He regularly dreamed, in snatches of sleep just before dawn, of driving around Washington while wearing his pajamas, and being stopped by the cops. They always kicked and punched him in these dreams, for no apparent reason. He hesitated to pull rank and tell them he worked for Lyndon Johnson, but then he did and they didn't care. Worse than the blows they delivered, their indifference and disrespect disturbed him. It didn't matter how hard he worked. He could never do enough. Then another disturbing thought: if they booked him, whom could he call? His wife wasn't here. "What does this all mean?" Brammer typed into a journal. "Someday . . . I will be alone and defenseless and inadequate to the moment. The more I will rage the more I will be put down."

As he worked through humid mornings in his office, writing memos, newsletters, press releases, and radio addresses for the senator, as he flitted in and out of the Robotyper room, the dream's brutal residue flaked away. Assured by George Reedy that the senator liked his draft of a speech, or invited by Johnson to a party in the country, he felt a rush of renewed energy, aided by another Dexamyl.

In the early months of 1958, he was primed to enjoy Lyndon Johnson as much as he ever had and as much as he ever would. Johnson had fully recovered from his heart attack and from the blunt humiliation of the 1956 presidential race. He was slimmed down, relatively healthy. He was not yet agitated about the coming campaigns of 1960. He had resumed his role as undisputed leader of the Senate. Politically, Texas was still firmly in the control of the Democrats (Barbara Bush recalled, "I can still remember when George and I volunteered to work at the polls during a primary election [in Midland in 1958]. Exactly three people voted Republican that day. The two of us and a man who you could say was a little inebriated and wasn't sure what he was doing.") By 1958, Johnson had parlayed his government connections into a cache of great personal wealth, using federally guaranteed cost-plus-profit contracts to acquire land and build on it, using federally licensed broadcast affiliations to expand his radio and TV networks, using federally subsidized equipment—as well as taxpayers' money—to promote his oil and gas deals. He reveled in his status as a Cold War hawk, whipping up "holy war" hysteria over what was, in Ronnie Dugger's view, "principally a disagreement [among nations] over how to modernize."

Full of magnanimity, power, and scotch, he would gather his troops, bellow at them verses from the book of Isaiah—*For are not my princes kings* (my hard-peckered boys!)—and pack the whole kit and caboodle off to a country retreat. On one such occasion, "LBJ had about sixteen Scotches but did not get drunk and never went to sleep. He talked all the way and was in high spirits," Brammer reported to Nadine. "He kept talking about me . . . and all I could offer was a sick smile." He wanted to buy Brammer a car. He wanted to buy him new suits. (Grand favors as forms of indenture.) On another occasion, he talked to his staff "very frankly about religion, about not having any. Everybody got drunk."

Briefly, Johnson appeared to value Brammer's political advice. He considered Brammer's idea that Padre Island be declared a national park, which would protect its pristine shoreline from overdevelopment by oil and gas interests. Ultimately, LBJ failed to pass any such legislation, and the island was not protected until 1962, under a proclamation signed by President Kennedy. Kennedy took credit for the notion, along with Senator Ralph Yarborough.

One weekend in early February, Brammer and other members of the staff accompanied LBJ to an overnight party at the Virginia home of George Brown (where Sidney had nearly drowned in the icy pond). "The Virginia country was beautiful after the snow," Brammer wrote:

> We got there about 5, immediately started drinking, had people waiting on us hand and foot, had a sumptuous meal . . . LBJ waved his arm about the room and said, "Here's how you forget. You sit here at a big dining table before a crackling fire and carpets three inches thick. Now tell me. Are you very worked up about the suffering in the world at this moment? That's what you got to watch out for."
>
> That man!

Johnson's presence always worked "like a shot of adrenalin" on Brammer. Even if "his personal magic last[ed] just about as long," something he would say or do would renew Brammer's faith in his essential goodness—as when Johnson remarked quietly, before the fireplace in Virginia, that his old nemesis Allan Shivers had been a skilled politician but lacked the one necessary ingredient for success: "Didn't love the people."

---

Back in Austin, Nadine failed to escape the political world. She needed extra money, so she went to work in the Capitol, doing clerical tasks. "The Texas legislature is not known for being a great deliberative body, and at that time it was more like one big party," she said. She was "living it up . . . trying not to think about the future." The "main concern" of each day was "figuring out where to meet in the evening or which party to attend" with "other young mothers my age who were also in damaged marriages, either waiting for divorce settlements or running from their situations by having affairs." Brammer's letters to her during this period often ended with him asking her how a particular soiree turned out, or whether she had sounded muted on the phone because of a hangover ("You weren't exactly making good sense").

She met attractive young legislators from all over the state. Already she knew Bob Eckhardt, from the *Texas Observer* team. Originally from Houston, he had just been elected to the House and was drawing attention as a brilliant legislative craftsman, owing to his lobbying experience and his understanding of political mechanics. Process always trumped ideology, he said. Nadine liked his genial smile, his slightly crooked bow ties, and his habit of not talking down to his two little girls, Rosalind and Orissa. He frequently brought the girls to lunch at Scholz's. One day, when he went to pay the check, the waitress assured him that a gentleman in the corner, a lobbyist, had taken care of it. Rosalind asked him whether the man was a friend. "Well, not exactly a friend, but he's interested in some of my legislation," Eckhardt explained. "Oh Daddy, he made a bribe!" Rosalind replied.

Nadine met Bob Hughes, a state representative from Dallas with a rather anemic voting record, usually in service to oil and gas interests. Hughes was gregarious, funny—and married—and he and Nadine promptly began an affair. "We weren't discreet," she admitted. "We partied with my friends, who soon became his friends, spending many afternoons on his boat on Town Lake . . . long good-byes, and wonderful dinners . . . charged with sexual anticipation."

Mike Levi, an academically trained philosopher and a rancher, opened up his Paleface Ranch to the young political crowd. The group used the grounds as a dance compound, a space for lavish barbecues. Sitting on over eight thousand acres along the Pedernales River, the ranch got its name from the salty-faced Hereford cattle grazing the riverbanks. Sometimes the parties lasted for days. Once, the members of the Modern Jazz Quartet, refused hotel rooms in Austin because they were black, moved into the ranch and played impromptu concerts for the partygoers. "We'd all pack a picnic and take the food out to little boats on the river," Nadine said. "They had fold-out beds on the boats. The Pedernales has these cliffs around it that are just incredibly tall. We'd pull up on a sand spar, start a fire, and cook steaks. Everyone would get kind of drunk and laugh and carry on. It was a magical time." Often, she and Bob Hughes slipped away from the steak dinners to watch sunsets, hold hands, and drink white wine on a hardscrabble hilltop.

Brammer learned of Nadine's indiscretions on visits to Texas to see the children. One weekend, on impulse, he bought a Vespa and rode all three kids around town on it, "in a highly dangerous and illegal manner," Sidney said. "We loved it!" He called himself their "derelict daddy," and they couldn't get enough of him. Worse than hearing about Hughes from his friends was hearing from Sidney how, on some mornings, she would awaken and walk into the living room to find her mother and this man passed out together on the couch.

In her memoir, Nadine underplayed Brammer's reaction to the affair: "He declared he was going to Dallas to confront the legislator about our behavior," she wrote. "Upon his return, I asked him how it went. Bill said, 'He's terrific. I think I'll divorce you and marry him.'"

She wrote that Brammer "was having affairs as well" in Washington, but it is clear from the couple's correspondence that whatever flings he had were glum responses to Nadine's indifference toward her marriage. Her activities, her flaunting of them in front of the couple's friends, occasioned sad, sometimes ugly fights whenever Brammer came to Austin. Shelby has vague memories of Nadine making him sleep in some kind of outbuilding behind the backyard. He wrote of arriving in town once and being locked out of the still, darkened house—Nadine off somewhere at a party—and falling asleep on the lawn. The next morning, he tried to pay attention to his children, Sidney crawling on his lap, grumbling about her brother's "grubby little-boy hands," staring at his wife, wondering when they had turned into Dick and Nicole Diver, dissolute in paradise. Then he would fly back to DC and send her conciliatory letters:

> I haven't had any revelations—except for the staggering revelation of finally being able to get through the barriers of pride and self-consciousness and *really* communicate . . . I don't want you to withdraw from anybody's glittering world. I don't want a simpering, sweet-innocent housewife type. There's no need to stay away from . . . anybody's parties or to feel you've got to be Mrs. Bill Brammer instead of Nadine. I *want* you to be Nadine—I've loved you for your vitality, intelligence, and your rare qualities as a mother. I just want you to respect first

> yourself and then others. You haven't been—you've been abusing yourself (and others) under the delusion you're being a "great, happy bird." The thing is, you *are*—there's no point in trying to prove it. When you do try, you're actually less free and vital than you would be if you just played it straight. What I mean is, that's not really living "life." It's giving vent to the self-destructive impulses that are in everyone, and the result is self-abuse, self-pity: rendering meaningless through mis-use and surfeit any real value freedom and vitality might ultimately have for you. Blah, blah blah . . . words are frauds, and I wish you and the children were here. I want to be strong; I want to be a real goddamned man; and perhaps if we can get this madness even partially resolved I can concentrate less on building up my own faltering reserves and more on bolstering and supplying yours.

He signed his letters "I vant you" and "sex things." Attempts to "*really* communicate" fizzled quickly, usually over money—a check he wrote Nadine bounced; his bad teeth got even worse and he had to sell the car in order to pay the dental bill—or tensions flared over an innocent remark from one of his children on the telephone that revealed they didn't know where their mother was.

He returned to the only thing he knew how to do: "I have worked every night this week on the book," he wrote Nadine, trusting the novel to be the answer to their problems. But the *novel* was a problem. The dialogue of his world-weary characters sitting in the Dearly Beloved Beer and Garden Party had improved with each new revision, but still lacked any point. These people were not Scott Fitzgerald's doomed romantics but rather a klatch of cynical drunks. He hadn't got the tone right. Too flip. Too flat. He needed a bigger vision (as did his tipsy friends at Scholz's, he thought). He set the pages aside and concentrated, once more, on the setting of a movie shoot. Politicians and screen stars—the similarities were obvious: the enormous egos, the need for adoration, the artificiality of the surface. What the story might be he still didn't know, but the models for his characters had been standing squarely in front of him, one of them quoting the book of Isaiah, the other harassing him for money. Critics have always cited Brammer's sensitivity to Lyndon Johnson as the genius at the heart of *The Gay Place*; equally as insightful are the portraits of Nadine apportioned among a number of female characters in the book, beginning with the actress Vicki McGown. In her narcissism, her desperate need to dominate men and situations, she is an embodiment of Nadine's beauty queen persona, the Duchess of Palms, isolated and silver tinted. Nadine's other qualities, the vitality and intelligence that Brammer so prized, he parceled out in other sections of the story.

He swiftly drafted a version of what became "Country Pleasures," book three of *The Gay Place*, featuring an LBJ-like governor on a visit to a Hollywood movie set in a southwestern desert. There, he encounters the larger-than-life Vicki. She is the estranged wife of his press aide, Jay McGown, and the mother of Jay's daughter. Two volatile personalities grappling for attention in an exotic locale: immediately, the writing pulsed with wild comic imagination. The pain at the center of the McGowns' marriage balanced the humor.

"I read [it] as it was written, in Billy Lee's apartment," said Larry L. King. "He got his energy then from candy bars and hot cherry Jello that he drank in a milk bottle, which was a little strange. He had more raw talent than any of us who came along later. But I thought, by God, if Billy Lee can do it, I'm going to work a little harder at learning my craft."

Initially, Brammer thought of the movie-story section as a stand-alone novel. In a letter otherwise concerned with debts and the worry that he might have to find a better-paying job, maybe in the Foreign Service ("all I think about is getting home to you and the kiddies"), Brammer told Nadine, "I finished the book Sunday 10 a.m. after working all night Saturday night and into the morning. The Memorial Day weekend gave me a lot of time. I worked all night Thursday night, all night Friday night after sleeping most of the day, and then Saturday night and into Sunday. My last four chapters were colossal. I edited the thing lightly Monday and shipped it off to Street yesterday."

"This was before the days of [the] widespread use of Xerox machines," said Brammer's friend Glen Wilson. "If you wanted a copy of something you could use an Apeco copying machine, but this was costly and time-consuming (you had to run the copies through a bath of developing liquid and then hang them up to dry). Mostly, you simply made a carbon copy. But Bill, in his eagerness to get on with his writing, didn't take the time to do this, so that his original manuscript was the *one and only* copy in existence." Brammer promised to send Nadine a carbon, but he never did, so Wilson may have been right.

The midterm elections distracted him from the anxiety of waiting for his agent's response to the new pages. Ralph Yarborough was running to keep the Senate seat he had won a year earlier in a special election. The liberals worried that the fix was in against their candidate, but Yarborough squeaked to victory. The only person who never doubted the outcome was LBJ, proving his political acumen once again, Brammer said. Brammer had serious misgivings about Yarborough. The man was probably too ideological to be "worth a damn" as a US senator—Johnson's view precisely. Such sentiments further distanced Brammer from his pals back in Texas.

Finally, James Street wrote to say he was not excited by the new material. "I am as lost as you about what to do with the book," he said. "I think the key problem is that the story is just too morbid. Jay deserves better than he receives, and without making him a character with whom the reader can identify, you lose a foil. You must have a healthy background against which you can operate your characters, and that ain't here."

"I don't want to think about it," Brammer told Nadine. "I couldn't possibly write it non-morbid with a 'healthy' background. I don't think Street and I are on the same vibrations . . . Anyhow, I am starting another book this week—another short one—just to get my mind off this publishing madness. Idiot agents make me morbid."

The new short novel would eventually coalesce into book two of *The Gay Place*, "Room Enough to Caper." It concerned a junior senator like Ralph Yarborough, trying to win an election against formidable odds (and paralyzing self-doubts). As in "Country Pleasures," the farce of political hijinks is tempered by the story of a sad marriage. The senator and his unfaithful wife fight over the well-being of their two little girls, and wonder where they went wrong.

Robert Penn Warren's *All the King's Men*, published in 1946, was an obvious model for the kind of novel that Brammer hoped to shape. He read and admired the book but found the first-person narration less compelling than the expansive point of view of *Tender Is the Night*. He was interested in an entire social milieu, not just a coming-of-age story. He absorbed a less well-known political novel, *The Caperberry Bush* (1954), by a former *Houston Post* reporter named Jack Guinn. A work of fantasy as well as a study of American politics, *The Caperberry Bush* tells the story of a truth serum placed in a metropolitan water supply, and the subsequent impact of complete transparency on a political campaign. The unspecified setting seems to be Oklahoma. Brammer liked the indeterminacy. The major importance of Guinn's novel to Brammer lay in the book's gleeful skewering of tony folks through lightly fictionalized portraits. In part, *The Caperberry Bush* was a roman à clef focused on the life of Oveta Culp Hobby, a wealthy and powerful Houstonian with extensive holdings in radio, television, and newspapers. Guinn's example further emboldened

Brammer to use Lyndon Johnson, Nadine, and his friends at Scholz's as character molds—so much so that when *The Gay Place* was published, Willie Morris, just back from a stay in Great Britain, took one look at the character Willie England and said to his friend, "Billy Lee, at least Thomas Wolfe changed the names and addresses."

Ultimately, Brammer's fictional governor, Arthur "Goddam" Fenstemaker, would not depend solely on Lyndon Johnson. Brammer was intrigued by Huey Long, Sam Rayburn, and Penn Warren's unforgettable Willie Stark. Life had provided the perfect climax for a political story: the deaths in office of FDR and Texas governor Beauford Jester. Reportedly, Jester had died on a train heading for Houston. "It was common knowledge in Austin newspaper circles that his mistress was on board with him, and that a friend of Jester's hustled her off the train before the body was removed," said Brammer's friend Anita Wukasch. Brammer kept track of these saucy details.

But it was the introduction of Johnson's personality into the rough scenes he had drafted again and again that finally made the novel gel (that, and Brammer's courage in exploring, wistfully, the collapse of his marriage). And it was Johnson who continued to dominate his daylight hours following the sleepless nights of work on the book.

"Johnson passed Hawaii last week in an hour and 45 minutes," Brammer wrote Nadine about the vote on Hawaii's statehood. "It took 50 years to get it there." And it had taken his staff's blood and sweat to prepare the vote. Under Johnson's brutal routine, staff members came and went, exhausted and traumatized. Brammer's officemate, Booth Mooney, left for a while. Brammer's workload doubled (with no increase in pay). Around this time, he became especially close to an eighteen-year-old intern, Michael Janeway, son of the economist Eliot Janeway and his wife, Elizabeth, a journalist and novelist. Michael was a "Holden Caulfield type." Even so, he was "more mature than most of our contemporaries," Brammer told Nadine. "You forget he's so young until you give him a couple of beers and realize you have a sudden drunk on your hands . . . I've been kidding him lately that LBJ probably has him picked out as a potential spouse for Lynda Bird, and he saw Lynda the other day and had to go sit down to get over his [frightened] dizzy spell."

Janeway considered Brammer his tutor in politics. Brammer would sneak him into Johnson's office at night. Breaking into the bourbon supply, he would refer to the room as a "Turkish whorehouse." Brammer "mixed an antic sense of humor and appreciation of our employer," Janeway remembered. "'Sweet Daddy Grace,' he sometimes called Johnson in conversation, after the outlandish black evangelist of the 1930s." The name suggested "Johnson's extremes, between shrewd political mastery and raw vaudeville, between near paranoia and overbearing exuberance."

The time was approaching when Johnson would need to organize his presidential campaign if he intended to run in 1960. The prospect made the senator increasingly tense and excited, often "sad-eyed as a spaniel," Janeway wrote. Johnson swung massively from declaring he had no designs on the White House to making his "usual wild plans about how he's going to change the world," Brammer said. "Hope he does it." Generally, Johnson fumed. Booth Mooney's biography of him, with which he had been pleased, now seemed to him sinister. Everybody stood against him. He became more snappish at his staff—nobody had thought this possible. Even Brammer's patience with him frayed, made more ragged by wakeful nights and scads of pills.

He wrote Ronnie Dugger, "I'm stripping my testes 14 hours a day in behalf of LBJ, of whom—to use one of his words—I'm [now] only moderately fond." Then he launched into a thorough consideration of the man. It is worth quoting at length. This was the Lyndon Johnson Brammer observed as his *Gay Place* portrait grew clearer:

> [I] judge from your editorials [in the *Texas Observer*] you're against him personally . . . the doctors are against him because he's for increasing Social Security benefits, East Texans are against him because he didn't sign the [southerners'] Manifesto [against desegregation], the Shivercrats are against him because he's an ADAer [a member of Americans for Democratic Action] and the ADAers are against him because he's a southern conservative.
>
> My opposition has a more selfish turn (I sold out my principles long ago). He works me too damned hard.
>
> Seriously, I don't know what to think of him. I've got a speech all prepared if he ever asks me (and he has been known to). I'm going to tell him he's the most incredibly able and well-equipped son of a bitch I've ever known. Exact quotes.
>
> He's a sick man. I don't want to oversimplify, and I'm not a snap analyst, but it's rather obvious that the thing that eats on him is a king-sized inferiority complex. He's got to prove himself, to bowl people over, plow 'em under. He has to keep people off balance; he has to reach the top—even if it's the presidency. He draws strength from other people's

weakness, and he must have adulation. And, of course, he's thin-skinned out of all proportion, as witnessed by the blood drawn from your *Observer* gibes.

He will forever be seeking and never quite finding (in sufficient amounts)—approval. OR, in the father image, a pat on his little horse head . . .

One thing this has done to me. Shattered all my illusions about the men I really cared about. It's rather shocking to see LBJ snap his fingers (literally) and watch Humphrey or Morse or Jack Kennedy jump (literally). He treats all of 'em—each and every one of 'em—each and every one of the 96—like children. Of course he flatters and badgers and gives them the usual treatment, but, still, there's that contempt. And perhaps he has to have that.

The newspapermen respect him, but all of them I'm pretty sure are quietly hating his guts. I haven't handled a news conference yet that there wasn't some little unpleasantry—you know, being not quite nice or showing just enough disrespect to the men of the press. I'm not saying he ought to be nice because they're newsmen—but, for God's sake, because they're human beings.

Nadine says it's a case of hormones—and LBJ's got too many. He just overpowers people with his manhood.

And you find yourself fighting to hold onto your own. You look around and see how he's spiritually castrating the rest of the people around you and it's a real battle. I've given him no backtalk (in fact he's been quite nice to me), but I have to concentrate on not jumping and simpering and clicking my heels like the others do when he lets fly a fart.

From the high point of his fascination with Johnson's skills during the passage of the civil rights bill in the Senate to the grim irritability of Johnson in precampaign mode, Brammer had bottomed out, with "near-fatal disillusion" about politics. On quick visits to Austin to see his children, he would sometimes escort Sidney to the state Capitol and tell her, "Don't take all this seriously, little girl—this is not something to be impressed by." Ever afterwards, Sidney said, "I [never] *could* . . . take it seriously. This indelible kind of attitude that he had given me—'It's just 9 to 5, it's not to keep the system going . . . No politician ever hung the moon.'"

He began to consider leaving LBJ and fleeing DC, a town that, more and more, seemed mentally feeble to him—historically, all the intellectuals, including the political experts (he may have been thinking of the Janeways), gravitated to New York, leaving behind the dregs, he would tell his friends. "So much of what passes for information in this city is not fact at all but simply a warmed-over combination of half-truth, informed gossip, and garbled surface event . . . Living here offers no special advantages for the Truth-Seeker: proximity only serves to give one the dubious sensations and satisfactions of knowing *first* what may or may not be happening in the halls of the mighty. We here in Washington are, all too often, simply misinformed faster than the folks out in the hinterland," he typed into a notebook. He wondered whether his servitude in the nation's capital had given him a "spiritual head cold or terminal angst."

He saw nothing to look forward to but "another round on the robo-typer." Everyone on the senator's staff had started to look to him like "Big Brother's half-sister."

Part of his growing discomfort had to do with fear: he believed he couldn't tolerate LBJ's misery, or the manner in which he would inflict pain on everyone near him, when he failed to receive the presidential nomination in 1960. And Brammer didn't believe he *would* receive the nomination. The Democratic Party was still enamored of Adlai Stevenson. "We are witnessing here a phenomenon of pentup [*sic*] frustrations which, I guess, we must blame old FDR for," he wrote in his notebook. "Everyone who lived through the R[oosevelt] Era feeling hurt and resentful because FDR wouldn't do what the New Republic people wanted . . . Well these people are now taking out their need to believe in an Idealistic, Dedicated, Sincere Liberal Leader on dear Adlai. He is perfect for the role . . . idealist, dedicated, sincere, and NICE. Of course he is nothing that FDR was: tough, perceptive, shrewd, brutal (the brutality of a thoroughgoing pro), wholly self-aware and capable of the most profound and far-reaching value judgments at the political levels (judgments which, for all his sensitivity and intelligence, Adlai seems altogether incapable of making)."

In this thumbnail sketch of a "thoroughgoing pro" (everything Stevenson was not), Brammer was naturally listing what he had learned from LBJ—and laying out the defining characteristics of his budding novel's central figure.

If he did leave Washington, what could he do? In preparation for a possible return to Austin (assuming Nadine would let him back into the house), he accepted a couple of small assignments from the *American-Statesman*. He profiled a local zoo, posing for a photographer with a bull snake wrapped around his neck. Journalism disgusted him just as much as politics.

He attempted to shake his blues with quick trips, whenever he could slip away from the Robotyper room without falling too far behind. These getaways did little to lift his gloom. "Went to the beach in Delaware over the weekend and zipped myself up in the sleeping bag," he wrote Ronnie Dugger. "Was . . . accosted by Negro homosexual at 2 a.m. under the boardwalk."

Finally, then, only writing could offer him "a glorious escape, an overcompensation through esthetic release." He told Dugger, "The act of creation has not much to do, I'm afraid, with Life itself." If he wasn't writing, he was "out of [his] mind." If the writing was perking along, he tended to exhibit social "neuroticism." He read the letters of Flaubert, which sent him back to *Madame Bovary*, to the measured tone and loving detail required to elevate what seems a trivial life into an existence worth assessing. He read Graham Greene's *The Power and the Glory* and *The Heart of the Matter*. "Greene in these two books is fooling around with real Art, and there is much of engagement and sacrifice and near-fatal disillusion in them," he wrote Dugger. "The first page of 'The Power and the Glory,' with its dusty buzzards flapping over a Mexican village, is about the most tremendous beginning of any novel in the English language outside the first page of 'A Farewell to Arms.'"

He read the book of Isaiah and the Song of Solomon, as much to tune his ear to the subtle rhythms infusing LBJ's speech as for the language and imagery. He copied into his notebooks phrases from the Bible:

*It is the glory of God to conceal a thing, but the honor of kings to search out a matter.*
*Let her breasts satisfy thee at all times and be thou ravished always by her love . . .*
*You have played the harlot with many lovers; and would you return to me?*
*Mischiefs of whoredom!*
*deliver me from out of the land of the wicked, redeem me from the grasp of the ruthless.*

Of that last line, he typed, "My own epigraph."

He also stayed current with the literature on Dexamyl and Benzedrine. A Harvard psychiatrist named Abraham Myerson, whose research had been funded by the Smith, Kline and French pharmaceutical company, claimed that depression was caused by the "suppression of natural drives to action," and therefore amphetamines, capable of adjusting the hormonal balance in the central nervous system, were the ideal therapy. Myerson's findings were available not only in medical journals, but also in full-page ads in mainstream magazines. In one ad, a grinning man, hands on hips in a supremely confident pose, blots out a gray image of his own sad face, as if his former unactive self were fading fast beneath the penetrating power of Benzedrine. Accompanying the picture is a comment from Dr. Myerson: "If the individual is depressed or anhedonic . . . you can change his attitude . . . by physical means just as surely as you can change his digestion by distressing thought." In another Smith, Kline and French ad, a smiling, aproned housewife cheerfully vacuums her floor while tentacles spread from her body like the arms of an octopus—a force field of happiness and energy. The accompanying text asserts, "Just one 'Dexamyl' *Spansule*, taken in the morning, provides daylong therapeutic effect. And mood elevation is usually apparent within 30 to 60 minutes." The millions of ad dollars worked. Enough amphetamines were sold to dose every US citizen at least forty-three times a year.

Brammer had no trouble getting doctors to prescribe the pills for him—physicians were just as swayed as anyone else by the money and the advertising campaigns, not to mention pharmaceutical lobbyists. Doctors believed amphetamines were generally beneficial for anyone, whether or not they had serious medical complaints. Through his friends in Texas, Brammer also had easy access to products from Mexico. Always ahead of the curve, he was already familiar with the rapidly developing, specialized vocabulary of "speed," long before that or any related terms became widespread: bennies, benzies, beauties, lidpopper lightning, skyrockets, sparkle-plenties. Sitting in Senator Johnson's office at night, he would put on a Paul Desmond record, pop a "Christmas tree" (a green-and-red Dexamyl), and hear the words of his novel, the lovely, flowing sentences, the music of his brain, brighten with electric clarity. His heart galloped. His breathing intensified, and his concentration blocked out everything but the page trembling in the typewriter in front of him. The paper expanded and filled the room, along with his unlimited confidence that he was producing the finest literature his country had ever seen.

And damn, if he didn't convince his agent this might be true. So what if he wasn't quite on the same "vibrations" as James Street? Brammer would shimmer enough for the two of them. He convinced Street not to give up on the evolving manuscript. The agent agreed to send it to Houghton Mifflin. Brammer had begun to believe his chances for publication were running out, so the waiting period when he knew that an editor was reading his manuscript felt more wretched than ever. He wandered aimlessly each day after the formal close of business in the Senate Office Building—from the Botanical Gardens to the National Gallery to the Smithsonian. He often spent hours in a penny arcade. "No word from the publisher, which is probably [the] reason I have been so unsatisfied all week," he wrote Nadine. "Thinking of taking up marijuana."

Finally, he heard from a Mrs. G. D. de Santillana at "Houston Muffin." She apologized for being slow in turning to his pages, but it was a busy season. She was "getting ready" to read soon. "You are being redundant when you refer to yourself as the 'perfect neurotic author,'" she told Brammer. "Just say author and I know all."

He tempered his anxiety with pills. He stayed busy by writing speeches for LBJ ("I am still feeding him stuff—some of it pretty good," he wrote Nadine) as well as forty new pages of a story about Governor Fenstemaker trying to get a junior senator elected to Congress. He titled the novella "If Ever Any Beauty." "It is pretty good and I am amazed at how I continue to gush," he told Nadine, hoping she would be impressed enough by his progress to let go of Bob Hughes and recommit to the marriage. "Gad! Your nymph-like romps at the Levi hole are unimaginably remote to me," he wrote her at one point. "Think I'm getting impotent. It's not that I'm being a prick but I'm suffering from corns, piles, heart murmur, mal de mer, weltschmertz, and LBJ-itis. Do you continue tranquil?"

To Ronnie Dugger he confessed his fears about his writing: "I am 'facile' enough, God protect me, but the intellect behind the prose is weak. Not inferior—just weak. Like a muscle never used enough, a little atrophied."

One early morning, just before dawn, on his way back to his apartment from the office, he walked into a tree and blackened his eye. His body was feeling just as weak as his mind. But on April 27, 1959, Mrs. de Santillana wrote, "We are very excited [by your manuscript] . . . I'm very excited to get something in the works on which we can give you the confidence of a contract." Two months later, she reported, "I have just finished IF EVER ANY BEAUTY . . . It is wonderful reading, it has swing and glitter and pace . . . In the fall we must get together. And talk about Arthur Fenstemaker, who is rapidly becoming my great American hero."

---

"I'm still not convinced" about the quality of the novel, Brammer wrote "Nudeena" in mid-July after visiting the Houghton Mifflin offices on

Park Square in Boston, but the editors' assistants and publicity people he had met assured him the work was very fine. The publisher had offered him a General Royalty Contract on June 22 for an "omnibus volume containing three short novels: 'The Gay Place,' 'If Ever Any Beauty,' and an untitled third related novel," all three "loosely tied together by the attractive, obliquely presented Governor Fenstemaker. It's a terrific idea, or so I think," de Santillana had told him. He received $750 on signing; on receipt of the final version of "If Ever Any Beauty," he would receive $250 more, $250 on receipt of a synopsis of the "third related novel," and a final $250 for the novel itself. He felt "goofily, placidly, statically happy," he told Nadine. "It must have been the rum. Mixed with dexamyl." He walked for hours, alone, along the banks of the Charles River. "It was all nearly as good and strange and tropical as two days in Istanbul," he said.

He wrote to friends: break out the casks of Amontillado!

On August 6, Anne Barrett, Mrs. de Santillana's editorial assistant, told Brammer the latest version of "If Ever Any Beauty" was "a little slow in getting off the ground, but the dialogue is good and Governor Fenstemaker contributes his usual magic touch as soon as he comes on the stage." The trouble, she said, was too many characters. It was hard to focus on any one story line.

Within two weeks, he had sent her new pages that "picked up [the story] enormously," she said. "This is partly because of Governor Fenstemaker, an absolutely wonderful man," but also because Brammer had sharpened the other characters, made them less passive. "I think you are on the right track," Barrett wrote. "We are all agog to read [more]."

Nadine, the reader who counted most with him, did not respond to the book's prospects with the same level of enthusiasm. Mostly, she wanted to know how quickly he would receive the rest of the money. His initial happiness evaporated. His depressions were exacerbated by the down periods following speed runs. "My feeling this week is no feeling, or rather the absence of feeling," he wrote Nadine. "Probably as a result of being so high for so long . . . And all the reasons were so shitty superficial, or ephemeral, or something . . . [I have] performed well for LBJ. There was a staff meeting called that I hadn't known about and I was included and they could hardly shut me up. LB [*sic*] was impressed, but I can't, at this point, remember a single thing I said."

In November, Nadine filed for divorce. She had gotten tired of Bob Hughes—it was obvious he would never leave his wife for her—but she wanted her independence from Brammer. Devastated, he wrote her parents, "I love her desperately (or perhaps the memory of her) . . . [but] I'll have to be rather frank . . . Nadine is beautiful and intelligent and loves her children. But she is also vain, arrogant, self-indulgent and self-destructive—and this last quality involves not only herself but the children she loves and her husband . . . She has hurt herself terribly in Austin."

He explained that word of her misconduct had reached him all year long in Washington: "Senator Johnson was even aware of it, and made it known to me that he thought I *ought* to do something about it." He railed against his old pals at Scholz's: "She has had at one time or another as corrupt and ruinous a circle of friends as any in my experience. Even the ostensibly 'good' ones get a kind of vicarious thrill from following Nadine's adventures and even encourage her in some of them." He was left with a dilemma: "I now find myself in a position of having to decide whether to play dead as I have for nine years or fight the [divorce] suit." He said his heart was broken: "She has done an awful violence to her children and pretty well crippled me career-wise as a consequence."

# 10.

"Neil's domestic problems with Andrea are artistically handled, and I believe that someday—outside the novel, of course—Neil and Andrea will come together again in love," Samuel D. Stewart, a New York editor for Houghton Mifflin, wrote Brammer in April 1960. It comforted Brammer to know that his revisions of the novel were proceeding apace as the book made its way toward publication, even if Stewart's comments were a cold reminder that domestic problems were more easily resolved on the page than in life. Neil and Andrea, characters in "If Ever Any Beauty," soon to be called "Room Enough to Caper," were barely disguised fictional surrogates for Brammer and Nadine—the junior senator and his wife, whose mutual unfaithfulness cripples their marriage.

Exhausted by his work for LBJ, bereft at the loss of his marriage and children (he knew he had neither the strength nor the standing to fight the divorce petition), but hopeful that he might soon make his living as a novelist, he seized the moment to leave the senator's staff. Michael Janeway's father, Eliot, dubbed "Calamity Janeway" by journalists for his consistently dire forecasts of America's economic future, published weekly financial newsletters highly prized by the political establishment. The newsletters were part of his Janeway Publishing and Research Corporation, operated out of his lush five-story townhouse on Manhattan's East Side. At Michael's urging, Eliot hired Brammer to write for him. In January 1960, Brammer moved into a small apartment at 65 Bedford Street in New York. Janeway gave him an office on the fifty-ninth floor of the Empire State Building. Mrs. de Santillana, who by then had met Brammer and warmed to him—signing her latest letters "Dorothy"—wrote, sympathetically, "New York is lovely and expensive and a long way from Texas if that is where your children are."

Nadine saw Brammer's move as a mark of instability. "I am broke, broke, broke," she wrote her folks, "but hope to hold out until I can get a paycheck of Bill's . . . The girls need shoes. I need *money*."

As for Lyndon Johnson, he was disappointed by Brammer's departure, the way a father willingly but regretfully watches his son strike out from home. Johnson always liked to say he didn't get ulcers, he *gave* them, but on the other hand, he never left anyone—people left *him*, revealing varying levels of disloyalty. He understood that when a fellow found a good opportunity, he needed to take it—but he reminded Brammer, *I can make you rich, boy, if you're smart enough to stick by the Great Man*, and who knew, maybe they would work together again someday.

"My father was an . . . eclectic meddler," Michael Janeway said. A student at Cornell (he never took a degree), briefly a communist (he "found it boring to distribute Marxist pamphlets in Harlem"), occasionally a journalist for *Time*, *Fortune*, and the *Nation*, Eliot Janeway developed a "personal style—writing and conversational—[that] hardened into a lordly, insistent certitude about life, and most particularly about the inner workings of politics and economics. This certitude he based on a unique access to information about what was *really* going on, together with a command of that information that left scant room for disagreement," Michael wrote. In other words, he was Johnsonian in his granitic presence and implacability. He had "moved swiftly, before he was thirty, from the determinism of Marxist theory in the face of capitalist collapse, into the power elite of the liberal New Deal and Roosevelt's administration of the war, and at the same time into the inner sanctum of Henry Luce, the conservative who set the haughty tone of *Time* magazine in the years of its greatest influence," Michael added. Little wonder that he assumed a "didactic" personality. Brammer had shifted from barely holding on in one gale to another. "Uncle Eliot is an LBJ type, and there's little repose for anyone when he is about. Which is most of the time," he wrote Nadine. "He is all right, though, and a good doctor-teacher." And he had taken a real shine to Brammer, as had Elizabeth, his wife. "Was planning on going to bed 8 o'clock New Year's Eve, which is what I did, except Eliot got me up at 10 to insist I go with them to a party. Dullest thing I've ever attended . . . and the only reason I did it was that it was given by the Sunday Book Editor of the Times." Elizabeth Janeway occasionally wrote for the *New York Times Book Review*, and hoped to get Brammer's novel some play there when the book appeared.

Booth Mooney, working once more for Johnson, came to town to consult with Janeway about the stock market. "I thought you were getting away from all those crazy people in Washington, and Janeway is as bad as Johnson," Mooney told Brammer. "But nicer," Brammer answered. Janeway took them to dinner at the Plaza, "where we sat between Edward G. Robinson and June Allyson and Janis Paige and Satchel Paige and Ethel Merman," Brammer recounted for Nadine. "I ordered a whole goddam pot of hot chocolate and embarrassed everyone. 'You got no dignity, Brammer,' Janeway says (he talks in inflexions [*sic*], like Salinger children). 'You got to crank it *up* and quit eatin' *Cokes* and *Snicker Bars*, for chissake, and go out and get *laid* . . .' He is very sensitive."

Soon, at Janeway affairs, Brammer met John Cheever ("he wanted to know all about Texas"), William Styron ("real whiskey gentry"), Lionel Trilling, Robert Penn Warren, and Alfred Kazin. He met Mort Sahl, who told him he was writing speeches now for Jack Kennedy. He reconnected with Robert Benton, now an artistic director at *Esquire* magazine. The two of them would meet for drinks in the late afternoons and go to movies together at the Museum of Modern Art.

"The Village is pleasant and not exactly the wicked and reckless place it is advertised to be," Brammer told Nadine. "I do some cooking in the evenings. I make grocery purchases when I get home after work—usually one can of something. I have to save my old cans because I am cooking in them. Very homey and domestic scene: three cans bubbling with corn, new potatoes, and tamales on burners that are about as adequate as a butane camp stove. Feel like I'm in a high class hobo jungle." He reported that "all is quiet except for the roaring in my ears."

One day on the street near his apartment he ran into a "wild looking woman . . . Tall, dark, hair down to bum, black mesh hose, purple bullfighter pants, no makeup except for eye gunk." He recognized her as an old classmate from Sunset High. She had moved to New York to become a painter. She invited him to a party at her Second Avenue loft, where he learned she had once been Jack Kerouac's mistress. He met Allen Ginsberg, "the 'I-have-seen-the-best-minds-of-my generation-shit-in-the-wastebasket-

and-eat-Sin-Sin' poet of worldwide beatnik phame," he wrote Nadine. One night he might spend an evening schmoozing with elites from the country's political and financial enclaves, the next he would be slumming with the "bohemian" crowd (just months before the eighty-five-year-old Herbert Hoover declared at the Republican National Convention that along with "communists and eggheads," the "Beats" were "one of the three most dangerous groups in America").

Almost daily, Brammer wrote the "Dear Wife of [His] Youth" detailed letters about his doings. The letters' most remarkable quality is their loving intimacy. In spite of the couple's pending divorce, his tone never changed—he communicated to her as if she were, and always would be, his best pal in the world. At first, he seemed to expect that their status as partners would not alter one bit, whether or not they were married. He told her about his apartment, "convertible couches and whitewashed walls and mosaic end tables and gilded mirrors from the Janeway basement." A phonograph that no longer played backwards, once the DC electricity had been converted to AC. "I have decked the bed with coverings of tapestry and carved works and fine linen and perfumed it with myrrh and cinnamon sticks," he wrote Nadine. "Hope you can someday come here when we are no longer man and bride and fill it all with love. Kiss my children."

He loved hearing about the kids. Mostly, Nadine shared news of their ailments. Sidney and Willie suffered frequent ear infections. Shelby had swallowed a dime and almost choked. Nadine needed more money. The legal proceedings were costly. "Want to get this stuff over with so I can pay off lawyers and love you a little better," Brammer wrote, "[though] I am not and never have been a well man."

For Valentine's Day 1960, he sent books to Sidney and Shelby. "Don't you forget that others like to receive Valentines . . . and especially don't forget big Mr. Willie!" he wrote to them. "You could have fun trying to tell Willie what Valentines are all about. You might, in fact, try to make a Valentine for Willie . . . and don't forget to make one for your Mother. You might, also, want to learn a little more about Valentine's Day—how we came to have such a day, its history, how it all got started. You'd find that sort of information in your Encyclopedia. Get Mama to look it up for you. If you remember enough of it, you could tell your class about it at school."

In the same letter, he encouraged them to paint pictures to send to him for his bare walls. "Paint one picture every day and you'll soon find you're painting better and better—and you'll also find you've suddenly got a great many pictures all your own!" He urged them to write poetry. "Poems are not too difficult to write . . . You can get a lot of fun out of writing . . . A hundred times a day even the dullest of us sees and hears and receives sensations, and anyone who is able to hold these sensations in the mind and observe them and turn them into words or pictures is a very special person indeed." As weeks passed into months, as the divorce went forward, as Nadine's responses to Brammer's letters grew chillier—and she resumed her affair with Bob Hughes—he pleaded with her less and less to come visit him in New York. He wrote her mother, "I know Nadine is better than she was a year ago. At the same time—and I don't think I'm a perfectionist—it doesn't strike me as being quite good enough. She continues going off on overnight weekends with Hughes . . . This no longer disturbs me quite as much emotionally as it did . . . The main thing, of course, is that she is giving a great deal more attention to the children. She's cut down on the drinking and partying, and that is a blessing." He wanted to minimize *his* excesses, too, but Janeway kept inviting him to parties to get him out of his lonely apartment. It *was* lonely, despite the kids' paintings on the walls, and—as he had done in Washington—he began to spend nights in his office rather than going home. Coworkers asked him whether they could use the apartment while he was away; sometimes he lingered at double features so friends could "pussytrack the bedspread," he said. For his depression, he asked doctors to fill as many prescriptions for amphetamines as they would. For a while, his communications with Nadine came down to, "COULD YOU TAKE THIS BY [YOUR] PHARMACY AT YOUR LEISURE AND HAVE IT FILLED AND MAIL TO ME? b."

---

Lyndon Johnson did not misread very many men, but Jack Kennedy managed to sneak up on him. It is possible that if Billy Lee Brammer, with his keen observational skills and cultural knowledge, had remained an integral part of Johnson's team, he may have been able to alert LBJ to Kennedy's threat. As it was, Johnson let himself be blindsided.

Everyone in the Senate knew that JFK's daddy had bought his boy a ticket to the fair, with money rumored to be earned from bootlegging (originally, the family plan called for Jack's late older brother, Joe, to grab the national glory). JFK was lazy, unserious, unengaged on the Senate floor. He spent much of his time in his office tossing a football with his friends. His Georgetown home was like a frat house. "[He is] weak and pallid—a scrawny man with a bad back, a weak and indecisive politician, a nice man, a gentle man, but not a man's man . . . pathetic as a congressman and as a senator," Johnson said of him: a pretentious playboy.

Kennedy bragged that if he didn't get a "strange piece of ass" every day (that is, someone other than his wife, Jackie), he couldn't relax. It was an open secret among his colleagues and the Washington press corps that he suffered from deterioration in his lumbar spine and from Addison's disease, a failure of the adrenal glands resulting in frequent fevers, nausea and vomiting, poor appetite, and chronic fatigue. (Addison's also gave him a copper-colored complexion that he allowed everyone to think came from his outdoorsy lifestyle.) On many days, he remained upright only because of back braces, cortisone shots, and—increasingly—the same amphetamines to which Brammer was steadily becoming addicted.

Johnson was a scotch man. Kennedy was all about speed. In addition to their regional and political differences, the men were prevented from fully understanding each other by the chemicals coursing through their systems—a not inconsiderable detail. The faster pace set by Kennedy's drugs of choice was more *of the moment* than Johnson's how-'bout-we-chat-over-a-little-branch-water jig. "Just like the rest of the culture, the presidency was in transition—and campaigning wasn't just whistle-stops any more. It was big media. It was television. It was jet lag all the time," said Sidney Brammer, repeating lessons learned from her dad. "The politicians in DC—these guys had to be jacked up round the clock."

And Johnson was missing the signals. One day in the Senate chamber, Kennedy told LBJ he would support him on a particular bill "even if it means going against the interests of my state." Johnson shook his head. "I can't let you do that, Jack. Your first duty is to represent your people. I never ask a man to vote for me when it means going against his constituents." Kennedy thanked him and walked away. Johnson turned to his brother, Sam Houston, standing nearby. "Who in the hell is he kidding?" he said. "That damned bill has nothing to do with his Massachusetts constituents. But he's sure learning how to spread the bull." This should have been a warning to Johnson that he was dealing with a smarter, craftier man than he realized, but he just could not take the grinning party boy seriously, even when Kennedy announced his candidacy for the presidency. Johnson could not conceive that the country would send a man with as thin a legislative record as Kennedy's to the White House. "It is the politician's task to pass legislation, not to sit around saying principled things," he insisted. In his mind, *he* was the obvious choice for president, the leader of the Senate, the person who had passed a civil rights bill against all odds. The problem was, he played coy, as he had in 1956. He was torn between his massive ambitions and his fear of humiliation if he failed to reach his goal. He wanted to be *asked*. He wanted to be *given* the party's nomination. He had earned it, damn it. Wishing to be courted, he went so far as to deny he desired the presidency whenever reporters asked him about his plans.

Brammer knew his heart. A year earlier, while still working for the senator, he had accompanied LBJ to the ranch for a fiesta honoring Adolfo López Mateos, the president of Mexico. In a move reminiscent of the 1948 campaign, when Brammer first saw Johnson in the flesh, LBJ hired a fleet of helicopters to fly over the small towns of Texas and deliver dignitaries to the compound, including the governor, Speaker Sam Rayburn, and the US treasury secretary. A red carpet on the lawn greeted the Mexican president. A mariachi band played, standing beside hundreds of pounds of steak on the grill. Brammer noticed a cloth banner stretched across the house's front entrance; it could not have hung there without the senator's knowledge: "Lyndon Johnson Será Presidente."

Like the press, the Kennedy clan wanted to know Johnson's intentions (his dithering had become "The Number One Enigma of United States Politics," said *Look* magazine). Bobby—Jack's de facto campaign manager—flew to the ranch one weekend to ask whether he planned to run. Johnson toyed with him, wouldn't say yes or no. This only increased Bobby's visceral hatred of the man: his southernness, his manners, his accent, his ego, his need for control. The *real* trouble between them? Bobby's towering insecurities and his flash temper matched Johnson's step for step. LBJ took him deer hunting. He placed a shotgun in his hands, showed him how to pull the trigger. The recoil knocked Bobby to the ground. Johnson laughed, helping him up. "Son, you've got to learn to handle a gun like a man," he said.

In the following weeks, Johnson continued to tell the press that he was not a candidate. Meanwhile, Bobby flew all across the country, lining up delegates for his brother in advance of the state primaries. He put together a "highly-financed new-style machine" and operated it with "brutal efficiency," said Sam Houston Johnson. "Lyndon stayed away from the primary races, never entered a single one. He knew, as does everyone, that it's possible to win all the open primaries and still lose the nomination because most of the delegates are chosen in closed state conventions, usually under tight control of party bosses . . . Senators and congressmen [gave] my brother . . . innocent assurances: 'Don't you worry about the people in my state, Lyndon—I'll have 'em for you when the time comes.'" For instance, Johnson had counted on Senator Tom Dodd of Connecticut to deliver his state's delegation, but to Dodd's surprise, John Bailey, the state chairman, had already "put together a slate favoring Kennedy." Bobby had beaten Dodd to the punch.

Later, when the campaigning was over, Kennedy liked to tweak Johnson by describing the 1960 presidential race this way: "I dreamed that the good Lord touched me on the shoulder and said, 'Don't worry, you'll be the Democratic Presidential nominee in 1960. What's more, you'll be elected.' I told Stu Symington [another candidate] about my dream. 'Funny thing,' said Stu. 'I had exactly the same dream about myself.' We both told our dreams to Lyndon Johnson, and Johnson said, 'That's funny. For the life of me, I can't remember tapping either of you two boys for the job.'"

"Johnson [always] ran on his record as the man who had made the Senate work. It gained him flattering articles in the magazines, but it did not win him sufficient [party] votes," said Harry McPherson. He was "mistaking power in the Senate for power in the country. The cockpit we watched with such fascination was in some respects a paradigm of the country. The issues fought out there were symbolic of those on the street. But it was finally not the street. It was a large room in Washington."

And Kennedy had transformed himself into a formidable national presence—energized, fleshed out by his drug regimen, newly confident, well financed by his father's resources, well coached by experts in the latest media, aware that his smile came across on television as dazzling and boyish and beautiful. "I have never seen anybody in my life develop like Jack Kennedy did as a personality, and as a speaker, and as an attractive person, over the last seven, eight years of his life," said Senator George Smathers. "It was a miracle." Another signal Johnson had missed: beneath the party-boy façade, on some fundamental level Kennedy was driven by the same urgent fear Johnson was—the certainty that his life would be short and he had to do whatever he could *while* he could. Johnson had his weak heart. Kennedy had his disease, his chronic pain. Both men were death-haunted.

A few weeks after Bobby's hunting fiasco at the LBJ ranch, Johnson flew to New York to court potential campaign donors (though he had still announced nothing). "I was invited to [a] reception in his honor at Gracie Mansion," Brammer reported to Nadine. "Lots of [wealthy] cats on hand to look the Big Pumpkin over. He did all right for himself, put on a good show, and didn't pick his nose or cuss out a photographer. Extra nice to me, as I expected. No one ever seems desirable until he's lost them. Wants me to come to Washington and work for him from time to time, doing some writing (probably helping them catch up on the mail—Walter [Jenkins] said they were way behind). He even asked Janeway, and Mr. J had to say yes, so I'll probably go down for a week sometime soon."

In fact, the invitation was welcome. Brammer had grown quickly restless while writing economic forecasts ("Cuba's oil grab is just a symptom of the Soviet Union's oil offensive"). He had gotten tired of being chastised by Janeway's secretaries for not keeping track of his business receipts.

But he found Washington just as dreary as ever. Johnson was driving himself, and everyone else, batty with his ambivalence about the presidency. "You've never had a heart attack. Every night I go to bed, and I never know if I'm going to wake up alive the next morning. I'm just not capable of running for the presidency," he would say to Bobby Baker one day. The next morning, "his attitude was, 'I'm not running, but I'm gonna win,'" Baker said. Under Johnson's orders, Walter Jenkins handed out wads of "hundred dollar bills to Johnson loyalists" and told them to "fan . . . out to many states" to lasso delegates.

Juanita Roberts tried to cheer the senator up one day by placing a few potted plants around his office. "Get those damn things out of here," he yelled at her in front of the staff. "I'm not running a greenhouse."

At a party one night, the wife of a staffer "got tight" and told Brammer "her life was a bunch of shit and why don't we go sit in a snowbank and screw," he wrote Nadine. The only good part about being on the Potomac again was the opportunity to fictionalize LBJ once more, forging the senator's words in letters to constituents and other folks. Brammer realized that long before he created Arthur Fenstemaker for his novel, he had been "creating" Lyndon Johnson—like a ventriloquist, throwing his voice on the page.

Janeway accosted Brammer when Brammer returned to New York. He wanted to know what the hell Lyndon was up to. That fellow was his own worst enemy, Janeway said. Johnson needed to cut the cloak-and-dagger bullshit, come right out and declare himself a candidate. Janeway, raised Jewish (though he always downplayed his background), strongly mistrusted Kennedy's Catholicism. He feared that a Kennedy administration would not be pro-Israel enough, whereas he had taken great pains, over the last few years, to educate Lyndon about the Middle East.

Finally, two months before the Democratic National Convention was scheduled to open in Los Angeles, Johnson admitted to his staff that he intended to mount a serious, all-out run for the nomination. Kennedy had most of the delegates sewn up, but if he failed to secure the nomination in the first round of convention balloting, Johnson could seize his chance. All bets would be off. Delegates would be free to flock to any candidate. Rather than directly oppose Kennedy during the first vote, Johnson preferred to remain underground and let somebody else fan the chaos. He worked to convince Adlai Stevenson's supporters to initiate a "Draft Adlai" movement, gambling that if Stevenson blocked Kennedy in the first round, Stevenson's supporters would come to their senses, realize that Adlai's moment had passed, and move to the Johnson camp.

"You ask about the Johnson prospects . . . I dunno . . . They are better since the U-2 incident, of course . . . Kennedy is hurt when people think of him standing up to the Russian K," Brammer wrote Nadine in late May. Kennedy had blundered badly, giving Johnson an opening. On May 1, Francis Gary Powers, the pilot of an American U-2 spy plane, got shot down while flying in Soviet air space. Immediately, Nikita Khrushchev canceled a scheduled Paris summit conference with President Eisenhower to discuss nuclear de-escalation. He demanded an apology from the United States. On the campaign trail, Kennedy criticized Eisenhower for authorizing the risky U-2 flight on the eve of the conference, and said if he were president, he would send Khrushchev his regrets. Right away, Johnson went after Kennedy for crumbling in the face of international threats. He suggested Kennedy was weak and unpatriotic. Khrushchev was trying to divide the American people, he said, and "we ought not to be doing the job for him . . . It was Mr. Khrushchev who . . . broke up the summit meeting by refusing to talk to the President other than in insulting language. It is not the American President who ought to apologize to Mr. Khrushchev. It is Mr. Khrushchev who ought to apologize to the American President." Audiences responded enthusiastically, shouting, "No! No!" at rallies whenever Johnson yelled, "I am not prepared to apologize to Mr. Khrushchev. Are you?"

"Johnson seems to have straddled the public consciousness again," Brammer informed Nadine. The "theme of unity crap" was working for him. Then LBJ asked Brammer to join the campaign. With Janeway's blessing, he did—postponing the proofreading of his novel's galleys. He worked with Janeway to arrange a meeting between Johnson and Adam Clayton Powell, a congressman representing Harlem. "We don't want to get the good niggers mad at us," Janeway said. Brammer haggled with Walter Reuther, the head of the United Auto Workers, on the phone: "The deal is Reuther promises no endorsement of anybody if Johnson can deliver on a version of . . . [an] old age assistance bill." Once again, he worked eighteen-hour days, failed to sleep, survived on Dr Peppers and pills. Johnson put on his Stetson, revved up the whirlybirds. In Idaho, Oregon. Just like old times.

And then the Kennedys bought the West Virginia primary: Johnson was convinced of this. "How the hell does Joe Kennedy move money around like that?" he bellowed.

Brammer wrote Nadine, "[We] were hoping to get some mileage out of [an] exposé of Kennedy buying [the] West Virginia election. All set for revelations. Then Ed Folliard of [the] *Washington Post* goes to West Virginia, and comes back to state, with all [the] prestige of [the] Pulitzer Prize behind him, that there was no such thing . . . West Virginia [was] strictly kosher."

Janeway fulminated, "An yew know whut—that goddam Folliard has got a sick baby, one of them cerebral palsied babies . . . An' we find out that Joe Kennedy done give a million dollars last week to the goddam National Cerebral Palsied Association . . . How's that for a high-class bribe?"

---

"MOVE TO KENNEDY NEARS STAMPEDE: JOHNSON SEEMS HEADED FOR POLITICAL ALAMO," read one headline just days before the convention began, in the Los Angeles Memorial Sports Arena. Los Angeles didn't look like the kind of city in which to anoint a national leader—"one has the feeling it was built by television sets giving orders to men," Norman Mailer wrote.

It didn't matter how many sweaty, boozy delegates Brammer collared on the arena floor, pushing them to switch their loyalties; it didn't matter how many nasty rumors the Johnson team spread about Kennedy's ill health; it didn't matter how often Johnson repeated to convention-goers, "I haven't had anything given to me. Whatever I have and whatever I hope to get I got through my own energy and talents. Now this young man I appointed to the Foreign Relations Committee claims he knows more about foreign affairs than I do. You know, there are some people who will throw crutches at their doctor and get smarter than their daddy." No matter: John F. Kennedy was going to be the bright new face (puffy with cortisone) of the Democratic Party.

Harry Truman, elder statesman, convinced that Kennedy was too green to assume executive leadership, complained that the convention was being run by the devil. Sipping scotch on a couch in his hotel room at the Biltmore, Johnson watched the first-ballot voting cascade away from him.

Brammer probably knew well enough to stay away from the Big Pumpkin the following day, far from the spray of his festering wound, so it isn't clear how much he may have witnessed of the vice presidential follies, but he certainly would have spoken to other staff members within hours, or minutes, of the swift and astounding developments: John Kennedy's request that LBJ become his running mate; Johnson's grousing that, in the words of former vice president John Nance Garner (from South Texas), the position wasn't "worth a bucket of warm piss"; Bobby Kennedy's frenetic attempts to undermine the offer; LBJ's reconsiderations (morbidly listing every male in his family who had passed away at sixty, ordering his staff to learn how many presidents had died in office). Was JFK's offer a mere courtesy to the majority leader, one he didn't think the senator would accept? Was the offer a pragmatic recognition that Johnson favorably balanced the ticket? Or did Kennedy fear Johnson would attempt to blackmail him with tales of his womanizing? Historians have puzzled over these matters ever since. On the ground, Johnson's staff viewed the situation much more simply: "John Kennedy obviously realized he needed Lyndon Johnson," said the senator's brother. "As a Catholic attempting to overcome an historical bias against people of his faith, he particularly needed someone to boost him in the Bible Belt of the South and Southwest." And why did Johnson say yes? "Most of the Texas staff accepted Mrs. Johnson's reason for his decision: the majority leadership was an exhausting job for one who had survived a heart attack. The Vice Presidency would give him relative peace and quiet," said Harry McPherson. "Others thought he had taken it out of a sense of duty: Kennedy could not beat Nixon without Johnson; to reject the offer would have been disloyal to the party."

Brammer saw through these rather pallid explanations. He agreed with Texas governor Price Daniel: "Something people always seem to forget when they talk about the vice presidential nomination being offered to Johnson is that, at the time, nobody in the Johnson camp thought there was any chance for John Kennedy to win the election . . . You can't really understand exactly what went on in [Johnson's] mind, and in the minds of the people surrounding him in Los Angeles, unless you realize that most of us were convinced that Kennedy *could not win* . . . The theory was that if he took the nomination and they lost, Johnson would be in better shape for 1964. He would have heeded the call. He would have gotten out and done his best . . . [gotten] his name before the people."

In the hours leading up to Kennedy's acceptance speech, Brammer got an earful about Johnson's decision. Eliot Janeway excoriated this sellout, this big galoot throwing his lot in with the damned *Catholics*! Phoning from Austin, Willie Morris, set to inherit the editorship of the *Texas Observer* from an exhausted Ronnie Dugger, wondered whether Johnson's move signaled a more liberal direction. Just how progressive *was* Kennedy? Morris was willing to give Johnson the benefit of the doubt, more than Dugger had been.

On July 15, in the Los Angeles Memorial Coliseum, John F. Kennedy spoke repeatedly of "revolution"—in technology, medicine, human rights:

> I stand tonight facing west on what was once the last frontier. From the lands that stretch three thousand miles behind me, the pioneers of old gave up their safety, their comfort and sometimes their lives to build a new world here in the West . . . Today some would say that those struggles are all over—that all the horizons have been explored—that all the battles have been won—that there is no longer an American frontier. But I trust that no one in this vast assemblage will agree with those sentiments. For the problems are not all solved and the battles are not all won—and we stand today on the edge of a New Frontier.

---

In the months ahead, Brammer campaigned across the country for the Kennedy-Johnson ticket, and he proofread galleys of *The Gay Place*. He had taken the title from a Scott Fitzgerald poem: "In the cool of the afternoon . . . / Under a white moon— / I heard Helena / In a haunted doze / Say: 'I know a gay place / nobody knows.'" A far more elegiac region than John Kennedy's New Frontier. "Title . . . gives me some anxiety, as it suggests a queer parlor," Brammer confessed to Ronnie Dugger. Dorothy de Santillana told him, "Don't worry": "I am laughing at the Fire Island connotation but I think that basically it won't affect the title. I'm sure none of our salesmen would ever make the identification!"

Brammer had completed three novellas, "The Flea Circus," concerning a young legislator named Roy Sherwood and his cronies at the Dearly Beloved Beer and Garden Party; "Room Enough to Caper," about the junior senator Neil Christiansen's reelection bid; and "Country Pleasures," focused on gubernatorial press aide Jay McGown's damage-control efforts at a wild desert movie shoot. Governor Arthur "Goddam" Fenstemaker dominates each of their lives. He works tirelessly to eradicate political corruption, pass civil rights and education bills, and nurture promising political careers. After many rewrites, the stories were "sharp, sensitive, comic in the right places, and touching," said Samuel Stewart, Brammer's New York editor. (He had caught Brammer's infectious humor and signed his letters "Francis Gary Powers"). Still, even at the proofing stage, some finishing touches remained: "You write such good dialogue that it is a temptation to use it as a crutch and to tell your story that way," Anne Barrett, de Santillana's assistant, warned him. He relied too much on exposition, as he had done in "Fight Team!," his college short story, and he needed to be more patient with physical descriptions. "We are all excited about the possibilities of this book and let's spare no trouble at this last stage of the game," Barrett said. "[And when you can,] get some rest—if that is possible in the rip-roaring set you write about!"

He had replaced James Street with a new literary agent, Elizabeth McKee. Robert Benton introduced them. "Way back in 1955, I had a leave from the army, got on a plane to Texas, and spent the night at Bill and Nadine's, but Bill was out of town somewhere," Benton explained. "I was doing some photography then, and I took some 'art' photographs of Nadine, which Bill didn't appreciate." Now, years later, here was a chance to make it up to him. "I'd done a children's book, *The In and Out Book*, with Elizabeth. I sent Bill to her. She convinced Houghton Mifflin to consider his novel for their annual award, which Philip Roth"—and Robert Penn Warren—"had won. I think sending him her way was the worst thing I ever did to her. He was always borrowing money. He had this way of talking people out of their shirts."

His expenses were mounting on the campaign trail—reimbursements wouldn't flow from Johnson's office for months—and then, in early October 1960 his appendix burst. "Sorry for the best laid plans but try to enjoy the rest," Dorothy de Santillana wrote to him at New York's St. Luke's Hospital, enclosing a check for three hundred dollars to cover his medical bills.

Within weeks he was on the road again with LBJ—in time to join the senator on his swing through Dallas. There, Brammer could enjoy his parents' tender loving care. Just days before the national election, Kennedy-Johnson trailed Nixon in Texas. Worse than losing the nation would be losing his home state, Johnson thought. "We put that son of a bitch on the ticket to carry Texas," Bobby Kennedy muttered every morning. If they lost, LBJ would never hear the end of it from this little twerp. Even if they *won* the White House, but wasted Texas—his influence in the new administration would be zilch.

"Lyndon, I believe you're cracking up," Kennedy said to his running mate when the cortege arrived in the Lone Star State.

"They're having a little disturbance at the Baker Hotel," a motorcycle policeman informed LBJ's driver as the senator and his staff approached downtown Dallas. Johnson was scheduled to hold a fund-raising luncheon at the Adolphus Hotel and to stay overnight at the nearby Baker. At the same time, a Republican Junior League event had been organized downtown. Young Republicans were handing out Nixon-Lodge pamphlets at the corner of Commerce and Akard Streets. Bruce Alger, the sole Republican congressman in the Texas delegation, known not for the legislation he had passed but for what he opposed—public housing, integration, Social Security, school lunches, and Medicare—exploited the coincidental timing to whip up a protest against LBJ. A charismatic and flagrant womanizer (according to the historian Steven L. Davis, his wife's divorce petition claimed that on the "evening [he] won his first election . . . he brought a prostitute to their hotel room, forcing her to watch as he made love to the woman"), his core constituency had always consisted of wealthy Dallas matrons. "The prettiest bunch of women I ever saw in my life," he addressed the Junior League crowd minutes before the senator's motorcade turned onto Commerce Street. Visible in the distance were Jack Ruby's strip club and, miles farther south, across the murky Trinity River, the rusted factory spires of Oak Cliff. "If Khrushchev could vote, he'd choose Kennedy-Johnson!" Alger yelled. The ladies cheered. As Johnson stepped from the backseat of his black Lincoln, with Lady Bird on his arm, they shouted, "Traitor!" "Judas!" "Pinko!" Alger waved a hand-lettered sign: "LBJ Sold Out to Yankee Socialists."

Later, newspapers named the female protesters the "Mink Coat Mob" (because, reporters said, many of the women wore furs purchased at Neiman-Marcus). The Johnson group tried to work its way through the shouting throng toward the Baker Hotel, Brammer still weakened from his hospital stay. Some of the women spat at the senator; someone grabbed Lady Bird's white gloves from her hands and threw them to the ground. "You ought to be glad you live in a country where you have the legal right to boo and hiss at a man who is running for the vice presidency of the United States," Johnson tried to assert above the taunts. "Turncoat Texan!" someone yelled. Later, as he made his way to the Adolphus luncheon, he waved away police escorts. "I asked the policemen to stand aside, because if the time had come when I couldn't walk unaided through the lobby of a Dallas hotel with my lady, I wanted to know it," Johnson said. Once more, Brammer glimpsed the man's intuitive genius. Johnson "moved with excruciating slowness through the chanting mob and the rain of spit," one journalist said. The senator knew how these images would play on television. "Let's just let them do all the hollering," he told his wife and his staff, staring at the cameras "with a martyr's embarrassed smile."

"It was the most triumphant half-hour of Johnson's career," Lawrence Wright recounted years later in *Texas Monthly*. "Overnight, he became an acceptable candidate to big-city Northern Democrats who had automatically hated him, traditional Democrats who had not (they now admitted to themselves) seen past the corn-pone mannerisms of L.B.J. to the winking F.D.R. inside him."

"If he could have thought this [incident] up, he would have thought it up," Bill Moyers said. Certainly, in the days afterwards, Johnson's staff exaggerated the violence that occurred, minimized the pushing and shoving *they* had done before Johnson called them off. In any case, though Nixon still carried Dallas in the national election, the presidency "was decided that day in the lobby of the Adolphus Hotel," Wright wrote. "It was the closest election in history . . . People said afterward that they were not voting for Kennedy as much as they were voting against Dallas."

Even Richard Nixon admitted, "We lost Texas . . . because of that asshole congressman, you know."

---

"Brammer . . . has jokingly told friends he may have to leave Texas once [his] book is published," the *Austin American-Statesman* said toward the end of the year, announcing its former reporter's prestigious Houghton Mifflin Fellowship. Images of the Mink Coat Mob may have flitted through Brammer's mind when he made this quip; more sorely, he fretted over Ronnie Dugger. How would he and the other Scholz regulars receive his affectionate but unflattering take on Texas liberals, his lionized Lyndon? At the Scholz Garten, "we felt betrayed" when Kennedy "picked Lyndon Johnson as his running mate . . . since Ronnie had led a principled charge against Johnson for six years," said Celia Morris; Ann and Dave Richards, leaving the beer garden "well-lubricated" one night, took a knife and cut down a banner on Congress Avenue that read, "Lyndon Johnson, a Leader to Lead the Nation"—they barely escaped the Austin police.

Brammer, "now a gray flannel executive for a New York research corporation" (i.e., no longer a real Texan), was once an ace reporter, said the Austin paper: "[He] slouched along at an indifferent canter and he spoke with apologetic quietness. These were deceptive characteristics. Brammer was actually as nosey as a reporter can be and stay within the law, and he was amazingly prolific. He could grind out copy like a player piano."

"What a formidable amount of work you have done! And how good it is!" Dorothy de Santillana wrote to him. "The total impact of reading the whole thing as one book was terrific. Many congratulations. I am sure you will be pleased at the book's public reception. I *know* it . . . Really, we are awfully pleased with you and proud of you."

He told Nadine he hoped to be filthy rich by the first of the year. He would shower financial blessings upon her—though he was already glimpsing what a "depressing business" the book trade could be. He had been turned down for a Guggenheim Fellowship. Eugene McCarthy had failed to respond to a blurb request. The *Ladies' Home Journal* had declined to excerpt the book because "it is much too rough and tough and cynical, in our opinion, for our ladies." So far, Elizabeth Janeway had been unable to convince the *New York Times Book Review* that his novel deserved notice. He suspected publishers that bought and sold review space in its pages. Politics, everywhere.

His divorce from Nadine would be final by June.

"I am sending you the first copy off the press of a wonderful new novel by someone called William Brammer," de Santillana wrote him on January 6, 1961. "I hope you will like it as much as I do . . . We are hoping for a splendid success."

Lyndon Johnson was about to become the nation's vice president. And Arthur Fenstemaker was about to be introduced to readers as the delightful governor of a country "most barbarously large and final."

# 11.

*The Gay Place*, "being three related novels," opens with one of the most stirring evocations of an American landscape in our literature:

> The country is most barbarously large and final. It is too much country—boondock country—alternately drab and dazzling, spectral and remote. It is so wrongfully muddled and various that it is difficult to conceive of it as all of a piece. Though it begins simply enough, as a part of the other.
>
> It begins, very like the other, in an ancient backwash of old dead seas and lambent estuaries, around which rise cypress and cedar and pine thickets hung with spiked vines and the cheerless festoons of Spanish moss. Farther on, the earth firms: stagnant pools are stirred by the rumble of living river, and the wild ferment of bottomland dissolves as the country begins to reveal itself in the vast hallucination of salt dome and cotton row, tree farm and rice field and irrigated pasture and the flawed dream of the cities. And away and beyond, even farther, the land continues to rise, as on a counterbalance with the water tables, and then the first faint range of the West comes into view: a great serpentine escarpment, changing colors with the hours, with the seasons, hummocky and soft-shaped at one end, rude and wind-blasted at the other.

That this contradictory continent, seen wide-angled as if from Lyndon Johnson's whirlybird, reflects the jumble of its inhabitants' social and political lives becomes clear soon enough—as does the realization that this will be an urban story, in spite of the natural setting so lovingly described at the outset. The focus of vision gradually narrows to settle on a "pleasant city, clean and quiet, with wide rambling walks and elaborate public gardens and elegant old homes faintly ruined in the shadow of arching poplars." Ruined, as well, by the fading of the old agrarian dream—forty acres for every family, ensuring them a stake in the democratic process; ruined as much as enriched by paved roads and electric wires, a complex of connections too weighty yet too incredibly swift to be burdened with oldfangled notions of back-to-the-ranch innocence. The book's bucolic beginning is interrupted—erased altogether from the rest of the story—by the banging of an old truck carrying "migratory cotton pickers," the modern face of agrarianism, past the Juicy Pig Stand downtown. The clattery engine awakens two politicians, the young Roy Sherwood, a legislator sleeping off a hangover in his car, parked in front of an all-night supermarket, and Governor Arthur Fenstemaker, "flounder[ing] in his bedcovers" in the governor's mansion a few blocks away. The lives of the downtrodden and the powerful are linked from this moment on, whatever else occurs in the narrative—a point underscored a few paragraphs later when the governor, demanding his morning coffee, asks his black butler, without irony, "You think it's gettin' better . . . Bein' a colored man. You think it's any better? . . . Of course bein' better still don't make it very good. I was thinkin' yesterday, signin' my mail, how I'd feel if I wrote a public official about, you know, my rights? . . . 'Try to make reasonable progress toward a solution . . . Sure keep your views in mind . . .' Why *God damn!* Some cornpone Buddha say that to *me*, I'd set a bomb off under him."

The butler grins at the governor. "I think most colored people vote for you . . . Even when you don't say things exact."

Whatever heroics this novel's characters may perform, we know from the start that they will not be unblemished.

Governor Fenstemaker—"'windowmaker' in Hill Country German, an illusionist and visionary," Al Reinert explains—winces at his coffee. "Nothin' tastes like it used to," he says. It is a sadly fallen world. But he has good works to pursue. "Goddam," he mutters. "Sir?" says the butler. "I'm just goddammin'." He puts in a call to Roy Sherwood, who, having caroused all night with his liberal pals and with his lover, Ouida (the "most eligible married woman in town"), is threatening to sleep away his day.

"Hell of a note," Fenstemaker says to him. "World's cavin' in all round us; rocket ships blastin' off to the moon; poisonous gas in our environment . . . Sinful goddam nation . . . laden with iniquity, offspring of evildoers. My princes are rebels and companions of thieves . . . " "Who the hell is this?" Roy asks. "Isaiah . . . The Prophet Isaiah."

So begins the action of "The Flea Circus," book one of *The Gay Place*. Fenstemaker has surveyed the Wasteland over which he presides (T. S. Eliot's modernist wordplay is part of the book's stylistic fabric). He has determined that he must pluck from among the "nutboy liberals" one who can help him counter the equally worthless conservatives in "gettin' [things] better." Specifically, he wants to pass an education bill. After much nudging, he convinces Sherwood he is the man to floor-manage the bill, despite Sherwood's lack of confidence. Sherwood's friend Willie England, editor of a liberal weekly newspaper—"happiest when anyone belabored him with the charge that he was a mere political propagandist"—also falls into Fenstemaker's orbit. "Oppose [my] goddam bill!" the governor tells the uncomprehending editor. "Those fellows in the Senate—they think this is all I want, they'll give it to me. But if somebody's runnin' round whoopin' about how good this is, settin' precedents and havin' a foot in the door and braggin' on how much more we'll get next year, then all my support'll get skittish and vanish overnight . . . Only don't oppose it too much, either. You raise hell and *your* bunch won't go along. They'll introduce their own bill askin' for the goddam aurora borealis. I need their votes, too. Just oppose it a little bit—oppose it on *principle*!" This was Lyndon Johnson's "half-a-loaf" politics to a tee—compromise, tweak the system for whatever you can get, then shout, "Victory!" The alternative was to end the session by passing no legislation whatsoever.

Ideally, "I want unanimous consent and dead silence!" Fenstemaker roars.

In the course of things, the governor and his new liberal colleagues abort a bribery scandal that threatens to undermine *everyone's* interests.

Sherwood is already jaded when we meet him. His life is "like high school, when boys and girls had crushes on each other from one semester to the next. Except that now [they had all] developed faint wrinkles" and an unseemly longing for material comfort. Under Fenstemaker's mentorship ("I been sucklin' my babes . . . Time the chicks got out the henhouse and foraged for themselves") he matures, emotionally, politically, but his changes only heighten his disaffection with "last week's illusions." His cynicism reaches fever pitch when the bribery scandal bleeds over into his love affair, when the cost of public life drains the vault of honest, hard-won intimacy. Sherwood thinks:

> [We] were all such amateurs . . . Risen out of innocence, out of grace, passing into awareness and a kind of hollow sophistication with hardly a corrupting experience . . . [And you] could trace the wornout course of [our] piddling derelictions right alongside [our] politics. It wasn't enough; not enough to break through into awareness and good intentions; not enough, moreover, to stand away and point to how the public and private business ought to be carried on, clucking your distaste and disapproval. It was insufficient—in fact, it was ruinous. [Roy] wondered about the Governor. Had he somehow managed to transcend into some blessed state, passed [us] all, perilously close to the abyss until reaching a point of holy ground from which he could view the whole speckled landscape, viewing it without a tyrannizing emotion? At least he remained operative—old Fenstemaker—he knew what absolutely had to be done . . . The truly able, it appeared, had only so much time to squander on disillusion and self-analysis . . . The truly gifted, as opposed to the merely clever, were too busy running things to be bothered.

Like Roy Sherwood, Neil Christiansen, in "Room Enough to Caper," struggles to revive in himself the will he once possessed to get things done—he cannot remember the "last time he'd seen real passion." Once, he had "really had it, whatever it was, in the make-up of some few men who seemed able to get high on their own adrenal fluids." Now the governor, hoping Christiansen will fight for reelection to the Senate (so that, through him, Fenstemaker can get a "nigger bill" passed), worries that the man has "run out of gas at the age of thirty-three." Also like Sherwood, Christiansen marvels at the governor. "*I* get down," Fenstemaker tells him. "God knows I get right down on the basement floor and want to cry and throw a bomb at the next Creeping Jesus who walks into my office with a long face and a longer hand out. But I get over it. It's a little song and dance I go through when somebody plays the secret music . . . Your job is to get elected and stay elected . . . When that's assured, you get good enough, mean enough, you learn to fend off all the bill collectors. They come around wanting the moon you give 'em green cheese and make 'em think that was what they were lookin' for all the time. *That's* what you do. That's what a professional *has* to do."

Christiansen's tank appears to have emptied because his political career may have wrecked his brother's life (his *brother* should have been the "poet-politician," but he died after fleeing home, working as a journalist covering revolutions in Latin America). Also, Christiansen's marriage is failing. When he isn't around, his wife, Andrea, does exactly what she pleases. She tells him "Life is awfully well ordered . . . I feel like a great happy bird." She asks him whether he wants a divorce, but the next minute she is "up against him, crying softly." "Oh, Neil, what's happened . . . ? How did this all happen . . . ?" she says. They lie "side by side trying to recapture whatever special emotion there had been for them. It seem[s] to be passing them by, just barely, and they [cling] to the heavy languor of the moment as if it [were] the real thing and they had won it for themselves."

Revisiting the "hills above the city and the winding river" where he courted Andrea as a young man, Christiansen discovers his memory has become a fading "old radio receiver picking up a distant signal." "Not so much long gone youth as adulthood never quite attained," he thinks, trying to pinpoint his problem. "If there had once been beauty . . . a fever for life and a search for a code of conduct, those private joys had long since been supplanted by trivial and lighthearted depravities." Here, Brammer's prose approaches Scott Fitzgerald's cold and wistful tone.

Through a series of dramatic maneuvers, the governor gets Christiansen reelected. Better than anyone, Fenstemaker grasps the country's social realignments: "Most of us came into town one Saturday a few years ago and stayed . . . We're urban, by god. All of a sudden the people in the metropolitan areas outnumber the rednecks . . . They come into town—they buy little houses and color television and Volkswagen cars." The old-style politicians are "still pitching to the Church of Christers and the pickup truck crowd."

Christiansen's victory is small comfort for him as he shuttles between his home district and DC, separated from his wife and children, a man forever in transit. Alone among the three books in *The Gay Place*, "Room Enough to Caper" does not begin with an overview of land, but rather with a claustrophobic snapshot—the interior of a cramped "old attack bomber," the senator's transport.

Brammer lends the events a strong mythic layering—this *Christian son* is thirty-three years old, the savior's age when he died. The senator's home visit takes place at Easter, the season of life reborn. Stated so baldly, these biblical elements sound heavy-handed, but they are given a light touch in the narrative, which veers into Joycean stream of consciousness when Christiansen returns to the Senate floor ("Can't seem to catch his eye.

Got hers—not his—got hers, we're exchanging looks in this great gilded chamber. All this quiet dignity . . . rich tradition . . . Get me a pint of Quiet Dignity, kid . . . hundred proof.").

In the end, Christiansen absorbs life's vast contradictions (Is marriage holy or a sham? Am I a good man or a pretender?). Either they will sap him or enable him to become an effective legislator. On the one hand, he expresses near nihilism: "Love was not the natural condition of man; neither was decency," he thinks. "They were inventions, illusion; and what was needed was not so much cerebration or good intentions as convincing stage props." On the other hand, he professes a guarded optimism. "I like the Senate," he says: "It's a nice place full of good and occasionally extraordinary men struggling with a hopeless and possibly unattainable noble ideal. The fact that the ideal *might* be impossible to realize doesn't undignify the effort. The nobility exists in our conscious effort to be decent men, to somehow transcend centuries of hopelessness and bad thinking and arrive at some approach to blessedness."

Like "The Flea Circus," "Country Pleasures" begins with an airy landscape, but the terrain has diminished, the mountains giving way to "sandhills and . . . gray dunes. Then there was only the tortured prairie grass, dust-bleached and brittle . . . shimmering in the new-visited heat, rising off the floor of the ranchland and collapsing again." The governor's wife, Sweet Mama Fenstemaker, gliding on a scorched desert highway in a limousine alongside her husband, and his brother, Hoot Gibson, and the governor's press aide, Jay McGown, says, "I keep thinking we're going back into the mountains . . . I keep thinking we're going back but we never seem to get there."

"It's because we're driving between two parallel ranges," McGown explains. "It looks like they come together up ahead, but they don't really—it's all an illusion." Thus, the physics of this exotic world, and the story that follows, have been settled.

The governor's entourage has arrived in the desert to observe a Hollywood movie shoot. The governor hopes to exploit the celebrities for whatever political gain he can wring from them; the visitors hope to take advantage of the governor's cash and goodwill.

McGown, we are told, has the "quality, characteristic of those constantly exposed to Arthur Fenstemaker, of having peered steadily at the scene of an accident, experienced a revelation, seen death and redemption, God and Lucifer staring back, and somehow, incredibly, survived." He feels glum as the group approaches the motion picture lot—"simulated adobe huts, plaster on plywood; balsa outbuildings and ersatz oil derricks chained to railroad flatcars." The star of the show is his estranged wife, Vicki, from whom he hopes to win a divorce and generous visitation rights to his child. He knows the next few days will not be pleasant. And perhaps he is worried for another, unstated reason. The governor does not quite seem himself. Old Arthur is human, after all, overworking, drinking too much, straining to balance his many responsibilities—in this case, trying to head off a protest march at the Capitol on the issue of school desegregation. Meanwhile, the Justice Department is threatening to enforce integration in his state, stirring up *everyone*. "Hell of a country," the governor mutters. "Hell of a goddamn country." He closes his eyes in the car, "holding [a] drink with both hands against his chest."

The movie's director, Edmund Shavers (the name is a deliberate echo of Allan Shivers), tells the governor he has a "good face." "He mentioned the possibility of including me in one of the scenes," Fenstemaker says. "Not really playing myself, exactly. Playing the governor of a state, though."

Illusions build upon illusions, like layers of smoke. Jay McGown believes the governor is *already* playing a role, just like his movie star wife: "They were not quite people, those two. They were a little hard to believe; each of them heightened by special technicolor effects," he thinks. (Vicki gets her bearings "from the [disorienting] mountains on either side of them," herding everyone into a country of misperception.)

But perhaps in an impure life, a life lacking innocence and nobility, the only way to approximate these blessed states is to imitate their gestures until we embody their attributes, however shoddily. Perhaps, in a fallen world, this is as close as we can get to the divine.

"Invited in" to the halls of power, Roy Sherwood might well become Prince Hal.

One day on the movie set—bright with its artificial sheen—a member of the governor's staff contemplates "Arthur Fenstemaker's transformation from timorous, picknose politician into . . . whatever it was that currently passed for greatness. The Presidency makes the man? Perhaps the movie queen story, drummed and repeated . . . over and over again, had made its impression on Vicki McGown's muddled intellect . . . to a point where Vicki could convince herself that she *was* a queen."

Late one evening, back in the Capitol, Jay McGown sits at the governor's desk, sipping the gentleman's booze (just as Brammer poached Johnson's bourbon at night in the Senate Office Building). But instead of wearing greatness until it becomes a second skin, McGown fears there is nothing inside him—or any of his contemporaries—but "dead remains." A world of Hollow Men, prancing in front of balsa-wood mansions.

Brammer's meditation on illusion reaches its peak with the introduction of Dead Man at the governor's ranch—a former bootlegger living on Fenstemaker's property. He once faked his demise to escape the law. His "death" indicates the passing of the rural way of life, just as his prolonged existence suggests the past's lasting, mythic power over our imaginations. *Do* we become what we replicate, what we project, or does hollowness hiss behind our sparkling facades? Brammer has animated this question with several vivid images—the movie set, Vicki McGown, Jay, Dead Man. Most pressingly, the inquiry is an attempt to locate the true nature of Arthur "Goddam" Fenstemaker, the window maker, the grand illusionist. At novel's end, *he* survives only as myth. His mortal self dies of a heart attack in the arms of a lover. He lies as we first encountered him, enmeshed in his bedcovers, "pale and blue in the soft light, bathed in the faint fragrance of woman, grinning at some great vague private joke."

---

"I suppose there was probably a lot of torment he channeled into his writing," Nadine said. "I was bored with his book . . . He'd been working on it for years and I just didn't want to hear about it anymore." But then "when I read [it] I felt like he ripped me off. He was using all my stuff." Nadine is Ouida, the unfaithful married woman in "The Flea Circus"; she is Andrea, the unhappily married mother in "Room Enough to Caper"; she is the beauty queen star, Vicki, in "Country Pleasures." Nadine's lover, Bob Hughes, shares some of Roy Sherwood's characteristics, as does Bob Eckhardt, though he always claimed he saw little of himself in the character. "I can't believe how much [Billy Lee] got in there," Nadine said. "He used *everything*."

Who's who in *The Gay Place* has long since lost its significance, or its ability to titillate, even for the surviving members of that period's Texas insiders. Jan Reid argues that the novel holds up and has remained in print more or less continuously for over five decades because "woven through it are themes that dominate our politics today: the siren's song of lobbyists' money, the ease of demagoguery, the lechery born of power, the cost of pursuing such a life on marriages and children. But at times these politicians do good things for the right reasons. *The Gay Place* succeeds because its characters have texture, resonance, and depth . . . You care about them."

For Southwest writers, the book came as a revelation. "Billy Lee's ghost still hovers over Texas," says Al Reinert. Aside from folklorists such as J. Frank Dobie, there "were no Texas voices with whom younger writers could tune their own talents, compare insights, from whom they could learn," Reinert writes. "Nor, more important, was there any tradition of or appreciation for the means and aims of honest writing: imagination, introspection, a deliberate search for models and values, for the grace and strength of true self-knowledge." Brammer helped establish a tradition of southwestern life and letters. Before *The Gay Place*, the "portrait of the Texan had always been made by others, from typecast actors to visiting reporters, sentimentally or cynically, but always superficially."

"Brammer's book got Texas right, but it was not just a regional novel," says William Broyles, cofounder of *Texas Monthly* magazine. "This book was written by a man who could have been our Faulkner or our Joyce . . . [with a] sensibility and a talent that could have, just possibly, made modern Texas as universal a landscape as the London of Dickens or the Spain of Hemingway . . . When I read *The Gay Place* . . . I was in college in Texas . . . and neither my professors nor my fellow students considered our own state worthy of study. We spent entire semesters, however, on the politics of Massachusetts mill towns or the literature of the English countryside, as if politics and literature were phenomena that always cropped up elsewhere. *The Gay Place* changed all that for me, and I stayed in Texas because of it."

Perhaps inadvertently, Broyles's comments reveal a long-held insecurity festering beneath much of Texas's cultural bluster—namely, the desire to be recognized by New York. What greater imprimatur than a New York publishing contract? Brammer benefited from the fact that *his* Texas—urban, hip, jazzy—resonated with the Eastern literary establishment.

The critic Don Graham pointed out that Brammer's book arrived in the same year that Larry McMurtry's first novel, *Horseman, Pass By*, was published, and a year after John Graves's pastoral elegy *Goodbye to a River* appeared. Both are fine books, but they "inhabit Nostalgia Ville," Graham writes, "a river, a ranch. But not *The Gay Place* . . . This is new Texas, ca. 1958, and Brammer's novel accurately predicts the continuing urbanization of the state." Perhaps for that reason, Dobie objected to the book. Its characters were "cheap," he wrote. They "drink and drink & drink to boredom & screw, & screw & screw to death." Like Lyndon Johnson misreading John F. Kennedy, Dobie missed the seriousness and depths of Brammer's project. In addition to its astute examination of American politics, its rebuke to literary tourists like Edna Ferber, *The Gay Place* "captures hints of cultural change ahead," Graham writes. "Hipsters and politicians talk of Zen and Buddhism and existentialism and jazz. There is a sense of imminent cultural revolution waiting just 'round the corner. Brammer knew . . . that the Eisenhower era was a lot more complex and interesting than retro television sitcoms would suggest. In 'Room Enough to Caper,' he also proved prophetic . . . Not until the Robert Redford film *The Candidate* would there be as searching a study of the politician as . . . a man capable of winning elections but without any sustaining vision, without any reason or motive to serve beyond ego satisfaction."

Not just in the manner of Fenstemaker's death, but also in the description of the protest march at the Capitol, Brammer predicted LBJ's future, the hallucinatory, musical rebelliousness of the decade ahead:

> Groups of people were gathering beneath the trees. It looked very much like an old-fashioned picnic for a time, but then these early crowds were swollen by later arrivals carrying placards and banners, painted bed-sheets and pasteboard signs. There were women and children sprawled out on the grass, watching from a distance and joining occasionally in erratic, short-lived marching formations and crazy snake-dances. There were some old men with cymbals and an ancient bass drum and a tarnished trombone. There were several clusters of people grouped around speakers, who stood on the hoods of cars waving their arms.

The novel's stream-of-consciousness passages sound like speed runs ("[Sex] . . . burrowing in the luxuriant folds of me, like bugs and slugs . . . under . . . lovely latticed porch steps"). In such prose, as well as in the "sad" figure of Kermit, the proto-hippie, a "genius gone to seed—gone slightly askew, in fact," Brammer sketched a prophetic vision of himself.

*The Gay Place*'s lasting legacy is all the more important in a culture in which "democratic politics is the country's national epic," according to Christopher Lehmann. And yet what a generally poor job our literature has done by that epic. The problem has been that most American writers "look upon the political process as a great ethical contaminant and task their protagonists with escaping its many perils with both their lives and their moral compasses intact," Lehmann writes. His 2005 essay, "Why Americans Can't Write Political Fiction," remains the most incisive discussion, to date, of Brammer's contribution to our literature. In the hands of most writers, Lehmann says, "bracing satires wilt into two-dimensional fables in which the same basic lesson is learned over and over again: spurn the process and save your soul."

In essence, American political fiction has been a series of children's books, unable to render (or even adequately face) the complexities of adult behavior.

The "one truly great modern American political novel [is] Billy Lee Brammer's 1961 *The Gay Place*," Lehmann claims. In it, "politicians are not the tempters in the garden of American innocence. They are moral protagonists": "As political animals, they're accustomed to honoring few clear distinctions between their messy, conflicted, adulterous, and boozy lives and their obligations to the public weal, and so they are not in the business of sacrificing one for the sake of the other. This means, among other things, that they have few two-dimensional virtues to jeopardize and no melodramatic Victorian corridors of power in which to sully themselves. Brammer's protagonists are all sublimely self-aware adults."

He concludes: "The genius of Brammer's novel is its willingness to wrestle openly with the implications of a tragic, divided political nature—not merely for stars of first magnitude like Fenstemaker but also for the many lesser political beings in his orbit, falling so continuously short of the glory. True knowledge of sin, after all . . . is the original force that sparked the . . . halting Puritan dalliances with formal democracy on the North American continent."

# 12.

On the eve of the book's publication, Brammer decided he had heard enough. First the Big Pumpkin and then Uncle Eliot: for years now, powerful, self-centered men had been haranguing him. "Janeway's nicer and nicer [but] I feel kept," he wrote Nadine. "[I] have got to get loose or I'll lose all my resolution."

It was time to think of himself—to *assert* himself—as a writer. At a "little cocktail party" thrown by the Janeways in an apartment "half the size of your living room," filled with Picassos, Chagalls, and Mirós, "two producers asked if my book would make a play, and I had to tell them I wasn't quite sure if it would even make a book."

He had mighty hopes for *The Gay Place*'s success, though he also feared that Houghton Mifflin, "which rarely spends money promoting books," would manage only to get him "a one column box in *Publisher's Weekly* or something." Even if royalties started rolling in, the checks wouldn't arrive for months yet. He had begun to draft another novel, but he couldn't afford to quit Janeway to work on it full-time. Nadine's divorce lawyer, a man she had met at a party at Paleface Ranch, was seeking child support payments of three hundred dollars a month. She said she needed a bigger house for the kids.

So, drifting away from Janeway rather than resigning in any formal sense, he went to work for Henry Luce. "I hope *Time* will lead you to Life and Fortune," Dorothy de Santillana wrote him. "The last thing he wanted to do then was work for *Time*," said David Halberstam, whom Brammer had befriended. "But they had this money box in the office, and he'd just grab a handful. He'd laugh and say, 'This may be the only time in my life I can take you to lunch.'" His political experience and his connections in DC made the Washington Bureau the obvious spot for him, so he moved again, settling into a back bedroom in the house of his friends Glen and Marie Wilson. Almost immediately, he wrote Ronnie Dugger, "I wish I could resign from the Luceville Establishment. One of the more depressing revelations which have come to me in my middle years is that people who pay you great to middlin' wages actually have the nerve to expect recipients to work backends off in exchange, not to mention expectation of whimpering, obsequious gratitudes." But he was reading a great deal—Talleyrand and Socrates—and he was working on his new book, a sequel to *The Gay Place*.

"Bill Brammer knows his people, politics, and native state of Texas, and has brought them to life Texas-style (on a grand scale) in three fast-paced novels in one book," Houghton Mifflin announced in a series of national ads—its official launch of Brammer. Advance sales to bookstores were higher than usual. "This isn't just another 'gifted' first novel to be reviewed and quietly forgotten. It's going to be a big book—our biggest fiction book scheduled so far—and we're excited about the possibilities," de Santillana told him. As she expected, the reviews were almost uniformly positive, and many were effusive (including—after all—a prominent piece in the *New York Times Book Review*: "Brammer has an authentic, even lyrical, writing talent"). "I don't know of another work quite like it," Gore Vidal wrote in *Esquire*. "[It is] an amiable, generous-minded, unpretentious novel which I enjoyed very much." "Mr. Brammer has crashed the literary world with a first novel worthy of careful criticism [and] wide readership," Roger Shattuck wrote in the *Texas Observer*. "By the time I'd read sixteen pages of 'The Gay Place,' I was on the Brammer bandwagon," said Maurice Doblier in the *New York Herald Tribune*. "Now that I've read the whole [thing] and wished there was more, I want to help drive it." Ernest B. Fergurson, writing in the *Baltimore Sun*, concluded, "It is a conscientious work by a young man unafraid to make his first effort a full-scale gamble," while Lon Tinkle, the *Dallas Morning News*'s respected book critic, declared *The Gay Place* "a first novel full of immense talent . . . Brammer can write with the best of them," he said. "[The novel] overflows with the vitality of creative gifts."

A student journalist at the *Daily Texan* remarked, "Pre-release, press notices to the effect that 'everybody's reading it' raise two questions: Has anyone finished it? How many have turned to Shakespeare's 'Much Ado about Nothing'?" Shattuck complained that the novel's "love duets" were "unconvincing" and that the characters could be unpleasantly materialistic. Other reviewers' criticisms ran in similar gullies, but in each case, negative remarks were balanced by praise for Brammer's lyrical ability and massive promise. *The Gay Place* earned notice equal to that of other important literary debuts of 1961: Harper Lee's *To Kill a Mockingbird*, Joseph Heller's *Catch-22*, Walker Percy's *The Moviegoer*. It was a Book-of-the-Month Club selection, along with Theodore H. White's *The Making of the President, 1960*. There was talk of a movie sale—maybe up to $75,000.

*Playboy* magazine wrote to Brammer's agent; the editors were "immensely responsive to the idea of recurring fiction from him," they said. "Our readers . . . are young, highly urban, extremely well-educated, predominantly of the young executive group, and not interested in finding in our pages anything to do with family life . . . we're a grand market for a man who has something he wants to say to other men."

Brammer's trip to Texas in the spring of 1961 for book-signing events in Dallas, Austin, and Houston caused him no small anxiety. "From reading an early version of some of the book I knew I would resent Bill's politics in the novel—both his contempt for the Texas liberals, so many I knew to be people I would go to the wall with, and his adulation, a kind of disillusioned hero worship, of his Lyndon Johnson figure, Governor Fenstemaker," Ronnie Dugger said. Still, when the two old friends met for a beer at Scholz's, Dugger just sighed, "You put in the good Johnson and left out the bad—and Bill agreed." That was it. They renewed their bond together. They toasted. Dugger had not missed Brammer's fantasy near the end of "The Flea Circus"—Fenstemaker joins the Dearly Beloved crowd to celebrate his ties to the liberals. It was Brammer's brief dream of bringing his worlds together.

In Dallas, his mother told him she objected to the name "William" on the book cover. *Darn it, we named you Billie Lee*! On the experience of returning home as a "Famous Arthur," the local-boy-done-good, he would write:

> It is a wonder that I survived [the place] at all . . . One ultimately forgets . . . how Dallas reached its full urban flowering under such decisive cultural influences as . . . John Wilkes Booth . . . the Everly Brothers . . .

> [and] Father Coughlin . . . I am suffering from what is known today as 'alienation' . . . Dallas is . . . a Can-Do, Wheeler-Dealer kind of a city, where a man with vision and determination and a good line of credit can make a bunch of money and wear Countess Mara cowboy boots and get all vomity drunk at Cotton Bowl games.

Austin seemed no less strange to him, since he was not returning to a wife but rather to an antagonist in a legal case. Nadine's lawyer was pressing him to waive his rights to *The Gay Place*, assigning half to her and half to his children. Nadine wanted to go house hunting for her and the kids—a house he would never live in. Not that he deserved to, he would admit whenever one of the children reminded him of his past visits. "When I was a kid, people would break into our house all the time, drunk after parties. Or they'd just show up and lose their minds," Sidney told me. "One time, in Austin—Bill had been dragging in and out at all hours—one night, I woke up and there was a black man huddled near the radio—sleepy, unsure, I said, 'Daddy?'"

Sidney took the dust jacket of her father's book to show and tell one day in her third-grade class. The flap copy called the novel "an important contribution to modern bacchanalia." "I don't know what bacchanalia means," young Sidney said, "but it *does* sound wicked."

---

The Kennedy White House—Brammer's new beat—was notoriously reckless and insouciant, but the press corps sat on the most revealing stories about it. Reporters failed to write the truth about the Kennedys for several reasons: generally, in those days, journalistic practices drew a line between public and private affairs—this was an unspoken understanding between the press and the subjects it covered. Reporters were as dazzled by the Kennedy family as the citizenry was—they wanted to play among the cool, cocky insiders along with Jack and Bobby. And finally, if a reporter *did* cross the line, Bobby would make him pay. Hugh Sidey, Brammer's thirty-three-year-old boss in the Washington Bureau, discovered this fact the hard way following a White House New Year's Eve party in Palm Beach. For months, Brammer had been telling Sidey how out of control the Kennedy bashes were. That night in Palm Beach, Sidey needed to speak to Pierre Salinger, JFK's press secretary, and his deputy, Andrew Hatcher, about a foreign policy story scheduled to run in *Time*. He searched for them at the party. "Salinger was off someplace with a girl who was not related in any way by law or by blood to him. Hatcher had gone to Jamaica with a bunch of models. I went around. There was nobody. Everybody partying," Sidey told fellow journalist Seymour Hersh. "I have to say that I did sense it was excessive and probably not the way to run a presidency. He was the leader of the free world and this was the height of the Cold War." Sidey wrote nothing about the party for the magazine, but he did send a somewhat jokey internal memo to his New York editors describing the shenanigans: "Not since the fall of Rome . . ."

Somehow, the memo leaked to *Time*'s most prominent advertisers, and word of this made its way to the White House. Bobby called Sidey to his office. "He was shaking," Sidey recalled. His aides had never seen him so furious. "If this were Britain or someplace, we'd sue you for slander," he said. "This is the worst thing I've ever read, Sidey. I thought you were fair up till now." "Bobby, I'm just reporting the feeling down there—what reporters are telling me," Sidey said. He suspected the Kennedys never forgave him for the incident, and he wondered how many stories he lost because of it.

The Kennedys' "bad boy" behavior didn't shock Brammer—he had seen clay feet crumbling all over Washington. And this was an intensely entitled bunch. What surprised him were his old boss's changing fortunes and his own. As vice president, LBJ found himself ignored in the White House, underutilized, laughed at. His skills on the Hill were wasted by the know-it-all Kennedys. "Uncle Cornpone," they called him, "Riverboat Gambler." "Every time I [come] into John Kennedy's presence, I [feel] like a goddamn raven hovering over his shoulder," he would grumble. Worst of all, the president was a "lightweight," a "sonny boy," a pup who needed a "little gray in his hair." Brammer heard from former colleagues that Johnson's misery led him to booze more heavily than in the past. His aides told stories of having to "lift him physically out of bed and pump his arms up and down to stimulate breathing and make him functional." One night, said an old Johnson staffer, "he went on an incredible toot . . . wandered up and down the corridors" of a hotel and snuggled into the arms of one of his secretaries in her bed "the same way a small child will snuggle into its mother's arms." Meanwhile, Brammer told Ronnie Dugger that he was enjoying the delights of literary success. He had to be careful or his novel-writing days would be over, he wrote. He was spending his time bedding a "good many dark-haired ladies," all of them in psychoanalysis. "Certain lack of tension in mah prose of the past few months . . . Art is long and poontang is fleeting, and we shall soon outdistance understanding. Are there any nice, simple, pure and uncomplicated lovers left in the world? I defer to your judgment."

In particular, he was dating a striking twenty-two-year-old brunette, a Radcliffe graduate working for Brammer's old friend Marcus Raskin under McGeorge Bundy in Kennedy's National Security Council. Her name was Diana de Vegh—"Diana the Vague," Brammer called her. East Coast royalty: Westover (a tony Connecticut boarding school), a stint at Harvard (where her father sat on economic committees). Just vain enough to be charming, often discreetly removing her glasses, without which everything was a blur, so as to appear more perfect in public. She told Brammer she had first met JFK when she was nineteen, still a student at Radcliffe. At a political dinner in Boston, "there was an empty place next to me and he came and sat down and . . . asked . . . who was I and what was I doing . . . I was just thrilled." This made Brammer curious to know how she had found employment in Washington.

One night, Hugh Sidey, working late, was stunned when Brammer walked into the Bender Building, *Time*'s office on Connecticut Avenue, and told him glumly, "Hugh, this is the darnedest thing." He had just learned that the young woman he was dating was also sleeping with the president.

---

"Power," she said when he asked her why she did it. "Nothing will come of it. But he has a hold on me."

Brammer figured literary stardom was *his* only hope of hanging on to this young beauty, especially since he was up against the president. He asked Elizabeth McKee to secure a contract from Houghton Mifflin as soon as possible for a second novel, but she urged him to be patient: "The second novel should be carefully thought about and planned, not rushed into . . . Now please don't be breathless and frightened and sure that no one will like it . . . You're a hell of a good writer and there's no doubt that this is your career."

More swiftly than he could have imagined, though, he went from being publishing's hottest new prospect to last season's biggest disappointment. In spite of the glorious critical response, and the book's initial appearance on a number of regional bestseller lists, sales began to ebb right away. On June 20, 1961, Dorothy de Santillana told him, "Your book has sold only 36 copies since I [last] wrote you the figures . . . I am afraid you must face the fact that from now on the momentum of sales has slowed down and not to look for much further royalty. This is the natural way of a book . . . sad but true."

She sent an internal memo to the company's executive committee, informing its members that Brammer had "telephoned wishing more money . . . He was confused with [his] statement." His profits from sales had diminished when bookstores returned their unsold copies to the publisher. "He is under financial pressure and requests immediate payment of all money earned," de Santillana told the committee. With its approval she sent him a check for $250. An expected payment of $1,250 for the paperback edition disappeared when unsold returns of the hardback rose to a debit balance of $93.33. Though hope remained of a movie sale, which might revive the novel's fortunes, and Houghton Mifflin continued to profess interest in Brammer's second book, the literary world had moved on. "He sent me a delightful picture of himself with his handsome children," de Santillana wrote Elizabeth McKee. But there was nothing she could do to scrounge more money. "These terms are incorporated into every contract and ubiquitously applied . . . Will you write him my personal regret that the facts are less than fancy could hope?"

In the interim, he had succumbed to Nadine's lawyer and waived all future rights to *The Gay Place*. (To date, the novel has been reprinted five times.)

In part, the publisher had counted on Lyndon Johnson's visibility as vice president to stoke initial book sales, but the editors had failed to foresee how thoroughly he would vanish in the role. The Kennedy magic enchanted the public now; Johnson's record as master of the Senate didn't matter. "[His] image is poor. The accent hurts. Even if we assume many people would say they have no prejudice against a southerner, the fact is that in this country the Texan is partly a comic, partly a horse opera figure . . . Johnson really does not have the requisite dignity. His personal mannerisms are destructive of the dignified image. He's somebody's gabby cousin from Fort Worth," Ben Bradlee (later editor of the *Washington Post*) wrote John Kennedy in the lead-up to the 1960 campaign; his sentiments suggested why a Johnsonian figure would always struggle to achieve hero status in American culture. But more than that, on the cusp of an incendiary new decade, there were "revolutionaries in Cuba who look[ed] like beatniks, [there were] competitions in missiles, Negroes looting whites in the Congo, intricacies of nuclear fallout . . . It [was] all out of hand, everything important [was] off-center," Norman Mailer wrote following the 1960 Democratic National Convention. A traditional politician with a "good, sound, conventional liberal record," laboriously working the system, could no longer ignite the body politic. The nation wanted a dazzling superman onto which it could project whatever images of its dream life flickered to the surface. Lyndon's hangdog, basset hound visage belonged to another era. Now was the time for a man who could illuminate "the long electric night with the fires of neon leading down the highway to the murmur of jazz," Mailer said.

*The Gay Place* offered jazz and speed visions of changing American dreams, but that was not the way the publisher packaged and sold it. In turn, in very short order—once the hero of Camelot was gunned down in Dallas—the culture would require much *more* than a superman. It would turn to shamans, gyring in swirls of psychedelic patterns, and Brammer would be there, laughing. But that is a story for later. For now, it "was a hero America needed, a hero central to his time, a man whose personality might suggest contradictions and mysteries that could reach into the alienated circuits of the underground," Mailer wrote. Old LBJ-style anticommunists had rendered themselves obsolete: "To anyone who could see, the excessive hysteria of [1950s Red-baiting] was no preparation to face [a foreign] enemy but rather a terror of the national self: free-loving, lust-looting, atheistic, implacable—[it was] absurdity beyond absurdity to label communism so, for the moral products of Stalinism had been Victorian sex and a ponderous machine of ideology. Yes, the life of politics and the life of the myth had diverged too far." Thus the stage was set for a hipster-president who could "reveal . . . the character of the country to itself," for a melding of "America's politics" with "America's first soap-opera, America's best-seller."

*Hell of a goddam country.*

---

Brammer had finished off Arthur Fenstemaker at the end of *The Gay Place* (perhaps recognizing more than even *he* realized the freewheeling new America Mailer described). Old Arthur "lay abed—grinnin', full of beans, cool and luminous, gaseous to the end . . . with a silver hairpiece, powder blue tint round the chops, stiffish in the limbs," Brammer wrote in a draft of his intended sequel. Early on, he decided to call the new book *Fustian Days*—the strange word meaning, in Brammer's political context, pompous or inflated speech: *also* a characteristic of fresh, hip America. The novel's story line remained sketchy at first, but Brammer knew it would involve the attempt of "the consorts . . . [the] princes and knights-errant, poseurs and pretenders and court jesters" to secure Fenstemaker's legacy now that the "king" had succumbed. Roy Sherwood, Neil Christiansen, Jay McGown reappeared. The fight for civil rights had been a running theme throughout *The Gay Place*; it is clear from early drafts that in the new novel Brammer wanted to explore broader struggles for equality, especially sexual freedoms. Sim Hester, a congressional assistant, is an openly homosexual character, strong, independent; the initial pages establish him as someone who will be called upon, in the course of the story, to perform acts of whatever passes for heroism in the compromised world of American governance.

From the start, most of the characters wrestle with self-imposed malaise, a torpor born of the helplessness they feel after Fenstemaker's death. "A compulsive phrasemaker, Roy has devised one for his own condition: he tells himself he is Hanging On for Dearest Life," Brammer writes—as if referring to himself, the author, in the act of composing these lines. "An unspeakable day already; he was confident it would soon get worse . . . He had begun to wonder if he would ever again recapture any of that high-flapping extravagance, the burbling, hilarious sense of well being, which had elevated and sustained him [in the past]."

In Washington, in the Wilsons' back bedroom, Brammer sketched beginning after new beginning, trying to get the novel off the ground. In certain passages, the writing soars, even more lyrically than in *The Gay Place* at its best. He remained *the* singer of the Texas countryside, as in this flyover description, the view from the plane of the prodigal sons gathering for Fenstemaker's funeral:

> [Below,] the tidal meadow and the dazzling azure crescent of the Gulf. Then west a little: an unspectacular stretch of dry-lime miles toward the recalcitrant cottonfields . . . rank grades of honeysuckle and wild hibiscus, old wheel-rusted roadscapes of hills and high plains still some good ways farther on . . . Bucolic vistas, mostly, relieved now and again by awful lacquered junkpiles of cities and towns: fresh-minted cosmic jokes of . . . tarpaper paneling and bug-flecked neon . . . and in between, the ancient interior seas: great stands of loblolly pine, collard fields and scuttled oilsump and all the wornout pastures overrun with buckeye and cinnamon fur, wood violet and displaced mountain laurel and occasional black-mottled tiger lilies.

A valedictory glimpse, to be sure. The mourners have arrived in this land to "look upon one last hill country funeral in the old-style—possibly before the country itself and its old, ancestor-holifying ways were banished and rejected altogether for the randier pleasures of tall buildings and tenements and . . . wonderfully indifferent sprawl."

The end of that passage captures the view from Brammer's DC office window and his gloomy state of mind. In addition to the drudge-slog of daily reporting, a *Time* man working the Kennedy White House had to endure belligerence. Scorn. Kennedy loved to court the press, but he never trusted the avowed Republican Henry Luce. "That damn magazine," Kennedy would say. *Time*'s reporters "file the Bible . . . and the magazine prints the Koran." Luce was "like a cricket, always chirping away." And yet he said of JFK, "He seduces me"—even *he* was not immune to the Kennedy charm. He assured Kennedy's father that *Time* would always "look favorably on Jack as long as he held a tough line on communism."

Kennedy was so busy seducing people that it was a wonder he got any work done at all. In Brammer's first days on the job, the administration faced the Berlin Wall crisis (in which US government officials publicly decried the sealing off of East Germany but were secretly relieved to see a tide of potential refugees contained, the situation stabilized) and the Bay of Pigs (the chaotic planning and indecisive implementation of which were hidden from Lyndon Johnson—a sign of the Kennedy brothers' contempt for him). In the disastrous aftermath of the Cuban invasion, Diana de Vegh's boss, Marcus Raskin, questioned in a meeting whether the administration had learned anything from its mistakes. Immediately he was told "there must be loyalty." He was barred from further White House discussions. His position in the National Security Council, and thus de Vegh's, became largely ceremonial from that point on, irrelevant to any actual foreign policy planning. De Vegh did not seem to realize this. Nor did she seem to realize, quite, how many other sexual affairs her president-boyfriend was pursuing. From friends and colleagues, Brammer knew, but did not report, what Seymour Hersh would make public many years later, that "Kennedy was consumed with almost daily sexual liaisons and libertine partying, to a degree that shocked many members of his personal Secret Service detail." Hersh said, "The sheer number of Kennedy's sexual partners, and the recklessness of his use of them, escalated throughout his presidency. The women—sometimes paid prostitutes . . . would be brought to Kennedy's office or his private quarters without any prior Secret Service knowledge or clearance." Brammer also knew that

Kennedy's private physician, Max Jacobson, known around the White House as "Dr. Feel Good," was giving the president regular amphetamine injections, sometimes as often as every six hours (Brammer recognized the fixed look in his eyes, the dry mouth). Bobby and others worried. Kennedy waved them off. "I don't care if it's horse piss" in those syringes, he told them. "It's the only thing that works."

It also made him restless. "You had to really work to keep his attention unless . . . he had something that he wanted from you. And then, boy, you were the object of extremely focused attention," de Vegh said years later. "It's everybody trying to be good enough [around him], smart enough, witty enough. I was trying to knock him out—to be terrific." The same behavior was "much more criminal in the case of Bundy and McNamara."

The writer-voyeur in Brammer was fascinated by these flirtatious dynamics. He pressed de Vegh for intimate details of her encounters with Kennedy. At the same time, he was genuinely fond of her. He didn't like competing with this much more glamorous, powerful man. Trying to view his situation with humor, to take it in stride, he wrote one of his Texas pals in July 1961 (on old LBJ stationery), "Jack Kennedy is down in the back, and this has apparently limited his roundering for he does not often call to bug his teenaged mistress to whom I am secretly engaged. Very late on a recent evening a voice that was unmistakably our Leader's reached me on the phone, inquiring of 'Diaawhnah.' (I started to say she'd gone to 'Cuber' for a week and a hawrf.) I informed him that she was in the bawrth, tidying herself, and he rang off rather abruptly."

The Jockey Club in the Fairfax Hotel near Dupont Circle—a place to see and be seen for the young political set—was one of de Vegh's favorite spots. Brammer would treat her to dinner, try to impress her with stories of his burgeoning literary success (avoiding his doubts and disappointments): his tremendous progress on the new novel, the tantalizing prospect of a movie deal for *The Gay Place*. Then they would retire to her little house in Georgetown to spend the night together. She would share with Brammer some of her pillow talk with the president. Brammer kept a notebook filled with details of her experiences and some of the word-for-word dialogues she reported to him ("Title for a memoir by Diana: 'Balling Jack'"). He encouraged her to be as accurate and thorough as possible (and urged himself "really to write, as beautifully as she talked it"). These late-night confessions seemed to bring her relief. They heightened the amorous tension between the two of them. Brammer referred to Kennedy as Tiger. Tell me about Tiger, he would say. He learned that while Kennedy was campaigning for the presidency, he would send a limo to pick her up at her Radcliffe dormitory; his aides finally told him this was causing talk on campus. "I thought he was a big joke at first . . . I had only contempt for politicians . . . But my god he just kept *selling* himself," she told Brammer. "Some evenings it was just one wild chase after another . . . Like a goddamn steeplething . . . He can also be very persuasive and charming when he wants to be. Makes you think you're the only person he's been thinking about for months."

Then he got elected. Brammer recorded de Vegh's story:

> Visiting the house on N. St. a few days before the Inauguration: Secret Service . . . reporters . . . huge crowds . . . embarrassment as she identified herself, ducked her head and headed up the stone steps . . . He was late to a dinner party by 2½ hours, and afterwards, heading out alone and down the street, wandering aimlessly through the frozen snow-garlanded Georgetown streets, she turned a corner and simultaneously heard the swelling chorus of cheers as the limousine sped past her and pulled to a stop midway down the block. And there he was again, descending from the gleaming car, being hustled past police lines, giving his little goodhearted tailback's stiffarm gesture to the whooping crowds. She turned round and headed back up the street, thinking she was away from it for another week, two or three weeks, a month or so, but the phone was jangling when she reached home.

On a moment's notice, she said, the president would invite her to the Lincoln Bedroom in the White House, the big, high-canopied bed: "[He] wants to know what I've been doing, who seeing, have I any lovers . . . Asks about . . . other girls."

Brammer captured the following exchange he had with de Vegh:

> *What does he want from you?*
>
> *Just to come running when he calls . . . When he needs me . . .*
>
> *Like the other night on Berlin?*
>
> *Yes.*
>
> *What would happen if I married you—or rather if you got married?*
>
> *He'd probably think that was just devine* [*sic*] *. . . Very good thing for his little [set-up] . . . and he'd just keep on calling.*

*And you . . . ?*

*I don't know . . . I honestly don't know. Perhaps I might . . . Just keep on running over when I get the signal?*

*What the hell is it that* holds *you? Sex? Is it* that *good?*

*My heavens, no. Might have been once, just after the first time . . . But no—I can't recall a time when one of our lovemaking sessions didn't find me at one point or another, either in tears or hysterics or both . . . I don't know what you'd call it . . . Fascination, maybe . . . conditioned on the man himself and how he's grown . . . Perhaps there's even some of that grisly business of simply wanting to be close to power or history or influence . . . I couldn't care less about any conventional middle way of life . . . I want either to stay close to this thing, you know really* see *what's going on, feeling his lousy masterful presence at all times. Either that, or disengaged entirely . . .*

She told Brammer the poor man couldn't make it from his bathroom to his bed without wearing a back brace.

He would ask her to come over; he would spill the news about some international crisis, and then he would expect her to make love to him to calm his nerves. "You know Sunday night when you . . . asked me if he'd called and I said no?" de Vegh told Brammer one evening. "Well, fifteen minutes afterwards he did . . . I had dinner there . . . You know, you heard, I guess, that the Russians announced resumption of nuclear testing . . . They test the super super bomb, the million megaton bomb, we've had it . . . That's what he told me . . . We've had it, he said, and he made about a dozen phone calls: Rusk, Stevenson, McNamara; Bundy came by, all the others. They've got to decide what to do in a few days. Then he said, come on Diana—just like that—and I said oh, no and burst into tears, and he said oh what's all this? Oh don't be that way, dear, come lie beside me, so I lay down with him and it was just impossible."

She wondered why she kept going back—"it's all such an ugly business." Surrounding him, "such terrible people, so many really ghastly people." Was she just a victim of the "Cinderella culture" that encouraged everyone to seek romantic fantasies—"dime-store folklore"—or "do I want to be around the inner circle when the bomb comes? I rather doubt they'd take me along in their helicopters to wherever it is they'll be going for the underground shelters."

One day she read in *Life* magazine how "Mrs. K . . . always goes to the Lincoln bedroom for inspiration, and I nearly flipped. If she only *knew* what's been going on in *that* bedroom! What a riot!"

Brammer jotted into his notebook another of de Vegh's reported exchanges with the president:

> *Baby, don't be a problem now . . . I've got too many problems.*
>
> *That's the whole point. We've both got enough problems now.*
>
> *Look, sweetheart, I've had troubles since all this started. My God, I couldn't begin to tell you—all the things—everything—that went to hell because of you. So much has been endangered during the last couple years . . . Godalmighty, any one of them could have meant the end of my career. Scares hell out of me to even contemplate . . . But Jesus, I've never thought of it being any other way. It was worth it—*you're *worth it.*
>
> *I think we're causing each other too much trouble.*
>
> *No, Baby . . . Forget it . . . Relax and be a good girl. You're absolutely all I want.*

He would weep and tell her they had to stop meeting for a while. Jackie was returning to town now after a lengthy vacation, Jackie needed attention.

Then he would weep and ask her to come back. "Told him we had to break it off, and he immediately asked if there was someone else. I said yes, and that I was thinking of marrying him . . . this one instance of love I've found has only made me conscious of how disproportionate, how distorted, my perspective had become . . . All he did was cry a little and ask if I was really in love . . . Then he offered to send me away, like some jealous Papa, and then he asked that we make none of it final until dinner next week . . . So there I was again . . . and the next time it was as if nothing at all had been said or promised, not only at his sexual beck and call, but apparently he wants me to procure for him, too . . . he just lunged [at me] . . . I was just a sack of potatoes . . . Finally I rolled off the bed and got dressed . . . and so here I am . . . all horsewhipped, like you say."

At one point, Brammer typed into his notebook: "waiting for d. and wondering about the differences between d. and n[adine]. Why no screaming sexual jealousy? more sophisticated now? no think so . . . no, can't really be sexually jealous in this instance, only concern for d's welfare and my own need to be always informed."

They *all* knew Ellen Rometsch—everyone who had worked with Bobby Baker through Lyndon Johnson's office. Rometsch was a Liz Taylor look-alike from what was now East Germany, with an astonishing capacity for partying and entertaining men. Baker would often bring his "girls," including Rometsch, to the Quorum Club, a hideaway on Capitol Hill where lobbyists and legislators unwound together after hours and where Baker frequently made legislative deals on behalf of LBJ and others—deals that often included private introductions to his "girls." "I must have had fifty friends who went with [Rometsch]," is how Baker once put it, "and not one of them ever complained. She was a real joy to be with."

As President Kennedy soon discovered. Brother Bobby understood that her East German ties risked exposing the president to charges of consorting with a communist spy, should word of his dalliance ever leak to Republicans. Bobby worked to get her out of Washington and to purchase her silence. Brammer knew her; he had heard rumors about her nights with JFK. Whether de Vegh knew her, he didn't know. Diana didn't want to hear of her lover's other conquests. Brammer said nothing on the subject—and respecting the journalistic ethos of the day, he didn't expose John F. Kennedy's secrets. At first, his Washington stories for *Time*—pieces he reported, filed by Hugh Sidey—remained solidly focused on public matters ("Beneath the suntanned surface, when U.S. citizens thought of their country there was uneasiness and discontent"). But Kennedy was too charismatic to be profiled, for long, in the traditional manner. Sidey had learned from his encounter with Bobby that certain lines could not be crossed; nevertheless, the handsome young president *cried* for personal asides, even in a hard-news context. Brammer's observational prowess (as well as his private knowledge) came in handy here. *Time* began to report revealing details: "The President moved easily, showing no signs of his recent back injury, and he half-smiled his recognition to White House regulars. Yet his face appeared puffy, and lined by new wrinkles, and his hands seemed to tremble slightly as he shuffled the papers before him." And: "Even in the midst of briefings, the President sometimes ceases to listen as he stares into space—apparently searching for the answer to some nagging problem." Hints of complexity, vulnerability, a life apart from the pressroom podium—incrementally, in the pages of a mainstream news magazine, the president was taking on the shadings of a character in a novel.

At one point, Willie Morris gave Brammer space in the *Texas Observer* for a satire on the administration. Entitled "Glooey," it takes the form of a one-act play, and it is the closest Brammer came to publicly revealing the White House's daily routine. As the play begins, the First Lady says, "He's been in the pool since the crisis started." A newsman wants to know, "What crisis she talkin' about?" "You got me there," answers the president. Kennedy did, in fact, spend many hours a week in the White House swimming pool, accompanied by a woman or several women, sometimes joined by his brothers Bobby and Teddy. The water was heated to ninety degrees to soothe his back. Jackie was not allowed near the facility when her husband made use of it. "When the president [takes] lunch in the pool with Fiddle and Faddle, nobody goes in there," said one JFK staffer.

Setting the scene of his play, Brammer writes, "Visible [in the] pool is a young man, surpassingly beautiful . . . also unimpeachably naked." The unusual second adjective here suggests, perhaps, Brammer's bitter attitude toward unfair privilege. JFK's recklessness was so worrisome to many members of the Secret Service, and to members of the press corps, that a sense of dread thickened the West Wing air. Additionally, Kennedy's amphetamine use had started to make him thinner. In Brammer's play, the president says, "Sometimes I see me dead in the rain." The First Lady responds, "Oh darling, don't talk like that." The vice president, standing to one side, contemplating "walking on the water," pipes up, "What's so awful about talkin' like that? Go on . . . talk like that some more." In just a few words, Brammer had captured the true dynamic of Camelot.

Johnson, well aware of Kennedy's sexual profligacy, sulked and seethed. "You know what he does at night?" he told Harry McPherson one day. "He gets in a convertible and he drives to Georgetown to see one of his girlfriends." He said Kennedy was "driving the Secret Service crazy. They are right behind him."

On another occasion, Johnson told Brammer, "J. Edgar Hoover has Jack Kennedy by the balls." CBS president Frank Stanton recalled LBJ exclaiming that "he was waiting for someone to blow the whistle on Kennedy. But the press was completely in Kennedy's hands and Johnson knew that." It is tempting to wonder whether the history of journalism might have been altered slightly—if the code of official silence might have shattered earlier than it did—if Johnson and Brammer had still been working closely as a team. But Johnson had been conspicuously cool to his former aide since the appearance of *The Gay Place*.

"You are dealing with a very insecure, sensitive man with a huge ego. I want you to literally kiss his fanny from one end of Washington to the other," Kennedy told his staff regarding LBJ. "I can't afford to have my vice president, who knows every reporter in Washington, going around saying we're all screwed up, so we're going to keep him happy." Kennedy also decided to get his second-in-command out of the way as often as possible so that Bobby wouldn't be tempted to joke about the man's "gilded impotency"—in turn, Johnson cursed "that little shitass," the president's brother. Kennedy arranged numerous foreign jaunts for LBJ, ceremonial visits centered on flying the flag. Johnson didn't want to make these trips—particularly to Vietnam, where Kennedy had just approved a nearly 300 percent increase in the number of American military advisers assisting the South Vietnamese army, along with an operation code-named Ranch Hand, a plan to spray herbicide defoliants in the countryside to deny Vietcong guerillas food and cover. Johnson told Kennedy that he didn't want to fly over there and get his head blown off. Kennedy laughed and said it was all part of serving his country.

Johnson took his spleen out on his staff. En route to Asia in May 1961, he ordered Horace Busby off the plane for some oversight the hapless aide had committed. "But we're over the ocean," Busby said. "I don't give a fucking damn!" Johnson exploded. Lady Bird prevented the poor man from being ejected midair. Overseas, Johnson broke every cultural taboo, manhandling women and children in public (including a "few fingerless lepers," according to his biographer Robert Dallek), telling confused crowds they could all be as rich as Texans if they would adopt the American way of life. He seemed genuinely happy only once, discussing rural electrification with Prime Minister Nehru of India.

Back in the States, he flew to Texas for a meeting with Dwight Eisenhower at the ranch. Brammer was among the reporters assigned to cover the event. Both men's destinies had altered radically, rising and falling, in a very short time. Their personal worlds, as well as the world at large, were about to make even more unpredictable twists: the period's discord would soon be crystallized in a comment made at a rock-and-roll concert by something called a Beatle: "The next song . . . is our latest record or our latest electronic noise depending on whose side you're on."

On the flight back to Washington from the LBJ ranch, Johnson, melancholy, miserable in his secondary role, mused to gathered reporters that he missed the massive staff he had commanded when he served as majority leader in the Senate. Nobody respected him now. Nobody ever stuck with him. "Billy abandoned me," he said suddenly, pointing at Brammer.

"I picked up your book the other day but I couldn't read it. You had too many dirty words in it."

Brammer didn't answer.

"When'd you write that book?"

"When I was in Washington."

"When you were working for me?"

"At nights."

"You should have been answering my mail."

This particular press conference ended. The plane landed. The two men never spoke again.

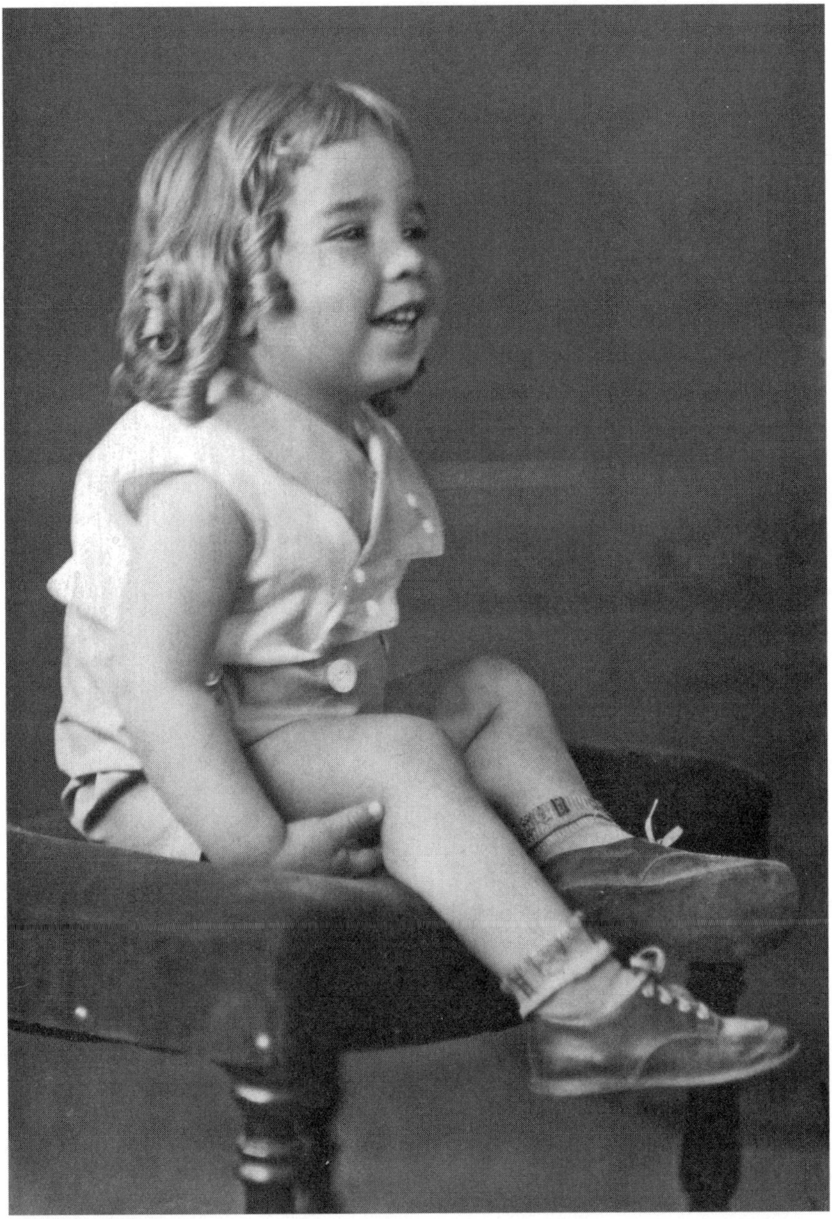

*Brammer's parents' house was part of a formerly middle-class, now workingman's, enclave called Oak Cliff in Dallas, next to a vacant lot and a winding little creek long dry. His father kept an extra fridge stocked with soda pop on a screened-in back porch—he was a plain fool for Hydrox and Dr Peppers. (Kate Brammer; all images provided by Sidney and Shelby Brammer unless noted otherwise.)*

*Brammer always referred to himself as a "menopause baby." As the child of older parents, he was doted on and left alone in almost equal measure. Hence, his frequent boredom. (Kate Brammer)*

*Brammer's mother Kate never spoke of her brief first marriage to a man she never named. He was the father of Brammer's older half-sister, Rosa. As a rather isolated child, Brammer used to love to go to the movies with his mother, often in the Texas Theatre with its ceiling of fake stars. (Rosa Gunnell)*

*Brammer grasped early that his father, a lineman for the Texas Power and Light Company, was a major agent of change, waving his wrenches and harnessing the power that brought the world, shouting, into the boy's room through the Crosley radio.*

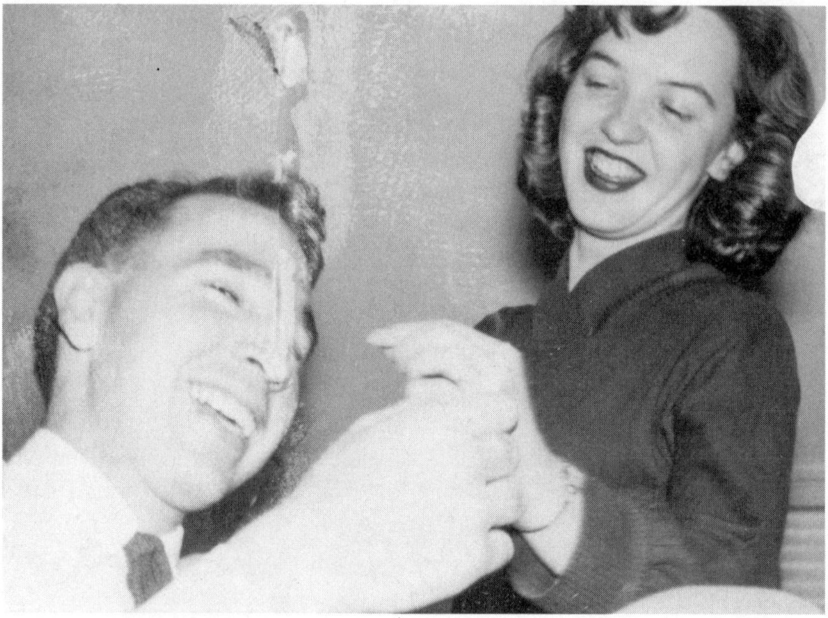

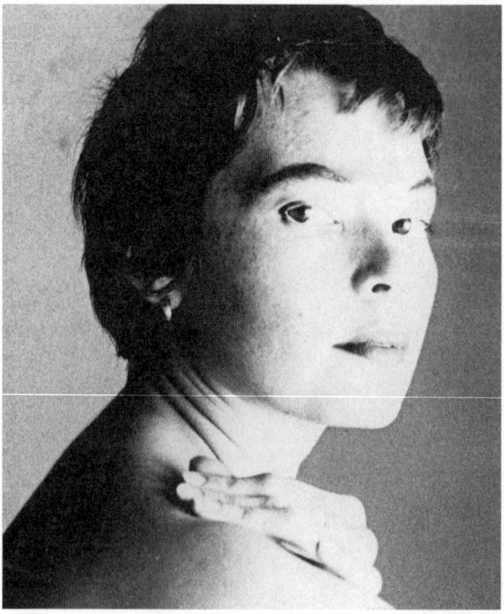

*"Charming, reckless, crazy Billy," Brammer's friend, Grover Lewis, called him. At North Texas State Teachers College, in the early 1950s, Brammer developed a "growing hipness about things in general," said his daughter Sidney.*

*Brammer's friend, Robert Benton, who later had a successful movie career, took this "art" photo of Nadine one night in the early 1950s when Brammer was out of town. Later, Brammer was not happy when he learned of the photo session. (Robert Benton)*

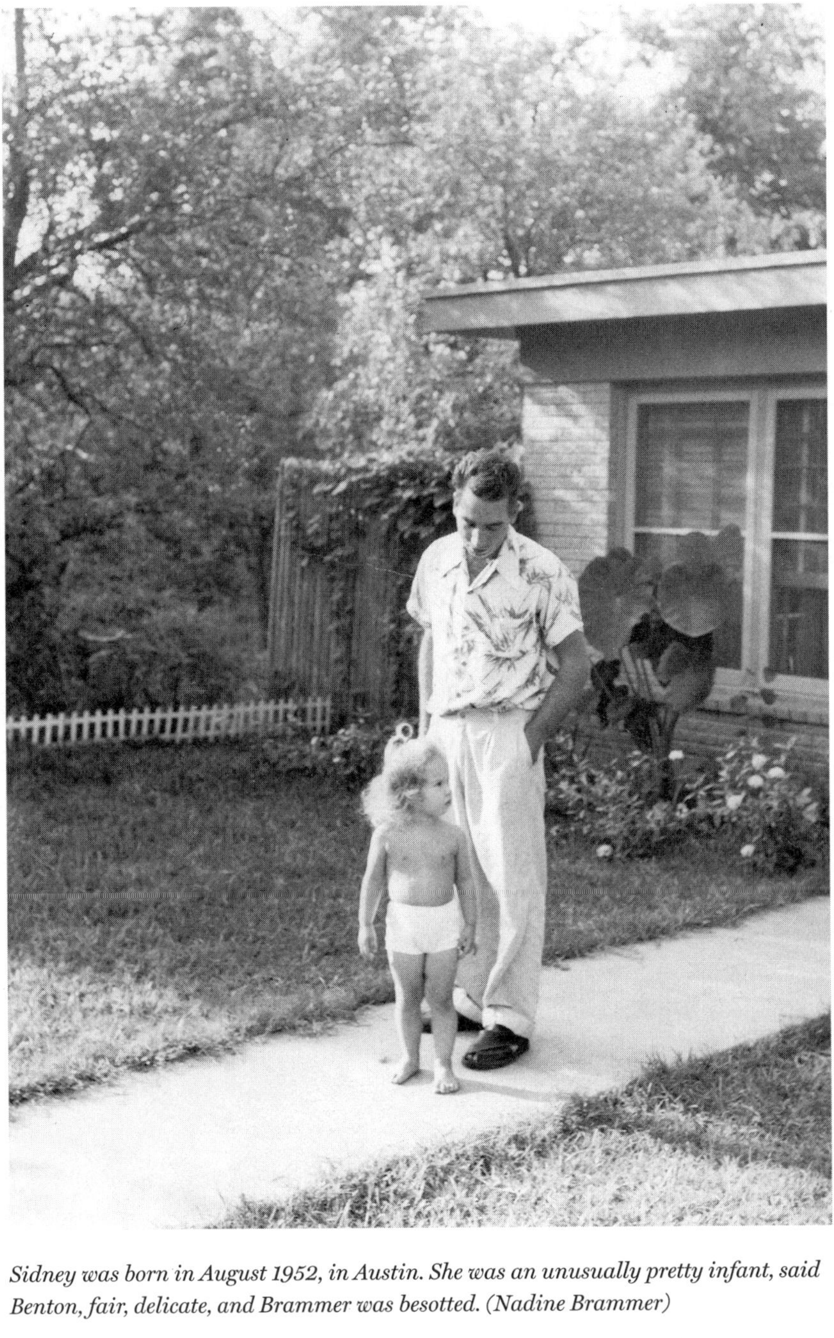

*Sidney was born in August 1952, in Austin. She was an unusually pretty infant, said Benton, fair, delicate, and Brammer was besotted. (Nadine Brammer)*

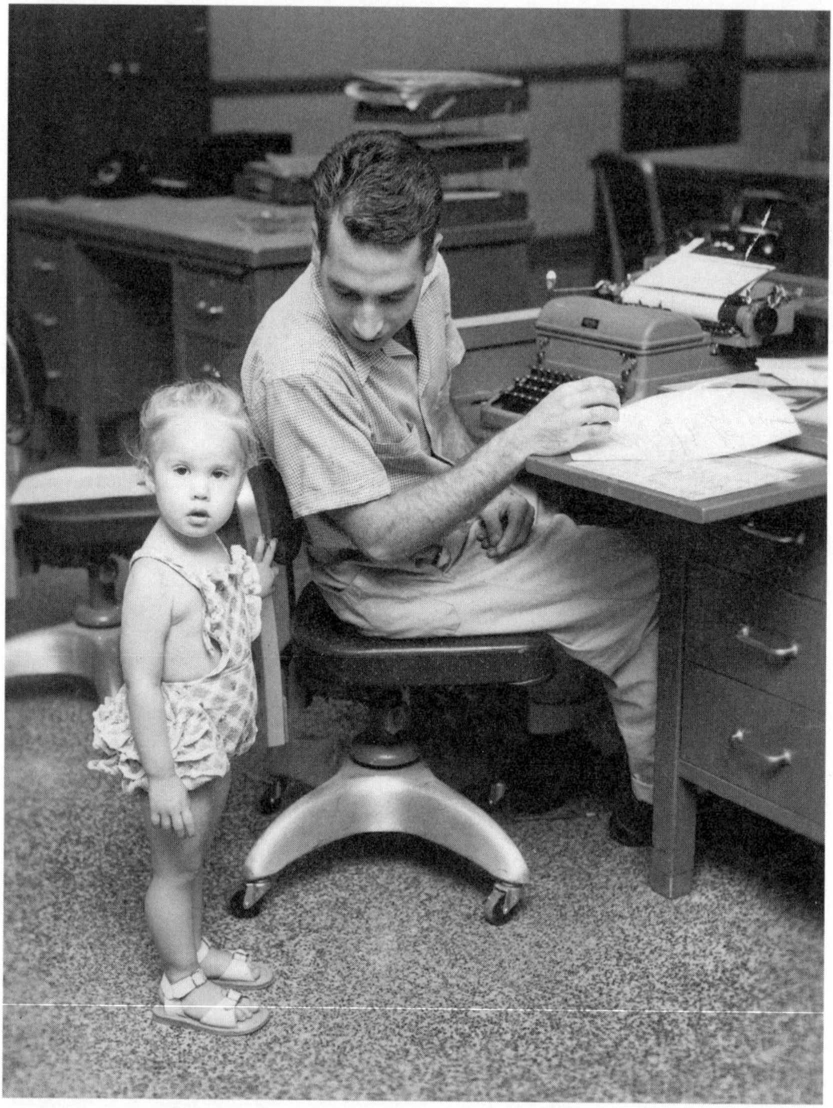

*When Sidney was a baby, Nadine shuttled back and forth between Austin and her mother's house in McAllen. She was unhappy staying home while Brammer worked during the day and went out with friends in the evenings. Brammer tried to make a home for the family in Austin, fixing up a study that Sidney frequently commandeered as a playroom. (Nadine Brammer)*

*Shelby, born in the summer of 1954, was as gorgeous as her big sister and just as beloved by her father. "I have no memories of Nadine and Billy Lee being together," Shelby said. "He's in DC and she's fed up." (Nadine Brammer)*

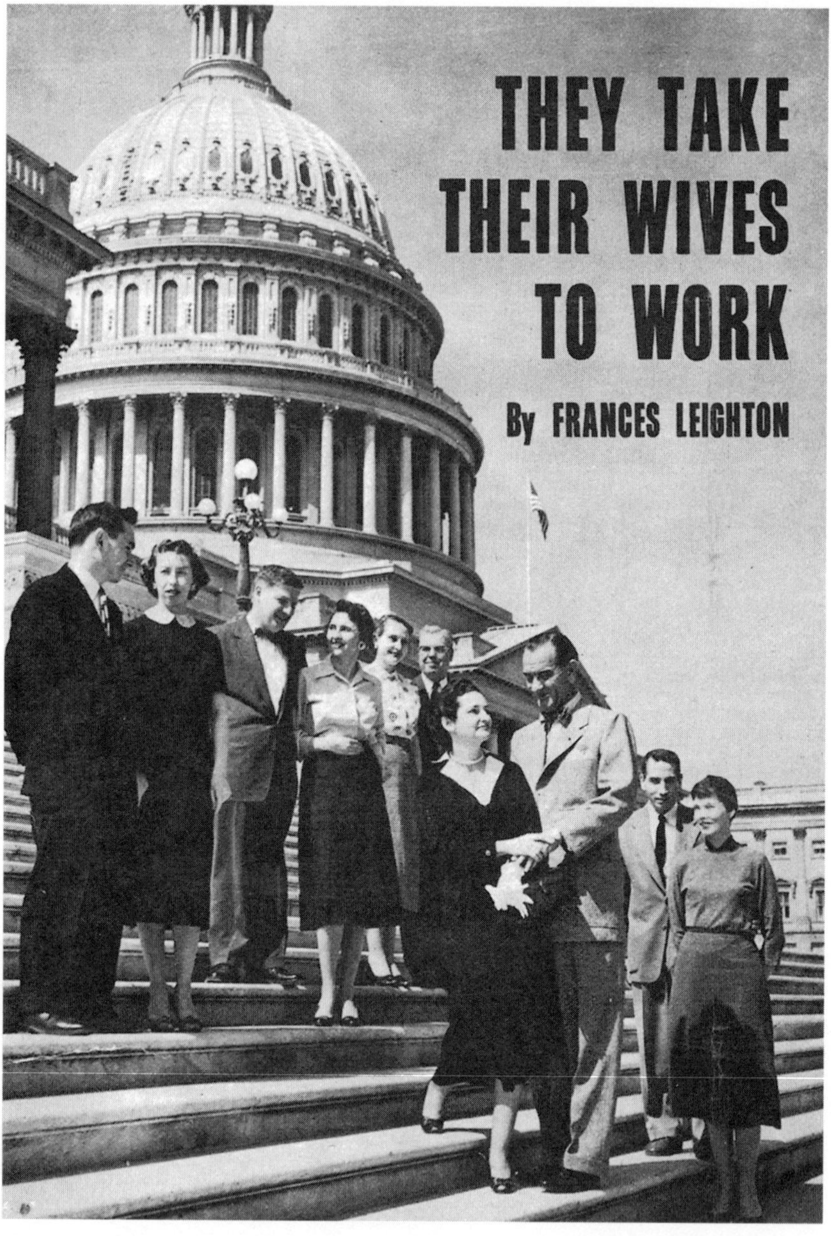

THEY TAKE THEIR WIVES TO WORK
By FRANCES LEIGHTON


*Lyndon Johnson hailed his policy of hiring couples as a progressive experiment in fostering "team spirit," but Nadine (lower right, with Brammer) admitted that this portrait of unity on the Capitol steps was an election year put-up job: "I was already straying sexually and emotionally."* (Courtesy of the publisher)

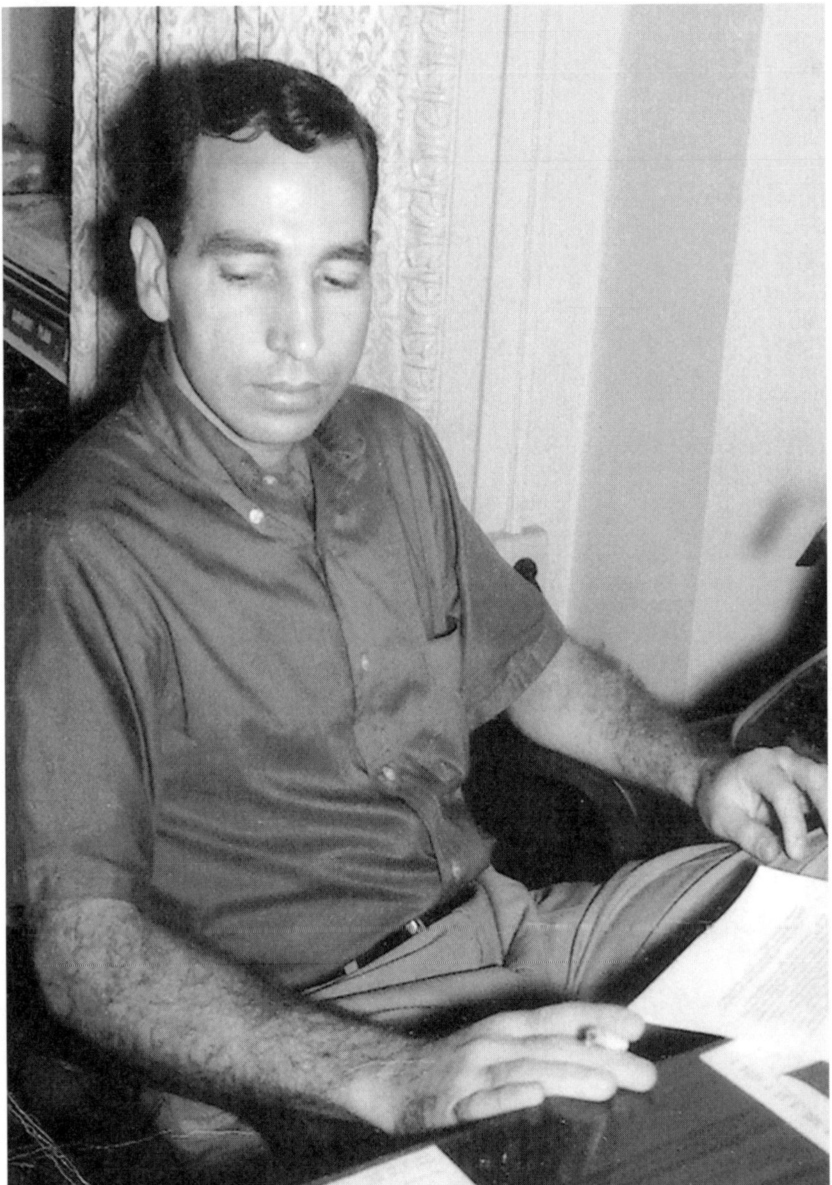

*Located directly underneath Richard Nixon's office, Brammer shared Room 201 with another Senate staffer and entertained colleagues by inviting them to come hear the "groan of vice-presidential plumbing." Here, Brammer wrote most of* The Gay Place *late at night, high on speed and swaying to the sound of Paul Desmond records.*

*"If you'll name that boy after me, I'll give him a heifer calf and he'll have a whole herd by the time he's twenty-one," LBJ told Nadine when she informed him she was pregnant and would soon leave his staff in Washington to return to Austin. At an early age, Willie became skilled at complicated magic tricks, which delighted Brammer. (Billy Lee Brammer)*

*Brammer campaigned for the Kennedy-Johnson ticket, delaying proofreading the galleys for* The Gay Place. *In Dallas, along with LBJ and Lady Bird, he got caught in the middle of an angry group of wealthy women who shouted curses at Johnson for "selling out" to Eastern liberals and communists. The press dubbed the group the Mink Coat Mob. (*Austin-American Statesman*)*

*Brammer's trip to Texas in 1961 for book-signing events caused him no small anxiety. He feared his old liberal pals might resent his politics in the novel, and he was not returning to a wife but to an antagonist in a divorce case. To top it all, his mother objected to the way his name appeared on the book cover, as "William Brammer." "Darn it, we named you Billie Lee!" she said.* (Austin-American Statesman)

*In January 1960, Brammer moved into a small apartment at 65 Bedford Street in New York and frequently went to movies with Robert Benton at the Museum of Modern Art. "The Village is pleasant and not exactly the wicked and reckless place it is advertised to be," he wrote Nadine. (Ina Backman)*

*Dorothy was a sorority dropout and an English major at the University of Texas when she met Brammer. After a mutual friend introduced them, she thought, "Ah, be still my heart. O English major heart." "Everyone in town knew who he was. I think I took the rollers out of my hair." Brammer wrote a paper for her, which earned a C+ for "poor sentence structure."*

*"Darthy, my love, I'm off to Washington," Brammer said. Dorothy asked, "What are you going to do with me?" He answered, "Well, I'll just marry you and take you with me." "I thought, 'Sounds like fun,'" Dorothy said.*

*The wedding was held in Dorothy's father's house in Houston and British-born classics professor John Sullivan served as best man. Sullivan's date was Barbara Jordan, who in 1966 would become the first African American woman elected to the Texas Senate. A friend later said, "I can just imagine Dorothy's father's reaction when he came to the realization he was throwing what was doubtless the first integrated wedding on his block."*

*In 1965, Brammer and Dorothy moved into the Daniel H. Caswell House at 15th and West Avenue in Austin, a turn-of-the-century Victorian / Colonial Revival home that was falling apart. It rented for $250 a month and became an epicenter of "wild abandon." (Bob Simmons)*

*Brammer grew a rakish mustache and bought new clothes when he took a job teaching journalism at SMU in Dallas. The city presented a "glum landscape," he mourned: "While not the unremitting drag I half expected, [it] is vaguely dissatisfying all the same. I had thought our friends in Austin, SF, NYC, etc. were troubled, sad, frequently depressing or boring. Much worse here." (Gary Cartwright archive and estate)*

*Brammer was a lifelong teacher, a companion, a grown-up kid, according to Shelby. "Whenever he was with you, his attention was focused solely on you," she said.*

*Robert Benton marveled that Brammer never made an enemy in his life. He took great care to maintain his friendships. His pal Tary Owens said he "was the only person about whom you could say, 'He stole my wife and I'm not mad at him.'" (Bob Simmons)*

*A literary celebrity, Brammer might vow to stay away from parties, but the parties came to him. One midnight, Jay Milner "found Billie Lee sitting alone in a corner" of his house drinking a Dr Pepper while a party caroused around him. "Am I this much fun?" Brammer asked his friend. (Bob Simmons)*

*Bud Shrake was covering sports for the* Dallas Morning News *when Brammer moved into Shrake's apartment in the early 1960s. It was through Shrake that Brammer met Jack Ruby (Shrake was dating Jada, Ruby's premier stripper at the time), and after the assassinations and LBJ's ascendency to the presidency, Brammer thought his life would turn around. No one had better LBJ stories than he did.* (Austin-American Statesman)

*"[Bill] got a lot of ego-satisfaction from being the center of attention with those guys," Sidney said of the time her father spent with this group of younger writers and their companions (Shrake, Kathy Lowry Deely, and Larry L. King, standing; Doatsy Shrake, Holly Gent Palmo, Pete Gent, and Brammer, seated). "They were big and drunk and loud. He'd sit quietly and then let out a pithy remark and they'd fall all over."*

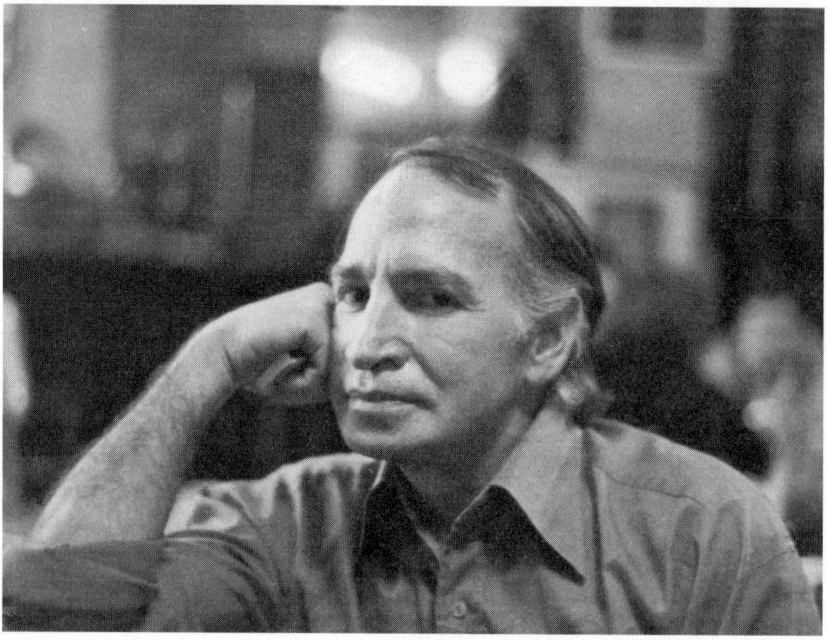

*"I saw that he'd gotten old," Sidney said. It became "almost painful to visit him in his rattrap apartments" but "one often had a* need *to see him—because Billie Lee had a way of getting to the quick of your deepest despond, making you laugh at it." (Wayne Oakes)*

PART THREE

# *ELECTRICAL VIOLATIONS*

# 13.

Katherine Anne Porter knew some things. She knew how to be a writer. She knew how to be a Texan. And she knew how to keep these burdens from crushing her heart. Brammer was impressed.

She warned him, though, "I've survived but I certainly haven't flourished": neither a Lone Star pedigree nor a lifetime of literary pursuits primed one for happiness in a country that laughed at both.

She had reason to be wary of young men from her home state who had just published acclaimed first novels: little time had passed since William Goyen, whose *The House of Breath* had dazzled critics a few years back, had wooed her and used her, latching on to her fame to make new professional connections. So when Brammer phoned the seventy-one-year-old from Washington, requesting an interview on behalf of *Time* magazine, she hesitated. Finally, she said, "I'm drunk as a coot but come on out. I'm not intimidated by reporters. It's just that they scare me to death."

She lived in a house on Q Street in Georgetown, but her publisher had found her a cozy hideaway room overlooking the harbor at Pigeon Cove, Massachusetts—a peaceful place for her to finish her long-awaited novel, *Ship of Fools*. Brammer met her there, and they sat together on a glassed-in porch above the Atlantic, watching the light change, discussing stories she had heard of exciting storms in the cove that could knock out the electricity for days. Immediately, she warmed to Brammer's quiet curiosity and his gentle manner. She chatted for hours: talking "[has] always been my sin," she told him.

She had spent twenty years, off and on, writing *Ship of Fools*—thirty if you counted the time she had wasted thinking about it without putting pen to paper. "It feels like the end of a very prolonged pregnancy," she said. Her advice to Brammer: always know your ending in advance. Write in "batches and binges"—however you can; it doesn't matter, just so long as you do it. She said she was "honestly so tired" now. She *did* have an idea for at least one more story, but the country was changing so much, getting so ugly and contentious, that she didn't know whether she could pull it off: "I would like to write about two wonderful old slaves who were my grandmother's companions, but someone is always giving a low name to good things and I suppose the N.A.A.C.P. would say I was glorifying Uncle Tomism."

Brammer admired her dignity—a combination of general defiance and proud decadence. She held her hands tightly in her lap as she sat in the sunset-on-the-ocean glare, wearing a simple black dress with flared sleeves and a string of pearls around her neck. She laughed easily, a sad sound. Her sudden expressions of pleasure looked anomalous on her sharp face. He hoped to be just like her when *he* was seventy-one. She had been the "architect of her own literary monument," he wrote for *Time*, the "sparing" designer of a "graceful, towering" achievement. Could he follow her writing wisdom, including the tip *Get out of Washington as quickly as possible*? The place was too corrosive for the fine sensibilities of a novelist, she said.

"Bill didn't really know how to go about being a famous writer," said David Halberstam. But he didn't need much nudging to leave DC. One of his last Washington pieces for *Time*, filled with crepuscular detail, revealed his numbed weariness: "It was a humid midsummer night in Washington. The city slept as best it could. On Capitol Hill the great dome glowed above an empty plaza. But in its nearly empty chamber, the U.S. Senate was in session—of a sort." These jaundiced sentences could have been lifted out of *Fustian Days*—the sense of a process exhausted and meaningless, lacking proper leadership. Fenstemaker was dead; Johnson was no longer majority leader. (Kennedy had sent the vice president to Berlin just to get him out of town; at the wall, LBJ had hoped to make a bombastic speech for freedom, but his security detail forced him to remain hunched in his car for safety reasons.) "Rhode Island's Democratic Senator Claiborne Pell, acting as presiding officer, nodded in his chair," Brammer wrote. "Democratic Whip

Hubert Humphrey and Republican Whip Tom Kuchal slumped at their desks, staring trancelike at nothing. And from his backrow desk, Wisconsin Democratic Senator William Proxmire talked and talked and talked, pausing only to sip butterscotch-flavored Metrecal."

Katherine Anne was right. Time to go.

---

Was it coincidence that within a few weeks of Johnson's snub over all the "dirty words" in *The Gay Place*, Brammer left Washington to join *Time*'s Atlanta Bureau? Was he forced out? Did he request a transfer? The answers aren't clear but, over the years, his move has added to the guesswork that Johnson's coldness was a major blow to Brammer's ego. David Halberstam disagreed. "I know that LBJ was *furious* about the book," he said—but not because of its content. "He was really angry that it was written 'on his time,' so to speak. But Bill was *amused* by Johnson. He saw him as a great circus performer, and understood completely that beyond LBJ's liberalism was egotism, narcissism and power lust. Bill knew Johnson 'back to the bed he was born on,' as Dylan Thomas wrote. Bill never lived in the shadow of LBJ, because he never took him all that seriously."

More to the point, "I don't think [Lyndon] ever read a book that was written about him," said Horace Busby. "Mrs. Johnson may have, but not Lyndon. He read . . . but not that kind of book. And Bill Brammer knew that about him. I don't think Bill's decline had anything to do with Johnson."

Nadine remained convinced it was Lady Bird who banished Brammer from the Johnson circle—for what he left *out* of the book as much as for what he put in. Sweet Mama Fenstemaker barely registers in the novel. According to Nadine, Brammer overlooked how much influence Lady Bird had on Johnson's career, the way women in those days were *always* undervalued in professional affairs.

In any case, Brammer moved to Atlanta in September 1961 to replace Calvin Trillin as the junior man in *Time*'s bureau there. (The other factor in this shake-up was Brammer's need to stay a step ahead of Nadine and Eliot Janeway. Nadine demanded child support; Janeway claimed he had been stiffed on professional expenses. "Houghton Mifflin and Eliot Janeway called and [have] been after me eagerly about whether they could reach you. Inasmuch as I believe these inquiries concerned finances due certain people from you, I was rather pleased to say I did not know where you were," Elizabeth McKee wrote to him.) Brammer's new boss, Simmons Fentress, a genial North Carolinian, a fisherman, quick to laugh, slow to pigeonhole people, welcomed Brammer heartily and told him they would be traveling *mucho*—civil rights battles were breaking out in the most surprising places.

Over the next few months, Brammer and Fentress would cover integration as it "[crept] across the U.S. South . . . school by school, counter by counter, bus by bus." They were on hand when a "small group of Negroes quietly slipped onto counter stools" in an Atlanta drugstore "and were served without protest." They watched the Memphis School Board voluntarily admit thirteen "Negro children" into the first grade; a nine-year-old white boy confessed to Brammer, "I'd rather be dumb than go to school with them." They filed reports on blacks being beaten in southern jails for the effrontery of trying to buy "new cars" in downtown lots. They witnessed the first integration of a public facility in Mississippi—the waiting room of a Greyhound bus station in McComb. They were set upon by self-described "young white trash" in Pike County, Mississippi, as they covered an integrated bus ride from New Orleans.

Brammer was among the first reporters to note the growing tension between "Southern Negro college students" who were "fed up with the slow, legislative approach . . . to desegregation" and Martin Luther King Jr.'s tactics of appeasement: "A segregation law is often declared invalid in the courtroom, after patient argument by the N.A.A.C.P., only to remain in force by practice. To fight segregation in their own way, young Negroes have organized themselves into a federation called the Student Nonviolent Coordinating Committee . . . Prestige among SNCC's tough and tenacious young Negroes is often measured by the number of times a member has gone to jail on civil rights charges." Brammer wrote that the students had accused King of being an Uncle Tom: "He was once the idol of young Negroes, but now many are beginning to turn against him. They charge that King is far more interested in giving speeches across the U.S. than in head-on action." He reported that King had moved his Southern Christian Leadership Conference headquarters into a "predominantly white office building in Atlanta, where he puts up with segregated toilets and restaurants," while SNCC's Atlanta headquarters were located in a "windowless cubicle in an all-Negro district." A SNCC supporter told Brammer how disappointed he was that King had failed to take a scheduled Freedom Ride into Mississippi. He had recently vowed to stay in jail after being arrested for protesting in Albany, Georgia, but then "meekly posted bond."

Between the bus rides and the demonstrations, Fentress asked Brammer to report on the spread of backyard bomb shelters in the South.

From his brother, Jim, who conducted stress analysis for NASA rocket projects, Brammer knew the bomb shelters were a lucrative commercial enterprise for the manufacturers, but they could never deliver on their safety promises.

Brammer profiled Edwin Walker, a renegade army general forced to resign by John F. Kennedy after publicly accusing Harry Truman and Eleanor Roosevelt of harboring communist sympathies. A staunch segregationist, he would lead riots at the University of Mississippi against the admission of a black student. Eventually, he would settle in Dallas, where he would stir strong anti-JFK fervor just days before the president's visit there in November 1963.

The road trips and the many assignments kept Brammer away from his Atlanta apartment much of the time. Small and sparely furnished, it was lonely. "There was a wistfulness in Bill [in Atlanta] right after the book came out," said David Halberstam. "[A] sadness that had to do with the breakup of the marriage, separation from his children, and being still a little in love with Nadine." He talked Diana de Vegh into flying down for a visit. She had finally ended her affair with the president, and fond as she was of Brammer, she doubted his long-term commitment. He would bring up marriage and then drop the subject. One day he was living in DC, the next he had moved to Atlanta. He was always on the road. De Vegh's father had just died—she was grieving, in addition to mourning the loss of her relationship with JFK. She said she needed some time for herself. She told Brammer she planned to spend an extended period in Paris.

Alone in his apartment, once she had left, he would clutter his kitchen and living room with open cans of Betty Crocker cake frosting, spoons stabbed into the thick, sugary goo, for when he got hungry or felt a craving for sweets.

---

A house on stilts: that was how the children thought of it. "Nadine just said one day, 'I'm going to San Antonio to marry Mr. Eckhardt. Someone will come take care of you for the weekend,'" Sidney said. She was nine. For the second time, Nadine had jettisoned Bob Hughes. While working in the Texas Legislature, she had spent many hours near Bob Eckhardt. He had offered her a secretarial position in his office; though she took a different job, she saw Eckhardt every day. She brought him coffee. She took a shine to his white linen suits and his red bow ties. She liked the way he rode his bicycle to work. She liked the way he cut his lunch bread with his pocketknife. As an older person, he seemed more grounded than her peers: "My experience with Billy Lee had convinced me men my own age were irresponsible." Most importantly, "I knew [Bob] had the potential to be a [US] congressman and I thought his chances for election were good," Nadine said. "He had a long record as an outstanding labor lawyer . . . [I decided] I wanted to go back to D.C. without having to work as a secretary or be separated from my children. I had some idea of how much work being a congressional wife would be after watching Lady Bird work so hard for Lyndon." So she hatched a plan: "Certain men wind up in the White House or Congress because of the influence of their wives."

"With both Billy Lee and Bob, Nadine saw herself as the muse," Sidney told me.

Nadine married Bob Eckhardt on March 8, 1962, after an extended vacation alone with him in Mexico. He had recently divorced his first wife, Orissa, who suffered from severe bipolar disorder (he used to find her wandering the streets of Austin at night). When Orissa discovered he had been carrying on a long-term affair with a former college sweetheart, her mental stability shattered. The marriage imploded. Eckhardt's daughters, Rosalind and "Little" Orissa, were fourteen and fifteen, respectively. Four years later, their mother would kill herself by slitting her wrists.

Following the divorce, and before taking up with Nadine, Eckhardt retreated to some wooded acreage he had bought on Cypress Creek in Harris County, northeast of Houston. Between legislative sessions in Austin, he camped on the creek among magnolias, oaks, beeches, and tall pines. He survived on bourbon and wine. Very little food. After his marriage to Nadine, he brought his new family to Cypress Creek. Sidney, Shelby, and Willie lived in a tent, then in a makeshift shack without electricity, and finally in a larger house that Eckhardt built featuring a big fireplace, a potbellied iron stove, and a tin roof. It stood high on telephone pilings above the creek waters. Willie learned to ride horses. The girls kept chickens. Whenever the legislature convened, they all moved to Austin and stayed in an apartment behind Eckhardt's mother's house. "We just swung back and forth," Sidney said. The schools in Harris County were "full of racists. It was a rude awakening for us. Life was tough. We didn't like Bob. He was cheap." He didn't feel he should have to pay for Nadine's kids—where was the damn child support Brammer had promised?

From her former husband, all Nadine heard was, "I adore you, so, have sent Bob Eckhardt a timebomb in the mail. Hope you don't mind."

Nadine's constant demands for support led him next to an unusual source of funding, the Central Intelligence Agency, though it is unlikely he knew where the money came from. Continuing a pattern he had started with Janeway, he simply drifted away from his *Time* assignments, without a word to Fentress or anyone else. (He *had* clashed, months earlier, with the magazine's New York editors over their restrictive style policies and their refusal to let him publish a profile of Arthur M. Schlesinger Jr. with *Esquire*.)

As he traveled, he charged expenses to his *Time* credit card, but he never checked in again, and he never returned to Atlanta. "At a certain point, it became clear that Billy Lee didn't think like other people," an Austin pal would say of him later. "Whether it was the drugs kicking in or his natural temperament as he got older, who knows?"

He spent a few months back in Austin, writing speeches for local politicians who failed to pay him when they lost their elections. He attempted to see his children while avoiding Nadine as much as possible. Then he returned to New York to visit Robert Benton. "I was living with Gloria Steinem then and she was working with this foundation that sent students to Europe, getting students from the East and West together," Benton said. A twenty-eight-year-old graduate of Smith, Steinem had met Benton while writing for *Esquire*. They shared a love of movies and fantasized about composing screenplays together. Then she went to work for the Independent Research Service, an organization devoted to promoting American participation in Soviet-sponsored youth festivals around the world. The goal was to inject anticommunist sentiments into the proceedings and to repair America's tattered moral image after recent racial violence in its cities. The organization was supported by US corporations, including the American Express Company, but most of the money came from the CIA. Steinem knew this—"Private money receded at the mention of a Communist youth festival"—but the activism was necessary, she felt, the trade-off worth it to bring young people together internationally. She revealed to few of the people she hired where their paychecks originated. "We all had dinner one night," Benton said. "Gloria asked Bill to go to Helsinki for the foundation." He would write anticommunist pamphlets and press releases for the Eighth World Festival of Youth and Students that summer—it was all to appear spontaneous, an outpouring of American enthusiasm by the young. Brammer agreed; the money was good (he understood it came from the State Department); he liked Steinem—tall, beautiful, with a gold streak in her hair and a dignified manner that reminded him of Katherine Anne Porter.

In May, he attended a meeting at Harvard to discuss with the conference organizers "issues central to the festival and to American participation in it." And then, to save cash, he took a tramp steamer rather than an airplane to Europe. It left from Mobile, Alabama, and would dock at Le Havre. He took along his portable electric Smith Corona typewriter and plenty of "heart medicine" (amphetamines). On the voyage, he would finish *Fustian Days*. At the end of the summer, he would return to the States with cash in his pocket and a completed second novel ready for publication.

The steamer turned out to be Katherine Anne's ship of fools—a motley crew of folks with little to say to one another. Bad plumbing; weak electricity flickering in and out. No electrical outlets for his typewriter. The boat made many unscheduled detours to pick up cargo. Then the engines broke down in the middle of the Atlantic. "He was just adrift," said Benton. He was three weeks late. "He missed the foundation's conference. He betrayed not only Gloria, but the entire United States government!"

The writer and filmmaker Warren Miller, whom Brammer had met in the States through contacts at Houghton Mifflin, was staying in Paris at the time. He awaited word of Brammer's European plans, hoping to see him. When no news came, he wrote Brammer care of the publisher, hoping the letter would find him: "Were you batonned by the Helsinki fuzz? Serves you right, buddy; you're always getting in on the wrong side, right when you should be left, left when you should be right . . . It's the beginning of the Brammer legend, fella."

On his own with a thousand dollars of CIA money in his pocket, Brammer followed the Hemingway-Fitzgerald trail through the Old World, "from the Ritz Hotel bar to the Goyas in the Prado," Al Reinert said. The novelist Merle Miller, another contact through Houghton Mifflin, wrote from Paris to recommend Torremolinos, Spain: "There are a lot of people in Torremolinos who talk about writing and who want to have written. But there are those everywhere. There are also a large number of people who drink all night and then get up around four every afternoon so they can talk about writing and drinking some more . . . I kind of liked it." So did Brammer. He wrote Miller from Spain asking when he could send some "broken-toe pills." Miller "looked through the medicine chest," he said, but came up empty: "instead, I am sending you condolences."

Brammer complained to Elizabeth McKee that he was "falling apart," skittering across Europe. A number of maladies afflicted him. Whether this was true or just a ploy to get her to send him money or pills isn't clear. She responded, in a letter addressed to "Broken-Down Bill," that "Eliot Janeway is raising hell with Houghton Mifflin about your debt . . . We are . . . giving him no information about where you are, your plans, etc. . . . I am sorry if you feel awful but I'm sure you're not a hypochondriac."

Though he had not written a word of fiction, he promised to deliver more pages of *Fustian Days*. Merle Miller wrote, offering tips for sustaining a long-term literary career:

> You are going to be in very bad trouble if you don't knuckle down with a clique. The big whing-ding of a clique . . . is the Academic Clique. The neo-critics fellows, the folks that review each others' books endlessly and favorably and who play with each others' quarterlies *all the time*. And if you don't know Katherine Anne or . . . Red Warren or Harv [Swados] or Saul [Bellow], well, you will be nipped, bud.
>
> What will happen to you is what happens to *me*, all the time. They either ignore my guts or hate them . . . well, fuck them, I guess.

Frightened by the man's bitterness, Brammer vowed to begin writing in earnest again. He went to Paris, where he *did* meet Harvey Swados. He reconnected with William Styron, whom he had met in New York through Eliot Janeway. He stayed with Diana de Vegh. She introduced him to the new friends she had made, including Vladimir Nabokov's brother. She was more beautiful and self-conscious than ever—distant, dreamy, still grieving the loss of her father.

He was amazed at how proud and unafraid black people appeared to be on the streets.

By summer's end, he had burned through his cash. He feared he was wearing out his welcome with de Vegh. Though he had no prospects in Austin, he longed to see his children. De Vegh bought him a flight home; in the next few months, his welfare would depend, in part, on another young Texan just learning to be a writer, Larry McMurtry. The two would meet at a party in Austin, spend evenings drinking at Scholz's, and finally move in together. Katherine Anne Porter—you met Katherine Anne Porter? Brammer's pals were impressed. That woman—well, she *knew some things*. It was said she had already ordered her own coffin, in anticipation of her final end, and she used it as a coffee table in her Georgetown house.

Brammer had returned to his home state without a new novel, but he thought he had found an epigraph for one, or perhaps a credo for the rest of his days. It was Yeats, "On Being Asked for a War Poem":

> *I think it better that in times like these*
> *A poet's mouth be silent, for in truth*
> *We have no gift to set a statesman right.*
> *He has had enough of meddling who can please*
> *A young girl in the indolence of her youth,*
> *Or an old man upon a winter's night.*

His first day back in Austin, he asked an old friend, "Do you know where I can get some speed in this town? I've been away for seven years. I work much better on speed."

# 14.

"Let me tell you about groupies," Brammer typed into a notebook. "Let me tell you about all the pussy in the world . . . delicious, sunkist, irresistibly-packaged, brand goddam new barely post-pubescent, super-wizard, gloryosky . . . Endlessly, night after limp-membered night . . . none of it at all remotely meaningful, reliant, memorable, touched with grace. Diverting, pleasurable—sure, I suppose. Passes the time."

This was literary celebrity, in Austin, for Billy Lee Brammer in the early months of 1963. Far from being ostracized by the old Scholz crowd for his portraits of people in *The Gay Place*, he was lionized. Austin had become his "spiritual property," according to Larry McMurtry. "Almost everyone seemed to be trying to prove, by the way they lived and talked, that Brammer had based at least one of the novel's characters on them," Jay Milner said. The book had drawn an "uncannily accurate picture" of the "way we very often perceived ourselves. We lived and worked in a more or less constant state of exultation and angst, a word I read for the first time in *The Gay Place*. And when we greeted each other, we said, 'Haw yew,' just like Billie Lee's characters did."

As much as the *old* crowd, youngsters and newcomers wanted a piece of Brammer. "Students, journalists, lobbyists and legislators were by nature a transient lot, and their social antics gave Austin a reputation as a night-life playground for those bright irresponsibles who passed through," wrote Jan Reid. At this time, Brammer was the brightest of the irresponsibles, and he wasn't just passing through. He *belonged* to the place. "Austin always seemed to embrace a star of the moment, someone everyone sought to wind up at the same party with . . . In the early and mid-sixties, it was Billie Lee and Willie Morris"—then editor of the *Texas Observer*—"[that] everybody wanted to hang out with," Milner said.

What made Brammer a star? *The Gay Place* "showed a generation of writers they could write novels about Texas, and editors in New York would publish them," said Bud Shrake, a frequent visitor to Austin. He was working as a sportswriter in Dallas. "The explosion of Texas writing was set off by Billy Lee." Shrake had met Brammer early in 1961 when Brammer dropped by the newsroom of the *Dallas Times Herald* to promote *The Gay Place*. Nadine had come along. "We noticed immediately how cute Nadine was," Shrake remarked. Back then, "I thought that for a writer from Texas to make any money, [his] novel had to be about John Wayne fighting a whole bunch of Indians . . . Talking to Brammer that day I realized that he had been writing stuff he knew about . . . I thought to myself, 'Well, it's a whole new world then.'" Would New York really take Texas seriously? Could Texas finally shed its inferiority complex?

Younger writers—fellow journalists—latched on to Brammer, thinking he could help them sell their manuscripts. "Ah wah, Billie Lee: You suffer an embarrassment of riches," his old DC pal Larry L. King wrote to him. "You will erect mountains of gold and marble and they will spill into the air untold streams of hot red jello water." He had been writing a Korean war novel. He pleaded with Brammer to submit it to publishers for him. Brammer found it a "confused work," but complied with King's "aggressive persistence," out of friendship.

And then when the movie director Martin Ritt came to town, along with Paul Newman, to scout locations for the proposed film of *The Gay Place*, everyone figured Brammer was about to become even *more* famous. Ritt had commissioned a script from the veteran Hollywood screenwriting team Irving Ravetch and Harriet Frank Jr. Newman would play Roy Sherwood. Jackie Gleason, fresh from his star turn in *The Hustler*, would bring Arthur Fenstemaker to life.

But more than these material trappings, "a rare charisma" accounted for Brammer's appeal, said Jay Milner.

> Strange and powerful. His compelling charm had something to do with the fact that he had written that famous book . . . But it was more than that. One friend, Jim Smithum, might have come pretty close to explaining [it] when he said, "Billie Lee is the most reasonable human being I ever knew." It could be that the crowd so often ended up at Billie Lee's simply because the lights were always on, but I think not . . . I never heard Billie Lee raise his voice, and he was one of the best listeners I ever encountered. He always appeared deeply interested in what you were saying and knew something about whatever you were talking about.

Additionally:

> Innumerable women felt protective of this quiet little man who had written the book that had moved them so and to demonstrate their dedication, they would volunteer to scavenge pills for him. Billie Lee's favorite scam was that he arranged "this great deal" for the temporary use of a friend's cabin in the hills [around Austin] and wanted to gather in a month's supply to go off by himself up there and finish his book. I [was] with him when as many as five women came by his apartment in one afternoon to bestow upon him a stash of cabin-in-the-hills, finish-the-book medication.

"I don't think Bill ever had an enemy in his whole life," Robert Benton said. "That's what makes him so interesting. You'd think that someone embarking on that path of self-destruction after he drifted back to Texas would make at least some enemies along the way, but he never did."

Finally, it must be said that timing contributed to Brammer's aura of fascination in early-sixties Austin. His arch storytelling style seemed unique because other writers had not yet exploited Texas's rich hypocrisies—the bad behavior of its politicians and religious leaders. Demographically, Texas became more urban than rural in 1950. A decade later, this population shift was producing striking cultural changes. Brammer was the most sophisticated, most literary example of a Texas boy from an essentially rural background to adopt an urban lifestyle, to loosen his grip on the culture's cherished traditions, to explore the latest fashions, gadgets, art, and music.

Barry Shank, an American studies scholar, once remarked that among certain Austin students in the early 1960s, folksinging became a particular "way of marking one's difference from the student body represented by fraternities, sororities, and football players. Students from small towns in Texas who felt that their lives differed from the conservative meanings traditionally available were attracted to . . . folksinging." It gave them a "beatnik" or "proto-hippie" status.

John Clay, a local musician friendly with Brammer and Janis Joplin, said many years afterward, "Looking back on the situation, it seems there was a generation gap affecting the early Sixties scene, but not like the one they talk about today. People like Janis and me . . . were rejecting the standards of our own generation." And they would naturally gravitate to a slightly older fellow following the same path, validating them and encouraging them to experiment still further. Brammer became their guru. Quietly, mostly by example, he led a growing "underground contingent of people—proto-hippies, I don't know what you want to call them—but there were a lot of people that were becoming more and more weird, student drop-outs, artists, writers, there were quite a few of [them]," said Tary Owens, an old high school friend of Joplin's who had migrated to Austin with her. Their group determined to make *all of life* a work of art.

Surveying his surroundings, shortly after meeting Billy Lee Brammer in the spring of 1963, Larry McMurtry said the creative possibilities of a place "fertile with conflict"—when it has reached a "stage of metamorphosis"—could not be underestimated, especially when "rural and soil traditions are competing most desperately with urban traditions—competing for the allegiance of the young."

---

Brammer "had a great talent for finding the best, most unusual, out-of-the-way houses and apartments," Jay Milner said. "He would find one and move in, but [then] . . . he would get evicted for one reason or another—often for too many parties or . . . his odd hours . . . I seldom saw him sleep. He always seemed to be getting ready to do something or was just finishing something. I [used to] drop . . . by his abode as late as 3:00 a.m., and found him brewing up a pot of chili."

Milner was a newspaperman and fledgling novelist. He tooled about town in a 1949 black Cadillac hearse he had bought at a used car lot in Dallas for seventy-five dollars. He met Brammer at an Austin club one night and soon joined the circle around him, most immediately Fletcher Boone, a struggling sculptor and painter who would later own an Austin restaurant called the Raw Deal (at one point, the restaurant featured signs saying "Billy Lee Eats Here"); Willie Morris; Bud Shrake and his sportswriting pal from Dallas, Gary Cartwright, whose facial features looked somewhat Asian and earned him the nickname "Jap." Like Brammer, Shrake and Cartwright were dedicated speed users. Amphetamines were "just out in the open in those days," recalled Cartwright. "Pro football teams literally had buckets of Dexedrine. You just walked by and grabbed a handful and didn't think anything about it." Generally, he and Shrake indulged in speed "so we could drink more and drink longer hours," Cartwright said. As sportswriters, "[we] could hardly avoid offers of free booze. Nearly every luncheon, press conference, or sporting event featured an open bar. Professional teams had hospitality suites. Some p. r. guy was always around to pick up the check." Jazzed by "heart medicine," Cartwright and Shrake performed adolescent antics such as prancing around naked at parties and staging silly acrobatics. Shelby Brammer, while acknowledging that her father was responsible for the choices he made—he could be plenty indulgent on his own—believed he became a "mascot of debauchery" for Cartwright, Shrake, and other young writers who sought his approval, plying him with more and more pills. Ultimately, he saw the trouble they were all slipping into. "Depressing," he wrote, "all these ancient children tossing down . . . stuff with as much single-minded and purposeful desperation and bleary-eyed disregard for their own good as some Third Ave wino."

---

Every year, at the close of the legislative session in DC, Willie Morris threw a party at his house in West Austin. He would announce the winners of his annual Neanderthal Awards, given to the dumbest, least effective Texas congressmen. The parties often ended with a drunken Neanderthal trying to impress Morris with his great intelligence: "Shoot fire, Willie, I've read *Prowst* and all them."

The 1962 bash was memorable for Jay Milner because Brammer was there—this was just a few months before he went adrift in the Atlantic on his way to Helsinki. Brammer was dating a UT undergraduate named Janie, whom he had just met. Late in the evening, Nadine showed up, insisting he drive to her house to babysit the children because she and Eckhardt wanted to go out. Brammer asked Milner to escort Janie home if he didn't make it back to the party. In fact, Milner took her to his place to listen to records. She passed out on his couch. Later, he learned his friend was very upset that she spent the night with him. He had sat in his car outside Milner's window, staring up at the light, "imagining lurid scenarios."

"I called him and we met at Scholz's," Milner said. "The misunderstanding was soon dispelled. Billie Lee was much too placid to successfully hold a grudge."

Still, in the wee morning hours, over bowls of cold chili, stoked by pills, Brammer could slide into amphetamine-laced paranoia and extreme bitterness. "Women are nine-faced bitches," he typed one night in his notebook of meditations on writing, love, and politics. What set him off was Janie's accusation that he was the "nosiest man in the world," hurled at him earlier when she had caught him riffling through *her* notebook. He had found there copies of his notes on Diana de Vegh's intimate conversations with Jack Kennedy. Janie harbored literary aspirations; she asked Brammer to edit rough drafts of the short stories she was trying to write. He felt she had genuine talent, but she didn't work hard enough and she drank too much (her one publication was a letter to the editors of *Life* magazine, printed when she was a teenager, extolling the virtues of Elvis Presley—"His belting style drives us wild. We have to do something. Kick the seat in front of us or let out a 'verbal yell' or something"). Now, after discovering her notebook, he wondered whether she was using him. That was the trouble with groupies. Maybe all she really wanted was to be the "Hemingway doomed bitch-heroine," he wrote. He warned himself, "[This is] not the kind of love you got to have . . . Also remember you don't need no more parties. You been there. Nothing really new. Just draggy . . . What you need is a lover, wife and intellectual helpmeet . . . You got problems enough (artistic) without taking on some 20 yr old pearl beer queen who seems [intent] on bitching up both your lives at least twice a week . . . Get your books done!"

The problem was this: all these "dissatisfied married women" were "depressingly easy marks," even for an "un-cool lump of romantic baggage" like him, he wrote. Then he typed a frank confession: "For crissake be aware of how really spooked you are on this stuff . . . Yr most serious . . . problem is N. angst, N. syndrome; all those open running sore places where once she gave it to you good and continuously . . . You['ll] never survive another marriage remotely the same as [the] last one."

He remembered how Nadine had accused him of naïvete whenever he asked her how she could sleep around so much. Friends had told him stories—Nadine bragging she would never divorce him because the setup was "too perfect" for her, having him far away, working to support her while she "stepped out on him."

He stuck a fresh page into the typewriter. He wrote that most of the women he met seemed irritated that he "might have the presumption . . . or simple human instinctual compulsion to love [his] own children." Why? At a club one night, a young woman had asked him, "But do you *really* care for them all that much?"

"How to answer," he typed:

> I couldn't begin to describe to her the complete sense of despair that would overtake me in ny or wash or atla when I had been separated from them for more than a few weeks and the outlook for ever getting back to them seemed utterly bleak . . . why are [these women] so infuriated by this love? A general distrust and dislike for Men or Man? or a feeling . . . of being challenged in the intensity (or lack of it) they themselves might feel about [their] own children . . . I do know that I am neither all that complicated nor insincerely, melodramatically sentimental . . . I simply love them . . . and I am in distress most of the time I am away from them for any length of time.

---

He could vow to himself to stay away from parties, but the parties came to him. One night, Milner stopped by with a friend, Malcolm McGregor, a House member from El Paso. Brammer was sitting at his Smith Corona, so the men decided to let him work. Just as they were about to walk out the door, "a gang of revelers from Scholz's invaded the place," Milner said. McGregor offered to kick everybody out, but Brammer said it was okay, they would drift away soon. "Shortly after midnight we drove back by Billie Lee's place just to check. Sure enough, the party was still going strong," Milner recalled. "We went in and found Billie Lee sitting alone in a corner, on the floor, sipping a Dr Pepper longneck. The clamorous party caroused round him, none of the exhilarated guests paying any attention to their amiable, but silent, host."

And there was the puzzling paradox of Billy Lee Brammer: he exhibited an essentially passive personality, always letting louder folks take center stage, yet on the strength of his quiet charisma and steady generosity, he was pivotal to his group's activities, a powerful social catalyst.

"I sat down beside him on the floor," Milner said. "He nodded, grinning his characteristically sheepish grin, and asked solemnly, 'Am I this much fun?'"

---

"I long to talk with some old lover's ghost," he wrote one night in his notebook, once everyone had left him alone, sitting on the floor with all his lights up.

---

"Something in him was letting go," Ronnie Dugger noticed. On one occasion, he lent Brammer a "book with Love and Lust, or some such, in the title." Brammer joked that he would return it "as soon as I've digested chapters on 'Alpha-type masochists, downhill phase.'" The loss of his marriage; the emptiness of his affairs; the effect of the drugs; the disappointments in the publishing industry—these developments combined with disillusionment in politics to set him adrift, Dugger believed. He remembered Brammer discussing the economics lessons he had learned from Eliot Janeway. "Gives you a new perspective," he said. "Lots of money made; lots of money lost; and all of life's fundamental aspects reduced to [the] question of whether slumps in hogs, cattle, corn, will put a Democrat in the White House. Nobody talks about civil rights except the *New York Post*." He had begun his adult life as a mild cynic occasionally capable of making idealistic gestures. Now he told his friends that politicking "caused brain damage." When Gary Cartwright insisted he had a duty to vote, he replied, "I choose not to choose."

Yet if Brammer was dissipating, "it was not dissipation in the normal Puritan sense of the word," said Robert Benton.

> I think the easy and superficial thing to say about Bill is that he went on some gigantic slide, or to say that he's a Texan version of Fitzgerald. I don't think so. I don't think Billy went through the sense of torment that Fitzgerald went through. I never knew him when he was not some kind of extraordinary optimist, or wasn't filled with a kind of hope or generosity toward everyone around him. In some ways, he's more like a Graham Greene saint figure than a Scott Fitzgerald tragic writer. If you had to find a literary analogy, that would be it.

Said Dorothy Browne, the woman who would soon become his second wife, "It wasn't 'letting go' so much as . . . he didn't believe in *wisdom* any longer. He accepted everything. He never moralized or condescended to you, he never made value judgments about things. I don't think he believed in good and bad. I know he didn't believe in right and wrong."

And "he wanted to see where the young were going," Sidney Brammer added. He recognized that "it was a new day. He experimented—he'd do anything, anything." He "couldn't keep up with the culture fast enough. He started speeding all the time, trying to stay up constantly to write about it. But he couldn't write it, he could only *live* it until it burned him out."

"I can see why he took amphetamines," Dorothy agreed. "He made a desperate attempt to be awake all the time . . . He was really trying to be a think tank, to take in as much external stimuli as he could possibly fit in." And he loved sharing his knowledge with everyone around him. "He was my graduate school," Dorothy said.

At about this time, he began to place on the wall wherever he lived a quotation from T. H. White—Merlyn the magician's advice that the "best thing for being sad" is to "learn something . . . That is the only thing that the mind can never exhaust, never alienate, never fear or distrust."

"Bereft of hope, denied wisdom by the history he was seeing, he reposed on learning as the only way to keep going," Dugger said.

---

"It seemed to me that Billy's enthusiasm had run down," said Larry McMurtry. "We were both, at the time, in respite of wives and money"—McMurtry's wife, Jo, had run off with a local poet—"and [we] shared a house on Windsor Road," along with McMurtry's baby boy, James. Brammer and McMurtry had both graduated from North Texas State; they had published their first novels in the same year; and McMurtry's book had just been made into the movie *Hud*, starring Paul Newman. The writers had much in common. Over kraut at Scholz's—laughing together at the congressmen brushing caliche off their pant cuffs so that no one would know they had visited the beer garden—McMurtry told Brammer of the year he spent in California studying with Wallace Stegner at Stanford University. There, he met Ken Kesey—a classmate at Stanford. He thought Brammer might like Kesey. They shared a passion for the "new." Maybe a trip out West would give Brammer some peace so that he could finish his book.

With increasing sympathy, McMurtry saw how wearying Brammer's life had become. As the "local culture hero," he was a "natural target for anyone in Austin who was aspiring, frustrated, or bored. The inrush of Wives threatened to wrench the hinges off the door" of the Windsor Street house, he said. Brammer "faced it with the courteous and rather melancholy patience with which he would probably face a buffalo stampede. In the wake of the Wives came a sweaty and verbally diarrhetic mass of bored or bitter professors, broke or bitter politicians, protohippies with beach balls full of laughing gas, and broke-bored-bitter young journalists who looked like they had been using themselves for blotters."

McMurtry sealed off his part of the house and "left Bill to cope with the crowd as best he could." Watching Brammer's escapades, he came to believe that Austin had an unhealthy "fascination with its own pubic hair, and a corresponding uneasy fear that its sexual development might stop just short of adequacy. Groupiness was endemic . . . In such a town the person who is sure of himself is apt to be literally crushed by the surging mobs of the insecure, all rushing to confirm themselves by association."

Overall, "I didn't know [Billy Lee] well," McMurtry explained in a letter to me, "but I knew him well enough to know that he wasn't going to make it."

The worst of it: "He wasn't getting anything back from his writing." That was clear. "He was working on *Fustian Days* and I read everything he had. The first hundred pages or so was just wonderful, actually better than most of *The Gay Place*. You could tell it was written from a genuine impulse, he still had his original momentum going. After that it petered out pretty quickly, so far as its narrative interest. There were maybe another hundred pages, but it was pretty bad. I felt that it was running down already. Billy felt it too, which didn't help. It just seemed like he was bored with it."

In reams of rough draft pages, now archived in the Southwest Writers Collection at Texas State University, it appears that the final section of *Fustian Days* to engage Brammer before he lost touch with the book concerned Arthur Fenstemaker's brother, Hoot Gibson, based on Sam Houston Johnson: "distinguished drinker, unfrocked charlatan, man-of-the-cloth gone sour then more than sweet again: sweet as can be. Hoot was an unqualified, straight-arrow example absolutely unto his lovely old self." Had Brammer finished the book, Hoot might have been its biggest hero, rescuing and advancing the late governor's civil rights legacy. Perhaps Brammer feared that Sam Houston would react to this book as Lyndon had reacted to the last one, and he couldn't have borne that. Or perhaps Brammer had put too much of himself into Hoot Gibson, a form of wish fulfillment: Hoot, he wrote, had reached such "dazzling heights of sobriety that it had been possible for him actually to *function*," to "contemplate such vague, frivolous notions as the larger responsibilities one . . . owed to oneself."

Late at night, all alone, Brammer hoped to reach that clarifying point of stability, but he couldn't quite make it. He was still the *old* Hoot, indulging because, whenever he was high, his "old pals look and feel and behave just a real whole [lot] pruttier than maybe otherwise." In keeping with his growing disillusionment, Brammer couldn't muster, anymore, the energy to mine politics as a literary subject: "Fenstemaker . . . was a deceptive old toad in his fashion, but fairly bubbling with good works when appraised next to his gnat's butt of a successor." One hears, here, Brammer's despair at LBJ's diminishment as well as his judgment of young Jack Kennedy.

Initially, the manuscript pages of *Fustian Days* arrived in a "very mangled state," Elizabeth McKee admonished Brammer. She paid a professional typist to redo them. "I think [Houghton Mifflin] would believe that you whipped [the pages] out very casually if I sent it in the same form as what you sent me." But soon she was singing the novel's praises. She said she couldn't wait to read more of it—that is, if he "didn't leave it with some pretty airline stewardess" on his flight home from Europe. If he would only write more chapters, she was certain she could pry a healthy advance from Houghton Mifflin. Dorothy de Santillana had read the opening scenes and loved them.

Editors called to pitch him publishing opportunities. James H. Silberman at the Dial Press wanted him to ghostwrite a memoir of Speaker Sam Rayburn by LBJ—*if* they could get LBJ's permission. When that didn't happen, Silberman mused, "Your reminiscences about life with the majority leader make me wish that we were talking about a memoir of life with Johnson written by you . . . it would be a wonderful book."

A Broadway producer tried to pursue a musical with Brammer called *Lovebucket*, based on a character Brammer envisioned who sounded an awful lot like Diana de Vegh. "I am already a little bit in love" with your character, the producer said.

Brammer never actually worked on any of these projects, but he kept the possibilities afloat, always evolving, hoping he could wrangle money out of people. Very often, he did. Elizabeth McKee began to doubt him. "In case you think our enthusiasm for FD [*Fustian Days*] is waning—you're wrong!" she wrote him at one point, subtly sounding an alarm, hoping against hope that he would deliver the goods.

Whenever he failed to squeeze funds from people for projects he proposed, he sought other favors. "As for the drug needs, there's a new clampdown on New York druggists and we are unable to fill your order, so we won't be any help to you there," one publisher wrote to him.

---

One chilly dawn, after a nightlong party, Milner sat with Brammer on a hillside overlooking Lake Travis. Brammer confessed he didn't know *how* to write a novel. The first one had been a series of feature stories pieced together. "He said that sometimes late at night, when he was alone at his typewriter and the pills were kicking in, he believed he could do it again, but in the cold light of day he was afraid he didn't know how," Milner recalled. Brammer remembered fearing, "Now they'll *really* take it out of my hide, expecting me to repeat it," when he'd read the first good reviews of *The Gay Place.*

Most often, in late '62, early '63, Brammer told friends that everything he wrote seemed too innocent to him now, the novel a naïve aesthetic form. He feared he couldn't create more literature, because he knew "too much."

---

Knowing too much was Janis Joplin's problem, too. In the oil-refining Gulf Coast town of Port Arthur, where she grew up, bored, breathing the hellish air, Baptist churches bricked up street corners. But Joplin knew where all the brothels were. And the gambling joints. "When we were in high school, the city was on the one hand very straitlaced. But on the other hand, the town was absolutely wide open. I mean, the hypocrisy just glared," said Tary Owens.

"A key to [Janis's] personality was that she could not abide hypocrisy," David Moriaty, another Joplin friend, said.

Worst of all were the mixed racial attitudes—*Love thy brothers and sisters*, but don't let the black ones near your churches or schools. On the high school debate team, "we weren't allowed to argue the pros and cons of integration," Owens said. "It was a given that integration was a horrible thing. The argument instead focused on whether you could get federal aid without having to integrate."

In this clamped-down atmosphere, Joplin found release listening to "race records" on the same border-blasting radio stations that Brammer had tuned to as a kid: 75,000 watts of Odetta, Willie Mae Thornton, and Leadbelly. How come she could listen to this stirring rock and roll at night but not sit next to a black classmate in school the following day? she wanted to know. Joplin's peers trailed her down the narrow high school halls shouting at her, "Nigger lover!"

In 1962 she made her way to Austin and to Threadgill's.

In living *The Gay Place*, Milner said, "We went to Mr. Kenneth Threadgill's on weeknights." Mr. Threadgill was the son of a Nazarene minister; he loved nothing more than to bring people together. He could always be "persuaded to sing along with his Jimmy Rodgers jukebox records," Milner said. He would yodel, do a bit of Hank Williams, dance a little jig, then return to his bartending duties beneath a giant ceiling fan that merely stirred hot air. Four gas pumps sat out front of the bar, from the building's former filling-station days, a TV antenna (connected to nothing inside) twisted atop the roof—here, Threadgill hosted truck drivers and ranchers who had come to town at night, treating them to country tunes and hootenannies. Threadgill was a serious follower of music; he became curious about the growing folk phenomenon among the nontraditional students in town, the crowd that was getting "more and more weird." Threadgill observed that despite obvious cultural and generational differences, and the rural-urban divide, the students, ranchers, and truckers all shared a sense of exile from the mainstream, and they all locked on to music as a significant identifier. The songs each group listened to shared basic chordal and rhythmic roots. Brammer had heard these similarities long ago on the radio—so had Joplin—when hillbilly bands played their versions of Deep Ellum blues. Slowly, Threadgill's "little bar became a haven for folk purists," Jan Reid said, and one night "a young regular named Julie Paul . . . brought Janis Joplin to meet Mr. Threadgill." Paul had passed Joplin hitching on the roadside and told her about the bar's impromptu music nights.

By the time Joplin reached Austin, "she was already neurotic with rejection," Reid said, "a fallen Church of Christ girl, a homely, overweight victim of the cosmetic fifties . . . She cursed like a sailor, drank anything she could get her hands on, wore no makeup, wore no bra. She apparently wanted just one person, damn it, to notice her. That person was Kenneth Threadgill."

She teamed up one night with two new friends of hers, a duo called the Waller Creek Boys, Lanny Wiggins, a banjo player, and a harp man, Powell St. John. It was the first of many gigs they would play at the bar. Whenever the older crowd got restless, heckling Joplin during her screechy rendition of "Silver Threads and Golden Needles," Mr. Threadgill shushed them. He let it be known that he considered Joplin to be like a daughter. She voiced the agonies of hell with the passion of a pilgrim who had glimpsed heaven's gates, he said. He upgraded the bar's electrical capacities and bought a brand-new microphone for her.

She hung out with the hub of Austin's misfits at a place affectionately called the Ghetto by its residents, a two-story wreck of barracks-style apartments on Nueces Street, near campus, each renting for thirty-five dollars a month. In the ramshackle structure there were only four actual apartments—maybe five (if you squeezed together hard enough)—but dozens of folks crashed there at any given time, and it was difficult to know who really lived on the premises, a fact not lost on Allen Hamilton, chief of police at the University of Texas, and Lieutenant Burt Gerding of the Austin Police Department, who surveilled the place intensely, suspecting subversive political activity, drug use, and illicit sexual practices. Aside from a few disorganized civil rights marches in front of segregated movie theaters, the Ghetto group was largely apolitical. Drug use? Certainly, though at that time, the head trip of choice was peyote, available legally and cheaply (ten cents a plant) at a nearby store called Hudson's Cactus Gardens. The Ghetto-ites tended to cut the drug's bitter taste by mixing it with store-bought molasses, whose sugar content actually counteracted the mescaline. Far more dangerous was the home beer brewing, done in an enclosed stairway; sometimes bottles would overheat and blow up, sending glass shrapnel into the ceiling. Sex—the cops' *major* obsession, according to the number of reports filed on it—did occur frequently, in spite of the rotting-kimchee-and-catbox odor permeating the corridors as well as most of the bedrooms, and the unsavory presence of semen-stained mattresses that no one bothered to change. Someone tacked a sign—"Main Ball Room"—on the avocado-green door frame outside the most-used space. In America, it was beginning to be "rumored that women could have orgasms," said Ramsey Wiggins, a sometimes Ghetto presence.

The evenings were joyous—sitting outside in mild weather beneath stately pecan trees (one dead branch spangled with condoms and beer caps), listening to Janis sing and the Waller Creek Boys blow and strum. Brammer's attentiveness impressed Joplin, as it did many other women. Together, they shared their childhood pleasures of listening to late-night radio. They enthused over Bobby Dylan's first album—Brammer introduced her to it. She told him how, in high school, she would drive with a group of guy friends across the Louisiana border and flirt with rednecks in seedy swamp bars, sometimes landing her buddies in brutal fistfights. She could cause as much trouble as Nadine, Brammer saw—except she didn't have Nadine's self-assurance.

She laughed when he told her how one day he had left a stash of pills in his bathing trunks and forgotten about them. He went for a swim in Lake Travis. The pills gummed together in one giant ball. Not knowing what to do, he popped the whole thing in his mouth: scum-water cookie dough. It was one of his finest highs, he said.

At the Ghetto, Brammer met Gilbert Shelton, then lead cartoonist at the *Texas Ranger*, a campus humor rag frequently shut down by authorities for its irreverence and obscenities. Shelton drew *Wonder Warthog*, a spoof of *Superman*. Later, he would spearhead the 1960s underground comics explosion. The philosophy of his most famous creation, *The Fabulous Furry Freak Brothers*, could well have evolved at the Ghetto: "Dope will get you through times of no money better than money will get you through times of no dope."

Brammer met Dave Hickey, an acquaintance of McMurtry's. Hickey would become a noted art and music critic. He would write the "best sentence ever to appear in *The Texas Observer*," McMurtry said—more wisdom from the Ghetto: "Even if one succeeds in making a silk purse from a sow's ear, there remains the problem of what to do with a one-eared sow."

Beneath the gently swaying pecan trees (a sweeter, more sacred scene than the White House swimming pool, Brammer thought), Brammer came to know Wali Stopher, after whom Austin's first head shop would be named; Chet Helms; Grover Lewis, his fellow literary refugee from the alleys of Oak Cliff; and a host of skilled musicians who would shortly—with a little help from Billy Lee—lead Austin into punk-edged psychedelia.

---

Here is a snapshot of Brammer's work desk soon after he took a job with the Long News Service in Austin, in the spring and summer of 1963, providing articles on Texas politics to the *New York Times*, the *Los Angeles Times*, the *Chicago Sun*, and several Texas dailies:

> a green paperback entitled *Sex-Starved Slut*; a sealed can of Betty Crocker cake icing; a Wyamine nasal inhaler [a nasal decongestant used as a stimulant]; a tin of Dexedrine; a two-pack of Twinkies, wrapped in cellophane; a yellow vial of RUSH amyl nitrate . . . three empty green bottles with prescription labels for pills [no one had ever] heard of; a white bottle labeled "Black Mollies"; and an unopened half-pint of Jim Beam.

These details appear in a short story by Tom Walker based on his work experience with Brammer. Eventually, Brammer disappeared from the news service as he had vanished from Janeway's organization and from *Time*. Like so many other ambitious young writers, Walker hoped Brammer would help him place his fiction with an agent. Courteously, Brammer made promises he couldn't possibly keep.

Meanwhile, Larry McMurtry had moved to Houston to take a temporary teaching position at Rice University. Brammer followed him to the city and, "with the use of many blankets, made himself an air-conditioned cubicle in the garage," McMurtry said.

A week or so later, Brammer drifted back to Austin. Just two years earlier, he had published one of the most critically acclaimed novels ever written by a Texan; publishers continued to call him with offers; he retained journalistic credibility; his community saw him as a hero—and yet, increasingly by choice (or as a result of choices he made), he was living largely like a homeless person. "He was still *sort* of Establishment, but he was poised to drop completely out of society," Sidney said.

He found a small apartment. A fellow he had met, Bill Beckman, a freelance cartoonist (later famous for cofounding the *East Village Other*), became a frequent companion. Beckman created a strip entitled *Captain High*, in which a superhero with an *H* on his chest swooped into crime situations, making them infinitely worse. Then: "Enter Enig-Man," a character based on Brammer. Somberly, Enig-Man would survey the rubble left by Captain High and mutter, "Hm . . . "

One night Beckman took Brammer to a two-story Victorian house near campus, by Scholz's, at the corner of 18th and Brazos. He said he knew the girls who lived there—UT undergrads. Brammer would like them. One of those girls, Dorothy Browne, a sorority dropout and an English major, was sitting on the living room floor, writing a paper on *Tender is the Night* for a class on the American novel. "Beckman brought Bill upstairs and said, 'I want you to meet Bill Brammer.' And I went, 'Ah, be still my heart. O English major heart.' Everybody in town knew who he was," Dorothy told me. "I think I took the hair rollers out of my hair. And we talked and we talked and he said, 'What are you doing?' When I told him he said, 'You can come on over to my house and I'll help you write your paper. You can study. You can be at one end of the house and I'll be at the other end 'cause I stay up all night and write.' I *did* go with him that night, and the next morning his landlady came by, and because there was a chick in the house with him all night, she evicted him. So the first night I met him, I got him kicked out of his house. Luckily, the downstairs at our place was for rent. He moved in, and it just started from there."

The Fitzgerald paper he wrote for her earned a C+ for "poor sentence structure."

When his children weren't staying at Bob Eckhardt's house on stilts, Brammer brought them over. Dorothy and her two roommates "were all such beautiful women," Sidney remembered. "Shelby and I were just in awe." The girls played a guessing game: which of the three women would their daddy marry? One weekend, Bud Shrake and Gary Cartwright arrived from Dallas for a visit. "When we walked in [to his place], there were three coeds sleeping in T-shirts and panties on a mattress on his floor," Cartwright recalled. "Each one was a knockout. 'Uh, how you doin', Billy Lee?' we said. Not too bad, evidently."

Then Nadine heard he was about to receive $25,000 so that filming could begin on *The Gay Place*. She took him to court, claiming she had the "right to know how much money he had received for the sale" of the book. "I want every little tiny bit of information I can get to let me know when my children will get what is coming to them," she told the Austin paper. The legal proceedings ended when Nadine's lawyer dispatched a sheriff to Elizabeth McKee's New York office to snatch the check—and the movie never got made. The official explanation was that a change in studio heads scotched the plans. Brammer remained convinced for the rest of his life that Lyndon Johnson blocked the project through his aide Jack Valenti, who had forged strong ties with the Motion Picture Association of America. (Valenti later led the group from 1966 to 2004.)

Brammer used Nadine's subpoena as an excuse to skip town. He remembered Larry McMurtry's suggestion that he visit Ken Kesey in California. Kesey had recently moved into a log cabin in the woods outside La Honda (on the San Francisco Peninsula, due west of Cupertino), on Route 84 just across a little drawbridge from a place called the Boots and Saddle Inn. He had strung Christmas lights in the ponderosa pines surrounding the cabin, and he had created a large metallic bird, strung between trees, whose wings people could flap by pulling a rope. He had also constructed on the grounds a human figure out of scrap metal, a man in a *Kama Sutra* love position. A garden hose wove through his limbs, spraying copiously day and night so that the man appeared to be experiencing a perpetual orgasm.

Here, Brammer met Jerry Garcia and others who had chosen to get "on the bus," in Kesey's words, ready to follow the mantra that Timothy Leary would later bestow on the counterculture: *turn on, tune in, drop out*. The California sunsets painted everyone's faces a natural Day-Glo orange. In the low evening light, Kesey looked just like the Big Pumpkin—hulking, meaty.

Even for *him*, Brammer "ran at a pretty high gear" that summer, said the Merry Prankster. The gnome-like Texan gobbled acid. He began to inject speed.

While he was tripping in the woods, *Esquire* ran a piece announcing "what every American writer of importance is working on at this point in our literary history." Included with notes on James Baldwin, J. D. Salinger, William Burroughs, and Henry Miller is mention of William Brammer's "humorous Washington novel," *Fustian Days.*

When Brammer returned to Austin in the fall, he threw himself into guru mode more passionately than ever. "He was always giving someone a new book or an obscure magazine piece or a newly released record," Gary Cartwright said. "I first heard about Bob Dylan and Ken Kesey from Billy Lee." He would sit downstairs in the big Victorian house, watching three color television sets simultaneously, volume turned high—"just like his old pal Lyndon, staying up for days on end out of sheer visceral concern that he might miss something," said Paul Cullum, a journalist pal.

"I think he wanted to be the Ken Kesey of Texas," said Bob Simmons, whose path had crossed Brammer's at the Ghetto. "He would have been embarrassed by the analogy, probably, but I think if you stepped back and looked at it, that was what he had in mind."

He had already entered local lore. Now he secured his place in history. The "first vial of blue liquid . . . LSD-25 . . . had arrived in Austin," wrote the musician and cultural historian Paul Drummond. "Exactly who was the first to introduce it has become a point of issue. Tary Owens amongst others claimed it came via an unexpected source—Billy Lee Brammer."

Every one of his surviving friends still remembers him walking up to them, at one time or another, saying, "Close your eyes and stick out your tongue."

"Oh yeah, he was always very generous with his drugs," Susan Walker told me. Walker would become one of Brammer's best buddies. "I'm pretty sure he gave Janis her first acid."

# 15.

Janis lore maintains that the Alpha Phi Omega fraternity at the University of Texas voted her the "Ugliest Man on Campus." Actually, she merely received several votes in the contest, perhaps an even greater insult. How this came to pass is a matter of some dispute. A few people insist that she put herself in the running as a joke, but most of Joplin's friends recall her being devastated. A few weeks afterward, she recorded on a reel-to-reel tape at a friend's house in Austin a song called "It's Sad to be Alone": "The dusty road calls you. You walk to the end. / It's sad, so sad to be alone." Seven days later, she left town with fellow Ghetto-ite Chet Helms, a rather confused young man who couldn't decide whether Saint Paul or peyote was his religion. They hitched to his mother's house in Fort Worth. Mrs. Helms looked Joplin over—pink sunglasses, blue workshirt revealing plenty of cleavage—and kicked them out of the house. Helms's brother drove them to the western edge of town, near dusty, reeking cattle stockyards, and left them. The state of Texas had never done anything for Joplin except make her wish she had never been born.

She and Helms thumbed their way to San Francisco, rumored to be friendly to folkies. On her first night in the city, she sang at a place called Coffee and Confusion in North Beach. The crowd, used to the whispering lullabies of groups like the Kingston Trio, ate her up.

Meanwhile, Brammer's up-and-down celebrity ride continued. Texas bookstores invited him for readings. Billy Porterfield, a young aspiring writer, remembered seeing him in Houston following an autograph event: "He walked onto the dance floor of the International Room at the Montague Hotel with his new love, Dorothy . . . Everything was new. His white suit and ice cream shoes, his lady, his book and his fame. Billy Lee was matching Fitzgerald and Gatsby, and I envied him his moment because he was truly talented and he had arrived . . . [He] was upright, prevailing. It seemed to me his star would last the night. But then, I was only thirty myself."

Claudette Coleman, one of Dorothy's roommates, couldn't believe her friend was now seriously dating this "old man" (Brammer was thirty-four at the time). "But he's so interesting!" Dorothy would say.

*Darthy*, he would call her. *Darthy, my love.*

"He was the gentlest man I ever knew," she said. "He was someone you could tell anything to. And most people did."

He was bad news to her father. He earned no money. After graduating from the university, Dorothy lived with Brammer. She worked for a while at the state Capitol for a young congressman named Charlie Wilson. Then her daddy called her home to Houston.

Brammer drifted up to Dallas. His parents still lived in Oak Cliff—his father was as generous as ever with cash, his mother willing to fix him a meal—and his pals Bud Shrake and Gary Cartwright, both suffering through angry divorces, shared an apartment on Cole Avenue near the SMU campus. They let Brammer crash there amid the beer cans and the bread crusts and the bits of greenish lunch meat scattered about the kitchen. They were covering sports for the *Dallas Morning News*, the city's ultraconservative newspaper. The publisher, Ted Dealey, after whose family Dallas's downtown plaza was named, regularly referred to John Kennedy in editorials as a "crook, a Communist sympathizer, a thief, and 'fifty times a fool.'" At one White House press luncheon in Washington, Dealey told the president to his face, in front of dozens of the nation's top newspaper editors, "We need a man on horseback to lead this nation, and many people in Texas and the Southwest think you are riding on Caroline's tricycle."

The sports pages were intended to provide relief from politics, but Cartwright and Shrake didn't see their job that way. "To us, sports were too dumb to take seriously," Cartwright said. "We only reluctantly permitted the actual score of any game to soil our sterling examples of prose." Cartwright, in particular, used his columns to crusade for integration. "Texas Negro athletes" barred from Texas colleges "would have been credits to any Southwest Conference school, both as athletes and citizens," he wrote. "We've all watched too much Amos 'n Andy . . . [and this] begats ignorance." His editors warned him off the story. Each week he received threatening letters from the Klan. Brammer's old friends Ann and Dave Richards had moved to Dallas from Austin. Ann founded the Dallas Committee for Peaceful Integration; when Cartwright and Shrake joined their protest marches, alongside several black citizens, the *Morning News* editors kept an even more watchful eye on them, as did the FBI. This was not considered proper behavior among the established professional classes in Dallas.

"Rightwing nutcases had captured [the city]," Cartwright complained. "A gang of wingnuts had surrounded the front entrance of the *Times Herald* building, where a man in a monkey suit did a jig and railed against integrating the races. Others, led by Congressman Bruce Alger, clogged downtown sidewalks and [spat at the visiting] Lyndon Johnson . . . General Edwin Walker, who had been cashiered from the military for spreading right-wing propaganda to his troops, was carrying on his campaign of hate from his mansion on Turtle Creek Boulevard . . . [He] flew his American flag upside down, his way of signaling that the nation was in distress." Amid growing social tensions in the city, the police force seemed nearly absent. Among newspapermen, it was common knowledge that ever since the days of "Cowboy" Binion and "Cat" Noble, the forces of good in Dallas and the forces of vice were densely intertwined, bound by a bribery system based on gambling and prostitution money. Sportswriters openly bet on games in the newsrooms, hosting visits from men with names like "Big Circus Face, Puny the Stroller, and Jawbreaker King." They would drop by on Saturday nights to "check scores on the UPI sports wire and collect . . . wages," and no one worried about getting busted, Cartwright said.

The bachelor pad he shared with Shrake and Brammer became the go-to place on Saturday nights after favorite clubs like the End Zone on Lemmon Avenue closed. The "living room would be full of famous athletes, coaches, billionaires, nightclub acts, artists, hoodlums, drunks, writers," Cartwright said. Clint Murchison Jr., owner of the brash new pro football team the Dallas Cowboys, frequently partied with the boys, as did the team's star quarterback, Don Meredith. Murchison's buddy Bob Thompson often dropped by—one of *his* "dearest friends was J. Edgar Hoover, who made numerous secret trips to Dallas and nearly always stayed in Thompson's guest bedroom," Cartwright claimed (this, even as Hoover's local agents monitored the political activities of the Cole Avenue crowd).

Staffers from the mayor's office showed up at the apartment with plenty of whiskey. Jack Ruby was a regular visitor. Cowboy players and Dallas cops filled his Carousel Club each night, getting free booze and time with some of the girls. Shrake had met him in the dark walk-up club over a bottle of $1.98 champagne and introduced him to his pals. Ruby was a hard man to take seriously, with his John Garfield fedoras and his wormy little habit of slipping promotional cards for his club into people's hands as he shook them. He seemed a silly braggart, waving a blunt finger in someone's face—a finger bitten off in a bar fight when he had first arrived in Dallas in the forties—to insist what a "classy joint" the Carousel was. Still, he could be generous with his time and offers of favors for people he liked. He didn't smoke or drink, but shared Brammer's fondness for Preludin (a drug related to amphetamine)—it "makes you a positive thinker," he would say, "you don't have any inferiority, your reflexes are great."

Speed made everyone "smart and funny, or so it seemed at the time," Cartwright said. "I felt like one of those perpetual-motion gadgets you see in novelty shops, moving effortlessly as long as the batteries last." Five-milligram Dexedrine pills were as ubiquitous at the Cole Avenue parties as pot and alcohol. Cartwright and Shrake brought the pills home from the Dallas Cowboys' training room—three five-gallon tin buckets hung near the entrance to the practice field, one containing salt tablets, another lemon-flavored vitamin C, and the third "heart medicine." Players, coaches, and sportswriters grabbed it by the handfuls and gobbled the pink pellets like jelly beans.

Speeding, after days with no sleep, Brammer entertained partygoers with tales of his Washington days: airplane jaunts to Hyannis Port with JFK, eighty-hour poker games with the press secretary, Pierre Salinger, and journalists hacking in a furor of Corona Corona fumes. "There's a 'New Frontier' joke," Brammer would say. "A woman who made three unsuccessful marriages complained to her psychiatrist that her first husband was a writer and therefore impotent, her second was an outright homosexual, and the third—the one she'd had such high hopes for—was a nice young man who worked in the Kennedy administration and who, on their wedding night, simply sat on the edge of the bed till dawn telling her how good it was going to be." He said he had once seen LBJ take reporters to the family quarters in the vice president's house when Lady Bird was asleep, wearing only a slip. Johnson held the bedroom door open so the newsmen could get a good look. "That's the best little piece of ass in Texas," he said.

In fact, Brammer knew darker stories about LBJ, and it concerned him that hints of them were starting to make their way into the national press. Billie Sol Estes, the West Texas agriculture king whom Johnson had once warned Brammer to steer clear of, had just been convicted of mail fraud in connection with mortgages on nonexistent anhydrous ammonia tanks, totaling millions of dollars. In Texas newspaper circles, rumors had recently surfaced that Estes once hired a hit man named Malcolm Wallace to kill a US Department of Agriculture official. The official was investigating Estes's questionable cotton allotment transfers (the man's death was ruled a suicide, even though he had been shot five times with a bolt-action rifle and had ingested a lethal amount of carbon monoxide). Further, it was alleged that Wallace also worked for Lyndon Johnson, dispatching his political enemies. Brammer found these stories ludicrous—though he knew that Wallace *had* been convicted of killing a man in 1951, a man who had allegedly romanced Johnson's sister, Josefa. He had received a suspended sentence with the help of a lawyer retained by LBJ. What Brammer did *not* find hard to believe was that Estes had illegally raised money for Johnson, as well as for Ralph Yarborough, and that the mail fraud conviction might lead authorities to evidence of it.

Moreover, even before Brammer left Washington, he had heard that Bobby Kennedy was looking for a way to drop Johnson as vice president during JFK's second term. Now the press was reporting that LBJ's old Senate aide Bobby Baker had come under intense scrutiny over bribery allegations involving several senators. RFK was working this angle, not only to nail Johnson but also to pressure Baker into keeping secret the president's affair with Ellen Rometsch. It was rumored that a Washington insurance broker was ready to testify to the Senate Rules Committee that he had made payoffs to Johnson, arranged through Baker, in order to supply the insurance on a massive federal construction project. At Johnson's insistence, the man had bought advertising on LBJ's Austin television station; he had provided Lady Bird with a state-of-the-art stereo system. If these details were true, and if the Billie and Bobby stories broke big in the press, Johnson could be facing indictments as well as the end of his political career. Despite Brammer's estrangement from the man, he could not help worrying about the Big Pumpkin.

---

That damned jicky place.

Aside from plenty of new concrete and cookie-cutter retail outlets on several street corners, Oak Cliff hadn't changed much. At sunset, yellow light from the tall lamps along a thin black fork of the Trinity River cast a sickly glow on the weeds. Decaying old houses, reminders of the past's foolish optimism, loomed on purple bluffs above the bridge across the water. Austin's Barbecue still looked like the kind of fake barn front found on a movie set for a story about a talking pig or something. The Dobbs House Restaurant remained, square and bland, on North Beckley, leaking stale odors of vinegar and grease.

As Brammer strolled the dusty roads of the old neighborhoods up the block from his parents' house, he may or may not have known, from conversations at the Cole Avenue parties, that Jack Ruby lived in a small apartment on South Ewing—Brammer's sister, Rosa, rented out a couple of row houses nearby. Ruby was exactly the kind of fellow you would *expect* to be hunkering in a dark Oak Cliff niche, a man on the edge, taking whatever he could take from the world. His apartment would soon undergo a sea change—not physically, but emotionally, psychologically, as would the Dobbs House, when, under police questioning, a young waitress would testify that Lee Oswald ate breakfast there frequently, sometimes complaining about his undercooked eggs. Oswald's room, in a house on North Beckley near the Methodist hospital, also close to Rosa's rental properties, would alter as well. Similarly, the Texas Theatre, where Brammer had first held hands with shy girls and marveled at the false, winking stars on its ceiling. All these places would enter the national folklore, superseding the Oak Cliff stories Brammer had heard as a child, about the old hard roads, about bank robbers with glittering hearts of gold, about the ghosts of slaves rising with evening mists along the edges of the viaduct. Now the stories would tell of Oswald's erratic movements through these sun-shriveled neighborhoods—movements so frantic and numerous that it seemed there was more than one Oswald—of mysterious sightings of him with unidentified figures, maybe even conferring with the policeman he would later shoot on Tenth Street, of secret meetings in Jack Ruby's apartment before and after Oswald's murder in the basement of the Dallas Police Department, meetings involving lawyers, cops, and reporters, and the strange disappearances, in years to come, of all the men who had attended those meetings. The truth of these stories, and many more, can never be proved or discounted, but the power of folklore is its mystery, its obsessive focus on a single event and the endless effects of that event, like ripples on the river after a body is tossed in the water.

---

A scrim of dust and lint covered the small stage at the Carousel Club. As the girls shook their hips and stamped their high-heeled feet, big brown clouds rose into the spotlight glare. It was hard for the girls to finish their routines without sneezing. The dancers' dressing rooms smelled of dog piss; the kitchen's concrete floor was sometimes smeary with the animals' waste. "I'll keep my dogs where I want to," Ruby yelled whenever the dancers complained. He was much more solicitous of his canines than of his employees. Most of the girls didn't bother to wash their clothes during the week; they slipped in and out of their dresses so often between sets that they would simply splash layers of perfume on the fabric until the sweet-sweat smell nearly overpowered the rooms' urinous traces. If Ruby offered one of the girls a ride home after work, she would refuse. Who could sit in that awful Olds, its plastic upholstery ripped apart by those fucking animals? It was so bad that the springs popped through the seats. But you couldn't say anything to Jack. He called the dogs his children. No one was allowed to trash his kids. "Don't you have children?" he'd say. "Don't you respect them?"

His favorite, a dachshund named Sheba, he called his "wife."

Bud Shrake sized all this up on his first night at the club, when he met Janet Adams Conforto there—Jada was her stage name. Jada's act "consisted mostly of her dropping to her knees and humping a tiger-skin rug, making orgiastic sounds to the beat of recorded jazz in the background," Gary Cartwright said. "Though the act was the reason customers paid for watered-down, overpriced drinks, it nevertheless drove Ruby crazy. He thought it far too obscene for such a swanky joint as his." Mainly, he feared that the cops—some of whom were among his finest patrons—would close him up. "He was all the time pulling her aside and telling her to tone it down. Jada, of course, told him to get fucked." Ruby had recruited her from Madame Francine's famous club in New Orleans, where he knew the gangster Carlos Marcello, and where Jada, too, had mixed with petty mobsters, running drugs for them from Mexico. He paid her twice as much as his other girls, even as his fights with her over the explicit nature of her act grew more heated. It got to where he would turn out the lights on her performance. And yet he knew she was his top draw. "She was a remarkable woman, with hair the color of Florida oranges—unrestrained, it could reach the floor—purple fingernails that could have shredded an armadillo," Cartwright said. "She usually carried a pearl-handled .32 in her handbag and loved to drive around town in her Cadillac convertible, completely naked under a mink coat." "It was, he noted, "a better act than Ruby paid for." At regular intervals, she would cross over into Mexico—occasionally dragging, for cover, a clueless Texas legislator she had managed to seduce—and slip back through Customs "with hundreds of pounds of the finest manicured pot anyone had ever seen," Cartwright said. What she didn't sell or turn over to the mob, she gave to her friends in Girl Scout cookie tins.

Shrake began to date her. She would come to the apartment. The party boys, the football players, the mayor's aides scrambled to get near her. In his gentle manner—sometimes so quiet that Jada had to lean close to hear—Brammer asked her serious questions and listened intently to her stories. He discovered she had a shy side, a faltering insecurity behind the brassy face. In that regard, she reminded him of Janis. Sometimes, on party nights, rather than face a roomful of drunks, she would hike up her skirt and slither out a back-bedroom window.

On other evenings, she would complain about her difficulties at the club. The dog shit smell; that damned Ruby always gazing through the dressing room doorway at her, as if he didn't get an eyeful whenever she took the stage. It was such a bitch, she said, applying false eyelashes in the club's low light, especially when she was flying on coke.

She told Brammer, Shrake, and Cartwright that they were making a colossal mistake by laughing at Jack Ruby. He was much more dangerous than they knew. Cartwright admitted later how surprised he was to hear of Ruby's connections with Meyer Lansky; with Cuban gunrunners; with Santo Trafficante (who would brag of his involvement in the JFK assassination, an unsubstantiated strand of the national folklore); with the FBI, as a failed informant, too willing to play both sides of any situation to be of much use to the agency. Ruby had just seemed such a clown, eager for recognition of any kind.

In early June 1963, Ruby boasted to friends that he would soon pay off all his federal tax debts. When asked where he would get the money, he clammed up. Later, Seth Kantor, an investigative journalist, reported that Dallas police lieutenant Robert L. May Jr. documented, for Police Chief Curry, a series of meetings that month at the Carousel Club between Ruby and a "large group of Chicago racketeers." We now know that, perhaps coincidentally, Chicago racketeers were holding meetings all over the country. These events took place within a few months of a visit to Bobby Kennedy's office by two CIA officials, who told Kennedy to stop the Justice Department's prosecution of a Sam Giancana associate. When Kennedy asked why, the officers told him that "the CIA had enlisted the gangster in a plot to assassinate Fidel Castro." The lines between certain parties in the US government and the mob—what Bobby Kennedy referred to as the private government—had blurred. We also know that Sam Giancana had been sleeping with a woman named Judith Campbell, who had shared the president's bed. Through her, and through the electronic wiretapping equipment the CIA provided Giancana, he was able, later, to track the president's travel plans before they were publicly announced, his movements from Chicago to Dallas. We know that a credible plot to assassinate John Kennedy in Chicago was discovered by authorities—apparently, it was scrapped for logistical reasons. We know that Giancana and his partners Santo Trafficante, Carlos Marcello, and Jimmy Hoffa had all expressed murderous rage at Bobby Kennedy for his relentless prosecutions of organized crime; we know that Hoffa had floated the theory that bumping off Bobby would bring the full power of the federal government down on them, but if JFK were somehow erased from the picture, Bobby would be just another lawyer.

Brammer, Shrake, and Cartwright heard none of these things at the time, but they did know, from Jada, that Ruby had expressed intense dislike of Bobby Kennedy—in contrast to the remarks he would make, following his arrest, that he had moved against Oswald out of love and sorrow for the Kennedy family. They knew the power of folklore to both reveal and conceal. They knew from their experiences as reporters that facts can slap you in the face and still you might overlook them. *No conspiracy that big could be kept hidden by so many players for so many years*, official history has claimed. A persuasive argument—but that was just it, Brammer would answer. None of what we now know was ever really secret. We knew it all along. Was Jack Ruby just a clown, or was he a seriously dangerous man? He was both, Gary Cartwright would tell you. And still it proved nothing.

On October 24, 1963, in downtown Dallas, Ann and Dave Richards attended a speech by Adlai Stevenson, extolling the United Nations. Stevenson was greeted, first, by "well-dressed young matrons" reminiscent of the Mink Stole Mob, jangling "their arm bracelets" and swamping Stevenson's words, Dave Richards said. Then raucous shouting began. "Kennedy will get his reward in Hell. Stevenson is going to die. His heart will stop, stop, stop. And he will burn, burn, burn," someone yelled. "Communist!" Traitor!" According to Richards, "a long banner was unfurled behind Stevenson which proclaimed 'Get the U.S. Out of the U.N.' The banner was positioned on the stage in such a way that it seemed as if it could only have been placed there with the assistance of the city personnel in charge of the facility." As police escorted Stevenson to a waiting limo, a woman spat in his face. Another hit him with a placard proclaiming, "If You Seek Peace, Ask Jesus." The crowd rocked his car before he was able to get away. "Are these human beings or animals?" he exclaimed.

"When Ann and I finally got out of the hall, we faced a group of men dressed as Nazi storm troopers marching in the lobby," Dave Richards recalled. "I went head-to-head with one of the Nazis. Weeks later, after President Kennedy's assassination, I was convinced that my confrontation had been with Lee Harvey Oswald." Whether this was really the case or an example of "just how deranging the place called Dallas could be in 1963," he couldn't say for sure later.

Stevenson, who knew the president planned to visit Texas within just a few weeks, urged him to stay out of Dallas. "There was something very ugly and frightening about the atmosphere," he reported to Kennedy's aide Arthur Schlesinger Jr.

---

Kennedy felt forced to visit Texas. He needed to settle the spat between Lyndon Johnson and Ralph Yarborough. LBJ had not been the southern vote magnet that Kennedy had hoped he would be—southerners *turned* on Johnson for joining Kennedy's camp. He was no longer a viable asset. Yarborough might be in a better position to deliver Texas to Kennedy in the next election; liberals had gained significant strength in the state's Democratic Party, and Yarborough was their man. Johnson, sensing his loss of control over the state's apparatus—his last grip on power—clashed with Yarborough at every turn. His prospects for prevailing looked bleak, especially in light of the pending investigations into Billie Sol Estes and Bobby Baker. Richard Nixon was telling the press that he thought JFK would drop Johnson from the ticket because he had become a political liability. LBJ would love to have seen "that little shitass" Bobby Kennedy reduced to being just another lawyer.

Jack Kennedy hoped to solve his election problem, retain the loyalty of both Senator Yarborough and Vice President Johnson, and secure the full trust of the Texas Democratic Party. It was a daunting task, and it would play out in a city that Adlai convinced him was "nut country."

---

The president's entourage arrived first in San Antonio. Reporters noted how incredibly thin he appeared. He gave a speech about the New Frontier: "It is an era which calls for action and for the best efforts of all those who would test the unknown and the uncertain in every phase of human endeavor. It is a time for pathfinders and pioneers." Lyndon Johnson stood behind him, noticeably inattentive, gazing into space, focused perhaps on his problems.

The president's car passed a small black boy on the street holding a sign: "G.I. families are segregated in San Antonio."

Next, a flight to Houston. Confederate flags flew along the roads into town, next to signs saying, "Texas Belongs to the South," "Coexistence is Surrender," "Kennedy, Khrushchev, and King," and "Watch Kennedy Stamp Out Your Business." At a gala dinner that night in the Rice Hotel, Nadine and Bob Eckhardt greeted the president and the First Lady. JFK talked about the nation needing "three times as much electric power as it has today, four times as much water, and that is why we are developing [several] Texas river projects . . . [and] creating Padre Island seashore." Jackie gave a charming little speech in Spanish. It was "more Castilian than the kind of Spanish we hear down [in Texas], and on this account it was difficult to understand, not only among those of us who know little of the language, but also among some of the Latin Americans around me [that night]," Ronnie Dugger reported. "But that did not matter, nor dampen the *Vivas* for her."

As the dignitaries left the hotel after dinner, they encountered several signs on the streets: "Cuba is a Cancer—Are We Going to Operate?"

Nadine turned to her husband. "I hope nothing happens to the president while he's in Texas," she said.

In both San Antonio and Houston, Ralph Yarborough refused to ride in the same car with Lyndon Johnson. The president insisted that in Dallas, damn it, they would sit together in the motorcade as a sign of unity: "It's ride with Lyndon—or walk."

The next morning, November 22, in Fort Worth on the way to Dallas, the president gave a speech recounting the increases he had ordered in military spending: more Polaris submarines, Minuteman missiles, strategic bombers, nuclear weapons, tactical nuclear forces, tactical fighter wings, combat-ready army divisions, strategic airlift capabilities, and special counterinsurgency forces in South Vietnam. Most of the pool reporters tittered about Jackie's strawberry pink dress and pillbox hat rather than take notes on the speech. Someone handed her a fat bouquet of roses. As Kennedy walked to the small plane that would take him on a short flight to

Dallas, an official gave him a Stetson. "That hat protects you against your local enemies," he said.

Earlier that morning, Kennedy had told his wife, "It would not be a very difficult job to shoot the president of the United States. All you'd have to do is get up in a high building with a high-powered rifle with a telescopic sight, and there's nothing anybody could do."

The previous week, his Secret Service detail, scouting locations, recognized that it was going to be shorthanded and would have to rely on local law enforcement for protection. It worried the president would be a sitting duck in Big D.

On the streets of Dallas, on the morning of November 22, protesters circulated hundreds of handbills featuring two grainy photos of Kennedy, mug-shot style, above the caption, "Wanted for Treason"—an effort coordinated by General Edwin Walker. At Dallas's Love Field, a man in the crowd waved a large Confederate flag. Kennedy moved from person to person, smiling and shaking hands. Ronnie Dugger wrote in his notebook, "Kennedy is showing he's not afraid."

Congressman Henry Gonzalez of San Antonio, who had accompanied Kennedy's entourage, said to an aide, "Well, I'm taking my risks—I haven't got my steel vest yet!"

Lyndon Johnson carried notes for a speech in his pocket, intended for delivery that night at a dinner in Austin. The speech concluded: "And thank God, Mr. President, that you came out of Dallas alive."

Nothing was secret. We knew it all along.

Glumly, Ralph Yarborough climbed into the backseat of a car with LBJ.

---

Midmorning, Bud Shrake arrived at his office at the *Dallas Morning News*. The day's edition had just printed, in detail, the route the president's motorcade would take through the city. It had printed an ad featuring a large picture of Kennedy surrounded by a thick black border and a list of grievances, the gist of which was that Kennedy had sold out the country to the communists. The ad had been paid for in part by one of the Hunt brothers, who were among the state's richest oil families, another of whom sponsored a right-wing radio show on KLIF. As Shrake glanced at the ad, he looked up to see Jack Ruby standing by his desk. Ruby wore one of his gangster fedoras. "I just want you to know that I'm not angry at you," he told Shrake.

The night before, Shrake had been sitting in his apartment with Brammer and Cartwright when he received a strange phone call from Ruby.

"Don't let that woman in your apartment anymore," Ruby said. "You better stay away from her if you know what's good for you."

Shrake asked, "Are you threatening me?"

"Oh no, I didn't mean for you to take it that way," Ruby answered. "I'm just telling you for your own good."

Now, in the *Morning News* office, he followed up with Shrake: "I just want to warn you about Jada. She works for the mob, you know, runs cash for them and runs dope for them. She can get you in really big trouble in no time."

The men chatted for a few more minutes, and then Shrake said he was going to go find a spot on the street to watch the presidential motorcade.

We know, from his account and from Cartwright's, where they were the rest of the day. They found a spot together near Turtle Creek. They waved at the president. "Kennedy looked directly at us, his famous grin flashing like a polished diamond," Cartwright said.

Shrake wrote, "The president's grey eyes . . . took me all in with an instant's deep gaze . . . and his lips moved a bit, the smile broadening, and he raised a finger and pointed at me . . . A communication flashed from him to me that said there you are you freak what a time you must have among these people I like you for it don't give up."

We know from the *Warren Commission Report* all of Jack Ruby's movements that day. At about the moment when Cartwright and Shrake were waving at the president, Ruby was still at the *Dallas Morning News*, placing an ad for the Carousel Club.

We know that Dave Richards walked from his law office to the corner of Main and Elvay to watch the motorcade. "The scene was a disaster," he said. "For whatever reason, incompetence or malevolence, the Dallas police had not cleared the street of vehicles. A city bus angled away from the curb was partially blocking Main Street, and no meaningful crowd control was in evidence." Ann, who had scored a ticket to the president's scheduled speech at the Dallas Trade Mart, awaited his arrival at the reception.

We know, from a Dallas police memo typed on stationery graced with the phrase, "The only reason you and I are here is to assist the people of Dallas," that at 10:45 that morning a pedestrian was struck on Atwell Street by a white Cadillac bearing Louisiana license plates and driven recklessly by a woman who "gave the name of Comforto or Contorto." She said she was a dancer at the Carousel Club (no longer true—Ruby had fired Jada). When asked whether she could be reached there that night, she informed the officers that the club would be closed—a curious detail:

it was Friday; numerous visitors were in town because of the president; the Carousel could reasonably expect a surge in business. The woman seemed frantic. According to the memo, she said, "Let's hurry up and get this over with, I have got to get to New Orleans." And then, like Janis, she scurried the hell out of Texas.

We know where all these people were. We don't know Billy Lee Brammer's whereabouts. He always claimed that he was riding in the second press car behind the president that day. He said he went to Parkland Hospital and was standing in the halls when doctors declared the president dead. He said he made it to the police basement, two days later, when Ruby shot Oswald. Journalists and historians have repeated his assertions as fact, but these writers have admitted to me they have no source other than Brammer, and they cannot corroborate his stories.

His name does not appear on any of the official rosters of news personnel assigned to cover the president that day. He was not, at the time, directly employed by any news outlet. Ronnie Dugger, assigned to the second press bus, did not recall seeing Brammer in the motorcade or at the hospital, but this meant nothing, he told me: he wasn't paying attention to other reporters, many of whom he knew. Gary Cartwright said he did not remember Brammer talking about the motorcade back at the apartment, but admitted that "memories of that day are pretty sketchy." He *did* recall the many phone calls Brammer received, right away, from New York publishers, all of whom wanted him to write articles or books about the new president, Lyndon Baines Johnson.

Was Brammer scamming publishers (as he had developed a nasty habit of doing by then), exaggerating his closeness to the story? Perhaps, but the phone calls attest that he did not need to do this. His LBJ connections gave him plenty of cachet. The publishers were coming to *him.*

One of the strongest arguments for his reliability was his restatement to Nadine, toward the end of his life, that he was indeed part of the motorcade that day. He no longer had any hope of impressing Nadine or of securing a publishing deal. There was no reason to lie at that point.

In any case, Billy Lee Brammer's movements in November 1963 entered Texas folklore, and there they will remain.

If he *was* in the second press car, or on one of the two media buses, he would have seen people suddenly break and run down Elm Street in the direction of the underpass. He might have witnessed, as Ronnie Dugger did, "a motorcycle policeman . . . rough-riding across grass to the trestle for the railroad tracks that cross the underpass." "He brought his cycle to a halt and leapt from it and was running up the base of the trestle when I lost sight of him," Dugger's notes recount. All the reporters were shouting, "What happened?"

We now know that as the motorcade passed through the little green patch of Dealey Plaza as the clock on the Hertz sign atop the Texas School Book Depository hit 12:30, John Connally's wife, Nellie, sitting in front of JFK in the limousine, turned to Kennedy and said, "Well, Mr. President, you can't say that Dallas doesn't love you."

We know that seconds later Kennedy raised his hands to his throat in a gesture of extreme distress, but he continued to sit stiffly upright in the rear seat of the car, unable to move quickly because of a canvas back brace he wore, a restrictive shoulder-to-groin contraption; he had recently torn a "groin muscle while frolicking poolside with one of his sexual partners," according to Seymour Hersh.

And then, as Bud Shrake wrote, "Pieces of skull sailed out of Kennedy's head. A red spray flew out as if a stone had been thrown into a pot of tomato soup."

Two cars back, Ralph Yarborough and Lyndon Johnson huddled together for safety.

A few moments later, at the emergency entrance to Parkland Hospital, Yarborough told Ronnie Dugger and a handful of other reporters, "I heard three loud explosions, like a deer rifle . . . You could smell powder . . . I decline to describe their condition. They were shot. It is too horrible to describe. They were seriously hurt . . . I can't tell you where . . . This is a deed of horror. This is indescribable."

Improbably—or maybe not—Jack Ruby was lurking in the hospital halls, wearing the fedora he had on that morning in the newspaper office, asking reporters he knew whether they thought he should close his club that night.

Other reporters said they had seen the president's limousine in the hospital parking lot. It was covered with blood and the scattered roses from Jackie's bouquet. Hugh Sidey, Brammer's old boss from the Washington Bureau of *Time*, entered a narrow hallway, saying he had just heard that two Catholic priests had given the president the last rites. Doug Kiker, a stringer from the *New York Herald Tribune*, shouted, "Goddamn the sons of bitches!"

Lyndon Johnson insisted that no announcements be made until he was safely on Air Force One.

Ronnie Dugger left quietly and filed his report for the *Texas Observer*:

"If a city has a conscience, Dallas is searching its conscience now... People there are trying to find words and purpose for their shame, or to deny it in suspicion that their fears have come to pass. A stricken city, confused, frightened, condemned the nation over, Dallas is now its own problem, and many of its people very well know it."

*City of hate*, Americans were calling Dallas now, according to the wire services.

"It wasn't a city of hate," Gary Cartwright wrote many years later. But "it was ignorant... [and] it had the heart of a rodent. In the subterranean tunnels of those proud spires of capitalism and free enterprise crawled armies of conmen and hustlers, cheap-shot artists and money changers, profiteers and ideologues, grubbers, grabbers, fireflies, eccentrics, and cuckoos. Dallas was just like every place else, except it couldn't admit it."

---

"Take the play away."

This was one of Jack Ruby's favorite phrases, learned as a child in rough Chicago neighborhoods. It meant: *Always hit first. Seize the initiative. Don't hesitate.*

Brammer, Shrake, and Cartwright had heard him say it many times.

Whatever play Ruby was hoping to take away now, he didn't appear to be impulsive about it. He became an immediate and persistent presence on the third floor of the municipal building once Lee Oswald had been apprehended in Oak Cliff's Texas Theatre and brought there for questioning. "[Ruby] was always at the center of the action, passing out sandwiches, giving directions to out-of-town correspondents, acting as unofficial press agent for District Attorney Henry Wade," Gary Cartwright said. He was also carrying a pistol. "Twice during a press conference Wade mistakenly identified Oswald as a member of the violently anti-Castro Free Cuba Committee. The second time a friendly voice at the back of the room corrected the D.A. 'No, sir, Mister District Attorney, Oswald was a member of the Fair Play for Cuba Committee.' The voice was Jack Ruby's. How did he know that?" Cartwright said.

Many people milling about the third floor wore red badges, indicating they had been part of the Kennedy motorcade. They all looked as though they had been shot through the heart. The water fountains, coffee machines, and soft drink dispensers had all been emptied or quit working. The hallways were starting to smell as sweaty-dank as the dressing rooms at the Carousel Club. Will Fritz, the stoic police captain who had once tracked Bonnie and Clyde and was now in charge of questioning Oswald, stared at the gaggle of reporters as if he wanted to march them all into Turtle Creek, but an officer near one of the stairwells was busy handing out press passes to anyone he thought he recognized or who could convince him of his legitimacy.

The ACLU asked Dave Richards's law partner to see whether Oswald wished legal representation. From his cell, Oswald sent back word that he wanted nothing to do with the ACLU.

Two days later, Cartwright and Shrake were in Cleveland to cover the Dallas Cowboys–Cleveland Browns game. No national tragedy was going to prevent the NFL from earning its profits. "When the team was introduced . . . at Memorial Stadium, some people booed and yelled insults, but most of them sat in silence, wondering what sort of people these were who could murder a president and then have the audacity to come play a football game," Cartwright recalled. Earlier, as he was pulling his briefcase and typewriter from the trunk of his car at the stadium, Shrake met him in the parking lot. "Have you been watching TV?" he asked. "That guy Oswald, the one they arrested?"

"What about him?" Cartwright said.

"Someone just shot him in the basement of the Dallas police station. And you'll never guess who it was."

"Jack Ruby," Cartwright said.

"The name just slipped out of my mouth," he wrote many years later. "Hundreds and maybe thousands of times I have reviewed that reply. What was I thinking? Why did Ruby's name slip [from] my lips? I didn't really think that Jack Ruby had killed anyone. Or did I?"

Brammer—a witness, he claimed—never wrote a word about the shooting. He never explained how he could have gotten into the basement that morning, though it wouldn't have been hard to do so, in all the confusion. Maybe he *did* have a press pass by then, from an officer on the third floor. Or maybe he bluffed his way in, like Jimmy Turner, a director for WBAP-TV in Fort Worth, who flashed a Sheraton Hotel drinking party pass at one of the harried guards. Or maybe he just walked down the stairs from the main building unchallenged, like Ike Pappas, a New York City radio reporter. It has remained a mystery how Ruby—armed—gained entry undetected, if he *was* undetected. Said Jesse Curry, the Dallas police chief, "It just seemed like an act of God that Ruby got in there."

"You all know me. I'm Jack Ruby," he said, sounding almost hurt, after he had pulled the trigger and been forced by several men to the ground.

A short time later, police officers located his white Oldsmobile parked nearby, in the 2000 block of Main Street. Uncharacteristically, he had left its doors unlocked. In it, among the eaten-up seats, was Sheba the dachshund, a holster for his snub-nosed pistol, a stack of parking tickets, $837 in cash stuffed in a paper sack, and several hundred promotional photographs of Jada.

Folklore's pleasures rely, in part, on the turning points in the narrative that change the characters' fates. Accordingly, the events of late November 1963 in Dallas, Texas, altered the courses of many lives. After hinting that he would spill all his secrets if he could be guaranteed federal protection ("I have been used for a purpose"), and after making several suicide attempts in prison—once by sticking his fingers in an electric light socket—Jack Ruby would die in Parkland Hospital on the eve of a new trial. The official cause was cancer, though he had complained of being poisoned. Jada would die in a traffic accident in Albuquerque, one of several JFK-related figures, according to the lore, to perish in mysterious circumstances.

The investigations into Lyndon Johnson's possible crimes soon ceased—*Life* magazine canceled a planned cover story on the allegations against him—and he finally achieved his cherished goal of becoming president of the United States.

The life of the nation would never be the same. "The subtext of everything I've written over the past thirty-something years cannot escape the gravity of the 60s, specifically the unparalleled weirdness a lot of us experienced when John F. Kennedy was assassinated in what was essentially our neighborhood," Gary Cartwright would say. "I think of the event as a great power outage . . . Until the assassination, everything in my world seemed clean, transparent and orderly. Nothing has seemed clean, clear, or orderly since."

He well remembered the day that he returned from covering the football game in Cleveland to find Billy Lee Brammer beaming in the Cole Avenue apartment. Publishers had been clamoring for him. The *Ladies' Home Journal* wanted him to write a profile of the new First Lady. James Silberman, the editor who had suggested the ghostwritten Rayburn memoir, was now working at Random House; he was ready to offer Brammer an $11,000 advance plus $1,000 for each completed chapter of an LBJ biography. Brammer grinned shyly. "I think I hit the jackpot," he said.

# 16.

Darthy, my love, I'm off to Washington, Brammer said.

Dorothy asked, What are you going to do with me?

He answered, Well, I'll just marry you and take you with me.

"I thought, 'Sounds like fun,'" Dorothy said. Life with Brammer was one "seamless" party. He owned twelve Brooks Brothers suits. "He loved to go shopping. It was great," Dorothy said. "Every time he'd get some money he'd go buy things. Twenty record albums, books, color TV. He was indelibly materialistic, but he'd give you anything. He certainly had an appreciation for the best in life." And, she believed, he was about to deliver on his literary promise by writing a biography of the new president—and earning even more money as fresh publishing offers arose. In meeting his children, she had to meet Nadine, who she found "scary as shit." Nadine and her friends were like the "witches in *Macbeth*," Dorothy said. "They were older, and they were rangy and mean and beautiful and smart." But Dorothy loved Sidney, Shelby, and Willie, and she would be living on the East Coast, thousands of miles from Nadine. She bought a pillbox hat for her wedding and talked her reluctant father into hosting the ceremony in his Houston house in early December 1963, just a few weeks after the Kennedy assassination and Brammer's new good fortune.

"[Dorothy's] father was, as I understood it, a fairly typical Texas businessman, in that he wanted nothing but the best for his little girl," Jay Milner recalled. "Billie Lee was a decade or so older than Dorothy . . . [and he] sure didn't look very prosperous." Aware that the prospective in-laws were plenty anxious, Brammer's friends "solemnly vowed to be on their best behavior at the wedding." Brammer's best man—a last-minute arrangement, since many of his friends couldn't make it to the hastily planned ceremony—was a British-born classics professor at the University of Texas named John Sullivan. He had a "bawdy laugh . . . [and] looked like Alan Bates in his prime," Celia Morris said. "Like the Beatles, fellow Liverpudlians with his gusto and whimsy, . . . [he] relish[ed] absurdity in whatever forms he found it." The character Godwin Lloyd-Jons in Larry McMurtry's fifth novel, *All My Friends Are Going to be Strangers* (about a promising young writer ruining his life), was based on Sullivan—an Austin college prof who refers to undergraduate girls as "fuckists." Celia was married to Willie Morris at the time, but she and Sullivan were having an affair. Brammer was the only person in whom the couple confided, over beers at Scholz's.

Sullivan "decided it would make a most admirable impression upon the family and friends of the bride for him to escort as his date to the wedding festivities a brilliant young lady lawyer . . . who was attracting attention around Austin those days because of her brains and eloquence. Her name was Barbara Jordan," Milner said. In 1966, Jordan would become the first African American woman elected to the Texas Senate. LBJ would consult with her regularly on his civil rights speeches. Many years later, only her failing health prevented Bill Clinton from nominating her to the Supreme Court.

Said Milner, "I can just imagine Dorothy's father's reaction when he came to the realization he was throwing what was doubtless the first integrated wedding on his block."

---

From January until April 1964, Brammer and Dorothy lived in the basement of Glen and Marie Wilson's house just outside Washington, DC. Meanwhile, fortunes had turned for several of Brammer's old friends. Bud Shrake moved to New York to write for Roy Terrell at *Sports Illustrated*. Willie Morris had become a new associate editor at *Harper's*. Gary Cartwright would move to Philadelphia to write for the *Inquirer*. Larry L. King had resigned his job as a congressman's aide to write full-time; right away, he sold a piece to Morris.

Along with most of the country's major magazines, *Harper's* expressed intense interest in whatever Brammer might produce on LBJ. Naïvely, Brammer assumed he could walk into the White House and interview all his old colleagues from Johnson's days in the Senate. George Reedy, now LBJ's press secretary, told him he was persona non grata—the only journalist in the nation officially denied access to the president. "Billy just couldn't believe it," Dorothy said. "Hardly anyone would talk to him. People he'd known for years. Everyone said it was . . . because of Lady Bird, but he never really knew." Reportedly, Lady Bird was "upset about Fenstemaker. Thought it was literally Lyndon."

Brammer never got near Johnson, Dorothy said. "What really hurt me was I took out of the novel everything that made the sonofabitch the sonofabitch he was, but the sonofabitch got mad at me anyway," he later told a friend. The *Ladies' Home Journal* abruptly canceled its agreement with Brammer.

Johnson, already campaigning hard against the Republican Party for the fall election, was struggling to keep JFK's former staff loyal to him and to prevent his bad blood with Bobby Kennedy from poisoning his political agenda. He had good reason to be wary of reporters, particularly those he believed had betrayed him in the past. The Bobby Baker scandals would soon pass, but not without frantic maneuvering by Johnson and his staff to quell rumors that Baker had provided abortion services for congressmen and the "girls" he had paired them with. LBJ wanted no word of these allegations to reach the press. Within a short time, he would be forced to arrange damage control over the arrest of his faithful aide Walter Jenkins. Jenkins was caught in a YMCA men's room performing oral sex on another man.

One imagines LBJ wishing to banish *all* journalists from his presence—any reporter could be bought with a cheap bottle of whiskey, he had always maintained. The scandals came on top of the normal interdependency of government and the fourth estate, which was often "grating," Harry McPherson said. "Was there another country whose leader was under such unremitting surveillance? . . . To succeed with the public, the President needed favorable attention from the press; to do its job the press needed news from the President. That they depended on, and yet constantly failed each other, made for mutual resentment."

Johnson complained one day to former president Harry Truman that his staff members weren't organized well enough to counter ambushes by people "put[ting] out these mean books . . . question[ing] my integrity and my honesty."

In point of fact, Brammer had handled him much less harshly than most other writers. Three books published in 1964 by far-right-wing authors strongly condemned the president. Phyllis Schlafly would severely slash Johnson's New Deal policies in *A Choice, Not an Echo*; John Stormer in *None Dare Call It Treason* accused the government of communist leanings; and J. Evetts Haley's *A Texan Looks at Lyndon: A Study in Illegitimate Power* revived rumors that Johnson may have masterminded murders in the Billie Sol Estes case. Haley charged Johnson with manipulating the Warren Commission and deliberately whitewashing evidence of a conspiracy—a conspiracy, Haley hinted, that may have involved Johnson.

By contrast, *The Gay Place*, released in paperback in 1964, depicted its "LBJ character . . . warmly," said *Time* magazine. Fenstemaker was "a little cruder than the real-life Lyndon, maybe kindlier, and he [stood] head, shoulders, and ten-gallon hat above all the other heroes of current political fiction." *Time*'s reviewer concluded, "The President might want to take another look at . . . [the] book." He ought to be "proud" of his portrayal in it.

But, like an errant son, Brammer had disappointed him. Johnson's grievance was personal. He could not forgive his "boy."

Was Brammer devastated by this rejection, so broken that he could never really write again, as the Billy Lee Myth has asserted ever since? "Sort of," Dorothy averred. "But, you know, the truth is, I think he burned out writing *The Gay Place*. He set up an office with collages on the walls and a typewriter and all the stuff to be a writer, but he'd stay up all night, and you'd just hear the electric Smith-Corona all night long, and in the morning, half of it was x-ed out." His increasing drug use only made the *X*s more numerous.

In late March, he *did* manage to write a review for *Book Week* on a volume of speeches by LBJ. Brammer began:

> Few men in our history have assumed the glorious and appalling burdens of the Presidency with the zest and confidence and maniacal energy of Lyndon B. Johnson . . . [He] does not seem significantly changed . . . by his experiences of the last three years since his rise to the Vice Presidency . . . He seemed from the first moments of awareness to have devised and maintained an attitude, a plan of operations . . . that could only have come to him through those powerfully developed instincts and interior qualities for which he is . . . famous.

The canned speeches collected in the volume disappointed Brammer. The real Lyndon Johnson could never be contained or conveyed by a prepared text. Brammer recalled fondly the impromptu moments he had witnessed as an LBJ aide, "a Burnet County Fair, a fish fry, a banquet in some dusty little gymnasium packed with more citizens than the town itself could claim." In such settings, when Johnson was connecting directly with people, "high on his own chemistries, smelling out his audiences," he could be endlessly captivating, and he held the crowds in "delicious thrall."

In part, writing this review was, for Brammer, an exercise in nostalgia—and an (unsuccessful) attempt to ingratiate himself with the White House. To publishers, it was further proof that Brammer understood the new president better than any writer in the country. He received a flood of responses to the piece—from *Harper's*, from Knopf, from Harper and Row, even from the publisher of the speeches, who noted ruefully that Brammer had slammed the book but clearly knew his subject better than anyone. They all solicited new work from him. None appeared.

Dorothy quickly soured on Washington: "I thought it was boring 'cause it was office gossip all the time. I was twenty-three, and it was weird for somebody my age who hadn't been much in politics before to live in Washington when everyone was breathing Johnson . . . Larry King was a good friend of ours, and Bob Novak, a bunch of folks . . . You know, it was fun, it was exhilarating, but it was also boring to me. I remember, before we came back to Austin, we had about two hundred dollars in the bank and we spent a hundred and fifty of it on a standard poodle. We were broke."

It wasn't despondency over LBJ that prompted Brammer to suggest heading back to Texas. "He figured if he was going to get so much money from the promised book advances, then we could live on that much money a lot longer in Austin, where our friends were, anyway," Dorothy said.

Brammer packed his typewriter, his rough drafts, and his notebooks. From that moment on, he would never again wear a Brooks Brothers suit.

---

The couple found a large apartment to rent in West Lake Hills in Austin. Once more, Brammer set up a study with his typewriter and stacks of blue, green, and pink paper on a cluttered desk, but nothing ever got finished. "Oh, I tried everything [to help him write]," Dorothy said. "Being furious. 'Okay, Billy Lee, we had thirty-one people in the house last night, none of those people again, they stay out of here, you're going to work!' Or I'd take a soft line, put food on the tray at his typewriter. 'Would you like a back rub?'"

To try to jump-start himself, he traveled to New York, hoping to rustle an assignment with Willie Morris at *Harper's* or his old boss, Roy Terrell, at *Sports Illustrated.* He wound up hanging out with Bud Shrake, introducing Shrake to his first vial of liquid LSD. High on the stuff one night, Shrake ran into two thugs on the street. They demanded all his money. "All my money?" Shrake stammered. "Well, I can't give you all my money right now. Some of it is at home. Some of it is in the bank. We could go to my house." Irritated by his rambling talk and frightened by his wide-eyed stare, one of the thieves muttered, "This guy ain't right," and the predators wandered off.

Together, Brammer and Shrake visited Millbrook, Timothy Leary's acid colony, based at a sprawling private estate just outside New York. They sat and watched "Leary in a white robe wandering through piles of totally doped out people on the vast lawn in the middle of the night," and then they left, Shrake said.

Returning to Austin, Brammer tried to maintain regular relationships with his children. Grudgingly, Nadine granted them short stays with him. "We would sleep at his apartment for weekends or overnights," Sidney said, "and I would become almost hypnotized by certain albums that he would play *all night long* while he worked, probably because he set the replay arm of the turntable. Some that come to mind: Johnny Hartman and John Coltrane, Trio Los Panchos, Stan Getz, Ahmad Jamal's 'Poinciana,' Chet Baker, Keely Smith, Ella Fitzgerald, Harry Belafonte." Nadine worried about releasing her kids to Brammer, even for just a few hours, because she saw what a sensualist he was: He "wanted to see, smell, feel and do everything there is to do. He was always going beyond any kind of limit." As for her, she was already restless in her marriage to Bob Eckhardt. "If Bob and I had been mature, thinking adults, we never would have married so quickly, or perhaps not at all," she said later. "I felt we had to deal with our growing problems: his daughters' difficulties regarding his new marriage, my feelings of unhappiness at being excluded at his daughters' request." But he would not agree to attend therapy sessions with her. His solution to marital tension was to drink. And Nadine was pregnant. On September 18, 1964—the day J. Frank Dobie, once Texas's greatest literary giant, died—she gave birth to a baby girl, Sarah. In spite of all their troubles, "Bob and I were proceeding on course, politically," Nadine said. "The tensions caused by our family problems didn't deter us from our mutual goal: getting him elected to [the United States] Congress . . . He had a wide group of supporters among Houston liberals, and although conservatives didn't like his politics they respected him personally. Bob was politically wily. He knew how to play to the media and get the most exposure out of an issue. He had good ideas but he sometimes lacked follow-through, relying on others to implement his actions."

That would be *her* job.

---

When he had come back from Washington—apparently rejecting, from that point on, any pursuit of steady, "respectable" employment—Brammer became a "flower child who never let his hair grow long or costumed himself for the part," Milner said. "[His] demeanor remained quiet and reserved. He was never verbose the way most diet pill addicts were. He listened and watched, somewhat tenaciously. People were always saying, 'Look at Billie Lee over there watching us.' I think most assumed he was gathering material. But looking back, I think he was living inside his head."

Milner noted it "wasn't a bunch of spaced-out druggies doing all this partying around Billie Lee . . . These were young, ambitious, sometimes hardworking journalists, trial lawyers and politicians who mixed and mingled with the college crowd. They were intellectually bent and liberally inclined, with a professional underdog here and there, and maybe one or two basic conservatives, tagging along for the good times."

Superficially, it looked as though Brammer had traversed the social arc from elite culture to counterculture: in fact, his trajectory proved that these apparently separate worlds were alike. The counterculture *was* the culture.

Bruce Jackson, a young sociologist studying folk music in the Texas prison system, came to know Brammer and attended a gathering at the West Lake Hills apartment. He described the experience in an article in the *Atlantic* entitled "White Collar Pill Party":

> Next to the candy dish filled with Dexedrine, Dexamyl, Eskatrol, Duspatal . . . near the 5 lb. box of Dexedrine tablets someone had brought, were two bottles. One was filled with Dexamyl Elixir. Someone took a long swallow from the latter, and I thought him to be an extremely heavy user, but when the man left the room a lawyer told me the man was new at it. "He has to be. One mouthful is like two pills, and if he was a real head, he'd have a far greater tolerance to the Dexedrine than the amobarbitol, and the stuff would make him sleepy. Anyhow, I don't like to mess with

barbiturates much anymore" . . . He took a drink from the Dexedrine bottle and said, "And this tastes better. Very tasty stuff, like cherry syrup. Make a nice cherry Coke with it."

Dorothy said she would fill her grandmother's antique cut-glass bowls with colored pills for the parties. Jackson watched guests pass around a copy of *The Physician's Desk Reference* as if it were the Bible and discuss the effects of mixing certain drugs, experimenting thoughtfully, in a spirit of scholarship and adventure. The atmosphere was mellow, the talk of politics and philosophy. "The group considered few human frailties totally gauche, but going to sleep was surely one of them ('You're not going to sleep, are you?')," Jackson wrote. Dorothy patrolled each room, flashing silver coffeepots.

"There [was] nothing wild about the party at all," Jackson reported. "None of the playing around and sexual hustling that several years of academic and business world parties had led me to consider a correlative of almost any gathering of more than ten men and women: no meaningful looks, no wisecracks, no accidental rubbing. No one had spoken loudly, no one had become giggly or silly, no one had lost control or seemed anywhere near it. Viewed with some perspective, the evening seemed nothing more than comfortable."

These were "socialized amphetamine users," disdainful of noisy, drunken affairs that got out of hand. At one point, Brammer passed around a small dish of capsules—"One a Days," he called them. Watching him, Jackson understood that Brammer didn't just wish to get high; he was "interested in perceiving the drugs' effects. He is an experimenter. Often he seems to be interested as much in observing himself experiencing reactions as he is in having the reactions."

The ritual was important: the use of a holy book (the *PDR*), the counsel of a medicine man, the communal sharing of sacred substances. Secret knowledge of trade names, contraindications, and optimum dosages was as prized as a sports fan's obsessive recitations of ERAs and batting averages. Observing Brammer that night, Jackson concluded that the dedicated pillhead took drugs not to escape but to "have an experience that is entirely one's own . . . No explanations or excuses [were] needed for what happens inside one's own head when one is turned on."

Brammer told him, "You'd better research the hell out of [this phenomenon] because I'm convinced that the next ruling generation is going to be all pillheads. I'm convinced of it. If they haven't dysfunctioned completely to the point where they can't stand for office. It's getting to be unbelievable. I've never seen such a [social] transformation in just four or five years."

---

Soon after Brammer's return from New York, Dorothy's former roommate Claudette married a man named Hugh Lowe. Claudette had worked for a while as a teacher; Hugh had served in the Peace Corps and dabbled in journalism (eventually, he would become a lawyer). Following their wedding, they decided to pool what money they had and go to Manzanillo, Mexico. "We were there for a month, and we got kind of bored, so we called Dorothy and Bill and said, 'Come.' So they came down and spent the rest of our honeymoon with us," Claudette said.

"I had written Bill a letter about all the vials or whatever the hell they called all that stuff on the shelves of the pharmacies there, and that prompted him to want to come to Mexico," Hugh recalled. "He showed up with the *PDR* under his arm. He was ready." Incrementally, laws were changing in the United States; new federal regulations required doctors and pharmacies to keep better track of Dexamyl prescriptions. Prices were going up. A gram of dextroamphetamine that used to sell for 50¢ was now bringing $10 at the corner druggist's. A $30 pound of Dexedrine could now fetch as much as $4,200 on the black market. Inexorably, for financial and political reasons, white-collar pill parties were beginning to resemble backroom speakeasies. Addicts were being redefined as criminals rather than as persons suffering from an illness.

So Brammer fled to Mexico as if seeking paradise. "He couldn't speak Spanish," Claudette said. "He'd walk into a pharmacy and point: 'I want that one!'"

"He was a real word player, and he just made up his own translations for things," Hugh said. "There's a Spanish phrase, *solamente una ves*, which means, 'Only one time.' Bill interpreted it as, 'I am merely a flower pot.' There was a slogan for Coca-Cola, *refresco mejor*, meaning, 'It refreshes better.' To Bill, *refresco mejor* meant, 'Give my girlfriend a drink.'"

He and Dorothy had brought with them the standard poodle they had bought in DC. They called her Rosebud. One night, a festival took place in a little village off the beach. Fireworks crackled in the sky, frightening Rosebud. She ran off. Frantically, Brammer enlisted the villagers to help him find the dog. With broad hand gestures, he signaled that he would offer some kind of reward. "The people were dragging every dog they could find up there, 'cause, hell, they got plenty of dogs," Hugh said. "They didn't know anybody ever try to *find* a dog. So somebody asked Bill about *la cola*. *La cola* is the tail—what color was Rosebud's tail, they wanted to know. And of course Bill took it literally: 'Cola? *Si*! Pepsi for everybody! Anybody who finds the dog—Pepsi-Cola!'"

In late 1964, when Brammer and Dorothy stayed with the Lowes in Mexico, the Pacific coast between Manzanillo and Zihuatanejo had not yet been trampled by American tourists. Electricity was sketchy inside the sandy little cove shacks. There was only the *shush* of the ocean, the cries of pelicans and gulls. Occasionally, on the radio, accordion music from one of the border stations. A smell of salt and brine. Bright green dawns exploding over distant black mountain peaks.

The novelist Robert Stone would make a similar druggy trip to Manzanillo with Ken Kesey, Ken Babbs, and Neal Cassady just over a year later. Of the atmosphere of the place he wrote:

> The high-intensity presence of Mexico was inescapable. Even in the barrancas of the wilderness you felt the country's immanence. Poverty, formality, fatalism, and violence seemed to charge even uninhabited landscapes . . . On certain mornings when the tide was low and the wind came from the necessary quarter, you could stand on the beach and hear the bugle call from the naval base in the city . . . The notes of the Mexican call to colors were pure heartbreak. They always suggested to me the triumphalism of the vanquished, the heroic, engaged in disastrous sacrifice.

Sometimes in the evenings on the beach, Brammer and Hugh enacted battle scenes and parody Broadway skits for their wives, using seaweed scraps, umbrellas, and costumes. They laughed, they joked, they chased the dog, they spent all their money—but Brammer didn't write much. As Stone would later say of Kesey, "It was impossible to tell if [this was] a stage of literary development, a personal Gethsemane, or an apotheosis. Some fundamental change seemed to be taking place in the world, and as he . . . watched the lightning flashes and the fires of [a distant] volcano, he pondered what his role in it might be."

---

Banished from the White House, Brammer turned from politics and embraced what he took to be a broader, more profound social revolution than any legislation could produce. But never, ever was he unaware of Lyndon Johnson.

On November 4, 1964, James Silberman of Random House wrote Brammer, at the Fraccionamiento Peninsula de Santiago in Manzanillo: "Just in case you didn't see the papers—or don't read Spanish—I know you'll be pleased to hear that your friend Mr. Johnson will be our President for the next four years at least. That means a book about him is still current. I wish I knew somebody that was writing one."

Johnson's decisive defeat of Barry Goldwater in the fall election followed his legislative victories in Congress, the passage of the Civil Rights Act, his declaration—finally freed by the Oval Office from the necessity of pleasing the Texas Democratic Party—that "I'm going to be the President who finishes what Lincoln began." It followed a stirring speech in New Orleans in which he chided southerners for their backward treatment of blacks ("Whatever your views are, we have a Constitution and we have a Bill of Rights, and we have the law of the land"). Brammer had watched parts of the speech on a flickering television set in Manzanillo. He called it the highlight of the autumn campaign, "a highlight any way you look at it . . . It galvanized me. I was ready to go out and kill. That's how great he was."

Step by sleepless step, Brammer was *tuning out. Dropping out.* Yet the Big Pumpkin still had the power to move him. Within a few months of Jack Kennedy's murder, Johnson wanted a slogan he could stick in his speeches to propel the nation "toward some distant vision—vaguely defined, inchoate, but rooted in an ideal as old as the country," said Richard Goodwin, a former JFK speechwriter. LBJ called Goodwin and Bill Moyers to the White House swimming pool one day. Goodwin said, "We entered the pool area to see the massive presidential flesh . . . the deep-cleft buttocks moving slowly past our unstartled gaze. Moby Dick, I thought." "'It's like swimming with a polar bear,' Moyers whispered." Johnson called to them, "Come on in, boys. It'll do you good," and he insisted they craft a phrase that would articulate his ambitions for a progressive social agenda. The "Great Society" was born.

From a bar in Manzanillo, on a black-and-white television set with just enough electricity to function intermittently, Brammer—in spite of his disillusionments, in spite of whatever he felt toward the man, a potent mix of anger and regret, of brotherly love—thrilled when Johnson challenged his listeners:

For a century we labored to settle and to subdue a continent. For half a century we called upon unbounded invention and untiring industry to create an order of plenty for all of our people . . . [Now] in your time we have the opportunity to move not only toward the rich society and the powerful society, but upward to the Great Society . . . For better or for worse, your generation has been appointed by history . . . to lead America toward a new age . . . So, will you join me in the battle to give every citizen the full equality which God enjoins and the law requires whatever his belief, or race, or the color of his skin . . . Will you join me in the battle to build the Great Society?

# 17.

"We were one of the generations to which the word 'Romantic' might be applied—the offspring of a period inclined by history to highly value the Dionysian and the spontaneous, to exalt freedom over order, to demand more of the world than it may reasonably provide. We saw—may we not be the last to see—this country as blessed in its most generous hopes," Robert Stone wrote. "Our expectations were too high, our demands excessive . . . Excess is always a snare for those who demand much from themselves or from life. Excess, in fact, is characteristic of romantics, of romantic generations."

Brammer well knew the histories of romantic generations, of their relationships to literature and to the lives of their nations. He had studied the eighteenth-century German writer Novalis, who said the cause of excess was "a higher sensibility": "All sicknesses resemble sin in that they are transcendences . . . Man wanted to become God"—and who could blame him? Man turned into God by taking opium or drinking wine. Brammer knew that Thomas De Quincey's *Confessions of an English Opium-Eater* (1821) equated higher consciousness with dream states; the book insisted that opium-induced writing—the use of "sympathetic ink"—was the surest way to trace the "faint and visionary colours" of one's otherwise unreachable dreams. Brammer understood that the fantastic tales of E. T. A. Hoffmann, of Poe and Baudelaire, came in part from the mythopoetic influences of opium or alcohol, that surrealism was born of drug-based trance states, that the holy madness of the Beats had been largely narcotic fueled. He learned that he was not the first to host the equivalent of a white-collar pill party, that the artistic world of nineteenth-century Paris frequently staged dignified, proto-psychedelic evenings: "My dear Théophile," the painter Fernand Boissard once wrote to the writer Théophile Gautier, "hashish will be taken at my house, Monday, September 3rd . . . Do you want to participate? If so, arrive between 5 and 6 at the latest. You will have your share of a light dinner and await the hallucination."

Brammer was not the first to retreat into the woods, like Ken Kesey or Timothy Leary, or to find a deserted beach where he could supercharge his consciousness and commune with his dreams. But even a romantic—especially one who was running out of money—could pine for "the worst things" of the world. Brammer wrote Ronnie Dugger from Manzanillo: "I miss . . . football games, TV shows, tamale dinners, most especially Dr. Pepper."

In early 1965, he and Dorothy returned to Austin.

---

In San Francisco, Janis Joplin and Chet Helms "walked right into a speed crowd," said Helms. Augustus Owsley Stanley III, who would become the West Coast's LSD guru, was running a methamphetamine lab. Joplin's new friend Linda Gottfried offered her handful after pretty handful of Owsley's pills; each time they took them, "We thought we were growing by leaps and bounds," Gottfried said. "We worked night and day. We did more paintings, more poems, and more songs." Another new friend of Joplin's, Diane Di Prima, said speed "made a particular kind of art, and a particular aesthetic, happen." Joplin put it this way: "A lot of artists have one way of art and another [way] of life. They're the same for me."

But by the spring of 1965, she weighed eighty-eight pounds. She wasn't sleeping, she wasn't eating. Her friends feared she was going to die. They threw a bus-fare party for her so she could ride back to Port Arthur, to her parents' house, and recuperate. "She gave me all this propaganda about going to college and becoming a secretary, going straight and never again trying to be a beatnik," said her high school pal Dave Moriaty. But Port Arthur was never going to welcome her. "She *still* looked different," complained Bob Clark, another old acquaintance. At about the time Brammer came back to Austin, so did Janis Joplin. Despite her professed desire to "will herself to be the kind of person who wanted that white picket fence . . . it didn't fly," Clark said.

Austin was changing. "The different threads of the underground were starting to coalesce, as art students, rock 'n' roll kids, beer-drinking cowboys and introspective peyote eaters all mixed and mingled, and country, blues, and folk, rock 'n' roll and R&B all went into the same pot," wrote the music journalist Ben Graham. At the center of it all, working as a silent catalyst, was Billy Lee Brammer: "Close your eyes and stick out your tongue!"

"I still don't know Bill's LSD connection. He had the stuff straight from Switzerland. He spread it all over town," said Madeleine Villatorro, the wife of Joplin's buddy Tary Owens. She did not believe that Brammer was just another bystander at the scene; he was, in fact, helping facilitate Austin's changes. "Meeting Bill was seminal for me—as it was for everyone else," she said.

Brammer and Dorothy would soon move into the Daniel H. Caswell House at 15th Street and West Avenue, near the campus and the Capitol. The Caswell House was a large turn-of-the-century late-Victorian/Colonial Revival home built by the former owner of a cotton oil manufacturing company. It had porches on two stories built on rusticated piers. At one corner of the house, a conical turret rose into the air. The place was falling apart—the couple rented it for $250 a month. Along with the Ghetto, it served as Austin's crossroads of enlightenment and diversity: the "social swirl of the liberals, the 'independents,' the academics, the folkies, the Rangeroos, the spelunkers, the writers, and of course the wild abandon that arrived with the availability of the birth control pill," Henry Wallace, a local musician, told me.

Brammer's drugs "landed like an electrical pulse," said Ed Guinn, a musician who would soon cofound one of the nation's first psychedelic rock bands—a band that Brammer would briefly manage. "The drugs just shook the whole strata of society. What was discreet and proper changed dramatically. It was not unusual for nineteen- and twenty-year-olds to be hanging with thirty-five-year-olds and having the same experience. I remember meeting lots of older people at Billy Lee's . . . Wavy Gravy, Jules Pfieffer, Congressman Charlie Wilson . . . Charlie, he smoked dope . . . We were all heads, on the same level, with the same understanding of political and social dynamics. There were plenty of narcs around, too, but we didn't have that paranoia back then. There was an old guy—he'd come round us up to shoot armadillos on the west side of Austin, 'cause he'd grown up shooting stuff. Maybe he'd been in Vietnam, I don't remember. But we'd get loaded and go shoot with him. There was a lot of that intermixing."

As for the affable host: "Billy Lee was a good old head," Guinn told me. "A good guy to be around. Comfortable. He was more sophisticated than all of us."

"Billy Lee was incredible," said Tary Owens. "We were all trying to have open relationships [back then]. But we hadn't learned yet that it causes too much pain . . . We all had to learn that the hard way." Billy Lee "was the only person about whom you could say, 'He stole my wife and I'm not mad at him.'"

"He was married to Dorothy. I was twenty-one or so. I'd been married to Tary for two or three years," said Madeleine Villatorro.

> Bill was living in that house on West Avenue at the time we got together. Tary was having an affair I didn't know about. He encouraged me to take LSD with Bill one evening. Bill was a very sweet person. A romantic type. He must have met a lot of women. He was a good listener. He was genuinely interested in what you had to say. He'd work hard to draw you out. I remember we talked about movies. He was very much into film. He said he used to go to movies with his mother when he was growing up. That's what he did with his mother. We spent the evening together. With the LSD, I didn't think of him as my guide, really. I just wanted to know more about him.

Dorothy knew he was having affairs. "He would do this thing about, 'I'm impotent . . . Well, honey, you can try, but I don't know if it's gonna work.' Lots of young girls fell for that. *Lots* of young girls," she said. He would play the old man addled by drugs; but in fact, he felt like Balzac—"to live means to spend oneself, more or less quickly," using whatever stimulants will lead you into a state of "extraordinary cerebral exaltation." It wasn't that he wasn't writing—every night, all night, he pounded out page after page, but then, "I'd wake up," Dorothy said. "He had an X on his Selectric typewriter . . . he'd just be holding it down, X-ing out everything he'd written. He'd write all night and have four sentences of it left by the morning."

He told a friend—acknowledging, perhaps, that the speed, which had helped him compose *The Gay Place*, was now working against him as an illness, pressuring him into compulsive perfectionism—that "a kind of new nitpicking disease [has] only recently descended on me."

---

"Writing is just so murderously hard for me . . . though my skull feels livelier than ever," he confessed to Larry L. King.

---

"When I was thirteen, in 1965, I had a vacation week from the boarding school in Austin that I was going to, St. Stephen's. Nadine and Bob lived in Houston, which was too far to go for a short break, so I went to stay with Bill and Dorothy," Sidney Brammer said.

> One of Bill's prized possessions around that time was a gigantic pair of stereophonic headphones. I was reading on his living room floor and felt him put these giant headphones on my head, and he asked, 'What do you think of this?' It was Dylan singing 'I Ain't Gonna Work on Maggie's Farm.' Now, I'd already become familiar with Dylan at that time via the radio, because I had a transistor with headset that I practically slept with, and I was a rock-and-roll station AM nut. So I knew 'Like a Rolling Stone.' But I had never heard the complete early Dylan albums. Well, I heard them that holiday, over and over.

On September 24, 1965, Dylan appeared at Austin's Municipal Auditorium with a band called the Hawks to perform a show that had been notoriously ill received at the Newport Folk Festival just two months before. Given the hostility to Dylan's new musical direction, given that this was Texas, he was nervous about playing Austin. Fearing snipers, two members of his backup band, Al Kooper and Harvey Brooks, quit the tour rather than play in the Lone Star State. "If they didn't like the president, what would they think of *this* guy?" Kooper said.

Dylan opened with a few solo acoustic tunes, and then he invited onto the stage Robbie Robertson, Rick Danko, Richard Manuel, Garth Hudson, and Levon Helm. They brought out electric guitars. They plugged in—and unlike audiences in other parts of the country, the Austin crowd "got it," Dylan said later. To date, it was the most enthusiastic response his electric music had received. Brammer loved the show. Gilbert Shelton, who was living in a carriage-house apartment behind Brammer's home, and Jim Langdon, a friend of Joplin's who was writing about music for the *Austin American-Statesman*, gave the concert rave reviews. KAZZ radio praised the performance. On the coasts, the die-hard folkies didn't understand what Dylan was up to, or they resented his tampering with folk purity, but "down South it was just another Saturday night," Helm said.

"It was so in-your-face," recalled Brammer's friend Angus Wynne, a twenty-one-year-old novice show promoter. "You couldn't really understand the words—quality concert sound systems were nonexistent back then—but you could feel the energy. It was like being knocked over by this big burst of sound." Wynne didn't know what he was doing, but encouraged by Brammer and others, he began to try to book name acts for Austin. After hearing "Like a Rolling Stone" on the radio, he checked the back of a Dylan record album and saw that the singer was managed by Albert Grossman. He called information, got Grossman's New York telephone number, and contacted him out of the blue. "When I . . . made my pitch, someone yelled to the other room, 'Hey, do you want to go play in Texas?' and someone yelled back, 'Yeah, sure.' That's how things went back in the days before big-scale national tours."

In Austin's music lore, Dylan's electric concert is often mentioned as a turning point in the city's musical maturation. But in fact, most of the local players—Henry Wallace (then known as Wali Stopher), Ed Guinn, Powell St. John, Jerry Jeff Walker, and Charlie Pritchard among them—were already intrigued by the "power of electric music," St. John said. "My thinking was that the sheer volume I could achieve electrically would compel people to listen to my message, whether they wanted to hear it or not."

Like musical blenders, amplifiers mixed folk riffs, cowboy yodels, prison laments, and the keening of the baby-done-left-me blues, patched in from the country on scratchy recordings by Mance Lipscomb, Lightnin' Hopkins, and Leadbelly.

Jerry Jeff Walker—"often surly, all too often drunk . . . commanded the management to turn off the air-conditioning so the crowd could hear his quiet songs," an "unreasonable demand" in Texas, Jan Reid wrote. Walker stood at the microphone all alone with his guitar, but his galloping folk style "fairly begged for bass and drum accompaniment. Though few people realized it, Walker sounded almost country."

"You're all just a bunch of fucking cowboys!" Sid Vicious of the Sex Pistols would chide an Austin crowd in 1978, but that was just it—in Austin, "cowboy" was more hard-core punk, more authentic, and more diversified than any of the showbiz anarchy pantomimed by Vicious. Austin's was a honky-tonk scene, a series of desperate gatherings in grimy watering holes to blow off steam at the end of the trail ride: in the mid-1960s, Texas's burgeoning psychedelic movement had lost none of that frontier ethos. Add to this the power of electricity—colored lights as well as the amplified music—stirred with the power of peyote, and sidewinder punk, and then Brammer came along, leavening the mix with LSD. On February 10, 1966, Jim Langdon used the term "psychedelic rock" in his Nightbeat column in the *Austin American-Statesman*, the first recorded use of the phrase; Austin had officially proclaimed itself the center of mind-altering sound-and-light experiences.

It all began with just a few people in just a few places. From Kerrville, Texas, came the core of the band the 13th Floor Elevators, raised on Baptist hellfire, Mormon modesty, and stories of Bonnie and Clyde's misadventures (one of the band members would eventually be shot to death in a domestic dispute), and enlightened by acid from Austin's streets: an amalgam of influences not just improbable, but damn near impossible, a music of weird, confused, unquenchable longing. Debuting in a club called the Jade Room, the Elevators "were the natural descendants of the country outlaws of the generation before them, and extolled the punk ethos a decade too soon," wrote Paul Drummond. Their songs were delivered with painful sweetness by Roky Erickson (fated to undergo shock treatments later, like Ken Kesey's misunderstood hero in *One Flew Over the Cuckoo's Nest*) and the eerie wail of Tommy Hall's electric jug. Up from Houston came the Red Krayola, dedicated to improvised sound collages, featuring Frederick Barthelme, the younger brother of Donald, who would soon make his name as one of the nation's most innovative short story writers (Frederick, too, would become a formidable literary figure).

A group called Shiva's Headband combined fiddles, harmonicas, jugs, and electric guitars on extended, half-improvised arrangements presaging the long, rambling sets of the Grateful Dead. In Austin's old honky-tonks, the Headband proved that hippie music could sell a lot of beer.

Brammer was particularly close to a band called St. John the Conqueroo, featuring, at various times, among others, Wali Stopher, Ed Guinn, and Powell St. John. For a while, the Conqueroo stayed in the Caswell House, using its vast rooms as rehearsal space, stocking its fridge with pitchers of acid-laced orange juice. Ed Guinn was a three-hundred-pound African American—the first "Negro" admitted into the University of Texas's Longhorn Marching Band. "They decided it was time they had a Negro, and I was the one. But I'll never forget that the first song they had me play in the band was 'Dixie,'" Guinn recalled. Within two months he had quit the Longhorns. Soon he dropped out of school. He had heard of the folk scene at Threadgill's (though Kenneth Threadgill, bold in so many ways, could not bring himself to let this big black man through his door). But

Guinn was warmly welcomed by the folkies turned acid rockers. "I felt no need to blow up their bucolic scene [at Threadgill's]. They were all my friends, anyway. I was already playing with all of them," Guinn said. Other clubs in town were slowly loosening their racial restrictions—the 11th Door featured Jerry Jeff Walker as well as Doc Watson, Lightnin' Hopkins, and Mance Lipscomb. The Conqueroo regularly played the I. L. Club on Austin's East Side, a mostly black venue (old men playing dominoes) suddenly filled with cracker hippies. "It worked," Guinn said. There were a few scuffles now and then, but the "place got pretty crowded, and Ira [the owner] was making money—as much money as you can make on fifty cents for a quart of beer. It was a slightly difficult marriage of the cultures, with the white guys busy protecting their girlfriends from the black guys, but basically it worked." While Lyndon Johnson was trying to engineer racial equality from Washington, DC, by passing the Civil Rights and Voting Rights Acts, Austin's psychedelic bands, high on Billy Lee's acid, were bringing the races together in joyous celebration of music. Neither legislation nor drugged euphoria could provide lasting solutions to the nation's social problems, but fundamental changes *were* occurring underneath the political hype and the hype of the media touting fads like, in 1967, the Summer of Love.

Men like Harvey Gann, head of the Austin Police Department's Vice and Narcotics Squad, claimed drugs were the greatest danger in the city's underground: "In 1955 you could name [all] the drug addicts. I only had four men on the vice squad and maybe two on narcotics, a small detail. [But] pretty soon things started developing . . . multiplying . . . spiraling." Others, like the city's surveillance officer, Burt Gerding, said the worst thing about the "Jack Kerouac crowd" was its political agitation—the ridiculing of authority, the antiwar statements in the underground comics floating regularly out of Billy Lee Brammer's house. The comics were drawn by "subversives" like Gilbert Shelton and published in the new alternative newspaper the *Rag*. But it was the integration of the races that caused the greatest tremors among Austin authorities, the potential power shift signaling that "majority" and "minority" might not mean much anymore, that economic order might no longer rest on recognizable social principles. "Nobody gave a fuck" about race or any other kind of difference, Wali Stopher told me: "We were in an alternate world with values opposed to the mainstream culture's worldview of how to live. What mattered was who had the best stuff at the best price or who had the money to buy whatever you had for sale. Nobody was filing income tax returns. We were just wheeling and dealing."

Shelton, Joe Brown, and Tony Bell (another Brammer tenant)—all formerly associated with the *Texas Ranger* and now with the more politically radical *Rag*—used earnings from their dealings to open what they called the Underground City Hall downtown, essentially a glorified head shop but also the headquarters of an imaginary gubernatorial campaign run by Oat Willie, a creation of Shelton's (with help from Brammer). Oat Willie's fictive biography had him attending the University of Texas but becoming radicalized after the Kennedy assassination and dropping out of society. His feet were permanently encased in a bucket of oatmeal on wheels. He never wore a shirt, and he was distinguished by his bulbous nose and caved-in chest. His campaign cry—conceived by Wali Stopher—was "Onward through the fog!"

To the city's officials, it seemed as though the underground economy, and its subversive political underpinnings, was an imminent threat to the traditional power structure. Surveillance increased around the Caswell House and the Ghetto. Those people were the "enemy" because they "started [a] cultural revolution, and I felt strongly about my culture," Burt Gerding explained. "The eyes of Texas are upon you—always!" the Ghettoites joked.

The clubs couldn't be closed for race mixing. They were careful to keep their liquor licenses up-to-date. So the places were often shuttered for "electrical violations"—vague charges of using too much wattage, too many cords.

Jim Franklin, a local artist who designed many of the first psychedelic rock posters for clubs in Austin and San Francisco, identified another source of worry for men like Gann and Gerding—their inability to understand the economic value system of this new "revolutionary" culture. "[It was] always an anticommercial scene. That's why most of the people who moved [to Austin] did so," Franklin said. "Most of the musicians are content to play the same clubs and just get by and smoke their dope and drink their beer. How do you take an atmosphere that's suspicious of capitalism and heavily anticommercial and market it?" (Perhaps this creeping attitude accounted, in part, for Brammer's growing passivity, as well.)

There were some exceptions to the rule—most notably, Janis Joplin. She returned to the stage, in Austin, in December 1965, at the 11th Door, just down the street from the New Orleans Club, where the 13th Floor Elevators were testifying night after night to the miracles of acid; on one occasion, Joplin sat in with them. By late May 1966, Chet Helms, hearing that she had rediscovered her performing ambitions, convinced her to return to San Francisco and audition for a band he was managing called Big Brother and the Holding Company. He assured her he could help her stay off drugs. He had become a rock-and-roll impresario, but even *his* pursuit of the dollar was halfhearted, spurred by a love of the music more than a love of money. And when, in just a short time, Joplin became a full-fledged star, nothing pleased her more than sharing her happiness with her old friends in Austin. "I'm the first hippie pin-up girl!" she wrote Tary Owens, referring to a poster of her nude that hung in dorm rooms all over the country.

Her pilgrimage, and that of Chet Helms, opened a rich cultural road between the Texas Hill Country and the West Coast. "There was a strong Austin to San Francisco axis," Willie Nelson said. "If San Francisco was the capital of the hippie world . . . then Austin was the hippie Palm Springs." Ben Graham agreed: "Much that would be celebrated and mythologized about San Francisco in the late sixties would be created by the hard work, talent and innovation of . . . Lone Star renegades," he wrote. Chet Helms and the Avalon Ballroom; Janis Joplin; Powell St. John and the rock band Mother Earth; Travis Rivers and the *San Francisco Oracle*. The 13th Floor Elevators and the Conqueroo played San Francisco, but—in the spirit of anticapitalism—made little effort to endear themselves to audiences there or to pursue the record deals suddenly gracing Bay Area bands that copied their psychedelic sounds. "We went out there and played in the park with Santana and Big Brother," Bob Brown, of Conqueroo, said. "We played better than any of them, but people just slipped right over us. 'We want the guys from California, bring on Big Brother.' And man, Big Brother was horrible. Those guys knew two or three chords apiece and couldn't even play those." Besides, "Haight Street smelled like piss . . . All the people we thought were running around with flowers in their hair were . . . lying around with needles stuck in their necks."

It was so much better in Austin, where the antimoney, antimedia ethos had—so far—prevented an excess of jealousy, competition, exploitation, grabs for attention. If the psychedelic illuminations of the Jomo Disaster Lightshow, created by the Austinites Houston White, Gary Scanlon, Travis Rivers, and Steve Porterfield, had been co-opted by Chet Helms and promoted by the press as San Francisco magic, well, that was okay, Chet was still one of *us*, and here in Austin the light shows were bathing our minds in brilliant rainbows, bringing us all together. "We found out that a strobe light could bamboozle a drunken redneck to the point that he couldn't throw an effective punch [at a hippie], and would sometimes even nauseate him to the point of regurgitating his beer," said Powell St. John.

No, it had never been about money—men like Harvey Gann and Burt Gerding would never get it.

Communion. That was the thing: "College frat boys, jazz musicians, hippies, older drinkers, cowboys . . . [and] it was, to me, surprising how well everyone got along," recalled Clementine Hall, wife of the 13th Floor Elevator's jug player. "I can remember one performance . . . There was a very odd phenomenon: we noticed that the kids were not dancing, but were standing in an orderly manner up front . . . At one point, they began, first a few of them and then all of them, rubbing the back of their necks. We did not attribute this to neck strain from standing too close to the stage, because even those pretty far away were doing it." Later, Tommy Hall said he had heard of a religious state, the Holy Ghost experience, Clementine explained. The Holy Ghost experience was "when a group or crowd of people suddenly and unexpectedly (and apparently independently of each other) all made the same gesture or action. This action was caused by a shared spiritual experience . . . He thought the kids were rubbing their cerebral cortexes because they were having a spiritual insight of some sort. He later jokingly referred to the event as being 'goosed by the cosmos.'"

---

Brammer still listened to jazz and classical records, Dorothy said, until one day a neighbor boy dropped by and gave him a copy of the Beatles' *Rubber Soul*: "From then on, it was rock 'n' roll all the time."

He had always shared his passion for new music with his children, particularly with Sidney, whom he saw often while she was boarding at St. Stephen's Episcopal School. "Since he was always a little ahead of his time, searching for the new, he could feel the culture changing," she said. "That meant, to some extent, seeing the end of the novel as a major cultural force. Around this time, he may have thought—about novels— 'Fuck this. I did it,' though from time to time he'd try out a new idea for a while. I never saw him depressed over the trouble he was having with his writing. Never remotely self-pitying . . . self-*deprecating*, yes."

She loved St. Stephen's, and her good grades made her eligible for a scholarship. Before the offer, Brammer had promised to pay her tuition—but then Nadine received a phone call from the school: "Bill had never paid the tuition and Sidney couldn't have the scholarship unless the previous year's fees were paid . . . typical Bill, living beyond his means in that old West Avenue mansion." She jumped into her car, furious, and drove to Austin from Houston with the intention of "beat[ing] him to a pulp," she said. "I entered the house like a madwoman yelling how he had betrayed Sidney. Bill, along with the hangers-on at his house, ran like cockroaches. I felt so sorry for Sidney because her father had let her down—though she didn't, and doesn't, want to think that."

"I couldn't stay mad at him," Sidney said. She was beginning to have adult conversations with her dad, sharing a mutual love of popular music and books. "I don't think I ever had a talk with him when he didn't turn me on to something new."

Addicts look for enablers, people they can manipulate in order to get what they want. From his children, and particularly from his oldest daughter, Brammer knew he could always receive forgiveness. The heartbreak he caused his kids, all their lives, was enormous. But the children were smart enough—and attuned enough to their father—to recognize that whatever absolution they offered him was willingly given, whatever the costs. "He told me, candidly, he had to take speed because it was the only thing that made him feel good," Sidney said. And she accepted that.

---

Bob Eckhardt could have paid for Sidney's schooling, but he continued to be a "cheapskate," Sidney said. He insisted he shouldn't have to support Brammer's kids. As for his *own* daughters, he and Nadine maintained a rigid stalemate with them. Rosalind, the youngest, "remained upset about our marriage," Nadine said. Eckhardt spent a lot of time alone with Ros, away from Nadine, while Orissa, the oldest, avoided them all as much as possible. Then the girls' mother committed suicide. "Bob certainly needed my emotional support," Nadine said, but the difficulties of raising her four children, trying to placate Eckhardt's kids, helping them cope with their grief, and keeping the house in Houston as well as the apartment in Austin when the legislature was in session took a toll on her. She sought relief by going after Brammer again for child support payments. She began an orderly record of all the bounced checks he had written. She threatened him with court. His defense was to erect a wall of good appearances. He told a newspaper reporter he was about to deliver to his publisher the manuscript of his long-awaited LBJ biography—the item made it into the *New York Herald Tribune*. From the Random House offices, James

Silberman wrote Brammer, "That certainly is cheerful news and we're keeping the office open 24 hours a day in anticipation of this event."

There was no LBJ biography.

Brammer did a favor for Bud Shrake in New York—he gave him a "letter of introduction" to Diana de Vegh, who had returned from Paris. Brammer hoped for favors in turn: "an Rx for heart medicine" and a well-paying assignment from *Sports Illustrated*. Shrake appreciated meeting de Vegh—"didn't make no grabs at her," he assured Brammer, adding, "[I told her] how you loved her. She 'ppeared to like that." He agreed that without "heart medicine . . . I get to feeling all sick and fainty and my head starts to bob . . . [A] famous arthur might be a big finely-muscled devilishly handsome guy on the outside but on the inside he is as skittery as a pregnant nun, consumed with fear and trembling." He was working on getting Brammer that prescription, but in the meantime, his editors at *SI* did have a story for him. So in August 1965, Brammer found himself hunkered in a small motel room in Los Angeles, there to profile a young heavyweight boxer named Amos "Big Train" Lincoln, Sonny Liston's former sparring partner. Big Train was born in Beaumont, Texas, but he fought out of Portland, Oregon. He had overcome a stained past—several service-station robberies—to become a legitimate challenger for the heavyweight title. Brammer liked the tall, skinny kid; Big Train appreciated Brammer's serious questions, his genuine interest. It was a good story, and Brammer was grateful for the assignment. Maybe he could pay Nadine enough to keep her off his back for a while.

Gary Cartwright had flown to LA to cover the Dallas Cowboys' summer training camp in Thousand Oaks ("We trained in southern California because there was no place in Texas that would allow black players to live during camp," said Pete Gent, a Cowboy receiver). Brammer phoned Cartwright and said that Big Train had "promised to introduce us to what they call soul food. We're going to a neighborhood called Watts." The men ate a gorgeous meal of steak, black-eyed peas, fried okra, cornbread, and apple pie. The following day, Watts was in flames. Brammer and Cartwright made their way back to where they had eaten, amid the tear gas and the National Guard troops. "We're tired of this shit!" an old black man with a "stubby gray beard" yelled at Cartwright. Another man screamed, "Cops treat black people like fucking animals."

Big Train sided with the people of the neighborhood. He took a chair and sat in the middle of a pawnshop with a shotgun on his lap to keep the shop from being looted in the rioting. "We let the devil in[to] Watts," he said. Brammer thought *this* was the story now, . . . but then he saw how Cartwright's account of the uprising got buried in the newspaper among classified ads. Black unrest was not a story that white readers were ready to hear, according to the editors. By then, Brammer had lost all interest in Big Train's bout with an unknown Peruvian fighter. Big Train himself no longer seemed to care. Brammer drifted back to Austin. No story ever got filed. Shrake, accustomed to Brammer's unreliability, didn't even bother to ask him about it.

Back in Austin, even the strobe-lit urban pastures where lions lay with lambs, mollified by fifty-cent quarts of beer, seemed to be crumbling under social pressures. Had the revolution been implemented too swiftly and with too much excess? Was it the race mixing, the mixing of rednecks and hippies, of whiskey and hashish, of young and old, of liberal and conservative, of politics and anarchy? Where was the center? Could it hold? On August 1, 1966, Charles Whitman, a twenty-five-year-old architectural engineering student and ex-Marine, decided the center was the UT Tower, and from its twenty-seventh floor he dispensed his judgment. He had been given the best of American military training; offered the finest American education; sold the best consumer products on the global market; prescribed the latest antianxiety amphetamines; and assured of his inalienable right to carry guns. From this mix, he hatched a plan to murder his mother and his wife, to climb the tower's stairs, dragging a footlocker full of weaponry and ammo, and for an hour and a half pick off people on the campus and the streets of Austin. Over fifty wounded. Seventeen dead. The first mass shooting in modern American history. A student ran into Scholz's, a few blocks away, screaming, "There's a sniper up in the tower! He's shooting people!" The midday drinkers laughed. "Yeah, right!" They raised their glasses of beer. Then they heard the sirens. People hid behind trees. Played dead on the curbs. There were no SWAT teams in those days—this was the incident that sparked the militarization of American streets—so people came running from their apartments and houses with hunting rifles, ready to return fire. Nurses in a nearby hospital thought somehow they had been transported to Vietnam.

---

Dorothy succumbed to the pressures building in her marriage: the all-night parties, the affairs. She was unhappy with Brammer for occasionally "imposing his will" on her, insisting on sex when she wasn't in the mood.

He responded that she was far too sensitive: "What if I had exposed you to one of Bud's orgy games, or needed a porno ritual to get it up?" he argued.

Her friend, and Brammer's, Fletcher Boone, a local painter, made a play for her, and she ran away with him to New York to stay in a fifth-floor walk-up in the East Village. "It's one of the moves I regret most in my life," she admitted. "It lasted about a month. Broke up Fletcher's marriage. Almost broke up ours."

From Brammer's point of view, it was one thing to have a fling in this period of open relationships, but quite another to take off with someone. This felt like the old days with Nadine. "He made up this thing . . . it was a novel he said he was writing. He sent me the pages," Dorothy said. "The hero's wife had left him for another man and moved to a fifth-floor walk-up in the East Village, and the hero had figured out how to get in the crawl-space above their bedroom and watch them at night. Billy Lee's letters would come and stack up, and they were devastating to me. And I'd go sit on the roof and, you know, with people burning cars in the street or something—it was New York—and read these letters. They were crushing."

He was injecting speed, sleeping only about three hours a week, stoking his suspicions, his bitterness, his paranoia. He signed his letters H. Melville, Braque, or Eric Clapton. In one conciliatory card, he told Dorothy he was "consulting with this shrink, who promises to disinter & unveil the *Real Me* . . . I keep arguing [with him] that messin' round hard with ladies is a drag . . . on account of how all them delicate, beautifully transitory lady parts don't turn me on, not remotely, being rather more strung out on the notion of their one or two damn-near indestructible Eternal Verities."

He stopped seeing the shrink after three sessions.

Alone in the big house in Austin, he brooded over advice he had received from Bud Shrake: "Women generally look for weakness in men; probe for the soft spot and vulnerability . . . Only a fool goes to a woman and says, 'I need you.'" In his notebook, Brammer wrote, "Shrake scares hell out of me . . . and I am just incapable of [his] sort of cool, nose-bleeding restraint. I am, rather, one of the world's foremost blurters."

To cheer himself up, he put his favorite quote from T. H. White's *The Once and Future King* in a brand-new frame and hung it prominently on the wall: "You may grow old and trembling in your anatomies, you may lie awake at night listening to the disorder of your veins, you may miss your only love, you may see the world around you devastated by evil lunatics or know your honor trampled in the sewers of baser minds. There is only one thing for it then . . . to learn. Learn why the world wags and what wags it."

He would take his kids to the Brick Row Bookshop, on a musty second floor above a drugstore called Faulkner's, and lose himself in old books. He tried to stay busy by managing the Conqueroo. Ed Guinn said, "He did two things for us"—in addition to supplying the band with dope: "He got us a gig on the San Antonio River at a club called, then, the Pink Pussycat. It was one of those failed sixties swingers' clubs, you know, 'swinger' in the sense of smoking jackets and cigarette holders. It was a gig with Doug Sahm and us. Then he got us a big write-up in the San Antonio paper, in the entertainment section. We had a cover photo with the band looking deranged."

Doug Sahm was a young singer-songwriter billed as the "Texas Tornado." He blended the hard-rock sounds of the British Invasion with Hank Williams's heartbreak ballads. Brammer imagined writing a "rocky roll" novel based around a character like Sahm. He dreamed of calling it *Rock of Aegis*.

He interested one or two publishers in the idea, Shrake said. Somehow, by flying to New York and arranging "great stacks of paper on the floor in a way that suggested . . . he had fifty chapters outlined," he convinced editors at the New American Library that he was nearly finished with *Fustian Days*. They offered him a $10,000 advance. (Texas sizzled, now, in publishing circles—Lyndon Johnson was president, and Katherine Anne Porter had just won the Pulitzer Prize for her *Collected Stories*.) Right away, Nadine got word of Brammer's advance, produced her records ("check dated August 19 . . . returned because of insufficient funds; check dated September 6 . . . returned because of insufficient funds"). She swore she was going to send all the documentation to Domestic Relations Court. Soon thereafter, Larry L. King mentioned in a letter to David Halberstam that "[Billy Lee] has disappeared into Texas Limbo again . . . of course, without writing a single one of the many lines he pledged to write if [NAL] would buy him": "He has got his parents trained so that they will not admit to knowing his whereabouts, nor even admit blood kin with him. One of these days when the Sheriff is gaining on him fast he'll pop out of the toolie bushes all goggly-eyed and abstracted and wanting to borrow $5 and to be hid-out. And of course I will loan him the $5, even if I have to borrow it, and will hide him out. For I am a Fool."

---

At about this time, Hugh Lowe landed a job doing public relations for the San Antonio World's Fair, Inc.—HemisFair '68—the first licensed world's fair ever planned for Texas. The event's theme was "The Confluence of Civilizations in the Americas." "I was head of the PR department, and I told them, 'Oh boy, Billy Lee is a top-notch writer.' I thought, 'I'll get his help on some of this stuff,'" Lowe said. So in late 1966, Brammer moved to San Antonio and found an apartment on Mulberry Street—a place designed by Allison Peery, the well-known architect in charge of creating many of the fair's pavilions. "I came back, tail between legs," Dorothy said. "'Just let me spend the night here,' I said to Billy Lee. He was gracious and let me come back home, and that was really the best year of our marriage, that year in San Antonio. I taught school, and he sort of worked at HemisFair. We still had rowdy times and lots of parties. But a lot of neat people worked at HemisFair, architects and historians and landscapers."

John Kriken, later a celebrated California architect, had been stationed by the army in San Antonio. "I found [it to be] a most interesting American city which was four hundred years old, with pieces of architecture that dated back to that time, and [it] had an incredibly beautiful river that went through the middle of it that had been landscaped by the WPA," he said. When he heard that HemisFair was looking for architects, he jumped at the chance to return to Texas. There, he met the "most interesting group of people . . . Allison Peery . . . Ralph Yarborough and Henry Gonzalez . . . Ronnie Dugger . . . All these people were cutting-edge liberals. It's not the way we think of Texas politics today." And then there was Billy Lee, the center of it all: "A really remarkable character. San Antonio was the beginning of my professional career, and Billy Lee was very much a part of that," Kriken told me. "Knowing him was a wonderful experience. He had a peacefulness and a calm that the rest of us didn't have. We were not in the same field of perception that he was. He always wanted to help and to do things for people. It was like he was always meditating and looking out for you: 'Is everything going okay?' And if it wasn't, he would at least talk to you about it. He was almost a father figure for others. A very quiet force." Kriken recalled getting too high at Brammer's house one night—he hadn't smoked marijuana in a while. "I walked outside and passed out. And Billy caught me before I hit the ground. He was quite athletic, still in good physical shape."

Lonn Taylor, an Austinite hired by the fair as theme development writer, knew Nadine and Bob because he had lived on Eckhardt's mother's property, in a renovated backyard apartment. Though he had spent many evenings at the Ghetto, he did not meet Brammer until he dropped by the Mulberry Street apartment. "The door opened and there was Bill, and very,

very loud rock music was blaring. You couldn't hear yourself talk," Taylor recalled. "I must have had a distressed look on my face. Bill came up to me with a pair of headphones in his hand and said, 'Here, this is what you need.' I put them on, and suddenly I was listening to Mozart. I thought this was the most thoughtful thing anyone had ever done for me. He was a sweet soul, a lovely, gentle man." And he seemed to know everyone. Taylor recalled seeing Dan Rather at one of Brammer's parties, leaning thoughtfully against the refrigerator.

But he knew Brammer wasn't cut out for the work. "[Part of our] job was to write proposals for commercial exhibits that would fit [the] theme—'The Confluence of Civilizations,'" Taylor said.

> Here is how it worked: the sales department would decide to approach the Goodyear Tire Company to buy exhibit space at the fair. They would come to me and say, "We want a proposal for a six-thousand square-foot exhibit for Goodyear Tires." I would sit down and write an eight-page concept statement about the history of rubber in the Americas; how the Mayas discovered it; how the Aztecs used it in their ceremonial ball game, etc. The sales department would take it to Goodyear and Goodyear would say, "Fellows, we're not selling Aztecs, we're selling tires. We want an exhibit with tires in it." I would then have to rework the concept statement to get tires into it. It was a highly frustrating job.

And Brammer had no patience with it whatsoever. Besides, he "regularly received packages containing bricks of hashish at his office address, sent through an embassy diplomatic pouch direct from Morocco," Taylor said. "At one point someone in the fair's public relations office circulated a list of adjectives to be used in press releases describing the fair. Brammer drew up a counter-list, which I wish I had kept because it would be a priceless piece of Texas literary ephemera. The only word I can remember that was on it was 'dithyrambic.'"

Brammer proposed a "Pavilion de Dope Fiend," showcasing people shooting up, preferably aided by "pre-pubescent noodie females"; also, the "Pavilion a Gone-Gone," "aimed at capturing the spirit and the enormous appeal of apple-cheeked, snug-dugged, tight sphinctered Teeny-Boppers and Apprentice Hippies." Needless to say, HemisFair refused Brammer's offerings.

One night, at the Mulberry Street apartment, "a bunch of us were listening to music and watching some of those old Cuban fuck movies . . .

grainy, black-and-white, and the guys all had their socks on—16-millimeter stuff, we were running it backwards—and there was a knock at the door," Dorothy said. "It was Kesey and the Pranksters. They had come to see Bill."

First, they had showed up at Larry McMurtry's house in Houston. "Ken called and said they were coming to see me; little did I know that the breeze of the future was about to blow through my quiet street," McMurtry recalled.

> A very few minutes later there it came, the bus whose motto was FURTHER. . . There were Pranksters sitting on top, waving at my startled neighbors with Day-Glo hands. Ken was playing a flute . . . My son, James, aged two, was sitting in the yard in his diapers when the bus stopped and a naked lady ran out [of the bus] and grabbed him. It was Stark Naked ([her name was] later shortened to Stark), who, being temporarily of a disordered mind, mistook him for her little girl. James, in diapers, had no objection to naked people.

Politely, McMurtry suggested his neighborhood might be a little staid for the group—perhaps they should go visit Billy Lee down by the Alamo. Kesey taught James his first word—"Ball"—and the bus pulled out of town.

When the Pranksters arrived in San Antonio, "every cop in Bexar County was right with them. About forty patrolmen," Dorothy said. "But eventually the cops stayed for our party. The Pranksters had a way of making friends." In a day or two, Brammer sent them on to Austin, to the Caswell House, where members of the Conqueroo were busy chugging lysergic-enriched fruit juice.

---

In what had become a deeply ingrained habit, Brammer simply wandered away from his job without completing anything or officially resigning. Before leaving San Antonio, though, he received a visit from his children. One day, "we were dropped off at the San Antonio zoo and given a phone number written on a matchbook, to call him when we got bored—a wrong number, as it turned out," Sidney remembered. "We set out on foot in the direction we'd come from and managed to find his apartment—20 blocks away in a strange city. We felt victorious and very independent. When we arrived, we found him sound asleep, oblivious to the fact that we'd never called to be picked up. (Believe it or not, sometimes even speed couldn't keep that man awake.)"

---

John Kriken had told Brammer about a California filmmaker he knew, John Korty, who was looking for a screenwriter for his latest project. Without a second thought, Brammer and Dorothy headed for Bolinas, a bucolic former fishing village turned Beat retreat then hippie hangout, thirty miles north of San Francisco.

The Indiana-born Korty had done animation work for early television, but then made low-budget feature films in California, working out of a barn in Marin County. "I . . . set [Brammer] up in a cottage [on Stinson Beach] and started paying him. I gave him a short treatment I had written and spent several hours explaining my ideas for [my] film. He went off to write," Korty told me.

"He wanted to make this movie called *Riverrun* and it was about this hippie couple wanting to have natural child-birth on a sheep farm. Well, you can imagine how Billy Lee took to that," Dorothy said.

"We [my film company and I] checked with him weekly and always heard that he was making progress," Korty said. "Unfortunately, he wasn't showing anything to us. More unfortunately, weeks later, when we demanded to see something on paper, it turned out he just had a page or two. This was in late November [1967] and we wanted to start shooting in January. My business manager terminated the deal . . . and I wrote the script myself in December. We gave him a minor credit for 'additional dialogue' just to avoid legal problems. I liked him as a person and enjoyed his stories about LBJ, but he just could not write on assignment."

"Korty and Billy Lee were not cut out of the same DNA," Dorothy said. "Bill's version of it was that Korty had no sense of humor. And so it didn't work out. And God, Bolinas was awful. Berkeley academics who had 'gotten back to the land,' growing their own cornmeal and stuff."

Off and on, Lawrence Ferlinghetti lived in Bolinas. Richard Brautigan. Robert Creeley. Members of the Jefferson Airplane. Hal Chase, Jack Kerouac's old buddy from Columbia University: he had become the character Chad King in *On the Road*. Among the mule deer and wild nasturtiums on the tip of the gorgeous peninsula, nestled within eucalyptus groves and low-tide mudflats, the locals set up crudely constructed sheds, painted the colors of the rainbow, so that townspeople could drop off free clothing for their fellow citizens: the ultimate in communal living.

Dorothy wasn't buying the place's self-image. "It was really heavy-handed. Smug. I was the librarian in a one-room schoolroom there. They gave me $5,000 to buy books for the school. And I thought, 'Well, a good place to start would be to talk to the sixth-graders—what books are fun for you?' And I bought a bunch of Nancy Drew mysteries. The school went crazy. 'Why didn't you buy any black history books?' It was the antithesis of laid-back Austin."

"Happenings" were a staple of evenings in Bolinas, musical improvisations in the parks featuring bongos, flutes, vibraphones—and in one locale, the "Eternal Machine," a pair of picnic tables rigged with nails, wind-up toys, spoons, castanets, pocket combs, and, according to one local artist, "a variety of woodwind reeds attached to industrial grade garden hoses." Brammer was not much drawn to these events. Instead, he remained distracted from his movie script by the presence of his old friend Bill Beckman, the cartoonist who had introduced him to Dorothy back in Austin. Beckman was a frequent visitor to Bolinas. He and Brammer shared ideas. From his rental house on a mesa overlooking the ocean, Beckman produced a tabloid called the *Bolinas Hit,* the first issue of which described how to manufacture LSD. It offered poetry, cartoons, a photograph of a dead whale's bloated tongue, and a picture of one jackbooted policeman kneeing another in the groin, accompanied by the caption, "To be right is the most terrific personal state that nobody is interested in."

Other cartoonists, artists, and writers from Texas made their way to the West Coast, in and out of Brammer's orbit—among them, Gilbert Shelton, Jack Jackson (who had once worked in the Texas Capitol and printed his alternative comics at night in its printing office, at full government expense), and Joplin's high school pal Dave Moriaty. Initially, they banded together to produce psychedelic rock posters. The printing press they installed in a warehouse on Potrero Hill in San Francisco, across the street from a trucker's bar, was insufficient for the close-register work the posters required, so the group published "comix" instead, and then antiwar texts, and texts on hallucinogenic chemistry and alternative spirituality. Shelton's comic *The Fabulous Furry Freak Brothers* became a nationwide underground sensation. Naked hippies danced on the warehouse roof. The truckers loved it. This was the birth of the Rip-Off Press and the *Rip-Off Review of Western Culture.* Dave Moriaty listed himself as the press's founding publisher. An elder guiding spirit, Billy Lee Brammer was named "Editor at Sea."

---

Fired from the *Riverrun* project, Brammer gravitated to San Francisco. He hung out with Chet Helms, Janis Joplin, other Texas expats. Around the Haight, Joplin had become famous for howling, growling, and moaning onstage; audiences encouraged her to shoot up or get drunk (Helms's promise to shield her from drugs had not panned out). She was infinitely more talented than the members of Big Brother and the Holding Company—they knew it, too. They tried to keep her in her place with macho posturing and endless tiffs over song arrangements. The band's hostile dynamic wore her down, but she maintained a tough exterior. Immediately, Brammer reconnected with the thoughtful gentleness she rarely showed others. She confessed to him that sometimes she *still* considered her rock-star career a kind of summer vacation, and she imagined returning to Texas, to school, to that mythical white picket fence.

Improbably, Chet Helms had become an icon of hippie existence in San Francisco; underneath his Afghan jacket and big black hat, he was still just a Fort Worth boy. Joan Didion featured him as the ultimate flower child in "Slouching Towards Bethlehem," her cover story for the *Saturday Evening Post*, hailed by the magazine under the cover line "The Hippie Cult: Who They Are, What They Want, Why They Act That Way." Helms was the mayor of Day-Glo, a rock-and-roll entrepreneur heading up the Family Dog, an entertainment collective, and the Avalon, a psychedelic ballroom. He had developed an aggravating relationship with Bill Graham, the other successful local concert promoter, founder of the Fillmore. Loosely, Helms partnered with Graham, sharing acts and planning events, but Graham always managed to undercut him financially. Graham could be ruthless. Helms admitted that he was a lazy capitalist. "My motivation—put very simply—I liked to dance and that was a very free space," he said. "It's where my body and my mind and my soul felt free. So I was creating an environment around myself in which I could dance." Also, "I was interested in the scene's potential for revolution. For turning things upside down, for changing values."

When Brammer arrived, Helms was enjoying a rare flush period. He operated a branch of Family Dog productions in Denver, located in a former Whiskey A Go Go club on West Evans Street. The dance cage still hovered above the stage. Another Texan living in San Francisco, Bob Simmons, a writer, photographer, and Bay Area DJ, said the Denver Dog's manager had been stealing from the till. Helms needed someone new. An acquaintance of his named Barry Fey, with solid experience as a booking agent, wanted the job. So did Brammer. Brammer wanted *any* job. Helms saw the "famous arthur" as a "cultural jewel" in his crown as the hip king of the West, Simmons said. He sent Brammer to Denver as Fey's partner. Simmons tagged along to keep an eye on them both.

Driving a shiny new Volkswagen bought with a salary advance, Brammer, high on acid, took Dorothy, Rosebud, and a second standard poodle to Denver in a raging snowstorm. He had not put chains on the tires. Dorothy suffered an anxiety attack and ended up, briefly, in a hospital in Cheyenne, Wyoming. The couple arrived in Denver in the early fall of 1967. The Family Dog sat in a formerly industrial area of town, a ragged, 2,500-seat venue. Its retooled opening coincided with rumors that Owsley Stanley had relocated his LSD lab to Denver. Perhaps for this reason, an aggressive member of the vice squad, John Gray, swore he would personally rid his city of all long-haired people. Owsley stayed out of sight, so the Family Dog became Gray's primary target.

Janis Joplin and Big Brother officially launched the new Dog, bathed in the "total experience theater" of a Diogenes Lantern Works psychedelic light show. In the next few weeks, Quicksilver Messenger Service, the Youngbloods, the Grateful Dead, Mother Earth, Jefferson Airplane, Buffalo Springfield, Canned Heat, Blue Cheer, and Van Morrison took the stage. Jack Jackson—originally from Pandora, Texas, just outside San Antonio—drew the colorful posters, using his trademark signature, "Jaxon"; instantly, the posters became underground collectors' items. Helms began to talk of opening a Family Dog "Crash Ranch" somewhere in the Rocky Mountain foothills where bands and their fans could commune together in the forests.

"Of course, Billy Lee had a fabulous time," Dorothy said. "He stayed stoned every day . . . It was the *music*."

"Bill wasn't really managing anything," Simmons said. "He wrote press releases, generally 'looked after stuff' in the office, kind of hung out and made the place groovy." Helms and Fey handled most of the booking. Brammer *did* send certain acts on to Austin; Sandy Lockett and Houston White had opened a psychedelic rock club called the Vulcan Gas Company (across the street from the hardware store that sold Charles Whitman his ammunition—following the shooting, the store's business boomed). Lockett recalled Brammer's enthusiastic recommendation of Johnny Winter.

"I remember how embarrassed we were the night the Fugs (who were personal friends) were playing, and the sheriff came and confiscated our box office receipts so that we couldn't pay the band . . . Still they played the show. Possibly to prevent a riot," Simmons said. "Or the night that

Chuck Berry [was scheduled] and wouldn't go on until fully paid. So we had to go outside and sell tickets to people in line to get enough money to pay him. Billy Lee with a cigar box soliciting teens for ticket money. Shameful business."

John Gray couldn't shut the place for underage drinking—the club didn't sell booze. But he harassed the young patrons with trumped-up charges of vagrancy, hitchhiking, insufficient ID. The members of Canned Heat accused him of planting pot in their equipment. Brammer tried to get a restraining order against him, but Gray maintained his pressure.

"Often, money disappeared down mysterious rat holes," Simmons said. He suspected that Brammer took some of it to buy drugs. "Luckily, Bill didn't know about the popcorn machine. Amazing how much a popcorn dispenser can make over a weekend of rock and roll. We were seldom paid, but I kept the key to the machine."

One day, "in the heart of a very cold winter," Simmons said, Brammer observed a "person of importance" in the Family Dog organization

> grab a groupie secretary, with whom he had no relationship at all, and drag her into a small alcove office that had a day couch in it. Twenty minutes later, [this person] and the secretary emerged from the office both looking a bit mussed. Bill remarked at the time that it reminded him of when he worked with Lyndon. "Lyndon had the same technique, probably developed by watching too many roosters mounting hens in the barnyard." There was no courting or foreplay. He sometimes just grabbed, and dragged a low-status female into a closet and functionally raped her: "I mean, what are they gonna say? Besides, he would reward them afterwards, as well."

Simmons recalled a good deal of Pumpkin lore. A few years later, back in Austin, he was studying a picture of Richard Nixon on the cover of *Time*. Brammer remarked to him, "It's really amazing when you think about it. The last two presidents of the USA have been functionally insane, and yet the American people don't seem to notice." Simmons answered yes, these men certainly *did* seem crazy. "Seems, hell," Brammer said. "They really are insane. I mean in a clinical sense."

Eventually, poor management and police harassment damaged the Dog beyond fixing. Chet Helms lost $85,000 on the venture. Brammer loaned "his nice VW to some Family Dog hippie employee who promptly went out and totaled the car," Simmons said. "Bill left broke and humbled, driving his mother's 1954 Chevy with his wife and two black standard poodles in the back seat—back to Austin where there were gentler folks and kinder weather."

One of the last shows he attended at the club was a performance by the Doors, on December 31, 1967. Jim Morrison, apparently bored with being a rock star, was drunk and hostile, unable to sing some of the songs, surly with the crowd. He kept swinging his microphone on its long cord over the audience, attempting to pop peoples' heads. He wasn't playing. He wasn't being funny. He was *after* folks. Brammer got especially nervous when Morrison mimed exposing himself onstage behind a leather jacket held to cover his waist. When the clock hit midnight, and 1968—destined to become one of the most turbulent years in American history—officially arrived, Morrison screamed, "We want the world and we want it . . . *now*!"

---

"The Democratic Party's goal is to build a great society which will give the maximum scope for humanity to flower," Bob Eckhardt had proclaimed when announcing his run for a seat in the US House of Representatives from Texas's Eighth Congressional District, in Houston. While Brammer was scurrying around the West Coast failing to write a movie script and bottoming out as a rock promoter, his children were being dragged from one raucous campaign event to another. They hated the meetings almost as much as Eckhardt did. "[Voters] demand that I demean myself. It removes their inferiority complexes," he said of campaigning. "They think, 'Yeah, he gets elected to that high and mighty office . . . but look how silly he looks jumping up as high as he can with his shirttail hanging out . . . look at him with his pockets all bulging with stuff about himself, trudging through the supermarket parking area.' It's sort of like a fraternity initiation. When you've done enough demeaning exercises to hate yourself and everybody around you, they think you're fit for their company—and I suppose you are." Once the reluctant candidate had successfully claimed his congressional perch, Nadine crowed, "I believed in my heart that my husband would never have been elected to the House of Representatives without my support . . . [I was] an integral part of his operation, an extension of his staff. We were a team and there would be no limits to what we could accomplish."

It did help that he had earned a reputation, in Austin, as a man who made things happen politically—passing an open-beaches bill, which prevented private interests from gobbling up beachfront property and excluding public access to it. His environmental legislation would serve as a model for many other states. He was celebrated as a witty and eloquent speaker, often quoting Shakespeare—"For God's sake, let us sit upon the ground and tell sad stories of the death of kings" (*Richard II*). He worked hard to nurture bipartisan relationships. One day he and Nadine invited Barbara and George H. W. Bush, also a House candidate, to a picnic on their Cypress Creek property. Eckhardt and Bush shared stories about the extremist "nuts" they had to appease in their parties. They became good friends.

On Election Day 1966, Nadine left her kids with a nanny for nearly a twenty-four hour period, overseeing ballot boxes at a polling station, morning and afternoon, and then in the early evening enjoying a boozy victory party at their campaign headquarters, and finally, at about two a.m., joining Barbara Jordan at *her* headquarters to celebrate her election to the Texas Senate.

"Before congress convened in January of 1967, we house-hunted in Washington and were lucky enough to find a charming place in Georgetown, just across the street from the house that the Kennedys lived in when Jack was in the Senate," Nadine said. It was a high-ceilinged four-story house built in 1815. The family flew back to Texas to pack. Then, "after three days in the car with all the children, we arrived in D.C. [from Houston] just in time for a snowstorm. We didn't care—we were in D.C. and it was snowing!" Nadine said. "We walked down the middle of N Street, sidewalks piled high with snow, to Martin's Tavern, President Harry Truman's old hangout, where we sat together and ate a good meal as we watched the [storm]."

Eckhardt quickly established himself as the House's philosopher-congressman. He insisted that every piece of legislation be carefully, articulately crafted and itemized. He believed the Great Society agenda had been hampered by LBJ's habit of being a "legislative entrepreneur—result-oriented." Excess: Lyndon's biggest problem. Too much, too fast. Civil rights. Medicare. The War on Poverty. "Too little . . . legislation [is] governed by a firm view of what a bill is supposed to accomplish and how . . . Congressional acts, like common law, ought to move carefully from precedent to precedent," Eckhardt announced. Each morning, he would put on his bow tie and ride his bicycle, equipped with a small whiskey basket in the rear, to his office in the Longworth Building. More swiftly than she would have imagined, Nadine found herself bored at home, stuck with tending the children. "Congress is set up to take care of the members *only*. Wives are accommodated to a certain extent, but on the whole, wives are dispensable," she said. "If a wife goes on a junket with her husband, the federal government cannot pay her way. I was sorely disappointed to find [Bob] going on overseas trips without me; most of the time we couldn't afford the extra ticket . . . We had many heated conversations that ended abruptly when Bob ran out of the house, late for some committee meeting."

She did get a few perks, courtesy of her old friend Lyndon: "LBJ liked to party and was a pretty good dancer. At one point . . . we flew on Air Force One with the president and members of the Texas delegation and their wives to dine and dance in Austin in honor of the president, and flew back to D.C. the same night in an alcohol-soaked time warp," Nadine recalled.

Initially, she worried about how Johnson would react to Eckhardt, the most liberal member of the Texas group, but he set her mind at ease. "He's a *bred* congressman," Johnson declared.

The president walked up to her at a Washington party one night, shortly after her arrival in the city. She hadn't seen him in many years. He pressed his whole body against hers and said, "You act like you like that guy you're with." When she told him she had a brand-new two-year-old, he quipped, "We're gonna have to fix you up with some of those things we send to India to keep 'em from having so many kids." Neither Johnson nor Lady Bird ever mentioned Nadine's "previous incarnation as a twenty-five-year-old secretary married to Bill Brammer," she said. "Nor did I."

# 18.

It had been a dozen years since Lyndon Johnson hired Billy Lee Brammer—in part to pressure Ronnie Dugger into softening his views of LBJ. Now, in mid-December 1967, Johnson was trying again with Dugger. "I want a friendly book," said the president. He had given his old nemesis access to the White House even though Dugger had been harshly critical of him in print for well over a decade and now proposed to write a biography of him. Johnson *needed* Dugger's approval; as when he had snatched Brammer from the *Texas Observer* in the 1950s, he craved liberal as well as conservative consent. He wanted the love of *all* the American people, especially now that chants of "Hey, hey, LBJ, how many kids did you kill today?" filled the streets of Washington. Concerned about his legacy, he had also recently tried to impress another educated liberal, Doris Kearns, a twenty-four-year-old Harvard doctoral candidate serving in the White House Fellows program. In a public meeting one day, she asked him, "Don't you understand—how can you possibly not understand—how deep and serious the country's opposition to the war in Vietnam is?" He aimed a look of barely checked anger at her, but months later he summoned her to the Oval Office. "I've decided to do some teaching when I leave office," he said. "I've always liked teaching. I should have been a teacher, and I want to practice on you. I want to do everything I can to make the young people of America, especially you Harvards, understand what this political system is all about." Kearns was an attractive woman; he said she reminded him of his mother; but most importantly, she was a principled person resisting him. More than a challenge, he took this as an affront, a rejection, an impossibility. Brammer had witnessed this pattern repeatedly: the Pumpkin's sensitivity to the pain of rejection drove him first to despair, then to obsequious charm with others, then to bullying.

Brammer had never resisted his tactics—he had simply, in Johnson's view, betrayed him, so now he was gone. Like Kearns, Dugger was still digging in, still writing. Still sorely in need of the Johnson Treatment. "Leading [me] through the White House as if he owned it . . . he cuffed [me] with his rough anger," Dugger wrote. "He occupied his rocking chair with an indifferent authority, as if, should it squeak, he would maul it. There was threat, ferocity, real danger in him."

Johnson tried to explain the war to Dugger. "We killed Diem. But we didn't have anybody in Vietnam to take his place, and we'd be a lot better off with him than we are now! Listen, if Ronnie Dugger's my lawyer, and we've got to kill him, we want to be damn sure we've got another lawyer before we [act]." After this little lesson in what sounded like Mafia ethics, Johnson slipped into the bathroom adjacent to the Oval Office, leaving the door wide open. He continued to address Dugger while he did his business. He compared the Vietnamese people to his grandson, Patrick Lyndon: "He takes one step, then another, and then another, but it's slow; it just takes time."

Later, in his upstairs bedroom, while being massaged by a "blank-faced boy, about eighteen," and watching news broadcasts on three television screens, Johnson extended Dugger's education. "Hoisting himself to a seated position on the massage table, facing me, he continued to challenge me as if daring me with his nakedness, his pot belly, his dangling legs, his power-glowing self. Though I knew he was a country boy, he looked and seemed to be, in these strange moments, a Chinese war lord," Dugger wrote.

"We killed Diem," Johnson repeated. "We killed Trujillo. We were going after Castro. Us liberals." Dugger knew what he meant. He meant, *How can you softheads still love those grinning Eastern rich boys then turn around and hate* me*? The Kennedys were murderers.* They're *the ones who got us into these damn messes.* I'm *trying to straighten things out.*

"No deal," Dugger said finally to the idea of writing a friendly book, subject to Johnson's approval. This ended his meetings with the president, but not before he got to sit down to dinner in the White House's family dining room, along with a couple of other reporters and LBJ. Dugger returned to the theme of treating the world's citizens as if they were America's children. Who were we to say they needed our help to take the next baby steps? "I knew I wasn't putting the question well," Dugger said.

"I know exactly what you're asking," Johnson answered. The dinner concluded when he "pushed completely back from the table . . . glowering at me," Dugger said. "He shouted at me with a terrible intensity, jamming his thumb down on an imaginary spot in the air beside him, '*I'm* the one who has to *mash the button*!'"

---

The Texas liberals that had always vexed Johnson were cockier than ever in Austin in 1968. One of the nation's most active chapters of the Students for a Democratic Society had formed on the UT campus. The *Rag* gave a strong voice to countercultural values, civil rights, student freedom movements, antiwar sentiments, and appreciation of acid music: "The USA will come together in psychedelic harmony at last. Amerika will break out in one huge smile and everyone will be stoned, high, fucked up, jacked out of shape, mellow, blasted." The Vulcan Gas Company drew bigger crowds than the Texas Capitol, despite the cops' attempts to convince patrons that light shows were likely to electrocute them.

At one point, Frank Erwin, a Lyndon Johnson confidant and chairman of the UT Board of Regents, tried to ban distribution of the *Rag* on campus. Dave Richards warned him that doing so would be an infringement of First Amendment protections. Nevertheless, Erwin took the "dirty hippies" to court. "BIG FUCKIN' DEAL" was the *Rag*'s response. Richards represented the paper. Depositions in the case reveal how far apart Lyndon Johnson's paternal America and the Amerika of the young hippies were. Asked by one of the university's lawyers what type of activity she engaged in, a member of the *Rag*'s ragged staff answered, "I am involved in political work." The transcript continued:

Q: What type of political work?
A: Radical political organizing.
Q: For who?
A: For the International Revolutionary Movement. I can't be any more specific than that, because there is no one organization I am working for.

Q: . . . Where do they headquarter?

A: . . . I don't know how abreast the Court is of what has been happening in the radical movement . . .

Q: What was the name of this group—International what?

A: It isn't the name of a group. That is just the label that I would attach to myself. You know, it is not an organization. It is not in organizational form.

Q: Is it a sort of factional group of SDS?

A: No, that was just my own description of myself of what I was doing.

Q: Do you have any immediate superior, or somebody over you here in Austin?

A: No.

A federal judge ruled that the *Rag*'s activities were protected by the First Amendment. Twice, the US Supreme Court upheld that ruling. "Of course, by the time of the final victory, my clients had drifted off, and *The Rag* had disappeared," Richards said. "I had no one to report to about my success."

And that was the rub. "Psychedelic harmony" lasted about as long as a green flash at sunrise in the skies over Manzanillo. Quests for enlightenment were hardening into addictions. "The 13th Floor Elevators were proselytizing LSD and taking it on a daily basis—and it did them all in," Tary Owens said. "Within a year, Roky had just gone into outer space . . . I remember at the time, thinking, what have I gotten him into?"

Shiva's Headband's leader, the psychedelic fiddler Spencer Perskin, kept getting arrested for marijuana possession, halting the band's career progress, and the Conqueroo burned itself out. "We didn't feel like we could play . . . unless we were carried in on stretchers," said Bob Brown. "That was the thing; music didn't sound good if it was just good music. It was supposed to blow your mind, mesmerize or milk you. We did that a few times, and we'd look out and there'd be people wallowing on the floor, writhing around, eyeballs rolling back in their heads. And that's what we wanted."

Exhausted and deeply in debt, the owners of the Vulcan Gas Company soon closed its doors.

It wasn't just youthful hippies watching the gaiety vanish from the scene. Their slightly older comrades, the Scholz liberals, the hip professionals experimenting with new lifestyles, and the conservatives tagging along for fun, were also fumbling to keep the party going. In one of its last gasps, the *Rag* bemoaned the "Pathetic State of Texas Liberalism, Today." In a reevaluation of *The Gay Place* for the *Texas Observer*, Ronnie Dugger wrote that Brammer's novel had brilliantly, prophetically grasped the "corruption of the Texas liberals . . . [They] are soft, too pleasure-seeking, well off, or easy to buy; they are not hard-eyed, and they deserve the politicians' contempt." He nearly wept over "Brammer's cry for innocence."

"When we got back from Colorado, that's when everything was really just falling apart between us," Dorothy said. "The drugs got more and more of a hold on him, and the talk was . . . you know, he started stealing stuff from friends and hawking it to buy drugs. He became pitiful and a real pain in the ass. As much as people tried to still love him and help him, there was no doing it."

Larry L. King remembered visiting Austin at around this time. He, Brammer, Dorothy, and several others ate a drunken meal in a darkened motel lounge, Brammer taking regular hits off his methedrine inhaler. Later, he popped an amyl nitrate cap under King's nose, causing King to feel as if his "earlobes [were] on fire." In a parking lot somewhere, Brammer "cornered a trio of edgy youngsters, railed on them that he was . . . [the] Governor . . . by God demanding they support his closing of godless whorehouses where red-blooded daughters of Texas, some of whose great-grandmothers had martyred themselves at the Alamo, were being held in white slavery by agents of the Kremlin and Marlon Brando."

Somebody suggested an orgy. The party retired to someone's house. Later, King came to consciousness in a room lined with guttered candles. Brammer crawled to him in the dark.

King asked if he had enjoyed the orgy. "I don't remember if I joined in," Brammer answered. "I meant to, I assure you. But I think I forgot. No, wait. I ran into [Dorothy] . . . and she spoke evil of my participation." At that point, Brammer rolled over and passed out. King rose wearily, stepped over him, and muttered, "Sleep on, faithful husband."

It was a long way from white-collar pill parties.

King had tried hard to help Brammer get on track with his writing. Before coming to Austin, he had written his friend:

> You know and I know and every bone in you knows that you were by talent and design meant to be a writer . . . I think the [problem] holding you up now is that writing isn't "fun." Well, fuck it being fun—it's more than that, it's important [because] you got more talent than most of us . . . You can write circles around Ronnie Dugger and Willie Morris

> and . . . Larry L. King and the only Texan I rank in your class is Larry McMurtry. You simply use the language better than the rest of us; you are better at form and technique . . . [But] all that is so much shit unless you work, Billie Lee.

Word had gotten out among publishers that Brammer was not to be trusted. He applied for a writing instructor post at the University of Texas and received a prompt rejection. He admitted to King that this sad turn damaged his already microscopic self-esteem.

In the meantime, Bud Shrake and Gary Cartwright had moved to Austin. They *always* wanted Good Ol' Billy Lee at their parties. "These guys who'd gotten rich writing for *Sports Illustrated* and writing crap and stupid novels," in Sidney's view. "There were *so many* drugs. It was so fraught. Rich guys with unlimited quantities of pot and meth."

(Darrell Royal, head football coach at the University of Texas, answered one of Shrake's party invitations: "I am sure we will not be able to stay for the entire party if it lasts eight years. Maybe you will permit us to come and go.")

Then, on the morning of March 29, 1968, Cartwright got busted for marijuana possession—a felony in Texas at the time, bringing with it a sentence of two years to life in prison. Lately, he had been doing some freelance writing for a political opponent of Lyndon Johnson's. "I recognized [my bust] as a time-honored method of operation in LBJ cronyland," Cartwright said. His arrest also suggested an evolution of police policies—the cops were going after higher-profile figures in the local culture now, not just kids on the street. "Famous arthurs" weren't protected.

Cartwright's friends gathered at Scholz's to collect donations for his defense fund and to talk legal strategies. Dave Richards, among others, agreed to represent him. Eventually, mistakes by the arresting officers—the lack of a search warrant, a false claim that Cartwright had tried to sell the dope—led to a mistrial. But the city's tone had darkened.

"Is There Life After Meth?" Brammer wrote—a partial draft of a short story meant to awaken his muse as well as to convince himself that the party hadn't ended (alternative titles were "Meth in the Afternoon" and "The Sickness Unto Meth"). The story began: "Now then golly goddam (hunkering closeby the electric typing machine before realizing, with imperfectly concealed melancholy, that one cannot simultaneously compose one's memoirs and clutch one's gleaming genitals—but I digress already . . .)" Digression was his subject and his method. This wouldn't end well.

He did manage to complete for the *Texas Observer* a piece entitled "Apocalypse Now" (years before Francis Coppola used the title)—a sardonic commentary on the changin' times: "It's possible . . . that America would forgive its youth, provided young people trim their hair, dress respectably, get some sort of job, and exhibit sufficient patriotic zeal for incinerating Vietnamese peasants." As for him: "I am tuned in, turned on and almost entirely bereft of any emotion save for such as might apply to geriatric disorders," he wrote.

This was a lighthearted take on what he had recorded more seriously in his notebook: "The plain hairy fact is I am 39 years old and reasonably happy to be there (specially to be there alive). I am close upon the great male climacteric, and it doesn't hang me up any more than does baldness, feeble-ness, alarming loss of my favorite teeth, or standing only four feet and two inches tall. Fuck all that . . . The measure of a man's maturity is revealed in an examination of his most blessed little enthusiasms. And it is here that I stand a giant among only a few slightly taller bastards."

He listed his daily substance intake: "Midafternoon dope, plus doughnuts, Coke, sausages, more dope, little hash, ½ tab purple acid, little wine, some rum, some . . . stew, beer, coffee, Desoxyn, nembutal . . . aspirin, more wine, much more grass," all before going to "two incredible parties" and ending the day watching a "freak futuristic sci-fi movie."

More and more, his notebook jottings revealed a greater honesty and a growing awareness that the drugs were not a path to "heightened perception" but were, rather, a sad escape from responsibility. "Anybody who has faced up to . . . reality, repeatedly over a number of years, is a very tired cat," he wrote. He had been fooling himself: "Suddenly I am aware that everyone is freaking out, cracking up, shedding skins, examining offshoots, testing improbably new atmospheres for toxic substances, shaking loose from such moorings as might be operative in marriages, romances, aging courtships, decaying orbits, wornout affairs, friendships, circles, tribes—even one's own responsibilities toward oneself."

He began to organize his notebook entries more precisely, trying to impose some discipline on his speeding concentration. He meditated on such topics as "Love, Politics"—and parallels between the two—on "Reconstituted Clichés, Literature, Personalities, Landscapes." He gave these meditations a title: "The Angst Notebook, or Avez-Vous Dexamyl?" Dimly, he conceived of "The Angst Notebook" as a possible publishing project, but mostly the remarks—sometimes whimsical, often somber—were Brammer's way of talking to himself:

> *Reject the conventional fictions of "unchanging human nature." There is no such permanence anywhere.*
>
> *The nature of vision is human and not chemical.*
>
> *True wonderment is not an ecstatic revelation but a hopeless ecstasy of longing.*

Contemplating the tensions in his marriage to Dorothy, he revisited, from a distance, his history with Nadine: "*They were not unsuited, they were not cruel, they were never, despite their sexual misadventures, in love with anyone but each other. But they could not keep the faith in any sense.*"

---

The reporter, a friend of Nadine's, knew her freewheeling attitudes. Still, she was surprised when Nadine told her, for the record, that her response to being neglected by her husband was to start an affair. "You have to work at a marriage—and that goes both ways," Nadine said.

Myra MacPherson, a former *Washington Post* and *New York Times* reporter, was writing a book called *The Power Lovers: An Intimate Look at Politicians and Their Marriages*. A number of Washington wives refused to speak to her, but Nadine admitted cheerfully that she had caught her husband, Bob, having affairs; that she had reciprocated on more than one occasion; that smoking pot or indulging in a few "Alice B. Toklas brownies" was the only way to get through "some of those God-awful functions" in town; that politicians were wedded to their jobs (e.g., full-time fund-raising); that politicians' wives were to be pitied ("You sit between some little gray men who talk about how they miss their golf course or how important they are on some damn inconsequential committee. Who wants to hear that?"); that "Congressmen make the worst Daddies in the world . . . they abdicated as fathers years ago."

Sitting in the Eckhardts' living room, conducting the interview, MacPherson was startled to hear Nadine say, in front of her husband, "'Good, supportive' wives are not necessarily happy." Clearly, Eckhardt was shaken. "He doesn't know what being a father's *like*," Nadine insisted.

She said she needed to remind him every day at home that he was *not* "the Congressman." He was simply Bob.

Smiling tightly, Eckhardt said, "You're bitter, baby."

"Well, who the hell raised these kids?" Nadine shot back.

The kids asked themselves that very same question. "We were moved around so much, left alone so often. For me, Georgetown was as extreme as the Haight-Ashbury," Sidney said. In an interview and correspondence with the author and in a reminiscence she wrote for the *Texas Observer* in 1995, Sidney explained what being a teenager in the Brammer-Eckhardt clan was like:

> We were living in DC with a liberal Texas politician-father, under a Texas president who was conducting a war we hated. It was *political* chaos, just as Bill was hopping from Bolinas to San Francisco to Denver, in the midst of tremendous *cultural* splintering. Society was fragmenting and getting polarized. Radicalized. I was sixteen. I went to all the antiwar marches, but in many ways, politics was not so much the answer anymore for young people. The *music* was changing, affecting so much else . . . It was amazing . . . [and] we might have been the only teens in the whole beleaguered USA whose old man was more hip to what was going on in the land than we were. Bill would send us posters and handbills from Austin, San Francisco, and Denver shows, and we would know about the bigger names, like Blue Cheer, Jefferson Airplane, Moby Grape, because they were playing the Ambassador Ballroom in DC, too, and I was listening to them on underground radio stations in the DC area, much like Bill must have stayed up as a kid listening to border radio. So me and my siblings had this connection with him.

"He had these reel-to-reel tapes with lots of underground radio on it," Shelby recalled. Willie remembered receiving from him, in the mail, "a box of eight-track tapes when he was living in California. He sent me Santana, Buffalo Springfield, lots of others . . . I thought, boy, that was a treasure trove."

"He was always offering knowledge," Shelby said. "He sent books—Vonnegut's *Slaughterhouse-Five*, *Where the Legends Die* [that is, Hal Borland's *When the Legends Die*]. I was always eager to take what I could get from him."

Occasionally, the children would fly to Austin to see him ("It seemed so sleepy compared to DC—like stepping back in time," Willie said). Brammer entertained them, pointing at Dorothy and shouting, "Look, kids, it's the evil stepmother!" Or he would arrive in DC for short visits with them, avoiding Nadine as much as possible. Willie was learning magic. Brammer took a keen interest in his skills. "Willie's little hands changed overnight, it seemed," Sidney recalled. "I remember watching him one day with a penny, and the penny disappeared. His hands didn't look the same. All his liminal muscles were loopy and streamlined." Brammer was delighted with him.

"When he was with you, his attention was focused on *you*," Shelby said. "He was great fun."

But Sidney never relaxed—"something was wrong" with her dad. "He'd be driving us home late at night, and . . . he kept dozing off . . . I kept saying, 'Daddy, wake up!'"

She was busy studying her mother and stepfather, too, learning the elements of intimacy. "Nadine liked brilliant, rather passive guys," she realized. These men's personalities were as frustrating as they were attractive to her mother, for the men weren't likely to devote any more time to parenting than Nadine did. Sidney's stepsister Orissa had lost an eye to cancer—her father had failed to arrange regular visits to the ophthalmologist after doctors detected an unusual spot beneath her cornea.

Sidney understood that "Nadine also liked *power*. She was drawn to the political world because she perceived that was where the power was."

To wit: She really believed she could influence American policy. "Jim Rowe, an advisor to President Johnson, and I had lunch occasionally to discuss the war," Nadine remarked in her memoir. "He was a hawk; he'd try to explain the various reasons why we had to stay in the war." She was convinced she could change his mind.

In 1968, her old pal Lyndon "seemed sad and tired," she said. "He had received many threats on his life, and the disapproval of thousands of young and not-so-young Americans was clear. It was painful to watch . . . his head bowed, his body contorted in an attitude of defeat and sorrow . . . Bob and I felt extremely conflicted [around him]. Although our allegiance was to President Johnson, we desperately wanted him to stop the war."

Johnson understood that, in the minds of most senators, the costs of Vietnam would erode the resources necessary to support the domestic agendas dear to him: "I knew the Congress as well as I know Lady Bird," he told Doris Kearns, "and I knew that the day it exploded into a major debate on the war, that day would be the beginning of the end of the Great Society."

For him, this was the equivalent of the loss of "psychedelic harmony": either green dawn or darkness. The Texan in him refused to accept a choice so stark—after all, as he had announced one day to soldiers on their way to Vietnam, his great-great-grandfather had died at the Alamo, accepting impossible odds (this was, in fact, a falsehood); he came from pioneer stock, men "who had a rifle in one hand to kill their enemies and an ax in the other to build their homes and provide for their families."

Whenever Nadine heard him sling such bull at social functions, she dismissed his "big daddy" talk. "The leaders of our country seemed like parents unwilling to open their minds to the views of the younger generation," she said.

---

At around this time, Brammer wrote in *The Angst Notebook*:

> It is absurd to say that there is anything properly described as youthfulness in the American outlook. It is not that of young men, but that of old men. All the characteristics of senescence are in it: a great distrust of ideas, an habitual timorousness, a harsh fidelity to a few fixed beliefs, a touch of mysticism. The average American is a prude and a Methodist and the fact is never more evident than when he is trying to disprove it. His vices are not those of a healthy boy but those of an ancient paralytic . . . If you would penetrate to the causes thereof, simply go down to Ellis Island and look at the next shipload of immigrants. You will not find the spring of youth in their step; you will find the shuffling of exhausted men. From such exhausted men the American stock has sprung. It was easier for them to survive here than it was where they came from, but that ease, though it made them feel stronger, did not actually strengthen them. It left them what they were when they came: weary peasants, eager only for . . . comfortable security . . .
>
> And out of that eagerness has issued many of the noblest manifestations of American Kultur: the national impulse to make, if not for long endure, war, the pervasive suspicion of all other nations, the short way with heretics and disturbers of the peace, the unshakable belief in devils, the implacable hostility to every novel idea and point of view.

---

Johnson confided to Doris Kearns that he didn't like to go to sleep. He didn't want to be alone. In sleep, he was tormented by terrible dreams, he said, particularly a variation of a recurring childhood nightmare in which he sat paralyzed in a chair on the open prairie while his father's cattle stampeded in his direction. In recent dreams, he was lying in bed, unable to move, in the Red Room of the White House.

To calm himself, upon waking from this vision in the middle of the night, he would grab a small flashlight and walk down a hall where a portrait of Woodrow Wilson hung on the wall. Standing alone in the dark, he would touch the portrait over and over, assuring himself that he was still Lyndon Johnson and that he was alive. *Wilson* was the one who was dead.

Johnson told Kearns he loved the sound of the wire tickers he had had installed in his bedroom next to his three television screens—AP, UPI, and Reuters. The tickers' musical rhythm sounded like friends tapping at his door. He would return to bed, feeling less lonely.

---

One day, Jay Milner walked into Brammer's house and saw him dancing to reggae music on the hi-fi. For nearly fifteen minutes, Brammer whirled around the room, all alone.

Later that night, just before going to bed, he scribbled in his notebook: "*Commies were right . . . Rock* is *subversive . . . visceral . . . lewd . . . decadent . . . raunchy . . . truly ecumenical and all-embracing.*"

---

Bob Dylan's lyrics (revolution, desolate souls, apocalyptic visions)—just what is the *appeal* of that damn stuff, Johnson asked Kearns. Why was popular culture so fucking *dark* all of a sudden? The songs, the books, the movies. "How in the hell can that creepy guy be a hero to you?" he asked her after they had screened *The Graduate* together at his ranch. "All I needed was to see ten minutes of that guy, floating like a big lump in a pool, moving like an elephant in that woman's bed, riding up and down the California coast polluting the atmosphere, to know I wouldn't trust him for one minute with anything that really mattered to me. And if that's an example of what love seems like to your generation, then we're all in big trouble."

He fumed that *he* had become the symbol of everything bad in the world. "I just don't understand these young people," he said. "Don't they realize I'm really one of them? I always hated cops when I was a kid, and just like them I dropped out of school and took off for California. I'm not some conformist middle-class personality. I could never be bureaucratized."

But the young had turned away from him. Eagerly, they flocked to "hipper" candidates. "Early on, I joined the 'Get Clean for Gene' movement," Sidney recalled.

"You know when I first thought I might have a chance [at the presidency]?" Eugene McCarthy told a reporter. "When I realized that you could go into any bar in the country and insult Lyndon Johnson and nobody would punch you in the nose."

Worse: even some of Johnson's congressional friends had abandoned him. Bob Eckhardt had begun saying in speeches, both in Washington and Texas, "The war poisons the wellsprings of the Great Society," "Our commitment is to humanity, not to any military junta." Eckhardt and his liberal allies endorsed McCarthy, claiming he "brought sense and reason to the Vietnam debate."

And then: catastrophe. Bobby Kennedy entered the race. Johnson had spent nearly six years trying to get the nation to stop acting moony over *one* Kennedy, passing legislation—on civil rights, education, health care—that JFK could never have gotten past his mother, and now *another* Kennedy, that little shitass, was going to grin and charm his way into the hearts of the electorate. He would "reclaim the throne in the memory of his brother. And the American people, swayed by the magic of the name, were dancing in the streets." It was too hard to bear. "How is it possible that all these people could be so ungrateful to me after I [have] given them so much?" Johnson asked Kearns.

> Take the Negroes. I fought for them the first day I came into office. I spilled my guts out in getting the Civil Rights Act [passed] . . . I tried to make it possible for every child of every color to grow up in a nice house, to eat a solid breakfast, to attend a decent school, and to get a good and lasting job. I asked so little in return. Just a little thanks. Just a little appreciation. That's all. But look what I got instead. Riots in . . . cities. Looting. Burning. Shooting. It ruined everything. Then take the students . . . I fought on their behalf for scholarships and loans and grants . . . and look what I got back. Young people by the thousands leaving their universities, marching in the streets, chanting that horrible song about how many kids I had killed that day. And the poor, they, too, turned against me. When Congress cut funds for the Great Society, they made me Mr. Villain.

It was a goddam stampede.

---

Brammer and Dorothy were thoroughly stunned on March 31, 1968, watching Lyndon Johnson announce on television, "This country's ultimate strength lies in the unity of our people. There is division in the American house now. There is divisiveness among us all tonight. . . . With America's sons in fields far away, with America's future under challenge right here at home . . . I do not believe that I should devote an hour or a day of my time to any personal partisan causes . . . Accordingly, I shall not seek, and will not accept, the nomination of my party for another term as your President."

---

Four days later, Martin Luther King Jr. was assassinated in Memphis. Johnson told Lady Bird, "Everything we've gained . . . we're going to lose tonight."

Ronnie Dugger was eating dinner with Nadine and Bob Eckhardt in Georgetown when they heard the news. They sat in front of a television, listening to reports that riots and looting were occurring in many American cities. Southeast DC was burning. (On a street in midtown Manhattan, Celia Morris shoved her husband, Willie, shouting, "You southern boys have a lot to be guilty about!")

Eckhardt rushed out of his house and bought a security bolt for the front door.

In the next few days, hundreds of African Americans erected plywood tents on the National Mall and camped there to protest poverty and racism. They called their encampment "Resurrection City." Eckhardt wanted to tour it, so one afternoon he and Nadine walked through the rowdy crowds. "We found ourselves surrounded by about twenty young black men with big 'fros—they were the 'marshals' on the site and had heard that there was a congressman on the premises," Nadine recalled.

> They began to shout at Bob, who was holding our three-year-old, Sarah; we were encircled and couldn't walk away. Bob tried to tell them he'd supported their political causes throughout his political career, but the men were so full of anger at Congress and the government in general that they weren't going to let a live one go. A man in a Malcolm X T-shirt was really giving Bob hell, so I screamed at him, "Stop giving this man shit! You don't know what you're talking about!" That got his attention, and he said to Bob, "I can't talk to you, but I can talk to your woman." Then he guided me to a tent where I could sign up as a volunteer, and we were allowed to leave peacefully.

In the following days, Nadine returned to Resurrection City with Shelby to cook pots of beans, distribute blankets and cots, listen to speeches and music. Blocks away, on Wisconsin Avenue and M Street, the National Guard teargassed antiwar protesters. Black students at Sidney's school set the building on fire.

At a White House dinner one night, Nadine admitted to LBJ that she admired the strong, principled folks occupying Resurrection City. He slumped and said, "Those people out there are electing Richard Nixon right now." Weeks later, authorities cleared the Mall, for "sanitation purposes."

---

In Austin, the police continued to surveil pockets of the counterculture where race-mixing and subversive planning might be festering. At Scholz's, the liberal claque ordered pitchers of beer and tried to remain optimistic about the country in spite of dark clouds (cities burning) on the horizon. Locally, new energy for progressive causes took the form of a revitalized *Texas Observer* under the editorship of Molly Ivins, a salty, smart-mouthed woman; and a new set of young lawmakers swore to propose a bold legislative agenda, putting civil rights front and center. Arthur Vance from Houston, cocky, movie-star handsome, had taken Bob Eckhardt's old Texas House seat.

"Bill and I met Arthur at a party, and Arthur had interesting stories to tell," Dorothy said. "He was smart, he read books. He did things like surf fishing in the Gulf. He was an Arthur Murray dance instructor. So Bill invited Arthur home one night. And Bill sort of set us up, really. He was a voyeur, is what he was. One night he told me, 'You know, Arthur's going back to his district this weekend [in Houston]. Why don't you ride with him? You want to go see your parents, don't you?' So that was sort of the beginning of that."

Within a few weeks, Dorothy had left the house she shared with Brammer and moved in with Vance. "No more Cuban fuck movies," she said wryly, by way of expressing her motivation.

"Ah, my god, it's appalling to reflect on the horrific things we imposed on one another, almost from the beginning. Small deceits, outsized conceits, vanities and punishments and harassments and untreaded hangups and that terrible burden of romantic illusion," Brammer wrote to her, shortly thereafter. "How the hell did we manage to hold on for so long . . . Something in me that refused to respond with masculinity to marriage; something in you that possibly required [a] sense of sin or outrageousness or unrequited backseat love."

He turned on the hi-fi each night and danced until he passed out.

---

Lyndon Johnson was asleep when his aides got the news of Bobby Kennedy's murder. Gently, they awakened him.

His old antagonisms toward Bobby wrestled with inner fears that America had become a "sick society." He tried not to intrude on the Kennedy family's grief, given how they felt about him. He stayed nearly out of sight at the funeral mass in St. Patrick's Cathedral. A few days later, in the Oval Office, he listened to a radio segment recapping Kennedy's death. Hugh Sidey reported that Johnson "stopped work. His head slumped way down between his knees as he listened, so low that those in front of the desk could barely see him. When it was over, he snapped the radio off, rose from his chair a stricken man, walked out of the French doors into the Rose Garden and stood there alone, silent."

Later, Johnson told Doris Kearns, "It would have been hard on me to watch Bobby march to 'Hail to the Chief,' but I almost wish he had become President so the country could finally see a flesh-and-blood Kennedy grappling with the daily work of the Presidency and all the inevitable disappointments, instead of their storybook image of great heroes who, because they were dead, could make anything anyone wanted happen."

---

On television, the "nation watched in horror as police billy-clubbed and tear-gassed young kids" at the Democratic National Convention in Chicago that August, Nadine said. "My children sympathized with the demonstrators, and so did I."

At that point, politics working within the system was just about over, Sidney said: "I thought, Screw this 'Clean for Gene' stuff." She switched on her rock and roll.

---

On his last full day in the White House, on January 19, 1969, Lyndon Johnson sat alone in the Oval Office. Painters and furniture movers dabbled elsewhere in the building, preparing for the transition to the Nixon administration. Johnson summoned Doris Kearns.

In the last few years, the president had needed a "resident intellectual," Harry McPherson believed, someone he could trust, someone to help him "'relate' to the intellectual community . . . [as] the war grew and university protests grew with it"; as poets and literary critics "took to the *New York Review of Books* to denounce Johnson as a preternatural villain, a monster who had seized on domestic liberalism as a cover for his stupid (or cunning, depending on the writer's needs) intervention in Vietnam."

Al Reinert agreed: "More than any other modern president [Johnson] was suspicious of writers, artists, intellectuals of all brands. Like a tragic flaw, it grew under pressure into paranoia—FBI files, small deceptions, larger ones—which came back on the rebound as a gap in his credibility." Now LBJ needed a writer to go through his papers, structure his story, and help him compose his memoirs. Years earlier, he had shunned the intellectual he once trusted most—the man, Reinert said, "who had seen into his soul more clearly than anyone else he had ever known." Johnson had stopped trusting "that part of himself that had trusted Billy."

But now he wanted to get his story out "from beginning to end." He turned to Kearns. "Those memoirs are the last chance I've got with the history books, and I've got to do it right . . . Will you help me?"

"Of course I will," she replied. She would be living and working in Boston, but she could arrange to spend weekends, parts of summers, and winter vacations at his ranch. It was settled. "Now you take care of yourself up there at Harvard," he told her as she left the Oval Office that day. "Don't let them get at you, for God's sake, don't let their hatred for Lyndon Johnson poison your feelings about me."

Over the next several months, on her trips to Texas, Kearns realized that it pained LBJ to relive his presidential years. More than that, he had begun to understand how damnably difficult writing could be. "Listen," he told her one day, "I've been reading Carl Sandburg's biography on Lincoln and no matter how great the book's supposed to be, I can't bring Lincoln to life. And if that's true for me, one President reading about another, then there's no chance the ordinary person in the future will ever remember me. No chance." He also worried that "no matter what I say in this book the critics will pull it apart. The reviews are in the hands of my enemies—the *New York Times* and the Eastern magazines—so I don't have a chance . . . I know the power of that group. Believe me, I know."

He looked much older than a man in his late fifties. He had pushed himself to excess, and he flinched, reflecting on everything now. Kearns saw that he "would rather be doing anything else than working on his memoirs." He would rather drink. Watch TV. He would even have preferred to listen to popular music.

"Anyone out there hear America singing?" Brammer wrote in his notebook as the weary decade neared its end:

> It would be comforting to believe that some middling residual oom-pah still obtained in this glorious commonwealth of polarized eccentrics, comforting, also, to believe that such Muzak as might be detected (yes . . . yes . . . but can you *dance* to it?) was given a more congenial reception than that which Mark Twain accorded the work of Richard Wagner, as an instance ("I understand it is much better than it sounds"). But no matter. I have aged badly and am long since overtaken with crippling sensory decrepitudes: I don't even hear mermaids singing over the incessant wheezing of my bronchial tubes.

PART FOUR

# *THE BODY ELECTRIC*

# 19.

"I saw that he'd gotten old. I thought, 'He's not in good shape,'" Sidney said. "He had a gray beard—he was putting mascara on it to try to look younger. You know, each time he'd visit us kids, or babysit our little sister Sarah, he wanted to come with toys and gifts and a little bit of cash for Nadine. He couldn't find a check to pay for the dentist, but he'd show up with these gifts."

After a while, as he "wore down," it became "almost painful to visit him in his rattrap apartments with the electricity turned off and no phone."

> We'd watch him poke through the wreckage of his bedroom for his Coke-bottle lens glasses or dentures (he'd had cataract surgery and lost his teeth by the age of 42) while we browsed through a cornucopia of literature that always seemed to have been flung in great disorganized piles into his living quarters. Once he'd gotten himself pulled together, we'd take him to eat Mexican food, or drive him to the store for more Dr. Pepper, or take him along with us to make some scene or another among the moveable feasts of Austin.
>
> As painful as it could be, one often had a *need* to see him—because Billie Lee had a way of getting to the quick of your deepest despond, making you laugh at it, turning it to your own best end.

Similarly, though he had been ostracized from the publishing world, he occasionally managed, against all odds and contrary to everyone's best interests, to charm an editor or an agent into giving him one more chance. At one point, an exasperated Elizabeth McKee wrote Herman Gollob, an editor at Harper's Magazine Press:

> He says he has written about half of a big rock-and-roll novel and he alleges he has been working on a journalism-as-literature textbook [This was a good five years before Tom Wolfe had a similar idea with his landmark anthology, *The New Journalism*]. He has a . . . contract with NAL dated December 15, 1965 for a $50,000 advance of which he received $14,000. NAL is now threatening legal action to recover it. Bill has had severe cataracts for the last several years but has had a final operation and is happy that he can see again! What do we do now?

Gollob could not be persuaded to risk anything on any of the alleged projects, but Brammer convinced McKee to secure for him an assignment from the *New York Times Magazine*. Bud Shrake reported to Larry L. King:

> [Billy] claims he is in truth going to write the story and get $750 and re-establish hisself and publish novels with high frequence. Says *Fustian Days* is back up to 200 pages and his rock novel is about the same. I have no doubt that if he ever were to finish *Fustian Days* it would be a good novel . . . Billy is amazing . . . he was in as bad a shape as I ever saw him, with eye & marital trouble and overloads of chemicals. Now he is coherent, can see and if he writes this stuff will probably save his [marriage] as well.

But Dorothy was long gone. Though still friendly with Brammer—and concerned about him—she was set to marry Arthur Vance.

Brammer never completed the magazine article.

"Some believe that Bill's greatest work was his own life, and that writing was only a facet of a rare gem of self," Sidney wrote years later in an appreciation of her father. But as the 1960s dwindled and the 1970s sputtered to a start, it became harder to maintain the guru role among so many burnouts. And *he* was beginning to crash. Austin's psychedelic moment—its bid to lead the country to a whole new way of life, first by colonizing San Francisco and then by spreading the love from coast to coast (on little tabs of acid)—was laboring to retain even a minor shred of brightness. Jan Reid, a freelance writer living in Austin, recalled seeing a sad show by the dispirited remnants of the Conqueroo at the Soap Creek Saloon: "The only interested people in the small crowd seemed to be Sandy Lockett [co-owner of the defunct Vulcan Gas Company] and their old patron Billy Lee Brammer, who had just missed a deadline for a magazine article about Texas' marijuana dealers because his teeth got so bad they required pulling. Lockett bobbed up and down behind the amplifiers, and Brammer grinned encouragement and approval through his new dentures." But the music, Reid said, was "dead weight."

One night, Jay Milner drove his old black hearse to Bud Shrake's place, where a party shook the rafters. Milner was about to move to Dallas to take charge as interim chair of the Journalism Department at Southern Methodist University. The department was on the verge of dissolving because of low enrollment and poor management; Milner had been hired temporarily to see whether he could turn things around.

At the party he bumped into Brammer. He had heard, from Shrake and others, that Dorothy had "run off to Mexico with a . . . member of the state legislature who had seen the light and joined the revolution for peace and good will—let his hair grow long and quit shaving his face," Milner said. "Billie Lee himself didn't volunteer all of this information. He never was one to bore you with his personal misadventures. That night . . . he simply stood around grinning sheepishly and looking downcast, while we all outsported ourselves trying to be amusing."

To Milner, Brammer had always been "our Norman Mailer. Quiet, yes, but he was out there amongst 'em." It was still true that "if you went anywhere that was anywhere, you ran into Billie Lee Brammer talk." Who better, then, to excite a moribund journalism program, Milner thought? Brammer's name "had drawing power, at least among people who read books, and I sincerely hoped SMU journalism students read books now and then. Besides, maybe the responsibilities of pedagogy would turn Billie Lee around." Milner sidled up to the silent, smiling man. He mentioned his idea. He described himself as old school—*he* could talk about examining public records for source material, interviewing subjects face-to-face. Brammer was cutting-edge—*he* could talk about the latest devices on the market, wires, minirecorders. Used to be, you would have to park yourself in a capital city to get the best story; now, like a fisherman reeling in a line, you could bring the story to you. The body politic had become the Body Electric. It needed a singer.

What did he think? As partners, they would be perfectly complementary.

Brammer shuffled his feet. Grinned wider. He asked Milner whether he had any speed. Within the month, he had moved to Dallas.

---

"It was incredible. Bill had actually gotten his shit together. I knew right away he'd make a great teacher. He had *always* been a mentor. He was a natural in that role," Dorothy said. He had written her in Mexico, asking whether she could scare up some cheap "heart medicine" for him. He said his escape from Austin had involved running from a "jackoff landlord . . . enraged by one of my famed bouncing rent checks," and a "deranged round of whimpering and packing." Preventing his "own imminent collapse" depended on the "availability of more new Chocolate mescaline (which serves as speed substitute, gives happy user the strength of ten, and turns scrotum into something very like tapioca pudding)." The two "lunatic poodles" had accompanied him to Dallas. Rosebud and Susie. Their demands exhausted him, but he was "propelled by cactus essence and possessed of a new typewriter ribbon." He was "getting busier, better, much too fucking sure of myself in all the wrong ways, and—for the first time in like ten years—dreaming some far-out shit." He said SMU "clutches me to its dowager bosom . . . as faculty member rapping at hysterical length about magazine journalism and something called 'Ethics.' Yeah." He said his new address was an apartment in an old house on Mockingbird Lane close to campus, fittingly enough near a Dr Pepper bottling plant—"Glass walls . . . [and] lots of recessed lighting which is doubtless splendid for seduction projects but absurd for reading, writing, picking hairs from TV dinners."

And oh, he added—when she got back to "soulful Austin," could she possibly contact his old connection down on West 33rd Street, near the bus stop, and score some brown mescaline for him (it cost twice as much in Dallas).

As the school semester neared its starting date, Kermit Hunter, the dean of SMU's Meadows School of the Arts, told Milner there were fifteen journalism majors. Milner could locate only five of them, and three of those had just switched their focus of study. To turn things around, he would need more help than he had thought. He hired an old friend of Shrake's, Pete Gent, a former Dallas Cowboy wide receiver who had studied advertising in college. Gent now ran a printing press with another Cowboy, Bobby Hayes. They printed rock-and-roll posters. As a football player, Gent had always antagonized the team's conservative coach, Tom

Landry. Gent smoked dope openly, along with his pal Don Meredith, the quarterback. Both men could be reckless on the field—sportswriters made regular bets on who was most likely to wind up in an ambulance before a game's fourth quarter, Meredith or Gent. Football was about "nourish[ing] desperate desires to be as alive as a man can be—to live each day as if it were the last—feeling life pumping through us," Gent said. His taste for extremes was as avid as Brammer's: "Anybody who makes it as a professional football player has survived the horror of real violence, facing the monster that lives in his heart."

He told Brammer he suspected the NFL had placed him under surveillance because he befriended black players. In the eyes of the league, race mixing was a bigger sin than indulging in narcotics. Cars followed him shamelessly. One night he caught a man staring into his house through a pair of binoculars.

Meredith quit the Cowboys rather than endure Landry's authoritarian regime. Soon afterward, Landry cut Gent. Because of his printing business, he didn't need the $200-a-month stipend from SMU, as Brammer did, but he wanted more time to finish the novel he was writing. He intended to expose the NFL as a microcosm of America: racist, rigid older leaders exploiting the young—wrecking their "livers, kidneys, and spines" in rituals of terrible violence—while the boys just wanted to party, to rock and roll, to use the substances that kept them upright on the field as a way to stupefy themselves at home. Brammer was fascinated by Gent's pursuit of excess and by the stories he told (did you know, Gent said, that Dallas "gave all the rookies the Minnesota Multi-phasic Personality test and a standard IQ test—all . . . weighted to make certain the blacks could deal with the pressure of living in the south"). Milner was happy to see his fledgling department click.

"Billie seems serious about wanting to do good so he can stay in teaching," Milner wrote Larry L. King. "It could be a good deal for both of us. If it got him in shape to finish a novel, it would be worth much."

Brammer grew a rakish mustache and bought new clothes. Almost immediately, though, his confidence crashed and his euphoria vanished. Dallas presented a "glum landscape," he mourned to Dorothy: "While not the unremitting drag I half expected, [it] is vaguely dissatisfying all the same. I had thought our friends in Austin, SF, NYC, etc. were troubled, sad, frequently depressing or boring. Much worse here . . . Appears that Dallas has embraced the manner and trappings of [the] movement while wholly dismissing any possibility of revolution." In this bleak city, he said, the provocative seeds of "hip/activist/weeniebob revolution are consumed entire, as by locusts." The young people here are "determined to get their capital gains and have their beads and bell bottoms too. One shortly expects Dailey Plaza [*sic*], site of JFK wipeout, to become gathering place for legions of spoiled, upper mid-class flower children bent on scoring tax-free zillions from . . . homegrown grass."

Over the Labor Day weekend, his friend Angus Wynne planned to mount a big international pop festival just outside Dallas at the Lewisville motorway, near where Brammer had married Nadine in 1950. The concert would feature "heavy cats like Janis, Winter, Grateful Dead," he said. "Should be instructive, enlightening experience—fashion and lifestyle-wise—if I can only keep my wits and what's left of perspective." The show might indicate whether "staid Dallas" had any chance at all of "apocalyptic revolution/reform," though he had "little conviction in any such notion." He concluded, "I am in extremity of woreout."

So was Janis, at the concert. She didn't see Brammer, or anyone else, after singing at three in the morning. The Dead did not appear to be grateful. The day was broiling. So was the night. Everyone listless. Dehydrated. Brammer tried to make out with three "barely post-pubescent" girls, but in fact he was sorely uninterested, his body incapable of stirring.

He had no better luck inciting "reform" in his house, though even before the semester began, the house had become "a gathering place for the disgruntled children and dilettante revolutionaries of Southern Methodist University and wealthy north Dallas," Gent wrote.

"The door was just literally open," Sidney said. Kids could come and go, doing whatever they pleased. Right away, the dean of the Meadows School and the local police arranged to watch the premises. The house was a rowdy outlier near an exclusive private campus ringed by giant fraternities and sororities.

In Gent's novel *North Dallas Forty*, the character Harvey Le Roi Belding is a portrait of Brammer during his SMU period. In Belding's house, Gent wrote, one might find on any given day a "female art major who fucked almost everyone that set foot in the house, something to do with her recent commitment to women's lib," or a male music student who "sat around writing poetry complaining of the injustice in his parents' threat to cut off his allowance because of his long hair and five-year probation for possession."

Belding/Brammer could usually be found "alone in the front room, reading *Rolling Stone* and listening to Leon Russell." He had given up on the kids' "dope-crazed fantasies of correcting the social ills of the great Southwest." He knew they were just biding time until they found "a nice uncompromising job with a big salary and an expense account." His only commitments were to "dope, rock music, young girls, anything else that would bring him intense if transitory pleasure."

As classes began, Milner wanted the program to emphasize reading. He had spoken to newspaper editors from around the country, and they all agreed that young journalists were weak in the basics—composing taut sentences, organizing paragraphs. These deficiencies reflected a lack of reading, unfamiliarity with classics in the field. Milner embarked on an idealistic crusade—to train a whole new generation of reporters—and he believed he had excited Brammer with this challenge. Early in the term, Dorothy came for a visit, to see Brammer off to a good start. She attended one of his classes: "He was wonderful. A wonderful raconteur. High-octane bullshit, you know: 'I cut this article out of the paper this morning,' and he would riff on it." She told Ronnie Dugger, " [H]e'd come into class with an article by Nicholas Von Hoffman. He would read it. They'd go out onto the grass and sit and talk about it. The kids would just open up. They loved it." He gave them Gary Snyder, Jerry Farber's *The Student as Nigger*, and, later, William Sparke and Clark McKowen's *Montage: Investigations in Language*.

Max Woodfin, who would eventually become a speechwriter for Barbara Jordan, took two classes from Brammer, Explanatory Reporting and Editorial Writing. "We were crammed into what seemed to be a storage closet," he recalled.

> We had a one-room lab, a long rectangular room with typewriters lined up on either side of it, so a person spoke to the class in this sort of U-shaped configuration with students on the left and right sides. It was awkward, but Billy Lee made it work. I never had a bored moment in his class. He had a calm demeanor. . . . He would often start with, "What do y'all want to talk about today?" . . . Early in the term, we had already figured out that class didn't necessarily start on time. Sometimes Billy Lee would already be there. Sometimes he wouldn't show up for ten or fifteen minutes. Or Billy would be asleep or hungover. We were a small group. We all knew each other. It wasn't a big lecture class, so we'd always wait for whatever was going to happen.

To fulfill one of the writing assignments, Woodfin interviewed and profiled a housekeeper on his dormitory floor. After class one day, Brammer asked him whether he would like to get some coffee or a hamburger. "I really think I can help this story," he said. He carefully edited the piece with Woodfin, concentrating on the big picture rather than on line-by-line choices. "He told me, 'You need to get into her head,'" Woodfin remembered. "I said I had no idea what that meant. He told me about being a better listener. About not being afraid of silences in an interview. He said many journalists make the mistake of trying to tell their subjects how much *they* know about a topic. They don't really listen."

Woodfin knew Brammer's own writing had stalled. "One day, Jay came into Billy's class. For some reason, they got off on the subject of writer's block: 'What happens when a story isn't writing itself?' At one point, Billy said, 'Hey Jay, how many pictures on your wall have *you* straightened?' Jay said, 'Yeah, that's one of my distractions.'"

Brammer announced one day that the students were in for a treat. "He was clearly stalling for some reason, but nobody knew why," Woodfin said. "The first student on his right was a young woman . . . If anyone could pass for a hippie at SMU, she could: beads, long red hair, barefoot or maybe she wore flip-flops—Mary Lou was her name. She said, 'Mr. Brammer, what's going to happen today?' He was building up all this drama. All the sudden, in walks Jay Milner with Ken Kesey. Some people knew who he was. Others had no clue. Mary Lou said, 'My God, Ken Kesey! What the hell are you doing in Dallas?' Without missing a beat, Kesey said, 'No, young lady, the question is: What the hell are *you* doing in Dallas?'"

Nearly every evening after work, Milner dropped by Brammer's place or Pete Gent's house. "We exchanged cosmic resolutions to all the world's problems as we listened to the high-impact music that was coming out at that time—Dylan, Rolling Stones, Kris Kristofferson, John Prine, the Beatles and the Byrds," Milner recalled. "Billie Lee's hi-fi system was in hock to . . . Gent . . . so we did our listening there." Gent regaled Brammer with stories of how the NFL—the "league that never disappoints"—was emblematic of "everything that's wrong with culture in America." When the cameras shut off after the game clock expired, he said, the players, still high on their capacity for violence, high on the pills that kept them going, high on coke, were naturally going to cause mayhem on the streets of our cities—like army veterans home from war but unable to adjust to civilian life. They were going to party hard, crash their cars, and kill innocent people. How many young phenoms have you read about who were arrested for reckless driving or for threatening people with firearms? Twenty-year-olds dealing drugs and conspiring to murder. It didn't matter how crazy these petty conspiracies were or even who pulled the trigger. The conditions were *set*. Things were going to happen, man. It was the goddam *culture's* fault. And if the kid was rich enough or famous enough, prosecutors would bend over backward not to convict. Hell, *that's* what these young journalists needed to be writing about. Get on it, Mary Lou.

Milner worried about the offbeat characters hanging out in Brammer's house. "In our hearts we empathized with [these] students"—the ones who "read underground publications, rejected materialism, hated the war, sneered at Campus Greeks," but this "did not sit well with everybody downtown, of course, or with our dean," he said. He worried about keeping Brammer on track. "Billie keeps asking me, because he is rather forgetful these days, what it is the course is about," he reported to Larry L. King. Sometimes Milner dispatched "a husky pair of varsity football players who were taking journalism classes to ensure that Mr. Brammer got to class on time." But on the whole, the operation ran smoothly and the program started to stir. Word spread across campus about Kesey's visit, about stimulating guest appearances by important editors such as Dwight Sargent from the *New York Herald Tribune*. The Journalism Department "entered upon a renaissance that began attracting some of SMU's better students," Milner said. "By the end of that school year, we had 125 majors and minors signed up for the next fall."

In mid-January 1970, the *Dallas Morning News* ran a splashy piece about the "bright lights" that had salvaged the Journalism Department and "lured an increasing number of students into journalism at a school which previously was not widely regarded in that field." Milner explained why he had hired Billy Lee Brammer: "I knew he'd read everything in print for the last twenty years." Brammer admitted that he had been wary of teaching: "I'm finding it easier now, but at first it was difficult dealing with kids who aren't kids. It's not the college I remember." Most students, he said, were simultaneously "very idealistic and cynical" about the average American newspaper.

In his notebook, this wry aside: "Teaching is the best thing I ever stumbled into . . . This past semester I taught public affairs reporting. Really a fine course for young people desperately eager to qualify themselves as third-rate reporters for any daily with monopoly domination of media in towns of 25,000 population or less . . . A sampling of my classroom quotes: 'I got a black cat bone. I got a mojo tooth. I got John the Conqueroo.'"

The program had garnered such positive notice nationwide that Bowling Green State University in Ohio approached Brammer, asking him to serve as writer in residence the following year.

---

"I don't know exactly when Billie Lee's determination began to unravel," Milner said. "Many students were telling me how interesting, and even inspiring, his classes were, but others were complaining that Billie Lee wasn't editing their copy in the newswriting lab. 'He just glances at my stories and says, "Looks fine to me,"' one worried coed told me. I checked into the situation, and soon decided to take over the lab myself for the remainder of the spring semester. By the end of the [school] year, Billie Lee was either missing class altogether or bumbling his way through them."

An accumulation of mescaline and speed and too many wakeful days had dropped him into a pit of bitterness, paranoia, and melancholy self-criticism. Dorothy had written to tell him that her relationship with Arthur Vance had exposed her to unpleasant talk from members of the old political guard. As a result, she felt unfairly targeted, uncomfortable, and uncertain how to move easily around Austin. This sparked reams of speed tips from Brammer—well-meaning advice that slipped into anger and self-pity. "A politician sensitive about his own integrity does not [compromise] his mistress . . . a man in love with a woman as vulnerable as you to unconventional behavior makes effective effort to protect his loved one from murderous gossip, unnecessary exposure, destructive guilt. Austin, particularly in its politics, is absolutely merciless in this connection," he began. Then, brutally, he rehashed recent history:

> You were a terribly fragile and exposed piece of goods all this past year, and I wish to heaven I could have looked after you more sensibly in San Francisco and later in Denver . . . I'm not condemning Arthur in the hope of improving my own standing alongside his conduct. That's irrelevant—I'm excruciatingly aware of how my own instability, thoughtlessness, and emotional paralysis combined to eliminate any hope for a viable marriage: no money, no children, meaningless sex, obsession with drugs, etc. What's at stake is your future.

Then he *did* attack: Arthur Vance possessed the "real charm, evident warmth, and the sort of vitality characteristic of every worthwhile politician I've ever known," he wrote.

> They are delightful people, but horrible things tend to happen to those around them. Look at the Kennedys; or Johnson, with an alcoholic brother, pillhead sister dead of misadventure, totally screwed up wife and children, best friend and top aide driven to eating a vice squad detective in a convenient YMCA; look at Eckhardt's wife, dead of suicide; or Nadine, every bit as miserable as [Eckhardt's ex] . . . the point is, a really ballsy politician's loved ones are mere extensions of themselves as heroic figures . . . They [the politicians] are propelled by notions of personal drama; the quality is close to being a prerequisite for office.

The letter continued for several single-spaced pages, advising Dorothy, sympathizing with her, quoting wise literature. And through it all, Brammer admitted he feared he was placating her to cover the absolute rage she provoked in him: "At some subliminal level . . . lurks [the] hideous suspicion that perhaps all this generous-hearted compassion is mere reeking bullshit and that my real motives constitute . . . [an] emotional bushwhacking to elicit sporadic bleats of pain from the lady. Jesus, I hope not."

He missed class after class to produce such letters—ironically, *writing again*, as Milner hoped he would do. The novelist Marshall Terry, chairman of the SMU English Department, a genial man with a great regard for *The Gay Place*, went to Brammer's apartment one day to try to persuade him to return to his teaching. It would be in everybody's best interest, Terry said—Brammer's, the students', the university's. Did he know how many people would be ecstatic to see him stabilize and publish another wonderful novel? Brammer thanked him for his generosity, his kindness and concern, and then went back to writing long, dense letters to Dorothy. It became apparent to Milner that Terry's plea had been Brammer's last best chance—the powers that be were poised to fire him. The SMU experience hadn't been a *total* washout: "I personally know of three students who were inspired by Billie Lee to read their first books. That alone is worth a lot," Milner reasoned. Still, he urged Brammer to waste no further time in accepting the Bowling Green offer.

One late-summer day, Pete Gent put Brammer on a plane to Ohio, "although he grumbled all the way to the airport that he'd prefer to stay and teach at SMU," Milner said.

---

Bowling Green, a former industrial town twenty-four miles southwest of Toledo, was "pretty, pleasant, seeming[ly] safe from hippie peril and riot squad assault," Brammer wrote Milner. "Improbably picturesque . . . [it was] the spit-niffling image of Anderson's Winesburg, Ohio, grotesques and all." Cornfields surrounded the prefab apartment building he lived in near the town's western edge, along with narrow, dusty roads traversed by the Amish's horse-drawn carriages. Watery local beer. Weak northern sun. Shaded woods. Early autumn snow. The coldest wind he had ever felt, slicing off the choppy gray surface of Lake Erie.

In a note on the menu, the sole Mexican food restaurant in town apologized to its customers for the food's exotic qualities, assuring them their health would not be imperiled by the chicken tacos.

More than once when he told someone he had come from Dallas, the person answered, "Oh. You're the ones that killed Kennedy."

In early October 1970, he heard that Janis Joplin had died of a heroin overdose, alone in a room at the Landmark Motel in Los Angeles. Her death occurred just weeks after she had returned to Port Arthur for her high school reunion and been ridiculed by her former classmates. Brammer sat, still and quiet, in his apartment watching the World Series on television, drinking Stroh's, playing Crosby, Stills, Nash, and Young or George Harrison's "My Sweet Lord."

He drove to Toledo. He bought a copy of *Rolling Stone* filled with Janis tributes. Chet Helms was quoted as saying he had last seen her a few days before she died. She had come into the Troubadour in LA wearing a bright red dress. "I just wanted to look good," she had said. "She seemed cheerful," Helms said, "but there was something . . . " At the end of the evening, she announced she was leaving. No one responded. No one offered to take her back to her motel. She slipped off, unnoticed.

Kenneth Threadgill told the magazine that Janis was a "wonderful old gal, just good common country people. I thought a hell of a lot of Janis."

Brammer turned up the Krishna chants, watched another strikeout.

On the narrow roads circling the cornfields, the horse-drawn wagons clattered past the town like little hearses, or the phantom contraption in that Emily Dickinson poem, the one where Death comes a-callin'.

He was spooked. He was bored. He missed his poodles (he had left the crazy dogs with his Dallas friends). He missed that special blend of Texas "rocky roll," the combination of "classic blues and boogie, bluegrass and coonass."

In a letter to Milner, he said time warps riddled the United States. Berkeley seemed four or five years ahead of SMU, which had only just reached the peak of hipness UT had achieved years earlier. "Bowling Green is somewhere there at hootenanny/Kingston Trio stage of... what the fuck was it?" he wrote. "Pat Boone perhaps, two three weeks overdue at the barber shop. The ladies are rather like Sandra Dee in miniskirt and training bra. My god I'm suffocating in all this interminable wholesomeness." He pleaded with Milner to please help him get back to Dallas. He signed the letter "Rotter-in-Residence."

Sidney informed him she had graduated from high school and gone to work in Senator Ralph Yarborough's DC office, supporting his reelection bid. In spite of her disillusionment after the Chicago Democratic Convention, in spite of serious doubts about the efficacy of establishment politics, she had decided to give the system one more chance. It was something to do now that she was out of school. She told her father she had trouble staying upbeat, with the interminable war in Southeast Asia, with Texas liberals facing stiff right-wing challenges in their district races. She was learning tough lessons: for decades, as long as conservative Democrats held sway in Texas, the Republican Party could never gain a toehold in the state. Liberals like Yarborough remained exceptions to the status quo, but his success, the success of the *Texas Observer*, and the liberals' increasing visibility caused blowback within the Democratic Party. In the event, Yarborough was defeated in the Democratic primary in 1970 by Lloyd Bentsen, a decidedly more conservative figure.

Brammer wished to lift his daughter's spirits, but he also wanted to give her his honest assessment of the state of the union. She had asked him, "Should I put off college for a while?" He wrote her, care of the senator's office, "You're currently living through a goddam revolution (now a couple or three years old—most revolutions last a discomfiting interval of time)—the most incredible, meaningful, provocative, and staggeringly *avant* or farrrr-outttt collective horror show ever recorded in [the] tidy, undistinguished history of this glorious republic of morons."

> The Civil War was merely a spastic interlude of provincial savagery... This one is infinitely worse in terms of its pervasive destructiveness, the brutalizing of collective sensibility, the profoundly upsetting *rapidity* of changes unfolding (each change producing still more change—and at continuously foreshortened intervals of time). It's the mother of apocalypse... combination fun house, plastic computer village and nightmare alley. It's all coming apart... [This] is bound to traumatize Americans into savagery or derangement or self-destruction... Indeed, we're behaving like spoiled, sadistic... storm-troopers even now, barely into

> the preliminary skirmishing, our *machismo* imperiled, our traditions subverted . . . I am frankly terrified, as revolutions, however glorious and overdue, are an interminable nightmare all the same . . . Do I club your hopes with too much pessimism? I don't mean any such thing, really . . . Lordy, I am terrible sorry to have got out of control that way . . . I can never seem to terminate the babble, once underway and flapping like sixty and wired with sufficient wattage to power the Grateful Dead . . . All I [wanted] to say was college is a worthwhile experience currently because the shit's coming down all over; and college . . . puts you smack in the action . . . To me, in any case, the learning experience is the biggest, baddest, most provocative turn-on available to the species . . . oh mah heavens, it is better than wine (not, decidedly, better than wommen, of course; too much to learn in that seldom-explored backwater even at this late hour) . . . [I] beg forgiveness for all my wretched excesses.

---

In the spring of 1971, Jay Milner worked a bureaucratic miracle on Brammer's behalf (taking advantage of a new school administrator, unfamiliar with the recent past). SMU reinstated Brammer as a journalism instructor. Right away, his rental house became another hippie hangout.

He was shooting "straight crystal methedrine . . . the napalm of all drugs," said Al Reinert, "a quarter-gram tapped into a spoon and dissolved in water, cooked on a flame to the color of milk and the warmth of blood, sucked with nervous fingers into the syringe, the arm quickly tied off, artery pumped-shot." He became more forgetful than ever. A local filmmaker had made a documentary about Ken Kesey and the Merry Pranksters. He asked Brammer whether he could screen the film in Brammer's house. On the night of the event, Brammer wandered in late and wondered "who the hell was showing movies in his living room."

Sidney came to visit, at loose ends after the failed Yarborough campaign. "Oh my God, she's got long hair!" Brammer exclaimed, greeting her. "He was trying to see where my head was at," Sidney said. "What's your favorite music? What do you like? Have you read my book? I wish you would." (Nadine had always told her she wouldn't like it.) Still the mentor, he gave her a copy of Rudy Wurlitzer's novel *Nog* as an example of revolutionary American writing.

Sidney's boyfriend thought he was "cool," but underneath the great simpatico relationship she enjoyed with her father, she knew she needed to keep some distance from him, for her own safety. She had an opportunity to enroll in classes at UT, so she and her boyfriend left for Austin. On February 23, 1971, within days of her departure, the police raided Brammer's house. He was "busted in the company of exotic plants and spices, syringes, et al.," Larry L. King informed Bud Shrake. Brammer seemed oblivious of his troubles. When his pals raised money to hire a lawyer for him, he frittered it all away. They tried again; when the lawyer contacted him, wanting to meet to plan a defense strategy, Brammer responded that "he was sorry but he had not been given enough notice and had big plans that night and could not see him. [The lawyer] was alternately wryly amused and properly horrified," King told Shrake.

At his friends' urging, Brammer finally engaged legal help. "No one wants to see the little bastard have to go to jail," Milner said, despite being burned by his buddy. A Dallas attorney got the charges reduced to a single count of marijuana possession. Brammer pleaded guilty and accepted five years' probation.

He decided to "have a garage sale and move back to Austin," Sidney said. "He told me, 'I'm really glad my parents didn't find out about the bust.' His father was blind and deaf at that point; his parents would soon move to Austin to be looked after by Bill's sister, Rose."

---

The arrest forced Brammer to confront his problems as honestly as he could. In a handwritten fragment tucked into his notebooks, he recounted his drug history: "Starting senior year in college I have been taking amplet or meth—legal at [the] time—regular use of prescribed narcotics . . . from early 50s through work on the Hill with LBJ, as [a] corres[pondent] for *Time* . . . through [the] 60s . . . to '72 when pressure came down on physicians' prescribing. Now after 25 years of sustained ingestion of meth and amplet, fair to say I have developed not an addiction, not even a metabolic dependence—but one hell of a reinforced and desperately fundamental well-oiled work habit and so much an integral part of rituals of writing and research as booze . . . notepaper, fresh type-ribbons . . . [drugs] suddenly no longer available—worse, poss[ession] of black market stuff . . . not for getting stoned but for simply getting—." Here, the fragment breaks off.

Worried friends confronted him: How could he wreck his mind and body so badly? Did he want to wind up like Janis? He answered, "Dope depends on what one brings to the experience: metabolically, chemically, intellectually, emotionally. It's awfully difficult to generalize on a subject with so many volatile elements, combinations, and variables." He agreed with Walt Whitman that "those who corrupt their own bodies conceal themselves"; on the other hand, corruption was not necessarily the end result of narcotics use, any more than was spiritual enlightenment. "The spiritual is none of our damn business," he insisted. Speed made his nerves taut. With Whitman, he would

*sing the body electric . . .*
*Food, drink, pulse, digestion, sweat . . .*
*The thin red jellies within you or within me, the bones and the marrow in the bones . . .*
*O I say these are not the parts and poems of the body only, but of the soul,*
*O I say now these are the soul!*

# 20.

Throughout the fall and winter of 1972, folks living along the banks of the Pedernales whispered that Lyndon Johnson was dying. Two years earlier, he had been evacuated to the Brooke Army Medical Center in San Antonio with chest pains. Ever since, he had been tottery, slow. He had grown his hair long in back, thin white wisps tickling his shirt collars—an aging hippie. Then, in June 1972, while visiting his daughter Lynda in Virginia, he suffered a severe heart attack. After a two-week hospital stay, he returned to his ranch.

He had spent the previous two years working with Doris Kearns on his memoirs. At the ranch, a "curious ritual developed," she wrote. "I would awaken at five and get dressed. Half an hour later Johnson would knock on my door, dressed in his robe and pajamas. As I sat in a chair by the window, he climbed into the bed, pulling the sheets up to his neck, looking like a cold and frightened child . . . He spoke of the beginnings and ends of things, of dreams and fantasies. His words seemed to flow from some deep well of sadness, nostalgia, and longing."

Early in 1971, he published the book of himself, the volume he hoped would correct all other impressions of him, including the comic one in *The Gay Place*. It was a dry, bloodless tome entitled *The Vantage Point: Perspectives of the Presidency, 1963–1969*. Kearns's view of the project can be surmised from a comment she slipped into the book from Marcus Cunliffe, a historian of American literature: "Political oratory was a variant of the tall tale. The tall tale spread West to reach heights of mendacity. It required a narrator and an audience . . . Was [the story] true? The question had little meaning. What mattered was the story itself."

For better or worse, in completing his personal and political lore, Johnson had brought his work to a close.

"I've got an instinct," he confessed to Kearns. He knew his successor in the White House, Richard Nixon, would slowly starve the Great Society until she was nothing but a shriveled old lady. "And when she dies, I too will die."

"Rumors were all over Austin that Johnson was calling in his oldest friends for last farewells, some of them friends he had broken with years before—Walter Jenkins, even Bobby Baker—trying to mend the fences of his cyclonic life," Al Reinert said. "All that winter Billy was obsessed with Johnson, pulling out old notes, old tapes, reading all the books and articles he could find, telling the old stories again."

A typed fragment wedged into Brammer's notebook reads: "It's come to that already, has it? Well, then, why the hell not. Recollect and re-experience, retrieve his bits and pieces and reassemble this ungainly, great-eared, goaty old squinch-eyed delegate from our boondock pathologies. Cut and paste and celebrate him now . . . [the] warts-and-all Big Pumpkin, commanding his colossal vanities and deceits, the mountain-sized eccentricities and sub-clinical derangements."

Would Brammer be invited for a valedictory visit to the ranch?

An LBJ staffer, Warren Woodward, had once said of his boss, "He collects people. And once he thinks he has collected someone, he can't ever really let him go. He has to get him back. Warehouse him on a shelf. He will be there if he's ever needed again. Or if company is wanted after everyone else has gone to bed. He has people on the shelf who have been waiting there for years. Waiting for his call."

The call never came for Billy Lee Brammer—perhaps because he couldn't be reached. Not easily. "Back in Austin, he was moving from place to place, living pretty much out of boxes," Shelby said. Aside from his best friends, only his probation officer knew how to find him quickly, to ascertain (according to the probation notice) whether it remained Brammer's "desire to become a peaceful and law-abiding citizen."

In mid-December 1972, Brammer glimpsed Johnson one last time, from afar. The occasion was a civil rights conference at the newly opened

LBJ Presidential Library in Austin, near the university campus. (During the library's dedication ceremonies, Johnson's old antagonists, "the antiwar demonstrators," included "a group of women dressed as witches who put a hex on the building," the writer Gail Caldwell recalled. "Six of them were arrested. A year later, a crack appeared in the structure that no one, not even the engineers, could explain.")

At the civil rights conference, Thurgood Marshall, Roy Wilkins, Hubert Humphrey, Earl Warren, Julian Bond, and other dignitaries gathered to reflect on and praise Johnson for his legacy in the fight for racial equality. Bond said he had often disagreed with Johnson, but "*By God*, I wish we had him [in office] now." Barbara Jordan called him a true revolutionary. The conference took place just five weeks before a cease-fire was announced in Vietnam and—almost simultaneously—Nixon announced his plans for unraveling the Great Society. Johnson would retreat to his ranch and indulge in paranoid visions of blistering betrayals by all the friends he had known. But on this, the last day of the civil rights retrospective, he wanted to bask in the glow of his best achievements as president.

His doctors had warned him not to attend the ceremonies—but if he *did* insist on going, not to exert himself by speaking. Nevertheless, he drove the seventy miles from his ranch to Austin in a punishing ice storm. He stood, wobbly and pained, to tell the crowd, "The progress has been much too small; we haven't done nearly enough. I am sort of ashamed of myself, that I had six years and couldn't do more than I did."

That man!

To Brammer, sitting silently in the back of the room, the event "had something of the air of a reunion of old classmates." The speakers were all impressive. But Brammer, still in thrall to the mighty Pumpkin after all these turbulent years, all the public and private hurts, said, "It remained . . . for Mr. Johnson himself to show why he loomed so much larger than President Nixon, who for all his efforts at lessening international tension and his historic trips to Peking and Moscow, still seems colorless, in much the same way that the current leaders of France pale before President DeGaulle and those of Great Britain before Winston Churchill."

For the fresh, new *Texas Monthly* magazine, Brammer penned the last words he would ever publish about Lyndon Johnson:

> [He] was in a mellow mood. He walked slowly, attentive to each step; his wife kept a sharp eye out for his every move and sign. He looked older, like, well, a statesman . . . His speech was something of a valedictory

> address, a retrospect by a man who had come a long way—in stature, in position and in understanding. This was not the President Johnson, exhorting us by his record, that we remembered, opinion poll in his pocket. He was even downright humble . . . If the rest of the participants had been rudderless and leaderless, looking back to the past and uncertain of the future, Mr. Johnson had some advice. "All is not lost . . . If they are going to dismantle all of this work we've done, why, then we need to bring it to the attention of the nation. You all get together and go see the President. He'll see you. And don't start out by telling him that he's terrible, because he doesn't think he's terrible. Just tell him, 'Mr. President, we know you want to do what's right, and we know it's a lot easier to want to do what's right than to know what's right.' And then you tell him what's right. He'll do it."
>
> Mrs. Johnson was standing by the podium now, and her concern was no longer hidden . . . She looked terribly proud of him, but also protective and worried. The President was not to be denied . . . "I can't provide much go-go anymore, but I can provide hope and encouragement—sell a few wormy calves now and then—to see that we continue."

Brammer concluded: "President Johnson was a giant, and remains one. What he did wrong, he did royally wrong; what he did right, he did royally right. Events are out of his control now, and we seem fated to be led by less imaginative, less colorful, less real people."

No records exist indicating that Johnson said hello to Brammer that icy December day, or that he even caught his eye. But once more, Brammer had observed the man closely, appreciated the fullness of his complexities, and turned him into words. In so doing, he said his good-bye and achieved a momentary grace. "The only person throughout the two-day seminar who said 'we shall overcome' was President Johnson," Brammer wrote. "He seemed to believe it."

---

"Hidy. Got any speed?" Brammer would greet his friends. At one party, Bud Shrake secretly followed his pal with a stopwatch. The longest interval, all night, between Brammer's requests for pills was twenty-three seconds. Dorothy, who had had a child, Lila, with Arthur Vance—she taught Lila to call Brammer "Uncle Looney"—said, "He was shooting crystal Methedrine and taking acid and mescaline at the same time. He was just a mess."

When he got desperate, he took his poodle's epilepsy medication. "One of the more improbable figures" around the Scholz Biergarten in those days was a 350-pound veterinarian named Louis Buck, Dave Richards recalled. He "made house calls and was much favored for this reason. It was rumored that he was the last-resort source for speed . . . in Bill's later years, dispensing pooch pep pills to help Bill through his darker days."

Sidney, now attending classes at UT, used to pop over to her father's house. He "could be passed out," she said. "I'd sit at his desk and talk out loud to him . . . He never fulfilled any fatherly responsibilities—except that he just gave me that solace all his life."

He told her he would always respond to her with "endless love and gentle schizophrenia." He gave her a copy of Thomas Mann's *Death in Venice*. The book featured a short story entitled "Disorder and Early Sorrow." "That's him," Sidney said. "He really got off on that line." In the story, a history professor named Dr. Cornelius finds his "sense of the eternal" in his "love for his little daughter," Ellie, the only part of him safe from the "wounding inflicted by the times."

Sidney offered to help him write again. She would take dictation from him, she said. He told her, "Honey, please don't worry about me." On another occasion, he said, "Stop being an overachiever and become a blissfully happy and reasonably well-adjusted hedonist like me."

In spite of his difficulties and afflictions, he always seemed "marvelously happy" to Nadine whenever she saw him in Austin. "He had a wonderful life," she believed. "Women just loved Billy Lee because they could . . . tell him anything. He never passed judgment. And he got off on everybody's story."

She wasn't grasping how, increasingly, his accepting nature was becoming an emotional distance, a consuming ambivalence about people and things, tempered by the drugs—and how, under certain combinations of drugs or in rugged periods between the highs, harsh judgments flooded his mind. From his notebook:

> Nothing turns one sour quite so suddenly and irrationally as the discovery that one's very best friends and lovers are fully capable of the most thoughtless acts, graceless presumptions, deceits, outrageous mindless vanities, stupefying betrayals, and self-serving transgressions. Never in my life have I endured any suffering imposed by persons for whom I felt any enmity. Invariably the killer *blows* have been indifferently laid

> on by those closest to me. Examples: Nadine . . . Fletcher . . . of course Dorothy. Never has any one of these people . . . expressed concern, professed regret, or confessed to the mindless self-indulgence of their chickenshit ways.

Perhaps this buried anger, weighted with parental guilt and fear of creditors, accounted for his compunction to wear a thick trench coat and hide behind trees when he approached Nadine's Georgetown house once in the early 1970s—presumably with the hope of seeing his children before Nadine saw him. He was "freaked out," he later told Nadine. Her friend Susan Streit, a UT grad who had come to Washington to work for Congressman Charlie Wilson, believed "Billy was afraid of Nadine because he always, *always* loved her."

Shelby, soon to graduate from Holy Trinity High School in DC, was seriously pursuing acting and playwriting. Brammer attended her performances and gave her flowers. He promised he would take her to the capitals of Europe so that she could dazzle all the boys with her beauty. She was old enough now to appreciate his "lovely sense of humor" and the fact that he "didn't bullshit"—unlike Eckhardt, who grumbled about having to pay her upcoming college tuition. She and her friends were casually experimenting with drugs, and she thought she "had a cool dad." "He *did* steal—not from me," she said. "He would take stuff, but then he'd pass it on. He had a voyeuristic 'what's yours is mine' thing. I remember going down to visit him in Austin once, at around this time, and he gave me a car, a Ford Falcon. I'm sure it was stolen. The stick shift was held on by a screwdriver, and a coat hanger kept the trunk closed. But—typical Billy Lee—it had a great radio and a wonderful set of speakers."

Willie, a quiet, reserved teenager, practiced his magic tricks, worked part-time at Al's Magic Shop on Pennsylvania Avenue, and avoided Eckhardt's political functions as much as possible. His stepdad did get him out of trouble, once, when he wrecked the car, by calling on a high-powered lawyer friend—to *that* extent, politics was useful. Otherwise, Willie wanted no part of it. At home, he was often left alone, not always aware of where his parents were. They were "forgetful," he liked to say. In public, he adopted a "cool" persona, but he admitted to friends that this was a protective front, a way of escaping the pressure to worship social status, which warped virtually everyone in Washington. As he got older, he appreciated visiting Brammer in Texas, where the people were "nicer."

More and more, Nadine preferred being in Texas, too. "None of that so-called big-time Washington social life had any basis in reality. It was hard to find real people . . . such a pile of shit," she reflected later. Besides, she had come to realize that Eckhardt was an alcoholic—"he didn't drink until 5 p.m., but then he slugged down two or three doubles in the office and moseyed over to a reception to drink and graze at some lobbyist's invitation." She grew bored and disenchanted. She initiated several new affairs ("How I had the time and energy to arrange these is beyond me—I can only conclude that they were the result of a volatile combination of an enormous amount of energy, raging hormones, and a deep insecurity"). She hung out with her friends—Molly Ivins, who told her, "If Bob had not been taken care of by good women all his life, he'd have been totally nonfunctional"; Susan Streit; Bob Sherrill, a Texas journalist, and his wife, Mary. Nadine and Streit liked to smoke pot together—to Eckhardt's embarrassment, especially one night when he came home, bringing for dinner "one of the Supreme Court justices," Streit recalled.

In her notebook at the time, Nadine wrote, "I am exhausted. I am on a downer about what a superficial life we have in Washington. I'm becoming more introspective and I'm afraid the more power Bob attains, the more he is seduced by 'power trip' sycophants."

Then Streit left for Texas. She moved in with a travel writer named Richard West, part of a coterie of journalists and artists gathering in Austin to begin a new venture, *Texas Monthly* magazine. Living in a guest apartment behind Streit's place, on Shoal Creek across from Pease Park, was Billy Lee Brammer. "I became close friends with Billy Lee," West said. "He was a dear, kind man, but a self-wounding figure, charming when high (never a better conversationalist), almost lifeless when not." Willie would visit, witnessing "several eye-opening episodes in that guest apartment"—adults coming and going in various states of dishabille, exploring alternate planes of consciousness. "Was *I* there?" Susan Streit asked him in my presence. "Sort of," Willie answered.

*Texas Monthly* was founded by Mike R. Levy, a twenty-six-year-old plumber's son from Dallas, a graduate of the Wharton School at the University of Pennsylvania and the University of Texas School of Law. He said he was "convinced that my state was ready for a really first class magazine that [would] appeal directly to the sophisticated, cosmopolitan folks that Texans have become." In other words, its intended readership was the generation of citizens first described in *The Gay Place*. Levy hired as his editor William Broyles, a former student of Larry McMurtry's at Rice University. He brought along Greg Curtis, a classmate from the McMurtry seminars.

"Neither Bill [Broyles] nor I had ever written for magazines," Curtis told me. "You know, when it came right down to it, it was all a bluff, in a way. We were *curious*, but we had no experience."

"Brammer was the second person I hired, and he gave the magazine everything he had," Broyles wrote later.

"Billy Lee really *had* done the writing, and so that was something in itself," Curtis said. "In that sense, he was enormously important to us."

Other young writers joining the staff—Al Reinert, Jan Reid—considered Brammer their mentor. "Billy was that which he'd never had himself: a resident guide, teacher, standard of comparison. He provided a homegrown role model, flawed surely, but that was a vital lesson in itself," Reinert said.

> I had been a cub reporter at the *Houston Chronicle* and managed to get myself fired because I had the wrong politics. I'd met Broyles and done a couple of assignments for him before the magazine went to press. Billy Lee took to me. He gave me advice, he edited me, and he gave me drugs. The first time I took LSD was at a *Texas Monthly* summer softball game. Billy Lee walked up to me and put a blotter on my tongue. I went out and tried to play outfield. *Very* long fly balls.
>
> He was an excellent editor. He had really lost the ability to write at that point, but he was still a careful reader and a kindhearted soul. He wanted to bring out the best in you. He concentrated on positive-energy rewrites. He was not a line editor, a pencil editor. He was a read-it-and-think-what-you're-trying-to-say editor. I'd never written magazine pieces before. Broyles had never worked a day at a magazine. Greg Curtis had been running a print shop in San Francisco. We were learning on the job. Billy Lee took us seriously.

"We had a sort of bullpen of writers," Curtis said. At first they all shared a single Selectric typewriter. There was a circulation manager and a salesperson "who had been married to Jayne Mansfield," he recalled. "He had this kind of zoned-out look. Probably, with Mansfield, he hadn't gotten much oxygen."

"It became clear that we had to take care of Billy Lee," Curtis said. One day, in an editorial meeting, Brammer sat back in a rickety rolling chair. He folded his hands behind his head. A few minutes later, he startled. "My hands!" he cried. "Where are my hands?"

Once, Curtis drove him to Houston "for an eye appointment. We came back . . . We'd been gone ten or twelve hours . . . and the record player in his apartment . . . you know how those old record players would work; the arm would come down and when it reached the end of the album, it would reset and play the album again . . . the record had been playing over and over all that time. All day, Bill's poor dog had been forced to listen to Fleetwood Mac."

But if you did take care of Brammer, he would tie you to a high standard of literary quality, Broyles said:

> He could sit for an hour reading a story, squinting through his cataracts, munching Tom's Peanut Patties and swilling endless Pepsi-Colas, and we would almost forget he was there; then, very patiently and politely, looking like a benign Mel Brooks, he would tell us in brilliantly succinct fashion just what the article needed. We already knew what was good enough; he taught us what was truly good, and that is the crucial difference . . . For a while I thought [his work] would be the first steps back on the road to his own literary recovery, but after a few months he just gradually stopped showing up, and we went on as best we could without him. I sometimes thought he had it in his mind that he had shown us all he could, and we had to do the rest ourselves.

The magazine's appearance coincided—probably not by accident—with a major shift in Austin's music scene. On November 27, 1972, Roky Erickson, judged legally sane and released from his electroshock therapy at the Rusk State Hospital in East Texas, reunited the 13th Floor Elevators for a show at Eddie Wilson's new venue, the Armadillo World Headquarters. The band's performance was ragged. The unbilled arrival of Willie Nelson, who played a short set before the Elevators hit the stage, completely eclipsed them. The era of pure psychedelia had passed; the Cosmic Cowboy had arrived. "Eddie Wilson . . . the ramrod of the operation, would try anything," Nelson said. As a young man, Wilson had tucked himself under Kenneth Threadgill's wing; he had watched how Threadgill pulled together different classes of people by merging seemingly divergent musical styles in his club. At the Armadillo, a warehouse near an old armory by a parking lot where people used to piss after shows at the Vulcan Gas Company, Wilson "booked acts from the Austin Ballet to Ravi Shankar to Bette Midler," Nelson recalled.

> Rednecks and hippies who had thought they were natural enemies began mixing at the Armadillo without too much bloodshed. They discovered they both liked good music. Pretty soon you saw a longhair cowboy wearing hippie beads and a bronc rider's belt buckle, and you were seeing a new type of person . . . I saw which direction this movement was going and threw myself in front of it . . . A new audience was opening up for me. I phoned Waylon [Jennings] in Nashville and told him he ought to come play the Armadillo. Waylon walked into that big hall and saw all those redneck hippies boogying . . . and he turned to me and said, "What the shit have you got me into, Willie?"

Bud Shrake explained why the armadillo became the natural symbol for Texas cowboy-hippies—they were both nocturnal, communal creatures, odd-looking but tougher than they appeared, and they liked to keep their noses in the grass. Jim Franklin, the former *Rag* artist who designed posters for the Armadillo and decorated the venue, said the Dillo was "where the 'necks met the heads." Cheap pot and cold beer—that was all it took, Eddie Wilson said, served in an updated state-fair-carnival atmosphere, like the old rodeo arenas that Brammer used to visit with his dad. In this stew of the traditional and the new, sincerity cozied up to irony. Barriers broke. One minute, a disc jockey at the Austin radio station KOKE wouldn't play Janis Joplin's posthumously released "Me and Bobby McGee" because it wasn't "country" enough; the next minute, George Harrison's "My Sweet Lord" dominated airtime because its slide guitar solo had just enough "country" to be authentic.

No single album captured the blend of irony and sincerity in Austin honky-tonks as well as Jerry Jeff Walker's *Viva Terlingua*, released in 1973. Jan Reid put it this way: Walker's version of Guy Clark's "L. A. Freeway" combined, in its instrumentation, the "jangling clash of the cultural influences on Austin music: a long-haired Teamster crazed by too much speed and too little sex, too stoned to move but in a hurry to get home." Moreover, while "any Depression Okie could identify with the lyrics, so could any freak who had ever made the mistake of driving an automobile under the influence of LSD."

Susan Streit heard the album and fell in love with the singer. A year later, she would marry him.

By the time Ed Guinn appeared on the cover of the *Austin Sun*, in April 1975, wearing an armadillo belt buckle, a cowboy hat, and a gun holster snugging two beer bottles, Austin's musical transformation was complete—this former member of the acid-soaked Conqueroo had become a Cosmic Cowpoke. Like the cosmopolitan chic in the pages of *Texas Monthly*, the cover photo suggested an even larger social shift: a citified African American could proudly, even if humorously, stand tall wearing a traditional trail-riding outfit—few people now questioned the blurring of such distinctions. Here was the *real* Great Society. Much excess, much self-destruction had been loosed to make it possible.

Among Willie Nelson's and Jerry Jeff Walker's most enthusiastic audience members were Texas state legislators, Capitol secretaries (with copies of *Texas Monthly* tucked into the outer pockets of their bags), and other young political professionals who—however career-oriented—liked to imagine themselves as cutting-edge. This desire to be fashionable had always characterized Texas liberals. Like the music, they were experiencing dramatic changes. Their long push to be recognized, their refusal to compromise—or to ever give LBJ a break—had driven many conservatives from the Democratic Party, increasing the Republicans' numbers. Though the liberals had made, and would make, several gains in the state, a backlash was inevitable. For example, Ann Richards's political career began with her relentless efforts to elect Sarah Weddington to the Texas House of Representatives. Weddington would successfully argue the Supreme Court case *Roe v. Wade*, which led to abortions becoming legal nationwide in 1973. Two years later, over beers at Scholz's, Gary Cartwright talked Richards into running for county commissioner. This set her on a path to becoming the governor of Texas—but as of this writing, Richards is the last modern Democrat to hold the office. The Republican Party now holds sway in Texas. In a sense, the liberals' excesses led to their self-destruction.

Billy Lee Brammer had become a local legend for his embodiment of excess. Jerry Jeff Walker met him one night through Bud Shrake. "We'd be out carousing around, going to try to find somebody who was still up or doing something—and there was always Billy Lee," Walker said. "He was just this comical speed freak in a garage apartment, looking old way before his time. You know, when you live day to day, the way he did, a year can be really long."

Gail Caldwell, a young writer drawn from West Texas to Austin in the early 1970s by the city's promise of "holy madness," encountered Brammer at Scholz's. It seemed to her that he was trying to conceive of strategies for staying out of trouble, but he was "not as strong as his worst impulses." She perceived greatness in him; she had heard the stories of *The Gay Place*; but she also sensed that he "had never recovered from his greatness." Neither politics nor art seemed to interest him anymore. The achievements had been made, the changes had been wrought. Now, all that remained was to live out the days. "I was twenty years younger" than Brammer, Caldwell said. "[I] had only just begun to understand how fine a book he'd written and how rough and sad the life had been."

---

"Austin knew and understood [Lyndon] Johnson better than Washington ever had, and a hush fell over the city as his funeral caravan moved out toward the Hill Country for the last time," Jan Reid wrote. Nadine and Bob Eckhardt had flown from Washington for the funeral. She had heard that LBJ's "unexpected death of a heart attack had occurred in much the same fashion and circumstance as the death of the fictitious Arthur Fenstemaker who died in bed with his secretary" in *The Gay Place*. The official word was that Johnson had been discovered alone on the floor of the bedroom at his ranch by Secret Service agents on the afternoon of January 22, 1973—the day the Supreme Court issued its ruling in *Roe v. Wade*.

"Steam rising from their tires, the vehicles [of the funeral cortege] moved out Highway 290 toward Johnson City, past the mock-western storefronts, the barbecue cafés, the last-chance mobile home lots, the quasi-luxurious tract residences, a fruit stand closed for the winter whose owners proudly displayed a pair of pruning shears with the notice: Hippie Clippers," Reid wrote. It was two days before the United States and Vietnam would sign the Paris Peace Accords. "The weather was miserable that morning, as if the ghosts of Johnson and Ho Chi Minh were waging one last frenzied battle, and once again, Ho had the upper hand. The rain was murderously cold, stubbornly refusing to freeze." Many of the mourners present had "cursed and hated Johnson at times," Reid acknowledged, "but he was still the mightiest of Texans."

# 21.

Eight months after Lyndon Johnson's death, "I conned *Texas Monthly* into sending me to New York to write about Walter Cronkite," Al Reinert said. "I stayed at the Chelsea Hotel—right before the Sid and Nancy days. Billy Lee showed up in New York soon after that. He was staying with a mistress he'd once shared with JFK, who was a wealthy socialite in the city now. She had a fancy place on the West Side."

An "Agreement to Return," filed with Brammer's parole officer, said, "I will make my home with Diana de Vegh" in her apartment on Central Park West. He was granted permission to travel by the State of Texas on September 26, 1973.

"I suppose I knew without wanting to recognize it that Billy Lee wasn't working for the magazine any more at that point," Reinert said. "He and I stayed in New York for six to eight months. He introduced me to Robert Benton. Billy Lee and I tried to write a screenplay together. . . . We never really nailed it. I had written a private-eye story for the magazine that Billy Lee really liked, and the screenplay was going to be based on that. We were working out of Benton's office."

"By that time, I had cowritten *Bonnie and Clyde* with David Newman, but the partnership was breaking up because he wanted to direct. I was looking for a new writing partner," Benton recalled. "Al had written a private-eye story, and we all thought we'd do that. We ended up in this fog. We had a wonderful time, and you had the illusion that the work was going well. It wasn't that it wasn't any good. It's just that it didn't go anywhere. As usual, Bill was blissed out, and his company was beguiling and extraordinary."

De Vegh had landed a spot in the cast of the television daytime drama *All My Children* (initially, Brammer reconnected with her when she appeared in Austin, in a play at the Country Dinner Playhouse). Nevertheless, she appeared to be restless. Acting suited her, but she still didn't seem certain of her long-term career. Clearly, she remained troubled by her old affair with Kennedy. "How do you settle within yourself a pattern of behavior that is a betrayal of someone else's trust?" she asked a reporter many years later. "There are 'arrangements' and there's a whole rhetoric and a whole kind of nonsense that people talk, but the basic act is betrayal. It's hard to be a person who is trustworthy, when in your own family you are not." She appreciated Brammer's willingness to discuss the vagaries of men and women, and she may have felt a nurturing impulse toward him, given the physical shape he was in. He had arrived at her door more as a friend than as a lover. He didn't try to minimize the toll the drugs had taken on him—"Absinthe makes the hard grow softer," he would say. He would fill de Vegh's antique crystal goblets with Dr Pepper from a can, sit back, and admire her austere beauty in the low candlelight of her dining room.

New York's literary culture didn't impress him any more now than it had in the past. "Elaine's is a pile of shit and the NYC literati ought to get its lumps for all their pompous 'lit'ry salon' self-indulgence. Hang around with a recorder and just *listen* to the bogus boilerplate that passes for La Belle Epoch," he wrote Grover Lewis. To Lewis, he also complained that the "timorous press and media barons had next to nothing to do" with the "Watergate Apocalypse," despite their self-congratulations, especially prominent within Washington and New York newspaper circles. Nixon had come "terrifyingly close" to getting away with everything, and would have done so but for a "single Federal judge, a couple of second-line reporters and a tough publisher of *one* paper." If Tricky Dick managed to escape prosecution, Brammer predicted he would be "trying to murder these people in years ahead."

He was paying attention to politics again. He was writing a little—he contacted Don Meredith about doing a piece for *Rolling Stone* concerning Meredith's decision to leave *Monday Night Football.* He was living in a safe, comfortable environment, under the watchful care of a friend. Shelby believed that if he had stayed in New York, he might have had a chance to turn his life around. But his mother died; he felt the pull of home. And under the circumstances—as de Vegh surely knew—betrayal of one sort or another was sooner or later inevitable. So Brammer honored the document he had signed, the one designed to keep him a reputable citizen. He agreed to return to Texas.

---

It was "one of those roads that made the state of Texas so proud. Graded about the time of Job and paved shortly after the electric cooperatives rendered kerosene lanterns obsolete and rural folks exchanged their outdoor crappers for septic tanks, it served the needs of the farmers and the ranchers and a few reclusive dope-dealers, ushering their produce to market." So Jan Reid described the trail to Dripping Springs, just off Highway 290 near the LBJ ranch, the path to the first annual Willie Nelson Fourth of July Picnic, a country Woodstock featuring sets by Waylon Jennings, Tom T. Hall, John Prine, Kris Kristofferson, and Rita Coolidge. "It was miserable and great," Billy Porterfield said later, "one of the glorious heathen stomps between the Americas of J. Edgar Hoover, Joe McCarthy, and Ronald Reagan." And it was one of the last glimpses of Texas that Brammer caught before decamping to Diana de Vegh's apartment in the fall of 1973. In need of money (*Texas Monthly* only paid about $250 for pieces he couldn't finish, anyway), he donned a floppy sombrero and a fat red bandanna, stood among air-conditioned Winnebagos in the dusty open parking lot, and hawked concert programs for Willie Nelson. As the sun baked his skin, he recalled standing as a boy in sweltering fields just like this—perhaps this very field—scratching the sticker burrs from his pants and watching as his father and his fellow linemen "clum some," stringing wires linking the past to the future.

But it was not this old-fashioned Texas he reembraced now, returning from the West Side of Manhattan. It was to the den of the Mad Dogs he came—in a back corner of the Armadillo World Headquarters, in the houses of his buddies Cartwright, Shrake, and Gent. With Dave Richards's help, the boys had legally declared themselves Mad Dogs, Inc., a loosely affiliated organization dedicated to producing entertainment and serving "writers, lawyers, artists, radicals, politicians, and other ne'er-do-wells." The group's rallying cry was "Doing Indefinable Services to Mankind." Their guiding principle was "Everything that is not a mystery is guesswork." They invested in the Armadillo, and Eddie Wilson gave them an office in the back. They drew up plans for an underground newspaper, a distribution center for pornographic movies, an Institute for Augmented Reality, and the Mad Dog Foundation for Depressed Greyhounds. They announced their intention to publish the prison poetry of the famous Texas stripper Candy Barr. They looked into buying a town in West Texas where "gambling, saloons, prostitution . . . dueling, spitting in public, lascivious carriage, cohabitation and every other wholesome vice known to man" would be legal. But mostly they got drunk and entertained one another at Scholz's, performing acrobatics or watching Ann Richards dress up as Dolly Parton.

"I was not terribly impressed with the Mad Dogs," said Shelby Brammer. "Bunch of silly old men getting wasted and wasting time. I was sorry when Billy Lee came back from New York and got involved with them all again."

Sidney, still studying acting at the University of Texas, wanted to visit her dad, but "I didn't like those people," she said. "Frogs in a self-satisfied pond. They treated Shelby and me . . . well, we were good-looking girls . . . and there's nothing worse than these leering old men, my father's friends, hitting on us. *And* treating us like children at the same time. It was so disappointing." (At one point, Shrake hired Sidney to do research for a historical novel he planned to write. He told her, "I want you to write the female dialogue for my novel.") She noted how readily her father meshed with the group: "Bill really did like the women in that scene. And he got a lot of ego satisfaction from being the center of attention with those guys. They were big and drunk and loud. He'd sit quietly and then let out a pithy remark, and they'd fall all over—he enjoyed that.

"Sometimes, I'd go to Bud's house, and Bill would be in one of his coma-sleeps," Sidney remembered. "I'd say to Gent, 'Tell him I dropped by and I'll come again later.' When I'd return, Bill had awakened and gone off to Dallas to check with his parole officer or something. I'd ask Gent, 'Did you tell him I'd dropped by?' In a drug haze, he'd half stir and answer, 'Huh?'" She feared her father was finally drifting away from her for good.

At the very least, he was risking hard jail time if he violated his parole. "One night I dropped by Billy Lee's, and he was on a little trip, and he asked me if I'd take him to 7–11," Susan Walker recalled. "It was eleven or twelve o' clock at night, and we get in my car and go to the store. I was so paranoid we were going to get arrested because he walked out with chocolate Popsicles, chocolate soda . . . which I don't know anybody who did *that* . . . and chocolate cake icing. I'd always ask him, 'Why do you leave your goddam spoon in the icing when you put it back in the fridge?' He'd say, 'I never know when I'm going to want just one bite.'"

He initiated a brief affair with Bob Eckhardt's eldest daughter, Orissa, who was living in Houston. "The thing with Orissa—that was a little *too* incestuous, even for incestuous Austin," Shelby remarked.

In Austin in mid-May 1975, Orissa's younger sister, Rosalind, married Stanley Walker, son of a legendary city editor at the *New York Herald Tribune*. An article about the wedding in the *Hays County Citizen* reads like a valediction for Brammer's generation of Texas liberals:

> Author Billy Brammer once wrote a book called *The Gay Place*, filled with charming, frisky people given to politics, romance, and beer drinking in the Austin setting . . . Last Saturday, at an Austin wedding on a hill above Barton Creek . . . people very much like those in the book (in some cases, identical to them) wandered around, sipping, chatting, laughing, remembering . . . Congressman Eckhardt, a Texas legislator of the "Gay Place" era, was at the wedding along with his present wife Nadine. So was . . . Ronnie Dugger . . . Molly Ivins; former state representative Arthur Vance and wife Dorothy. This is not to mention Brammer himself, who padded about with modest mien, thinking who knows what thoughts, as he gazed on the scene, and on the two women to whom he had been married in earlier times: Nadine Eckhardt, mother of his children, and Dorothy Vance. More than a few probably looked at Brammer, too, wondering if he would pull his magic again sometime, and make them live, in a book.

Soon after the wedding, Nadine's marriage to Eckhardt finally exploded, in another set of incestuous maneuvers. Nadine, bored with her husband and with Washington politics, had moved back to the Eckhardts' property in Houston. Eckhardt called Celia Morris in New York, having learned of her split from Willie. He told her his marriage to Nadine was a "legal fiction" at this point; they stayed together for the sake of their daughter, Sarah. Eckhardt and Morris became lovers. When Nadine found out, she filed for divorce. She claimed the family houses in Houston and a generous amount of child support. Morris was furious when Eckhardt acceded to all of Nadine's demands. On one occasion, he returned to New York after a weekend in Texas spent fighting with Nadine, sporting a large black eye. He told Morris a horse had reared on him. "If you think I'm taking a Texas Congressman to a New York cocktail party with a crazy story about getting a black eye from a horse, you'd better think again," Morris told him. She married him eventually, but the seeds of their future difficulties had been cast.

---

"[Texas] has had no Homer. Many bards, yes; innumerable village raconteurs, yes; and even, arguably, a few decent writers; but no Homer, and no Faulkner, either . . . no single, greatly-told tragic story. Texas in effect has no vital past." So wrote Larry McMurtry in the *Atlantic*. The piece appeared two months before Rosalind Eckhardt's wedding. He pilloried the state's fathomless self-admiration:

> If I were to choose one example of the Texas penchant for ludicrously overestimating local achievement, my example would certainly be the city of Austin. The Texas intellectual community treats Austin not merely with fond regard but almost with reverence; this, in my view, is the intellectual equivalent of thumb-sucking. My own feeling about Austin is that it is a dismal, third-rate university town . . . I don't believe it can claim a single first-rate artistic talent, in any art . . . [I]t is a soft-minded city that thrives not because of its intellectual standards, but because of the absence of them.

"Billy Lee was wounded by that *Atlantic* piece," Jan Reid said to me.

> Absolutely wounded. It was a direct attack on him, and everybody in Austin knew it. People were mortified on his behalf. Let me tell you something about McMurtry. Until his son and grandson became noted musicians in Austin, he had this thing about the town. He hated it because his wife had done whatever she did, you know, ran off with a poet or whatever. His time here had been very unhappy and he took it out on *everyone*. After Billy Lee was gone, McMurtry was kinder to him. He dedicated his novel *Somebody's Darling* to him. He has praised *The Gay Place* repeatedly in print, for over forty years now, as one of Texas's finest novels.

Yet in a letter to me dated January 22, 2015, McMurtry claimed he had never read Brammer's novel. Clearly, he nurtures mighty ambivalence toward Billy Lee Brammer, from residual competitiveness, painful memories, or something else.

In any case, however accurate its portrait of Austin, McMurtry's *Atlantic* piece would have fulfilled a greater purpose than literary skirmishing if it had prevented Brammer from becoming one of Texas's tragic stories. For a while, it seemed to create that effect. On a scrap of paper in his notebook at the time, squeezed over the address of Doris Kearns, Brammer wrote: "Has to do with not being afraid. Or if you are afraid, not letting it show." Kearns had collected the notes she made when she helped LBJ compose his memoirs; from these observations, she had produced what she called a psychohistory of his presidency, *Lyndon Johnson and the American Dream*. She presented Johnson as a true schizophrenic—alternately, a blustering bully and a paralyzed child. Brammer saw an advance copy of the book. Perhaps he recognized this was the volume *he* should have written. If he had not fallen out with the man, *he* might have been the intimate confidante living at the ranch during Johnson's last days. Brammer proposed taping an extensive interview with Kearns "in which we trade off tales of Pumpkin legedermain [*sic*] and endeavor to confront the unmasked LBJ and shared adventure of experiencing him." Surely, *this* was the great tragic story of Texas—of the nation—that McMurtry wanted.

A *Playboy* editor bit. He encouraged the project. Brammer spent several weeks typing up "Strategies for Pumpkin Article and Doris Kearns Material"—numerous sheets of notepaper covered with dense, single-spaced outlines for an in-depth essay. Though it was simply a set of notes, it was clear, well organized, meatier than anything Brammer had produced in years. Johnson remained his most urgent subject. In laying out questions for his proposed interview with Kearns, he said he wanted to know how she had become the "mother figure to the world's biggest baby." "Did she ever get him to discuss intimate biz which find no place in book but illuminate reality of meaningful relationship with Pumpkin (as opposed to brief, brutal never-satisfying conquests characteristic of so much of his time and emotional energies . . .)." "Push [Kearns] for more concrete illustrations of disorder, instability, paralysis in Oval Room."

For his part, he could supply plenty of illustrations of how "simple distortions of the truth" were a "matter of routine" for Johnson. For example, Brammer recalled how LBJ had developed his ranch lands "as if reclaiming his 'home' turf: an aristocratic family gentry pose which he more than half believed. Truth: family relentlessly commonplace; never possessed land in sizable amount, repeatedly in financial squeeze cause of father's speculation and money panics in early part of century." "Shacks on ranch cited [by LBJ] as his birthplace. Corrected by mother."

On a subsequent page, he recorded, "Doris perceives J as devoid of racism . . . not convincing. Not racist in pure sense, but assuredly flawed by preoccupation with racial or genetic stereotypes (smart Jew lawyers, bomb thrower libs, fuzzy thinkers, can-do men, etc., lazy mex . . .)." In a note on "final draft additions," Brammer concluded that Johnson was a "sophisticated professional who could be unmasked as a helpless, out-of-touch provincial outside [the] disciplines of his crafty, arcane professionalism." He was only four years older than JFK, "but light-years removed from K's sensitivity to the mass consciousness of turbulent Sixties. J no sense, never, of these transformations—still in tune with a bucolic Sat Eve Post cover of an America in which citizens honestly believed in July 4th rhetoric."

As the notes accumulated, as he expended more energy reassessing his old friend and antagonist, Brammer seemed to lose some essential part of his will. He could not overcome whatever fear he felt when contemplating the completed project. He would not see it through. The pages ran out; finally, the typed lines gave way to a barely legible scribble: "One learned a lifetime of lessons from Lyn., and one paid a murderous fee for one's wisdom—in still another lifetime of mindless abuse and petty humiliation."

---

Shortly after the Kearns notes peter out, a page in Brammer's notebook reads:

> Only then, when hands pulled behind and cuffs slapped on, did it occur to me that we were up against some genuinely impatient, pissed-off plainclothes lawmen. Shit. Blubbering, blood dribbling down face, into eyes, blinding, [I] was searched and shoved inside patrol car. At length, we proceeded back round to [the] res, where everyone headed inside except for me and a single patrolman. Perhaps half hour elapsed, passed out a few times, finally cops reappeared, hauled me out of car, asked my name, once again searched me and this time discovering pack of approx. 27 gms. of meth. At this point they yelled a lot of intemperate shit at me . . . and finally sent me to [the] Examining Room—couple hours, diagnostic x-rays, finally to city jail and a place to fall out.

According to Al Reinert, Brammer had impulsively caught a ride that night with a friend—presumably one of his dealers—"who proved to be the subject of a statewide police alert and was soon zooming down South

Lamar in Austin barely ahead of several patrol cars. Following the inevitable smash-up, there was a bit of a shoot-out, Billy huddling all the while on the floor of the back seat frantically groping for the plate-glass bifocals he needed to see with. He looked so incredibly harmless that not even the police could take him for a criminal."

"He was such a trickster," Nadine said. "He'd play on people's sympathies."

It was true, Reinert said: "His many friends were galvanized by pity. Sympathetic journalists censored news of his arrest, several lawyers offered to defend him, bail money was gathered, congressmen and authors voiced respect and even awe for the writer he had once been—all in tones of sorrow for the man he had become."

On the advice of District Attorney Ronnie Earle, Brammer pleaded guilty—on November 22, 1976, the anniversary of the Kennedy assassination. He was fortunate to slip by with five more years' probation (by this time, he also had on his record a shoplifting charge—he had walked out of a Texas State Optical shop with a pair of glasses). As with his first arrest, he was glad to know his parents would not learn of the incident. His mother had died when he was living with Diana de Vegh in New York. His father was beyond grasping much of *anything* now, spending his final, frail days in Austin, cared for by Brammer's sister, Rosa. No amount of electricity in the world could penetrate H. L.'s blindness. "It was really important to Rosa that Billy Lee would come visit his dad, that he stay and have dinner, and he did. He was good about it. In that way, he was a good son and brother," remembered Rosa's daughter, Kathy Gunnell. No one said much at the table. His legal troubles never came up. "Oh, Rosa worried about her brother. His parents always did, too," Gunnell said. "They just wanted to make sure he was safe, had a place to live, had food, had a car. Rosa never really talked about his problems. She just said he lived a 'bohemian lifestyle.' A writer, you know."

Like Sidney, Shelby and Nadine figured writing might save him. Together, they decided Brammer should coauthor a book with Nadine, "a joint memoir about the 'different trips' we had taken during the previous decades," Nadine said. "We thought the contrast would be illuminating" between Brammer's counterculture prowling and Nadine's "congressional wife thing." Nadine pulled together notes from her Washington eras—the parties with LBJ, the workings of the Senate, the illicit affairs of congressmen, the conversations with Daniel Ellsberg (another man for whom she claimed to have played the muse, reportedly telling him that "it would take some event outside of Congress to get us out of Vietnam"; within days, he had released the Pentagon Papers).

One afternoon, excited by the possibilities of the book project, she and Shelby dropped by Bud Shrake's place in Austin to share their idea with Brammer. "I remember it was a Sunday. There were these outdoor stairs. We climbed them, and Bill came to the door," Nadine said. "I talked to him for a while." But then she got the sense that he and Shrake were with a girl, and the three of them were probably engaged in some unsavory game. "Oh my god, I don't even want to know what was going on," she said.

She invited Brammer to move into her spacious house in the Houston woods for a while so that they could work on the book together. "I told him I would nurture him, feed him, and so forth . . . trying to get him on a schedule," Nadine said.

He drove down, bringing a young girl with him. Nadine insisted on a strict nine-to-noon routine, and then a break for lunch. Afterward, they would resume talking and writing together for a few hours in the afternoon. On the first day they drew up a time line. Nadine double-checked facts. He assured her he *had* been riding in the presidential motorcade on the day Kennedy got shot.

The next morning, he didn't show at nine. Nadine found him asleep in his room. "He was really like a little old man. He'd get up and look like he just felt terrible, creakin' around, you know. He was aged beyond his years. He'd been jacked around by cops." She discovered she really enjoyed talking to him: "He'd resolved a lot of things." But he insisted he couldn't write without speed. She offered to take him to a hypnotist who had recently weaned her off cigarettes.

"What shall we work on?" the hypnotist asked Brammer.

"I want to work on my nonproductivity," he said.

Nadine suggested he also try to lose his kleptomania.

"No, I want to keep that."

"As soon as the hypnotist began to speak, I went under and got my stop-smoking message reinforced," Nadine explained. "But as we got into the elevator to leave, Bill pulled out a cigarette and lit it."

"Ha ha, you didn't get me!" he said.

He needed to go to Austin to check with his parole officer. As soon as he left the house, Nadine found he had stolen an old pellet gun of her father's and a few other items he would probably sell for drugs. When he returned to Houston, she confronted him with evidence of the theft. "Insulted and angry, he left the house during the night," she said. "That was the last time I saw him alive."

---

As soon as they were done with the house, once they had all moved on, the place would be uninhabitable for years, maybe forever, until some good soul tore the place to the ground. In the basement, empty two-liter plastic bottles lay beside scattered rolls of aquarium tubing, rusty needle-nose pliers, funnels, Baggies, coffee filters, lithium strips, and little powdered piles of Drano crystals, solvents sitting next to engine starting fluid, boxes of Sudafed and 120-milligram twelve-hour pseudoephedrine. The fumes had seeped into the walls, throughout the house, until the walls, full of carpenter ants—a low, munching hiss—were barely more than pure, hardened smells, evil spirits engulfing the odors of vomit, old shoes, stale clothes. Any new family moving into this house—a suburban split-level on Devonshire, "on the downward slope of its life-cycle," Sidney wrote—had better not bring a dog. Within days, the poor dog would perish from chemical poisoning. Any child's toys placed in these rooms—rag dolls, plastic trucks—would need to be tossed. Over-the-counter inhalers would be essential to any family living here, for it was a dead certainty that each member of the family would develop respiratory problems. In Texas, landlords and Realtors were not obligated to warn young couples that the dream house they had just rented or purchased had once been a meth lab, never sufficiently sanitized. "Regulation" was a dirty word in Texas. Any congressman attempting to pass legislation protecting consumers would find himself blocked by powerful lobbyists from the real estate industry No one really kept track of how many houses, apartments, hotel rooms—or for that matter, open fields, creeks, and drainage ditches—were invisibly ruined by pharmaceuticals.

Periodically, Mexican authorities stopped traffic on the unmapped back roads leading from the mountains of Michoacan to the Pacific coast. There, Chinese ships offloaded precursor chemicals that then made their way to Austin via Nuevo Laredo in the packs of families emigrating from the poor town of Luvianos for construction work; the immigrants, having no choice, were also used as mules by the region's many drug cartels. Whenever these crackdowns occurred, pseudoephedrine got scarce on Austin's streets: the "shake and bake" method of making crank, ice, and crystal, using the plastic bottles, was threatened. So Brammer's new friend, John, a man, Sidney wrote, with "no other cultural apparatus for forming friendships" than cooking meth, substituted phenylacetic acid in the process. He and his fellow smurfer, a dodgy guy named Jerry up from Houston, who shared the house with Brammer and John, carefully measured out sixteenths or eight balls. They figured a two-pound bag of the stuff might bring in ten thousand to twelve thousand dollars.

At this juncture, "low-level violence and motel drug deals were probably an everyday part" of her father's life, Sidney said. Most of his former connections had either quit using or died. The house on Devonshire became a center of grisly capitalist exchange: John supplied the drugs, and Brammer—still enough of a local literary legend to attract young followers, girls "talking the libber talk but walking the groupie walk"—"got John laid," Sidney said.

Shelby came by the house one day to tell her father she was moving to New York to act, to write, to immerse herself in the theater world. "He was surrounded by boxes of his stuff. He was so proud of me." It was the last time she would see him. "When I arrived in New York, he sent me some crystal meth as a present. I was in a show. I took it beforehand. I got so sick I wound up in a medical clinic. But that was what he had to give at that point."

Most of his old friends tried to avoid him now. "He would come around . . . He'd want to sell you things," Hugh Lowe recalled.

> The things weren't worth anything—it was a way of trying to get some money without simply asking for money. He'd make these collages, boxes with collages pasted all over them, pictures from magazines and things . . . just speed activity, you know, gotta move, gotta move, gotta dance. They were funny, up to a point, strange little images, but they were one-time jokes. It got so you just didn't want to deal with him anymore. He was pitiful, he was down . . . but never really *horrible*, if you know what I mean. He just wasn't himself. Kind of a shell. But no one I knew ever criticized him, other than to say, "The poor guy's ruining himself."

When Brammer's father died in the fall of 1977, Brammer drove to Dallas in a falling-apart Chevy. He moved back into his parents' house in Oak Cliff for a few months—mostly to sit alone in the dusty rooms and eat Twinkies, Sara Lee pies, and cake frosting, determining what he could remove from the old homestead. He dumped "table lamps . . . sepia portraits of his pioneer grandparents, his father's World War I doughboy jacket, his brother's World War II medals, [and] his own Sunset High School baseball uniform" into the Chevy's trunk, said Al Reinert. He returned to Austin and conducted a bizarre mobile garage sale. "Sometimes I think [this] was Billy's revenge for all the gloomy pity we dumped on him," Reinert said. "He sure didn't take much pity on himself, and while he may have viewed his situation as uncomfortable, or unbecoming, he certainly never thought of it as tragic."

---

Eddie Wilson's Raw Deal restaurant, a pork chop and steak house, had become a new "in" place for politicians, lobbyists, artists, and writers. It was located on Sabine Street near a police station; inside, a sign above the door said, "It'll Be Better Next Time." This referred to the food but might well have expressed its diners' take on the previous decade. Ann Richards celebrated her election to the Travis County Commissioners Court at the Raw Deal; Molly Ivins showed up with her mongrel dog, Shit; Marge Hershey, a journalist and ACLU activist, entertained people with stories of her distant ancestor, Dr. Mudd. Dr. Mudd had attended Abe Lincoln's dying assassin, John Wilkes Booth, she said. The Raw Deal featured Brammer in its advertising—the chance to eat with Billy Lee was a heavy local draw. Billy Lee, Jerry Jeff—like these salty ol' monikers, the place was *authentic*, it was *Texan*, it was *cool.*

"Billy Lee [was] a fantastic conversationalist" over supper, said Michael Eisenstadt, a regular at the eatery. "He knew everybody from everywhere, what they had done and written, and he never, *never* spoke about his personal problems, which were legion. This was on Friday nights at . . . [the] Raw Deal. He once offered to trade his portable tape recorder for my roommate," a comely young lady.

With so many old anarchists and hippies moving into the mainstream—owning restaurants, running for office—the time seemed right for a new, upscale alternative newspaper. Jeff Nightbyrd, a former leader of the SDS and the *Rag*'s cofounder, launched the *Austin Sun* in the mid-1970s. One of his first goals was to score a piece by the legendary Billy Lee Brammer. Jan Reid had just published a comprehensive history of the Austin music scene entitled *The Improbable Rise of Redneck Rock.* The book was also an elegy for lost dreams: "The world we inherited was a large, disordered mess, and Texas was neither worse nor better than other places," Reid wrote. Our disillusioned generation was drawn to lonesome ballads in "American taverns," just as our forebears had been at the end of nineteenth-century cattle drives, places that had "something Puritan" about them, "a darkness without intimacy, as if shame were a requirement for being there."

Reid's understanding of the music and of cultural loss appealed to Brammer, and he agreed to write a review of the book for the *Sun*. It was the last writing he would publish. "From Janis and Threadgill through the acid rockers and up to Willie Nelson's succession of shit-kicker outdoor agonies—the story is as energized and affecting as the music itself," he wrote. Nightbyrd was thrilled with the piece, and so was Reid. Like others, so many times before, they believed this assignment might reintroduce Brammer to the muse. "I'm sure he had dark nights of the soul, but he didn't have that tortured writer sense about him," Reid said. "I think he was doing what he wanted to do. He was embarrassed that he didn't have more money. But he was happy."

Yet even this short review had cost him plenty of sweat. Before finishing the piece, he missed several deadlines. Worried, Nightbyrd sent an aide to Brammer's place one day to check on his progress. Music was blaring, and Brammer was sitting at his typewriter banging a tambourine on one knee while pecking out the review with one index finger.

For pocket cash, he went to work washing dishes and assisting the chef at the Driskill Hotel—one of LBJ's favorite old watering holes. Wells Teague, a writer assigned to profile the Driskill for *Texas Parade* magazine, told the journalist Michael Erard:

> I was interviewing whoever I could find there in the restaurant. I'd interviewed the manager, but I had the run of the place, so I talked to whoever was around. When I went back in the kitchen, there was a fellow with this big rack of ribs. He had on a white coat and one of those big hats that cooks wear, and he was just a real nice fellow. We chatted a minute about the operation. When he told me his name, I said, "You gotta be the writer. I've read some of your stuff." He said, "Yeah, that's me." And that's all he said . . . It was real apparent he wasn't too proud of what he was doing . . . He was mild, and a nice guy. Last time I saw him, he disappeared into the innards of the kitchen . . . to deep-fry several pounds of Port Lavaca breaded shrimp and a box of meat and shrimp egg rolls.

"His friends' refrigerators [became] swollen with stolen hams, huge buckets of shrimp Newburg, and occasional champagne magnums," Al

Reinert recalled. "Billy himself never wavered in his preference for cake frosting and Pepsi; rather he used his booty to barter for drugs."

A former colleague from his *American-Statesman* days, Anita Wukasch, tried to rescue him. "I may have been his last journalistic employer," she said. "At that time I was working for the Southwest Educational Development Laboratory, an entity created as part of the Great Society. Carol Hatfield, Liz Carpenter's niece, asked me, 'Do you have *anything* for Bill Brammer to write? He's making salads at the Driskill Hotel, and we know that will never do.' So I commissioned Bill to write a proposal to the Department of Education for funding of a bilingual project . . . Time went by. No proposal . . . On the very last day [before the deadline], here Bill came . . . and [the proposal] was . . . poetic."

He continued to fill pages in his "Angst" notebook (single-spaced, no punctuation, heavy *X*s), but by now he was typing frightened rants (Nadine remained the center of many of these: "She will by god drink yer blood for starters and serve whut's left for bleeding Mary cocktails"). The house he shared with his new friends, John and Jerry, sat near a federal building out by the airport. He feared authorities kept him under constant surveillance. A woman named Jodi moved into the house, spending most of her days walking topless through the poisoned rooms—Sidney called her, simply, a "crack whore." Brammer told Jodi he thought he had experienced several ministrokes recently. He thought he was losing vision in his left eye. He did not want to see a doctor, not only because he had no money, but also because he feared a physician's careful probing would "set free a malignance of such rapacious nast[iness] and bestiality that I will be consumed."

In one of her last encounters with him, Dorothy saw him at a party at a motel across the street from the LBJ Library. In the pool area, he walked out onto the diving board, fully clothed. He took off his shirt. "He made a perfect dive," Dorothy said.

"The part of him I never could get was why he so relentlessly strove to quit this fascinating world," Sidney said. "During the Vietnam era, he'd console my sensitive teen-activist agonies by telling me how Stendhal postponed suicide again and again because of his curiosity about the political situation in France. Stendhal wanted to see what would happen next."

"I don't know how much he was looking to stick around," Shelby said. "If I'd have been him, I'd have been bummed. He had so much potential, and he lost everything. He missed out on *us*. I have to think . . . He died penniless. He died alone. There had to be a part of him that thought, 'Fuck.'

I don't know. But I never heard him articulate it. Always, it was, 'I know where I'm at. As long as I've got my perspective, I'm all right.'"

He called Sidney one day in early February 1978 and told her he had some money in his room—presumably, from a drug deal—and he wanted her to have it. He wanted to help his children buy a house. He wasn't making much sense. She didn't know whether to believe him about the money. She told him, "Please, get some sleep." A few days later, she telephoned the house. A new Richard Dreyfuss movie had just opened locally. She thought her father would like it, and she called to see whether he wanted to go with her. She couldn't reach him, so she went by herself to a midnight show. "Next morning, he called, incoherent, about the money again. That afternoon, February 11, he died," Sidney said. He was forty-eight years old.

She got the call from John. In a short story she wrote later, based on the events of that day, her "John" character says, "Somethin' kinda bad has happened . . . The police'll probably want something like a next of kin."

According to the police report, John knocked on Brammer's bedroom door at about 4:50 p.m. and entered when he got no response. He discovered Brammer gasping on the bed. He attempted mouth-to-mouth resuscitation, and then he phoned for an ambulance. Sidney believed he spent some time cleaning up the house before calling anyone. A homicide sergeant named Manley Stevens told the *Austin American-Statesman* that "several bottles of vitamin B-12 and a syringe were found in the room . . . It appeared that Brammer had been on his bed reading. Several books were found near his bed. 'It looked like he had been lying [down] with his shoes off.'"

In fact, he had been reading the letters of Ezra Pound: "The intelligence of the nation [is] more important than the comfort or life of any one individual or the bodily life of a whole generation."

The official cause of death: acute methamphetamine intoxication.

Sidney "drove around the block three times before I stopped [at the house]," she said. "Casing it, because I didn't want to get in trouble. Sure enough, the place was swarming with cops."

A young police officer leaning on the porch's wrought-iron railing asked whether he could help her. When she informed him she was the dead man's daughter, he led her gently inside. The medical examiner suggested she might not want to enter the bedroom. When the homicide sergeant asked whether her father had a history of health problems or drug abuse, she pleaded ignorance. She remembered her father's phone calls, telling her about the money. In his suit coat in the closet, rolled into a sock, she found three thousand dollars in cash. Every penny of it would go for burial costs. One of Brammer's old girlfriends, a woman named Janie, sat with Sidney in the house. At one point, Janie noticed John remove a bag full of a white substance from one of Brammer's down vests. Sidney collected some of her father's items, including a few of the books and a portable TV, and left.

In the following days, she realized John "was not [being] upfront with me about Bill's share of the meth lab product." The three thousand dollars wasn't enough—she needed still more to pay for the memorial service and for transporting the body to Oak Cliff, to be buried alongside Brammer's parents. "I was the one who had to shame [John] into returning Bill's share," she said. "My shakedown went something like: 'If you want the TV, you'll have to come over here and take it from me, asshole, and while you're at it, bring me the money or the drugs, or you're going to hear from some friends of mine you don't want to meet.' Need I mention that I was an acting major at the time?"

John was arrested a year later in the very same house, in a drug raid. The "cops found him crawling out of a bathroom window with a Russian submachine gun," Sidney told me. "[He] never seemed to be a very bright man."

---

"In his own way, Billy died singing, like William Blake. It was the rest of us who mourned," Al Reinert said, in a mighty effort to soften the tragic circumstances.

Brammer's memorial service in Austin, on Valentine's Day 1978, drew "veteran legislators, dope dealers, musicians, innumerable married women who came alone, and anyone in Austin who claimed to be a writer," Reinert said. Cartwright was there, and Shrake. So was Ronnie Dugger. Ann and Dave Richards. Bill Broyles, Pete Gent, Jay Milner. Dorothy, Celia Morris, Nadine. Willie, nineteen, was the only person who cried. The others, grieving silently, seemed to feel as Larry L. King did: "Well, hell, Billie Lee has been looking for it a long time. I guess he finally found it."

"Billy Lee didn't look like himself in the coffin," Shelby said. "Somehow, his dentures hadn't made it to the service."

Lyndon's brother, Sam Houston Johnson, tottering on two canes—he would be dead within the year—gazed mournfully into the casket for a long, silent beat, then he turned and gave Sidney a devastated look.

Marge Hershey delivered a brief eulogy:

> Brammer was a gentleman and he was above all gentle. He was a teacher that all of us learned from. It is not surprising that he died reading and surrounded by books. His children and his friends recall his always giving you . . . what you needed—it might be a poem, it might be a toothbrush, a ride in the middle of the night. His generosity was as infinite as his mind was curious. There are many adjectives that can be used to describe Brammer—grace and courage. Grace and courage during many years of physical pain, near blindness and heartbreak. All of his life he lived on the edge. He suffered but his grace was such that he was not despondent . . . He was civilized and he helped us all be a little more civilized when we were in his presence.

Friends toasted Brammer's memory at the Raw Deal. Shelby rode in a car to Dallas with her Aunt Rosa to see the body laid to rest in Meditation Park at Laurel Land Cemetery in Oak Cliff. "It was a cold and windy day. There were maybe a dozen people at the graveside. Not many people from Austin. No wives." Brammer's old friend Angus Wynne said a few words, and then the tiny crowd dispersed.

# *EPILOGUE*

## *The Great Society*

Billy Lee Brammer had a talent for being on the scene when cultural change occurred, and his closest friends believed he was a catalyst for change, yet it is natural to wonder what would have been different if he had not been around.

A question that haunts most of us, about ourselves. A question that haunts literary biography.

Brammer once attempted to frame his place in history. He did so in his notes for the book Nadine wanted him to write with her: "Bestowed from birth with a lucy-in-the-sky twinkle, and irreverence for everything, [Brammer] bounced around the sub-culture after leaving LBJ, writing unfinished masterpieces by the score, ingesting hogsheads of drugs and acquiring a local image of the best approximation of guru and human wonder around." Fourteen years after Brammer's death, on assignment for *Texas Monthly*, Grover Lewis agreed to return to the old Oak Cliff neighborhoods where he and Brammer had been raised. When they were kids, Lewis said, the "No. 1 rule was: Don't mess up. If you swerved from the True path, you messed up. Above all, you had to 'cut it.'"

After the unraveling of the Great Society, most of the blocks "were streaked with phantasmagoric blight and filled with desperately poor and sometimes dangerous people—the latest incursion of have-nots from *jacales* and East Texas slums," Lewis said. Brammer's neighborhood, a collection of shabby lots, was peppered with "For Sale" signs. "I groped for terms to encompass the scope of the disaster: *systemic collapse, municipal cancer, de facto apartheid, social time bomb, a thousand points of dark*."

He visited Clyde Barrow's grave, a weedy, nearly forgotten relic of Depression-era folklore long since eclipsed by the ever-growing noise of Oswald-Ruby conspiracy theories. And then Lewis sought out Brammer's plot, next to his working-class parents. "It was early in the day, hushed and cool with a sheen of dew still glistening on the lawns. There was no one around so I just started talking to him," he wrote:

> "Can I come in for a second," I asked, "share a few bad tidings? There's trouble in River City, Billy Lee. Everything has gone to shit and flinders. It's the rankest times I can remember—lean and mean and scary everywhere . . . Well, it's a jicky age. The fat cats and rulingcrats and gravy-sucking pigs [have] robbed the country blind . . . Dallas looks about half torn down and half rebuilt, although it's still the same white man's city with the Trinity as a sort of moat. Oak Cliff is gone or sinking fast . . . Hell, [we've] even lost Stevie Ray Vaughan . . . People don't talk much about race anymore, but it's still the great divide, and nobody—white, brown, or black—will let go of it . . . If they can't find a common ground as generic humans, they might as well pack it in and head for the graveyard."

Lewis pulled his coat collar tight around his neck, turned and started to walk away. He stopped, his boot heels sinking half an inch into the mushy ground. "Speaking of which," he said to Billy Lee, "you sure messed up, boy."

# *ACKNOWLEDGMENTS*

I first read Billy Lee Brammer's *The Gay Place* as a teenager trying to educate myself in West Texas, at around the time I also discovered Larry McMurtry's early novels. That it was actually possible to write about where you came from, even if where you came from was by any reasonable standard a wasteland, was a life-changing revelation to a book-obsessed boy living in the parched Permian Basin.

When I arrived at Southern Methodist University, in 1973, desperate to find other misfit writers on campus, I learned from my teacher Marshall Terry that I had just missed Billy Lee and his classroom antics, but his legend became very much a part of my SMU experience. I spent late nights in the Fondren Library reading Billy Lee's *Texas Observer* pieces, and often meandered over to Oak Cliff just to see the "other" side of the river. A few years later, when another teacher, Jack Myers, arranged for me to study briefly at Bowling Green State University in Ohio, I learned that once again I had followed, and just missed, Billy Lee.

In the summer of 2012, at the Rainier Writing Workshop in Tacoma, Washington, I met Sidney Brammer, and we got to talking about her dad. From those conversations this book was born. It has come to fruition because of the generosity, openness, and honesty of Sidney, Shelby Brammer, William Brammer Eckhardt, and Nadine Eckhardt. Naturally, memory, history, and scholarship cannot escape the snares of subjectivity; any interpretative errors of people and events within these pages are entirely mine and not the fault of the Brammer family.

Dorothy Browne and Jan Reid welcomed me cordially into their home to share their stories and insights. Jan's biography of Ann Richards is a model for any contemporary biographer. Susan and Jerry Jeff Walker arranged a Billy Lee remembrance for my benefit, where I met some of the early stalwarts of *Texas Monthly* magazine, whose writing remains an inspiration. Hugh and Claudette Lowe graciously shared many of their memories with me. The warmth and candor with which people spoke about Billy Lee was consistently remarkable.

At the Southwestern Writers Collection, at Texas State University's Wittliff Collections in San Marcos, Texas, Steven L. Davis, Katharine Salzmann, and Jonathan Watson were beyond patient with me.

Colleen Mohyde of the Doe Coover Agency has worked tirelessly, out of the goodness of her heart, for my chimerical pursuits.

David Turkel was a marvelous companion in the wilds of Austin. Alejandro Escovedo and Jerry Jeff Walker have provided the mental soundtrack.

I am grateful to Robert Devens at the University of Texas Press for his enthusiasm and his skilled, steady guidance. My gratitude, as well, to the UT team for their excellent work: Nancy Bryan, Derek George, Kip Keller, Robert Kimzey, and Cameron Ludwick. Robert Draper gave the manuscript a helpful read, as did Gregory Curtis.

Many people responded kindly to my queries and interview requests. In addition to the Brammer family, I am especially indebted to the following: Robert Benton, Dorothy Browne, Gary Cartwright, Gregory Curtis, Ronnie Dugger, Ed Guinn, Faye Kesey, John Korty, John Kriken, Claudette Lowe, Hugh Lowe, Larry McMurtry, Robert Paige, Jan Reid, Al Reinert, David Richards, Bob Simmons, Lonn Taylor, Marshall Terry (rest his gentle soul), Calvin Trillin, Madeleine Villatorro, Jerry Jeff Walker, Susan Walker, Henry Wallace, Eddie Wilson, and Max Woodfin.

For me, personally, this book is a reckoning, of a kind, with my Lone Star upbringing, so I must thank my grandfather, Harry Tracy Daugherty, for instilling in me an abiding curiosity about politics, history, and culture, and my mother, father, and sister Debra for making our all-too-fleeting time on the land memorable.

Ted Leeson and Betty Campbell have been dear and necessary companions for over three decades. My sweet old pal Michelle Boisseau taught me, as she left it all behind, that sadness can be a form of soaring. For their sustaining friendship during the course of this project, my love to Suzanne Berne, Kathy Brisker, Aaron and Brenda Brown, Brandon Brown, Molly Brown, Kevin and Amy Clark, Jay Clarke, Nancy Cook-Monroe, Kris and Rich Daniels, Barbara and Gordon Grant, Karen Holmberg, David and Lindsey Huddle, Jon and Martha Lewis, Dinah Lenney, Creighton and Deborah Lindsay, Martha Low, Fred Mills, Scott Nadelson, Bob and Mary Jo Nye, Elena Passarello, Lia Purpurra, Jen Richter, Sue and Larry Rodgers, the entire Sandor family, Keith Scribner, Dana Smith, Tom Stroik, and David Turkel. For reintroducing me to the glories of the American Southwest, a special tip of the Stetson to Jon Sandor and Maryann Wasiolek.

Love and devotion to Hannah and Arlo Mullin, and to Charlie and Joey Vetter. And to my beloved partner, Marjorie Sandor, something like *dayenu*: even a little would have been enough.

# *NOTES*

PROLOGUE: NEW FRONTIERS

1 *Despite the desperate gravity*: Steven M. Gillon, *Lee Harvey Oswald: 48 Hours to Live* (New York: Sterling, 2013), 47.

1 *tumultuous atmosphere*: President's Commission on the Assassination of President Kennedy, *Report of the President's Commission on the Assassination of President John F. Kennedy* (hereafter referred to as the *Warren Commission Report*) (Stamford, CT: Longmeadow, 1993 [1964]), 200.

2 *unlike Grand Central Station*: Ibid., 201.

2 *Initially no steps were taken*: Ibid., 204.

2 *Newsmen wandered*: Ibid., 202.

2 *anyone could have entered the building*: Gillon, *Lee Harvey Oswald*, 60.

2 *stubby little guy*: Ibid., 81.

2 *My name is Jack Ruby*: Ibid., 62.

2 *At no point*: Ibid., 80–81.

3 *patsy*: Ibid., 160.

3 *If you fellows are here*: Gladwin Hill, "President's Assassin is Shot to Death in Corridor of Jail by a Citizen of Dallas," *New York Times*, November 25, 1963, available at nytimes.com/learning/general/on this day/big/1124.htm.

3 *identified news media*: *Warren Commission Report*, 212.

3 *was not challenged*: Warren Commission exhibit number 2056, November 30, 1963, available at history_matters.com/archive/jfk/wc/wcvols/wh24/pdf/wh24_cc_2056.pdf.

3 *an old insurance card*: Warren Commission exhibit number 2057, December

11, 1063, available at history_matters.com/archive/jfk/wc/wcvols/wh24/pdf/wh24_cc_2057.pdf.

3 *He used to* tell *people*: Sidney Brammer to the author, e-mail, February 2, 2015.

3 *Brammer . . . was at Dallas city jail*: Steven L. Davis, *Texas Literary Outlaws: Six Writers in the Sixties and Beyond* (Ft. Worth, TX: TCU Press, 2004), 148.

3 *Oh yeah*: Al Reinert to the author, e-mail, March 9, 2015.

3 *It would surprise the hell out of me*: Hugh Lowe, interview by the author, April 10, 2015.

4 *Dorothy Browne*: Dorothy Browne, interview by the author, April 9, 2015.

4 *trickster*: Nadine Eckhardt, interview by the author, December 5, 2014.

4 *Brammer's is a new and major talent*: A. C. Spectorsky, quoted on the dust jacket of *The Gay Place* by William Brammer (Boston: Houghton Mifflin, 1961).

4 *the best novel*: Willie Morris, quoted on the cover of *The Gay Place* by Billy Lee Brammer (New York: Random House Vintage, 1993 [1961]).

4 *a classic*: David Halberstam, ibid.

5 *He's been shot*: Gillon, *Lee Harvey Oswald*, 124.

5 *jicky*: Grover Lewis, "Cracker Eden," in *Splendor in the Short Grass: The Grover Lewis Reader*, edited by Jan Reid and W. K. Stratton (Austin: University of Texas Press, 2005), 261.

5 *Billy Lee was always ahead of the game*: Davis, *Texas Literary Outlaws*, 364.

5 *as personally responsible for American history*: Ronnie Dugger, *The Politician: The Life and Times of Lyndon Johnson* (Old Saybrook, CT: Konecky & Konecky, 1982), 13.

5 *when the culture came a' callin'*: Shelby Brammer, interview by the author, December 5, 2014.

5 *as Ginsberg was to the Beats*: Davis, *Texas Literary Outlaws*, 362.

5 *No one, I repeat no one*: Dorothy de Santillana to Bill Brammer, June 3, 1960, Brammer Archives, Southwestern Writers Collection, Texas State University, San Marcos, Texas.

6 *We stand today*: John F. Kennedy, "1960 Democratic National Convention Acceptance Speech," Memorial Coliseum, Los Angeles, California, July 15, 1960, audio-video and text available at americanrhetoric.com/speeches/jfk1960dnc.htm.

## 1.

9 *There could be a spell*: Eudora Welty, "Livvie," in *The Collected Stories of Eudora Welty* (New York: Harcourt Brace Jovanovich, 1980), 229.

9 *Bottle trees*: Ibid.

9 *cries of outrage*: Ibid., 237.

10 *lived in a world*: Grover Lewis, "Goodbye if You Call That Gone," in *Splendor in the Short Grass: The Grover Lewis Reader*, edited by Jan Reid and W. K. Stratton (Austin: University of Texas Press, 2005), 233.

10 *This is an overgrown country town*: Horace McCoy, *No Pockets in a Shroud* (London: Serpent's Tail, 1998 [1937]), 24.

10 *old lady seers*: Bill Minutaglio and Steven L. Davis, *Dallas 1963* (New York: Twelve, 2013), 32.

10 *coughed up by the dust storms*: Lewis, *Splendor in the Short Grass*, 230.

10 *The world beyond the horizon*: Ibid., 233.

10 *on the scout*: Ibid., 234.

11 *Snopesy little-jackleg*: Lewis, "Cracker Eden" in ibid., 249.

11 *menopause baby*: Nadine Eckhardt, interview by the author, December 5, 2014.

12 *first elevated railway*: Matthew Hayes Nall, "Oak Cliff, Texas," *The Handbook of Texas Online*, tshaonline.org/handbook/online/articles/hvo43.

13 *nightmare light*: Jack L. Brown, Jr., "Electrifying Dallas," in *Legacies: A History Journal for Dallas and North Central Texas* 7, no. 2 (Fall 1995): 5.

13 *The lightning*: Ibid., 6.

13 *Dallas must have the best*: Ibid., 7.

13 *Texans, Let's Talk Texans*: Robert L. Johnson, *Texas Power and Light Company, 1912–1972* (Dallas: Texas Power and Light Company, 1973), 70.

14 *We were ten years old*: Marjorie Stallard Mayr reminiscence, Brammer Archives, Southwestern Writers Collection.

14 *Water, water everywhere*: Ronnie Dugger, *The Politician: The Life and Times of Lyndon Johnson* (Old Saybrook, CT: Konecky & Konecky, 1982), 212.

14 *Now, Lyndon*: Ibid.

15 *set aside their corrugated washboards*: Ibid., 213.

15 *one bird dog*: Johnson, *Texas Power and Light*, 58.

15 *junk [their] oil-burners*: Mary Estelle Gott Salterelli, *Historic Hood County: An Illustrated History* (Dallas: Burwell, 2009), 50.

15 *Although rough winter weather*: "Company Is Building a New High Line to Hillsboro," *Corsicana Semi-Weekly Light*, January 14, 1947, 4.

16 *We followed the electric lines*: Mayr reminiscence.

16 *You know what T, P, and L*: Ibid.

16 *They rodeoed on weekends*: Ibid.

17 *father/son pair*: Ibid.

17 *Just as sailors disdain*: William Wister Haines, *Slim* (New York: Pocket, 1947 [1934]), 138.

17 *Steer Stadium*: Larry Bowman, "Night Baseball Comes to Dallas," in *Legacies: A History Journal for Dallas and North Central Texas* 7, no. 2 (Fall 1995), 12.

## 2.

18 *Once upon a time*: Billy Lee Brammer, "Salvation Worries? Prostate Trouble?," *Texas Monthly*, March 1973, texasmonthly.com/the-culture/salvation-worries-prostate-trouble.

18 *We talked many times*: Sidney Brammer to the author, e-mail, January 19, 2015.

18 *out there on the wretched edge*: Brammer, "Salvation Worries? Prostate Trouble?"

19 *But stop right there; A man is as old as his glands*: Ibid.

19 *I salute the Empire of Texas*: Franklin Delano Roosevelt, cited in Jason Mellard, *Progressive Country* (Austin: University of Texas Press, 2013), 19.

19 *Mexico's radio outlaw*: Brammer, "Salvation worries? Prostate Trouble?"

19 *goat gland transplantation; taking the goat testicle*: Ibid.

20 *Texas country tradition*: Kevin Pask, "Deep Ellum Blues," *Southern Spaces*, October 30, 2007, southernspaces.org/2007/deep-ellum-blues.

20 *Last Christmas*: Lyndon Johnson, "Tarnish on the Violet Crown," excerpted in *Literary Austin*, edited by Don Graham (Ft. Worth, TX: TCU Press, 2007), 50–51.

21 *recognized him at once*: Grover Lewis, "Cracker Eden," in *Splendor in the Short Grass: The Grover Lewis Reader*, edited by Jan Reid and W. K. Stratton (Austin: University of Texas Press, 2005), 259.

22 *softly undulating sentences*: Al Reinert, "Billy Lee," *Texas Monthly*, February 1979, texasmonthly.com/politics/billy-lee-2.

22 *too much of the cowboy*: Mellard, *Progressive Country*, 28.

22 *exiled from [his] own birthright*: Ibid.

22 *It never occurred to me*: Billy Lee Brammer, "Down a Bytrail," *Texas Observer*, July 24, 1964, 27.

22 *original teller should have told it*: J. Frank Dobie, cited in Francis Edward Abernathy and Carolyn Fiedler Satterwhite, *Texas Folklore Society, 1943–1971* (Denton, TX: University of North Texas Press, 1994), 90.

23 *has never been wholly comfortable*: David Richards, *Once Upon a Time in Texas: A Liberal in the Lone Star State* (Austin: University of Texas Press, 2007), 135.

23 *tried to build a Maginot line*: Mellard, *Progressive Country*, 94.

23 *homemade fascists*: Ibid., 36.

23 *nigger-lover*: Ibid., 96.

24 *you were forever defined*: Lewis, *Cracker Eden*, 257.

24 *where a lot of [poor] families*: Ibid., 248.

24 *football fraternity*: Ibid., 257.

24 *stiff old biddies*: Ibid., 256.

26 *one of Brammer's classmates*: Robert Paige to the author, e-mail, February 12, 2015.

26 *faint sucking noises*: Horace McCoy, *No Pockets in a Shroud* (London: Serpent's Tail, 1998 [1937]), 18.

26 *when you crossed the viaduct*: Ibid., 170.

3.

28 *Charming, reckless, crazy Billy*: Grover Lewis, "Cracker Eden," in *Splendor in the Short Grass: The Grover Lewis Reader*, edited by Jan Reid and W. K. Stratton (Austin: University of Texas Press, 2005), 259.

29 *somnolent backwater*: Grover Lewis, "The Legacy of Huckleberry Finn," in ibid., 237.

29 *kind of gulag operation*: Ibid., 239.

29 *the pool and its canopy*: Ibid.

29 *freighted toward business*: Ibid., 240.

29 *interest in jazz and be-bop*: Sidney Brammer to the author, e-mail, January 19, 2015.

29 *A report card*: Brammer Archives, Southwestern Writers Collection.

30 *At Hiroshima*: Lyndon Johnson campaign speech, 1948, cited in Ronnie Dugger, *The Politician: The Life and Times of Lyndon Johnson* (Old Saybrook, CT: Konecky & Konecky, 1982), 21.

30 *All his life Billy could remember*: Al Reinert, "Billy Lee," *Texas Monthly*, February 1979, texasmonthly.com/politics/billy-lee-2.

30 *[Johnson's] queer new machine*: Ibid.

31 *Johnson . . . won a piece of Billy's heart*: Ibid.

31 *populist-cowboy conservatism*: Sean Cunningham, cited in Wayne Thorburn, *Red State: An Insider's Story of How the GOP Came to Dominate Texas Politics* (Austin: University of Texas Press, 2014), 88.

31 *What's best for Texas*: Rentfro B. Creagor, cited in ibid., 52.

31 *About my background*: Lyndon Johnson, cited in Dugger, *Politician*, 25.

31 *a wild Christian*: Ibid.

31 *a trifling, undirected, boozing redneck*: Robert Sherrill, *The Accidental President* (New York: Grossman, 1967), 26.

32 *He was trying to better humanity*: Lyndon Johnson, cited in Dugger, *Politician*, 92.

32 *political idealism with defeat*: Ibid.

32 *[If] you stand by your principles*: Lyndon Johnson, cited in ibid., 93.

32 *There is no force*: Ibid., 60.

32 *"Boll-Weevil" Democrat*: Richard Kleberg, cited in Gary A. Keith, *Eckhardt: There Once Was a Congressman from Texas* (Austin: University of Texas Press, 2007), 38.

32 *His work habits*: Ibid.

32 *I'm crazy about my work*: Lyndon Johnson, cited in Dugger, *Politician*, 165.

32 *dream began of an America*: Ibid., 115.

33 *the Ten Commandments and the Golden Rule*: Jimmy Banks, *Money, Marbles, and Chalk: The Wondrous World of Texas Politics* (Austin: Texas Publishing, 1971), 82.

33 *Please pass the biscuits, Pappy!*: Ibid.

33 *Next time, sit on the ballot boxes*: Franklin Roosevelt, cited in Banks, *Money, Marbles, and Chalk*, 86.

33 *I'll tell you this*: Lyndon Johnson, cited in ibid.

33 *politically essential plunge into the Pacific*: Dugger, *Politician*, 250.

33 *one of the least deserved*: David Halberstam, cited in ibid., 252.

34 *Landslide Lyndon*: Banks, *Money, Marbles, and Chalk*, 88.

34 *I was beaten by a stuffed ballot box*: Coke Stevenson, cited in ibid.
34 *Billy . . . was not so naïve*: Reinert, "Billy Lee."
35 *A regional rhetoric*: Dugger, *Politician*, 142.
35 *received his being*: Ibid., 27.
35 *an intellectual* and *an athlete*: Nadine Eckhardt, *Duchess of Palms* (Austin: University of Texas Press, 2009), 15.
36 *[He] looked to me like a Dallas hood*: Ibid., 17.
36 *until he spoke*: Ibid.
36 *I had never met anyone like Billy Lee Brammer*: Ibid., 15.
36 *We were copacetic*: Nadine Eckhardt, interview by the author, April 8, 2015.
36 *If you look at photos of Bill*: Sidney Brammer to the author, e-mail, January 19, 2015.
36 *very straight girl*: Nadine Eckhardt, interview by the author, December 5, 2014.
36–37 *Everyone loved Bill*: Eckhardt, *Duchess of Palms*: 22.
37 *restlessness . . . simmered*: Ibid., 18.
37 *One night he told me*: Ibid.
37 *We were just bizarre enough for each other*: Ibid.
38 *[He had] a desire to harm me*: Ibid., 8.
38 *I began to truly hate him*: Ibid., 7.
38 *I escaped his advances*: Ibid.
38 *Success, I concluded*: Ibid., 10.
38 *first sexual feelings*: Ibid., 12.
38 *time I was thirteen*: Ibid.
39 *all kinds of weird stuff*: Eckhardt interview, December 5, 2014.
39 *Always, on the way home from the Monte Carlo Club*: Ibid.
39 *Guys loved me*: Ibid.
39 *I managed to avoid real sex*: Eckhardt, *Duchess of Palms*, 14.
39 *chosen Duchess of Palms*: Ibid.
39 *his whole effect*: Ibid., 16.
39 *he seemed to be more certain*: Ibid., 19.
40 *passing cars on the wrong side of the road*: Ibid., 17.
40 *What the hell are you*: Ibid.
40 *We just wanted to keep having a good time*: Eckhardt interview, December 5, 2014.
40 *My mother didn't like Bill*: Ibid.
40 *Call it impulse*: Eckhardt, *Duchess of Palms*, 19.
40 *We were stupid*: Eckhardt interview, December 5, 2014.
41 *What Makes a Top Newsman?*: Southwestern Writers collection, Texas State University, San Marcos, Texas.
41 *His copy was messy, but it was always good*: Eckhardt interview, April 8, 2015.
41 *Everyone had their stash of diet pills*: Jay Dunston Milner, *Confessions of a Maddog* (Denton: University of North Texas Press, 1998), 96.
41 *I used [them]*: Nadine Eckhardt, cited in Jan Reid, "Return to *The Gay Place*,"

*Texas Monthly*, March 2001, texasmonthly.com/the-culture/return-to-the-gay-place.

42 *His mother would cry*: Eckhardt interview, December 5, 2014.

42 *gave Bill a car*: Ibid.

42 *was entirely unable to manage money*: Eckhardt, *Duchess of Palms*, 21.

42 *everything from a Morris Minor*: Ibid.

42 *more pleasant life for us*: Billy Lee Brammer to Nadine Brammer (Eckhardt), 1951, Brammer Archives, Southwestern Writers Collection.

43 *What's this all about?*: Thomas Fensch, "Precocious 'S.I.' Adjusts to New Times," *Houston Chronicle*, November 30, 1997, available at articles.sun-sentinel.com/1997-11-30/entertainment/9711260199_1_sports-magazine-country-club-sports-life-magazines.

43 *had a touch of irony*: Ibid.

43 *Once the deadlines had been met*: David Sikes, "Oso Pier, Then and Now," *Corpus Christi Caller-Times*, November 28, 2015, caller.com/sports/outdoors/oso-pier-then-and-now-25399698-bba0-0294-e0530100007f5d25-357392971.html.

44 *What a ghost town*: Eckhardt interview, December 5, 2014.

## 4.

47 For background on Austin, I drew on Don Graham's excellent edited collection *Literary Austin* (Fort Worth: TCU Press, 2007).

48 *impulsive poet*: A. C. Greene, from "The Founding of Austin," in *Texas Sketches*, reprinted in Graham, *Literary Austin*, 6.

48 *founded on beauty*: Ibid.

48 *rolling and picturesque*: Frederick Law Olmstead, cited in Don Graham, "City of Words," introduction to *Literary Austin*, xi.

48 *killed off all the Indians*: William Sidney Porter (O. Henry), "Austin. A Brief Glance at Her History and Advantages," *Rolling Stone*, June 9, 1894, 1, reprinted in Graham, *Literary Austin*, 3.

48 *Texas is an eternal synthesis*: Mary Lasswell and Joe Pool, from *I'll Take Texas*, reprinted in Graham, *Literary Austin*, 55.

49 *more Baptists than people*: Bill Moyers, cited in Wayne Thorburn, *Red State: An Insider's Story of How the GOP Came to Dominate Texas Politics* (Austin: University of Texas Press, 2014), 7.

49 *We [were] arbiters of manners*: Eddie Wilson, cited in Larry L. King, *In Search of Willie Morris: The Mercurial Life of a Legendary Writer and Editor* (New York: PublicAffairs, 2006), 53.

49 *The beer garden was shielded*: William Brammer, *The Gay Place* (Boston: Houghton Mifflin, 1961), 21.

49 *Record music*: Ibid., 19.

49 *The soul of the place was found in conversation*: David Richards, *Once Upon*

*a Time in Texas: A Liberal in the Lone Star State* (Austin: University of Texas Press, 2002), 81.

49 *Our politics were pure*: Ibid., 83.

50 *The Lyndon Johnson forces*: Ann Richards, from *Straight from the Heart: My Life in Politics and Other Places*, reprinted in Graham, *Literary Austin*, 83.

50 *Eisenhower Democrat*: Ralph Yarborough, cited in Jimmy Banks, "Marathon Runner," in *Money, Marbles, and Chalk: The Wondrous World of Texas Politics* (Austin: Texas Publishing, 1971), 58.

50 *put the jam on the lower shelves*: Ralph Yarborough, cited in D. Richards, *Once Upon a Time*, 6.

50 *He's a drag*: Billy Lee Brammer to Nadine Brammer, May 9, 1960, Southwest Writers Collection, Texas State University, San Marcos, Texas.

50 *Most of his old friends*: Banks, *Money, Marbles, and Chalk*, 58.

50 any*where in the world*: Lyndon Johnson, cited in Ronnie Dugger, *The Politician: The Life and Times of Lyndon Johnson* (Old Saybrook, CT: Konecky & Konecky, 1982), 371.

50 *for a final shoot-out*: Ibid., 370.

50 *There was a real magic*: Nadine Brammer, cited in Al Reinert, "Billy Lee," *Texas Monthly*, February 1979, texasmonthly.com/politics/billy-lee-2.

50 *I thought they were the ideal married couple*: Robert Benton, interview by the author, May 6, 2015.

51 *We used to joke about creating a wall chart*: D. Richards, *Once Upon a Time*, 81.

51 *He could be stiller than anybody*: Celia Morris, *Finding Celia's Place* (College Station: Texas A&M University Press, 2000), 108.

51 *Although he did not seem personally driven*: Ibid., 109.

52 *How are you, you old horse fucker, you*: D. Richards, *Once Upon a Time*, 82.

52 *Someday, somewhere*: Lyndon Johnson, cited in Dugger, *Politician*, 371.

52 *I sensed was true*: Morris, *Finding Celia's Place*, 109.

52 *True fiction gives us* and other story analyses: class notebook, Fall 1951, Billy Lee Brammer Papers, Southwest Writers Collection, Texas State University, San Marcos, Texas; hereafter cited as Brammer Papers.

53 *It is one o'clock*: Billy Lee Brammer, "Fight Team!," Brammer Papers.

53 *I tried to show*: Brammer to Steffan, ibid.

53 *The theme*: Ibid.

54 *Keep trying to get a unity of theme*: Steffan to Brammer, ibid.

54 *Was the description*: Brammer to Steffan, Ibid.

54 *Well, here I am again*: Ibid.

54 *Just keep your eyes*: Steffan to Brammer, ibid.

54 *The city lies*: Brammer, *Gay Place*, 4.

54 *more charming and less destructive*: Larry McMurtry, "Ever a Bridegroom: Reflections on the Failure of Texas Literature," *Texas Observer*, October 23, 1981, available at www.texasobserver.org/ever-a-bridegroom.

54 *On brilliant mornings*: Brammer, *Gay Place*, 4.

54 *He knew every new product*: Nadine Eckhardt, *Duchess of Palms* (Austin: University of Texas Press, 2009), 21.

54 *I knew we were doing something wrong*: Ibid.

54 *There's nothing wrong*: Ibid., 20.

55 *He always wanted children*: Ibid., 21.

55 *Rooter-Pooter*: Bill Brammer to Nadine Brammer, n.d. [1951], Brammer Papers.

55 *I'm strangely bored*: Nadine Brammer to Bill Brammer, n.d. [1951], ibid.

55 *Have you decided*: Nadine Brammer to Bill Brammer, January 7, 1952, ibid.

55 *all we need is* money: Nadine Brammer to Bill Brammer, n.d. [1951], ibid.

55 *Yesterday I discovered*: Bill Brammer to Nadine Brammer, n.d. [1951], ibid.

55 *I feel not so good*: Nadine Brammer to Bill Brammer, n.d. [1951], ibid.

55 *Got you many kinds of prayzunts*: Bill Brammer to Nadine Brammer, n.d. [1951], ibid.

55 *Be good to your phallus; Let's do it; Su 'concubina'; Virgin Mary*: Letters from Nadine Brammer to Bill Brammer, Brammer Papers.

55 *My phallus*: Bill Brammer to Nadine Brammer, n.d. [1951], ibid.

56 *Went to town yesterday*: Nadine Brammer to Bill Brammer, n.d. [1951], ibid.

56 *I'm glad*: Ibid.

56 *Be happy*: Bill Brammer to Nadine Brammer, n.d. [1951], ibid.

56 *In fact, at one point*: Eckhardt, *Duchess of Palms*, 21.

56 *Love and nice things*: Bill Brammer to Nadine Brammer, n.d. [1951], Brammer Papers.

## 5.

57 *On January 25*: Nadine Brammer to Bill Brammer, January 7, 1952, Billy Lee Brammer Papers, Southwest Writers Collection, Texas State University, San Marcos, Texas; hereafter cited as Brammer Papers.

57 *dirty solid pink*: Bill Brammer to Nadine Brammer, n.d. [January 1952], ibid.

57 *You are a genius for finding it*: Nadine Brammer to Bill Brammer, January 10, 1952, ibid.

57 *said Robert Benton*: Robert Benton, interview by the author, May 6, 2015.

58 *Thought of you*: Nadine Brammer to Bill Brammer, n.d. [1952], Brammer Papers.

58 *Pay begins at $335 per month*: Bill Brammer to Nadine Brammer, September 5, 1952, ibid.

58 *Am having little sex dreams*: Nadine Brammer to Bill Brammer, September 8, 1952, ibid.

58 *Am generating energy*: Nadine Brammer to Bill Brammer, September 15, 1952, ibid.

58 *My dear friend:* Lyndon Johnson to Bill Brammer, January 26, 1953, Nadine

Eckhardt Papers, Southwest Writers Collection, Texas State University, San Marcos, Texas; hereafter cited as Eckhardt Papers.

58 *present requirements*: Major General Robert E. L. Eaton to Homer Thornberry, January 29, 1953, ibid.

58 *My dear friend*: Lyndon Johnson to Bill Brammer, February 1953, ibid.

59 *Have been staying out*: Bill Brammer to Nadine Brammer, n.d. [1953], Brammer Papers.

59 *singer-songwriter Doug Sahm*: Doug Sahm, cited in Sidney Brammer, interview by the author, December 6, 2014.

60 *wound through its nightclubs*: Barry Shank, *Dissonant Identities: The Rock 'n' Roll Scene in Austin* (Hanover, NH: Wesleyan University Press, 1994), 15.

60 *I've got sort of a study fixed up*: Bill Brammer to Nadine Brammer, n.d. [1953], Brammer Papers.

60 *John the Baptist; Copulation*: Ibid.

60 *excellence in writing*: *Austin American-Statesman*, December 17, 1952, A17.

60 *exuberant happiness*: "Three AP Awards Won by American-Statesman," *Austin American-Statesman*, January 10, 1954, A1.

60 *Bill, you weren't even there*: Anita Howard Wukasch, "The Image of LBJ in Billy Lee Brammer's *The Gay Place*," unpublished paper provided to the author by Nadine Eckhardt.

61 *I'm gonna give you a liver pill*: Block Smith, cited in Celia Morris, *Finding Celia's Place* (College Station: Texas A&M University Press, 2000), 59.

61 *greatest man in America*: Hugh Roy Cullen, cited in James McEnteer, *Deep in the Heart: The Texas Tendency in American Politics* (Westport, CT: Greenwood, 2004), 85.

61 *if our grandfathers*: Ibid.

61 *appalling travesty*: Cited in Morris, *Finding Celia's Place*, 59.

61 *done more to destroy*: Cited in McEnteer, *Deep in the Heart*, 85.

61 *Negro children*: Cited in Morris, *Finding Celia's Place*, 66.

61 *Robert Benton said*: Benton interview.

62 *I loved that Nash convertible*: Nadine Eckhardt, interview by the author, December 5, 2014.

62 *[Our] children claim*: David Richards, *Once Upon a Time in Texas: A Liberal in the Lone Star State* (Austin: University of Texas Press, 2002), 79.

62 *We [became] . . . the Texas equivalent*: Nadine Eckhardt, *Duchess of Palms* (Austin: University of Texas Press, 2009), 23.

62 *elusive, quixotic, irresistible to men*: Ibid., 22.

62 *intrusive . . . verged on voyeurism; set me up*: Ibid.

62 *we lied to ourselves*: Ibid., 24.

62 *uncomfortable; fun and games; He saw me enjoying myself*: Ibid., 24–25.

63 *shit-house liberals*: Cited in Morris, *Finding Celia's Place*, 60.

63 *working for Mr. Yarborough*: Jimmy Banks, *Money, Marbles, and Chalk: The Wondrous World of Texas Politics* (Austin: Texas Publishing, 1971), 21.

63 *He underwent a vasectomy*: Shelby Brammer to the author, e-mail, April 21, 2015.

63 *he must have felt*: Ibid.

64 *I need some clarification*: Bill Brammer to Nadine Brammer, October 26, 1954, Brammer Papers.

64 *I am missing*: Ibid.

64 *Bill walked into my life*: Ronnie Dugger, "To a Novelist Dying Young," *Washington Post*, June 18, 1978, F1.

64 *kamikaze liberal*: Lyndon Johnson, cited in Larry L. King, *In Search of Willie Morris: The Mercurial Life of a Legendary Writer and Editor* (New York: PublicAffairs, 2006), 50.

64 *ashamed of my culture*: Ronnie Dugger, cited in Brad Buchholz, "Ronnie Dugger: The Free Man," *Austin American-Statesman*, April 29, 2012, statesman.com/news/lifestyles/ronnie-dugger-the-free-man-1/nRnMw.

65 *platoons of energetic women*: Wayne Thorburn, *Red State: An Insider's Story of How the GOP Came to Dominate Texas Politics* (Austin: University of Texas Press, 2014), 66.

65 *Frankie . . . was to Texas*: Cited in ibid., 111.

65 *panzer troops*: Bob Eckhardt, cited in Gary A. Keith, *Eckhardt: There Once was a Congressman from Texas* (Austin: University of Texas Press, 2007), 3.

65 *spunk*: Ibid., 125.

65 *We will serve no group*: Ibid.

65 *If ever a rattlesnake rattled*: Ronnie Dugger, "LBJ, *The Texas Observer*, and Me," June 6, 2012, *The Rag Blog*, www.theragblog.com/ronnie-dugger-lbj-the-texas-observer-me.

66 *I do not agree*: Ibid., 126.

66 *Dugger dug his talons*: King, *In Search of Willie Morris*, 51.

66 *little star in the murky night*: Keith, *Eckhardt*, 126.

66 *He was a relaxed, soft-spoken fellow*: Dugger, "To a Novelist Dying Young."

66 *going regularly, unfailingly bump*: Bill Brammer, "A Personal Reminiscence," *Texas Observer*, August 25, 1961, 5.

66 *total commitment*: Ibid.

66 *Without remarking he would go*: Dugger, "To a Novelist Dying Young," F2.

66 *He came [to me]*: Ibid.

66 *If he seemed a bit overmuch*: B. Brammer, "A Personal Reminiscence," 5.

66 *I exempt Billy Lee*: Ronnie Dugger to the author, e-mail, February 23, 2015.

67 *provocative but clearly doomed*: Dugger, "To a Novelist Dying Young," F2.

67 *Dugger [gave] far more*: B. Brammer, "A Personal Reminiscence," 6.

67 *drives and demon-lusts*: Ibid.

67 *We are a bunch*: Bill Brammer to Nadine Brammer, n.d. [1955], Brammer Papers.

67 *swacked*: B. Brammer, "A Personal Reminiscence," 6.

67 *rather disappear into oblivion*: Buchholz, "Ronnie Dugger."

68 *he was hell-bent on the presidency*: Dugger, "LBJ, *The Texas Observer*, and Me."

68 *[Democratic] party and the nation*: Robert Caro, *Master of the Senate* (New York: Knopf, 2002), 473.

68 *No one maintains*: Dugger, "LBJ, *The Texas Observer*, and Me."

68 *I damned Johnson*: Ibid.

68 *Lyndon Johnson loathed*: Bill Moyers, cited in "Moyers, Hightower, Northcott Weigh In on Dugger," *Austin American-Statesman*, April 29, 2012, statesman.com/news/lifestyles/moyers-hightower-northcott-weigh-in-on-dugger/nRnMz.

68 *was like reading the Old Testament prophets*: Ibid.

68 *rotgut*: Dugger, "LBJ, *The Texas Observer*, and Me."

68 *to conceal his leftist treachery*: Dugger, "To a Novelist Dying Young."

68 *It was two or three weeks*: Bill Brammer, "Call to Greatness Muffed by Mr. Mitty," *Texas Observer*, February 28, 1955, 3.

69 *The State of Texas*: Bill Brammer, "The Soapbox Scalawags," *Texas Observer*, April 11, 1955, 3.

69 *They stuck a shaft in the ground*: Bill Brammer, "A Joyous Holiday Announcement," *Texas Observer*, April 18, 1955, 2.

69 *The scene is a lonely, submerged, oil-rich beach*: Bill Brammer. "Let Us Pray: A Play in One Act," *Texas Observer*, April 25, 1955, 1.

69 *There is a certain intimidating circumstance*: Bill Brammer, cited in Dugger, "To a Novelist Dying Young."

69 *hysterical, No-Think*: B. Brammer, "A Personal Reminiscence," 6.

70 *A Department of Public Safety narcotics agent*: Bill Brammer (unsigned), "State Dope Agent Kicked Latin but Is Cleared in Court Charge," *Texas Observer*, June 27, 1955, 4.

70 *Communist, Communist, Communist*: Bill Brammer, "Tom Reagan's Story," *Texas Observer*, April 11, 1955, 6.

70 *We've got everything under control here*: Bill Brammer, "Coercion in Rusk," *Texas Observer*, August 17, 1955, 1.

70 *old Jesse's private sideline*: Bill Brammer, "Jesse James Likes His Work," *Texas Observer*, June 13, 1955, 1.

70 *huckster*: Bill Brammer, "Hit 'Em Where They Live: The Political Hucksters II," *Texas Observer*, May 9, 1955, 4.

70 *in trouble* and other quotations from "The Green Board": Bill Brammer, "The Green Board," *Texas Observer*, May 23, 1955, 1.

71 *He was a very special person*: Nadine Eckhardt, cited in Dugger, "To a Novelist Dying Young."

71 *missing ingredient*: Bill Brammer, "A Fragile Subject," *Texas Observer*, August 17, 1955, 2.

71 *a slightly sad-eyed* and all other quotations from "Crume of Big D": Bill Brammer, "Crume of Big D," *Texas Observer*, September 28, 1955, 6.

72 *Billy was the first genuine*: Willie Morris, cited in Dugger, "To a Novelist Dying Young."

72 *Nadine told her parents*: Nadine Brammer to Nadine Cannon, n.d. [1955], Brammer Papers.

72 *we speak of the [Texas] slums*: Ronnie Dugger, "The Slums of Texas," *Texas Observer*, September 28, 1955, 4.

72 *[My] column is not for or against*: B. Brammer, "Crume of Big D."

73 *His top administrative assistant*: Caro, *Master of the Senate*, 503.

73 *socialism*: Ibid., 605.

73 *reactionary and racist*: Dugger, "LBJ, *The Texas Observer*, and Me."

73 *richly-conceived and rottenly written*: Bill Brammer, "Enormous, but Incredible: On Rereading Giant," *Texas Observer*, July 4, 1955, 7.

74 *Americans were about to be trapped*: Dugger, "LBJ, *The Texas Observer*, and Me."

74 *He asked me to go with him*: Nadine Brammer interview, December 5, 2014.

74 *townspeople [hadn't] changed much*: Bill Brammer, "Unworldly Little Marfa," *Texas Observer*, June 27, 1955, 1.

74 *mesquite-studded and stunted ranches*: Ibid.

74 *Some miles out from town*: Bill Brammer, "A Circus Breaks Down on the Prairie," *Texas Observer*, July 4, 1955, 4.

74 *a sham*: Ibid., 5.

74 *It's here*: Ibid., 4.

75 *so the moviemen simply sprayed*: Ibid., 5.

75 *dispatches from Marfa*: Steven L. Davis, *Texas Literary Outlaws: Six Writers in the Sixties and Beyond* (Fort Worth: TCU Press, 2004), 35.

75 *every bit as pretty*: B. Brammer, "A Circus Breaks Down on the Prairie," 5.

75 *A kind of fuzzy-cheeked*: Ibid.

75 *on the Worth Evans ranch*: Ibid.

75 *Earlier in the year, Governor Shivers*: Don Graham, introduction to William Brammer, *The Gay Place* (Austin: University of Texas Press, 1995), xxv.

75 *like a great landlocked whale*: William Brammer, *The Gay Place* (Boston: Houghton Mifflin, 1961), 416.

76 *It don't tumble*: Ibid., 424.

76 THE TEXAN WHO IS JOLTING WASHINGTON: *Newsweek*, June 27, 1955.

76 *the FBI or 'The Lobby'*: B. Brammer, "A Personal Reminiscence," 5.

## 6.

77 *It was once barren*: Lyndon Johnson, State of the Union Message, 1965, cited in Bill Porterfield, *LBJ Country: The Country That Shaped a President* (Garden City, NY: Doubleday, 1965), n.p.

77 *Heart Attack Drops Johnson*: Robert Caro, *Master of the Senate* (New York: Knopf, 2002), 626.

78 *I would rather face ten*: George Reedy, cited in Jan Jarboe Russell, *Lady Bird* (New York: Scribner, 1999), 178.

79 *Where are you, Bird?*: Ibid., 176.
79 *love letter*: Ibid., 178.
79 *I have been sitting here*: Lyndon Johnson, cited in Caro, *Master of the Senate*, 638.
79 *kind and obliging*: Bill Brammer, "Lyndon Comes Home," *Texas Observer*, August 24, 1955, 1.
79 *My dear friend*: Lyndon Johnson to Bill Brammer, February 1951, Nadine Eckhardt Papers, Southwest Writers Collection, Texas State University, San Marcos; hereafter cited as Eckhardt Papers.
79 *After hearing*: Nadine Eckhardt, *Duchess of Palms* (Austin: University of Texas Press, 2009), 25.
79 *We'd all heard*: Nadine Eckhardt, cited in Al Reinert, "Billy Lee," *Texas Monthly*, February 1979, texasmonthly.com/politics/billy-lee-2.
80 *Lyndon Johnson's relations*: *Dallas Morning News*, October 23, 1955, part 4, 1.
80 *Bill Brammer, associate editor*: *Texas Observer*, November 2, 1955, 1.
80 *the senator's Austin office*: *Corsicana Semi-Weekly Light*, November 18, 1955, 12.
80 *instinctively and intentionally*: Joseph Califano, cited in Caro, *Master of the Senate*, 637.
81 *journalist Jan Jarboe Russell*: Russell, *Lady Bird*, 178–179.
81 *welcomed [Billy Lee's] careful perspective*: Reinert, "Billy Lee."
81 *We were a couple of snobby*: Nadine Eckhardt, cited in ibid.
81 *It seems to be the tendency*: Lyndon Johnson, editorial, cited in Ronnie Dugger, *The Politician: The Life and Times of Lyndon Johnson* (Old Saybrook, CT: Konecky & Konecky, 1982), 119.
81 *Billy understood himself too well*: Reinert, "Billy Lee."
81 *At some point* and all other quotations and details of Dugger's visit to the LBJ ranch, unless otherwise noted: Ronnie Dugger, "LBJ, *The Texas Observer*, and Me," June 6, 2012, *The Rag Blog*, www.theragblog.com/ronnie-dugger-lbj-the-texas-observer-me.
82 *why he, the Senate majority leader*: Dugger, *Politician*, 92–93.
82–83 *[Billy] was fully aware*: Reinert, "Billy Lee."
83 *he played every part*: Dugger, "LBJ, *The Texas Observer*, and Me."
83 *bourbon and branch water*: Larry L. King, "Bringing Up Lyndon," *Texas Monthly*, January 1976, texasmonthly.com/politics/bringing-up-lyndon.
83 *Yes, by God*: Ibid.
83 *Come on home!*: Ibid.
83 *Robert Caro reported*: Caro, *Master of the Senate*, 635.
84 *charming, reckless, crazy*: Grover Lewis, "Cracker Eden," in *Splendor in the Short Grass: The Grover Lewis Reader*, ed. Jan Reid and W. K. Stratton (Austin: University of Texas Press, 2005), 259.
84 *I had seen people smoke*: Bobby Baker, cited in Caro, *Master of the Senate*, 617.
84 *Make sure Lady Bird*: Russell, *Lady Bird*, 177.

84 *Daddy, it sure is nice*: Caro, *Master of the Senate*, 633.
84 *political issues were [not] cast*: Harry McPherson, *A Political Education: A Washington Memoir* (Boston: Houghton Mifflin, 1988), 85.
85 *Pow Wow on the Pedernales*: Bill Brammer, "Pow Wow on the Pedernales," *Texas Observer*, October 5, 1955, 1.
85 *could be felt all the way*: George Reedy, cited in Caro, *Master of the Senate*, 641.
85 *think that you, Adlai*: Ibid., 642.
85 *looked fit*: Brammer, "Pow Wow on the Pedernales," 1.
85 *We here at the* Observer: Bill Brammer, "That Old Depleted Feeling," *Texas Observer*, October 12, 1955, 3.
85 *spared the carnage*: Bill Brammer, cited in Ronnie Dugger, "To a Novelist Dying Young," *Washington Post*, June 18, 1978, F2.
86 *Some of our friends*: Eckhardt, *Duchess of Palms*, 25.
86 *what stale enthusiasms*: Bill Brammer, cited in Dugger, "To a Novelist Dying Young."
86 *I defended my friend*: Ibid.
86 *genuinely a literary person*: Ibid.
86 *wanted a conservative personal life*: Ibid.
86 *An eight-hour man*: King, "Bringing Up Lyndon."
86 *back in the saddle*: Caro, *Master of the Senate*, 647.
86 *A natural gas bill*: Ibid.
87 *cushy, luxe Brown & Root plane*: Eckhardt, *Duchess of Palms*, 25.
87 *It didn't look like any plane*: Sidney Brammer to the author, e-mail, May 1, 2016.
87 *most unusual boss* and all other quotations from "They Take Their Wives to Work": Frances Leighton, "They Take Their Wives to Work," *Corpus Christi Caller-Times*, August 26, 1956, 66.
87 *I was already straying sexually*: Eckhardt, *Duchess of Palms*, 30.

7.

88 *Rube Goldberg–looking thing*: Nadine Eckhardt, interview by the author, December 5, 2014.
88 *Johnson worked*: Ibid.
88 *My dear friend*: Ibid.
89 *case letters; warm letters*: Booth Mooney, interview by Thomas H. Baker, December 31, 1979, Lyndon Baines Johnson Presidential Library Oral History Collection, posted at lbjlibrary.org.
89 *she regretted to report*: Sam Houston Johnson, *My Brother Lyndon* (New York: Cowles, 1970), 265.
89 *archivality*: Ibid.
89 *could get Ronnie Dugger to soften*: George Reedy, interview by Michael L. Gillette, October 14, 1983, George Reedy Oral History Interview X,

Lyndon Baines Johnson Presidential Library Oral History Collection, www.lbjlibrary.net/assets/documents/archives/oral_histories/reedy/reedy%20web%2010.pdf.

89 *Bill was an extraordinarily acute observer*: Ibid.

90 *crystal chandelier*: Bill Brammer, cited in Ronnie Dugger, "To a Novelist Dying Young," *Washington Post*, June 18, 1978, F2.

90 *I only think about politics*: Nadine Eckhardt, interview by the author, December 5, 2014.

90 *consume[d] his staff as fuel*: Harry McPherson, interview by Michael L. Gillette, September 19, 1985, Harry McPherson Oral History Interview VII, Lyndon Baines Johnson Presidential Library Oral History Collection, www.lbjlibrary.net/assets/documents/archives/oral_histories/mcpherson/MCPHER07.PDF.

90 *As a human being*: George Reedy, cited in Mark Updegrove, "Cruel to Be Kind: LBJ behind the Scenes," *Alcalde*, February 20, 2012, alcalde.texasexes.org/2012/02/cruel-to-be-lind-lbj-behind-the-scenes.

90 *Clean up your fucking desk*: Lyndon Johnson, cited in Robert Caro, *Master of the Senate*, (New York: Knopf, 2002), 126.

90 *I hope your mind*: Ibid.

90 *God, you're stupid!*: Ibid., 127.

90 *Jumbo*: Nadine Eckhardt, interview by the author, December 5, 2014.

91 *hard-peckered boys*: Bill Brammer, "Sex and Politics," *Texas Monthly*, May 1973, texasmonthly.com/articles/sex-and-politics.

91 *Johnson had no concept of order*: Reedy interview.

91 *You felt that the world*: Caro, *Master of the Senate*, 126.

91 *enthralled by Johnson*: Willie Morris, cited in Dugger, "To a Novelist Dying Young."

91 *He is just about 50 feet away*: Bill Brammer, cited in ibid.

91 *Empty Coke bottles*: Harry McPherson, *A Political Education: A Washington Memoir* (Boston: Houghton Mifflin, 1988), 121.

91 *Bill Brammer's eyes*: Ibid.

91 *Washington is hideous*: Bill Brammer, cited in Dugger, "To a Novelist Dying Young."

91 *We [had] been young and liberal*: McPherson, *Political Education*, 4.

92 *was working hard*: Glen Wilson, "Waldron, Brammer," unpublished reminiscence, 3, June 24, 1992, Larry L. King Papers, Southwest Writers Collection, Texas State University, San Marcos.

92 *I am almost finished*: Bill Brammer, cited in Dugger, "To a Novelist Dying Young."

92 *glib talkers*: Al Reinert, cited in Steven L. Davis, *Texas Literary Outlaws: Six Writers in the Sixties and Beyond* (Fort Worth: TCU Press, 2004), 42.

92 *he admitted to Dugger that*: Bill Brammer, cited in Dugger, "To a Novelist Dying Young."

92 *my prose took a turn*: Ibid.

92 *I am desperately fearful*: Dugger, "To a Novelist Dying Young."

92 *I am two chapters short*: Bill Brammer, cited in ibid.

92 *It was one thing to sit*: McPherson, *Political Education*, 5.

93 *I know every son of a bitch*: Lyndon Johnson, cited in Joe Phipps, *Summer Stock: Behind the Scenes with LBJ in '48* (Fort Worth: TCU Press, 1992), 41. Phipps accurately recorded many Johnson sayings later repeated by others.

93 *My people aren't sending me*: Ibid., 21.

93 *LBJ seems to have strangled*: Bill Brammer, cited in Dugger, "To a Novelist Dying Young."

93 *Johnson is in his element*: Ibid.

94 *either . . . Fitzgerald*: Ibid.

94 *Perhaps I'd better start all over again*: Ibid.

94 *I suggested to [Johnson]*: Mooney interview.

94 *Having the normal amount of human vanity*: Anita Howard Wukasch, "The Image of LBJ in Billy Lee Brammer's *The Gay Place*," unpublished paper, provided to the author by Nadine Eckhardt.

94 *I could write a book*: Bill Brammer, cited in Dugger, "To a Novelist Dying Young."

95 *funky*: Wilson, "Waldron, Brammer," 4.

95 *footed cast iron bath tub*: Ibid.

95 *She was a large woman*: Sidney Brammer to the author, e-mail, May 1, 2016.

95 *Someone had given me*: Ibid.

95 *lechery was frequently a topic*: Nadine Eckhardt, *Duchess of Palms* (Austin: University of Texas Press 2009), 30.

95 *LBJ could grope*: Ibid.

96 *It happened so fast*: Nadine Brammer, cited in Jan Jarboe Russell, *Lady Bird* (New York: Scribners, 1999), 171.

96 *Honey . . . do you want to*: Eckhardt, *Duchess of Palms*, 28–29.

96 *Everyone grew mellow*: Ibid., 29.

96 *When're you and me*: Ibid.

96 *I think Johnson was . . . very much*: Reedy interview.

96 *I think Johnson was taken*: McPherson interview.

96 *high that [came] from flirting*: Eckhardt, *Duchess of Palms*, 30.

96 *ferried press releases*: Ibid.: 31.

96 *This was heady stuff*: Ibid.

96 *I felt love for Bill*: Ibid.

97 *It was intoxicating*: Ibid., 31.

97 *Bill was miserable*: Ibid., 39–40.

97 *to go crawling in*: Barbara Raskin, cited in Tim Warren, "Barbara Raskin Paid Her Dues as Writer and Political Insider," *Baltimore Sun*, September 16, 1990, articles.baltimoresun.com/1990-09-16/features/1990259110_1_raskin-brammer-women-of-washington.

97 *drank [themselves]*: Larry L. King, cited in Davis, *Texas Literary Outlaws*, 40.

98 *Lyndon perceived Bill's intelligence*: Nadine Eckhardt, cited in ibid., 39.

98 *Boy*: Ibid., 45.

98 *Billy Lee would ask Johnson*: Nadine Eckhardt, cited in Dugger, "To a Novelist Dying Young."

98 *Who are you?*: Ibid. This routine between LBJ and Brammer is included in "President Glooey," a January 1963 satire that Brammer wrote for the *Texas Observer*.

98 *We'd go out to the ranch*: Nadine Eckhardt, cited in Davis, *Texas Literary Outlaws*, 39.

98 *You gotta* give *something*: Eckhardt interview, December 5, 2014.

98 *waited on [Johnson]*: Ronnie Dugger, cited in Davis, *Texas Literary Outlaws*, 41.

98 *After the lengths*: Bill Brammer to Nadine Brammer, n.d., Billy Lee Brammer Papers, Southwest Writers Collection, Texas State University, San Marcos; hereafter cited as Brammer Papers.

99 *"questionable" civil rights record*: Eckhardt, *Duchess of Palms*, 36.

99 *disability*: Eckhardt interview, December 5, 2014.

99 *Come, let us reason together*: Ibid.

99 *Shivers charged me with* murder: Ronnie Dugger, *The Politician: The Life and Times of Lyndon Johnson* (Old Saybrook, CT: Konecky & Konecky, 1982), 341.

100 *There was no evidence*: Ibid., 340.

100 *Johnson . . . enjoyed Brammer*: McPherson interview.

100 *On trips home to Texas*: Jan Reid, "Return to *The Gay Place*," *Texas Monthly*, March 2001, texasmonthly.com/the-culture/return-to-the-gay-place.

100 *The only way you're going*: Ibid.

101 *What would you teach*: Eckhardt interview, December 5, 2014.

101 *Look at George*: McPherson interview.

101 *Hubert!*: Eckhardt interview, December 5, 2014.

101 *trying to get some Senate business*: Brammer, "Sex in Politics."

101 *I haven't got time to worry*: Ibid.

102 *I think . . . [an] ambivalence*: Reedy interview.

102 *I will gut him*: Eckhardt interview, December 5, 2014; see also Phipps, *Summer Stock*, 70.

102 *I got bored*: Sidney Brammer to the author, e-mail, May 1, 2016.

102 *I was in a purple sock-dress*: Sidney Brammer, interview by the author, December 6, 2014.

102 *I was never more frightened*; *I meant for the scene*: Ibid.

103 *Am being good* and all other diary entries by Nadine Eckhardt: Nadine Eckhardt Papers, Southwest Writers Collection, Texas State University, San Marcos; hereafter cited as Eckhardt Papers.

103 *entertaining the Texas Correspondents*: Ibid.
103 *It is the 1956*: Brammer, "Sex in Politics."
104 *sit down to pee*: Ibid.
104 *were certain obstacles to overcome*: Bill Brammer, "Some Reflections on the Texas Campaign (Viewed from a Safe Distance)," memorandum to Lyndon Johnson, May 11, 1956, Brammer Papers.
105 *"straight" wife*: Eckhardt, *Duchess of Palms*, 38.
105 *I had fantasies of leaving Bill*: Ibid.
105 *tried going to a psychologist*: Ibid.
105 *She took care of [her husband's] business*: Ibid., 37–38.
105 *creative relationship*: Ibid., 44.
105 *Is* that . . .: Eckhardt interview, December 5, 2014.
106 *Dear Gary*: Eckhardt Papers.

8.

107 *If you'll name that boy*: Nadine Eckhardt, *Duchess of Palms* (Austin: University of Texas Press, 2009), 42.
107 *in her usual freewheeling style*: Shelby Brammer to the author, e-mail, April 21, 2015.
107 *arrived home before I could*: Nadine Eckhardt, interview by the author, December 5, 2014.
108 *Coonass Gothic*: Ibid.; see also William Brammer, *The Gay Place* (Boston: Houghton Mifflin, 1961), 244.
108 *How do you like our bizarre house?*: Billy Lee Brammer to Nadine Brammer, April 4, 1957, Nadine Eckhardt Papers, Southwest Writers Collection, Texas State University, San Marcos; hereafter cited as Eckhardt Papers.
108 *Your sojourn here*: Nadine Brammer to Billy Lee Brammer, April 5, 1957, ibid.
108 *I have no memories*: Shelby Brammer, interview by the author, December 5, 2014.
108 *He [decided] he would hide*: Brammer, *Gay Place*, 376–377.
109 *Perhaps . . . one of those big*: Ibid., 377.
109 *His favorite was* Tom Terrific: Shelby Brammer interview.
109 *he drove up in a black Fiat*: Eckhardt interview, December 5, 2014.
109 *favored lady visitors*: Billy Lee Brammer, "Sex in Politics," *Texas Monthly*, May 1973, texasmonthly.com/articles/sex-and-politics.
110 *the biggest raise*: Nadine Brammer to Nadine Cannon, December 1957, Eckhardt Papers.
110 *Life is hideous here*: Billy Lee Brammer to Nadine Brammer, April 4, 1957, ibid.
110 *I got alternately charming, tight*: Ibid.
110 *classic; I am amazing*: Ibid.
110 *needed a break from child-rearing*: Eckhardt, *Duchess of Palms*, 42.

110 *passed a pleasant weekend*: Ibid., 43.

110 *kept his hands to himself*: Ibid.

110–111 *I went out with my friends*: Ibid.

111 *You are invited to an* ORGY: Billy Lee Brammer party invitation, Eckhardt Papers.

111 *When Lyndon was at the ranch*: Eckhardt, *Duchess of Palms*, 43.

111 *From time to time, Nadine*: Eckhardt interview, December 5, 2014.

111 *Let's sneak away to Mexico*: Billy Lee Brammer to Nadine Brammer, August 1957, Eckhardt Papers.

111 *he was always snooping*: Eckhardt interview, December 5, 2014.

111 *I groupied him*: Ibid.

111 *It was the most strenuous*: Eric Sevareid, cited in undated clipping file, Eckhardt Papers.

111 *It is all mixed up*: Billy Lee Brammer to Nadine Brammer, n.d. [1957], ibid.

112 *misgivings that it's uneven*: James Street to Bill Brammer, March 28, 1957, Billy Lee Brammer Papers, Southwest Writers Collection, Texas State University, San Marcos; hereafter cited as Brammer Papers.

112 *considerably impressed*: Robert D. Loomis to James Street, October 9, 1957, ibid.

112 *I am really going into*: Nadine Brammer to Nadine Cannon, n.d. [c. 1957], Eckhardt Papers.

112 *[A]ll I ever hear from liberals*: Lyndon Johnson, cited in Robert Caro, *Master of the Senate* (New York: Knopf, 2002), 832.

112 *not gonna keep taking the shit*: Michael Janeway, *The Fall of the House of Roosevelt: Brokers of Ideas and Power from FDR to LBJ* (New York: Columbia University Press, 2004), 157.

113 *600,000 more*: Ibid.

113 *break the virginity*: Eckhardt interview, December 5, 2014.

113 *LBJ fooled hell out of Eisenhower*: Billy Lee Brammer to Nadine Brammer, n.d. [1957], Brammer Papers.

113 *Civil rights bill passed last night*: Billy Lee Brammer to Nadine Brammer, September 10, 1957, Eckhardt Papers.

114 *all too sophisticated*: Billy Lee Brammer, cited in Steven L. Davis, *Texas Literary Outlaws: Six Writers in the Sixties and Beyond* (Fort Worth: TCU Press, 2004), 44.

114 *Brammer has more wit*: Henry Holt response, cited in ibid., 43–44.

## 9.

115 *They don't mix*: William Brammer, *The Gay Place* (Boston: Houghton Mifflin, 1961), 230.

115 *asses for aides*: Nadine Brammer, cited in Ronnie Dugger, "To a Novelist Dying Young," *Washington Post*, June 18, 1978, F2.

115 *Nadine is just a bitter*: Ibid.

115 *Ever'body screws*: Bill Brammer, "Sex in Politics," *Texas Monthly*, May 1973, texasmonthly.com/articles/sex-and-politics.

116 *big, grubby manuscript*: Billy lee Brammer to Nadine Brammer, n.d. [1958], Billy Lee Brammer Papers, Southwest Writers Collection, Texas State University, San Marcos; hereafter cited as Brammer Papers.

116 *I think now*: James Street to Billy Lee Brammer, January 13, 1958, ibid.

116 *People keep feeling sorry*: Billy Lee Brammer to Nadine Brammer, February 25, 1958, ibid.

116 *What grim slobs*: Billy Lee Brammer to Nadine Brammer, n.d. [1958], ibid.

116 *He made a beautiful speech*: Billy Lee Brammer to Nadine Brammer, January 8, 1958, ibid.

116 *I am lost*: Billy Lee Brammer to Nadine Brammer, n.d. [1958], ibid.

116 *Maybe I'll get the book published*: Billy Lee Brammer to Nadine Brammer, June 4, 1958, ibid.

116 *I was having a ball in Austin*: Nadine Brammer, interview by the author, December 5, 2014.

116 *That evening, Nadine sat*: Shelby Brammer to the author, e-mail, December 8, 2014.

117 *What does this all mean?*: Billy Lee Brammer, notebook entry, n.d. [1958], Brammer Papers.

117 *I can still remember*: Barbara Bush, cited in Wayne Thorburn, *Red State: An Insider's Story of How the GOP Came to Dominate Texas Politics* (Austin: University of Texas Press, 2014), 68.

117 *holy war; principally a disagreement*: Ronnie Dugger, *The Politician: The Life and Times of Lyndon Johnson* (Old Saybrook, CT: Konecky & Konecky, 1982), 387.

118 *LBJ had about sixteen Scotches*: Billy Lee Brammer to Nadine Brammer, n.d. [1958], Brammer Papers.

118 *very frankly about religion*: Billy Lee Brammer to Nadine Brammer, n.d. [1958], ibid.

118 *The Virginia country*: Billy Lee Brammer to Nadine Brammer, February 3, 1958, ibid.

118 *like a shot of adrenalin*: Billy Lee Brammer to Nadine Brammer, n.d. [1958], ibid.

118 *Didn't love the people*: Billy Lee Brammer to Nadine Brammer, February 3, 1958, ibid.

118 *The Texas legislature*: Nadine Eckhardt, *Duchess of Palms* (Austin: University of Texas Press, 2009), 50.

119 *main concern*: Ibid.

119 *You weren't exactly making good sense*: Billy Lee Brammer to Nadine Brammer, n.d. [1958], Brammer Papers.

119 *Well, not exactly a friend*: Gary A. Keith, *Eckhardt: There Once Was a Congressman from Texas* (Austin: University of Texas Press, 2007), 149.

119 *We weren't discreet*: Eckhardt, *Duchess of Palms*, 50.

119 *We'd all pack a picnic*: Nadine Eckhardt, interview by the author, December 5, 2014.

120 *in a highly dangerous*: Sidney Brammer, "My Old Man," *Texas Observer*, April 21, 1995, 20.

120 *derelict daddy*: Ibid.

120 *He declared he was going*: Eckhardt, *Duchess of Palms*: 51.

120 *was having affairs as well*: Ibid.

120 *grubby little-boy hands*: Sidney Brammer, interview by the author, December 6, 2014.

120 *I haven't had any revelations*: Billy Lee Brammer to Nadine Brammer, n.d. [1958], Brammer Papers.

121 *I vant you; sex things*: Brammer Papers.

121 *I have worked every night*: Ibid.

122 *I read [it]*: Larry L. king, cited in Jan Reid, "Return to *The Gay Place*," *Texas Monthly*, March 2001, texasmonthly.com/content/return-gay-place.

122 *all I think about*: Billy Lee Brammer to Nadine Brammer, June 4, 1958, Brammer Papers.

122 *This was before the days*: Glen Wilson, "Waldron, Brammer," unpublished reminiscence, June 24, 1992, Larry L. King Papers, Southwest Writers Collection, Texas State University, San Marcos.

123 *worth a damn*: Billy Lee Brammer to Nadine Brammer, n.d. [1958], ibid.

123 *I am as lost as you*: James Street to Billy Lee Brammer, n.d. [1958], Brammer Papers.

123 *I don't want to think about it*: Ibid.

124 *Billy Lee, at least Thomas Wolfe*: Willie Morris, cited in Don Graham, introduction to *The Gay Place* (Austin: University of Texas Press, 1995), xvi.

124 *It was common knowledge*: Anita Howard Wukasch, "The Image of LBJ in Billy Lee Brammer's *The Gay Place*," unpublished paper, provided to the author by Nadine Eckhardt.

124 *Johnson passed Hawaii last week*: Billy Lee Brammer to Nadine Brammer, March 1959, Brammer Papers.

124 *Holden Caulfield type*: Billy Lee Brammer to Nadine Brammer, July 22, 1958, ibid.

124 *Turkish whorehouse*: Michael Janeway, *The Fall of the House of Roosevelt: Brokers of Ideas and Power from FDR to LBJ* (New York: Columbia University Press, 2004), 166.

125 *sad-eyed as a spaniel*: Ibid., 167.

125 *usual wild plans*: Billy Lee Brammer to Nadine Brammer, March 1959, Brammer Papers.

125 *I'm stripping my testes*: Billy Lee Brammer to Ronnie Dugger, cited in Dugger, "To a Novelist Dying Young," F3.

125 *[I] judge from your editorials*: Ibid.

126 *Don't take all this seriously*: Ibid.

126 *I [never] could . . . take it*: Sidney Brammer interview, December 6, 2014.
127 *So much of what passes*: Billy Lee Brammer, notebook entry, n.d. [1959], Brammer Papers.
127 *spiritual head cold*: Ibid.
127 *another round on the robo-typer*: Billy Lee Brammer to Nadine Brammer, February 11, 1959, Brammer Papers.
127 *We are witnessing here*: Billy Lee Brammer, notebook entry, n.d. [1959], ibid.
127 *He profiled a local zoo*: See Bill Brammer, "Coxville Zoo," *Austin American-Statesman*, April 16, 1959, A13.
128 *Went to the beach*: Billy Lee Brammer to Ronnie Dugger, cited in Dugger, "To a Novelist Dying Young," F3.
128 *a glorious escape*: Ibid.
128 *The act of creation*: Ibid.
128 *neuroticism*: Ibid.
128 *Greene in these two books*: Ibid.
128 *phrases from the Bible*: Billy Lee Brammer, undated notebook entries, Brammer Papers.
128 *My own epigraph*: Ibid.
128–129 *suppression of natural drives to action*: Abraham Myerson, cited in Nicolas Rasmussen, "America's First Amphetamine Epidemic, 1929–1971: A Quantitative and Qualitative Retrospective with Implications for the Present," *American Journal of Public Health* 98, no. 6 (June 2008): 974–985, available at ncbi.nlm.nih.gov/pmc/articls/PMC2377281.
129 *If the individual is depressed*: Cited in ibid.
129 *Just one 'Dexamyl'* Spansule: Cited at amphetamines.org/dexamyl.html.
130 *No word from the publisher*: Billy Lee Brammer to Nadine Brammer, March 1959, Brammer Papers.
130 *getting ready*: Dorothy de Santillana to Billy Lee Brammer, April 2, 1959, ibid.
130 *I am still feeding him stuff*: Billy Lee Brammer to Nadine Brammer, April 17, 1959, ibid.
130 *It is pretty good*: Ibid.
130 *Gad!*: Billy Lee Brammer to Nadine Brammer, n.d. [June or July 1959], ibid.
130 *I am 'facile' enough*: Billy Lee Brammer to Ronnie Dugger, cited in Dugger, "To a Novelist Dying Young," F3.
130 *We are very excited*: Dorothy de Santillana to Billy Lee Brammer, April 27, 1959, Brammer Papers.
130 *I have just finished*: Dorothy de Santillana to Billy Lee Brammer, June 26, 1959, ibid.
130 *I'm still not convinced*: Bill Brammer to Nadine Brammer, n.d. [1959], Brammer Papers.
131 *omnibus volume*: General Royalty Contract between Houghton Mifflin and Billy Lee Brammer, June 22, 1959, ibid.

131 *loosely tied together*: Dorothy de Santillana to Billy Lee Brammer, May 19, 1959, ibid.

131 *goofily, placidly, statically happy*: Billy Lee Brammer to Nadine Brammer, n.d. [July 1959], ibid.

131 *a little slow*: Anne Barrett to Billy Lee Brammer, August 6, 1959, ibid.

131 *picked up [the story] enormously*: Anne Barrett to Billy Lee Brammer, August 22, 1959, ibid.

131 *My feeling this week is no feeling*: Billy Lee Brammer to Nadine Brammer, n.d. [1959], ibid.

132 *I love her desperately*: Billy Lee Brammer to Nadine Cannon, November 17, 1959, ibid.

## 10.

133 *Neil's domestic problems*: Samuel D. Stewart to Billy Lee Brammer, April 12, 1960, Billy Lee Brammer Papers, Southwest Writers Collection, Texas State University, San Marcos; hereafter cited as Brammer Papers.

133 *Calamity Janeway*: For an overview of Janeway's life and career, see Kenneth N. Gilpin, "Eliot Janeway, Economist and Author, Dies at 80," *New York Times*, February 9, 1993, B7.

134 *New York is lovely*: Dorothy de Santillana to Billy Lee Brammer, December 18, 1959, Brammer Papers.

134 *I am broke, broke, broke*: Nadine Brammer to Nadine Cannon, December 20, 1960, ibid.

134 *My father*: Michael Janeway, *The Fall of the House of Roosevelt: Brokers of Ideas from FDR to LBJ* (New York: Columbia University Press, 2004), xi.

134 *found it boring*: Ibid., 92.

134 *personal style*: Ibid., 99.

134 *didactic*: Ibid.

134 *moved swiftly*: Ibid.

134 *Uncle Eliot is an LBJ type*: Billy Lee Brammer to Nadine Brammer, January 4, 1960, Brammer Papers.

134–135 *Was planning on going to*: Ibid.

135 *I thought you were getting away*: Booth Mooney, cited in Billy Lee Brammer to Nadine Brammer, n.d. [January or February 1960], ibid.

135 *where we sat between*: Ibid.

135 *he wanted to know*; *real whiskey gentry*: Ibid.

135 *The Village is pleasant*: Ibid.

135 *all is quiet*: Ibid.

135 *wild looking woman*: Billy Lee Brammer to Nadine Brammer, January 4, 1960, Brammer Papers.

135 *the "I-have-seen-the-best"*: Ibid.

136 *communists and eggheads*: Marcus Boon, *The Road of Excess: A History of*

*Writers on Drugs* (Cambridge, MA: Harvard University Press, 2002), 259. Boon mistakes J. Edgar Hoover for Herbert Hoover. For clarification, see Rob Johnson, "Did Beatniks Kill John F. Kennedy?," *Journal of Beat Studies* 2 (2013), available at questia.com/library/journal/1P3-3141292771/did-beatniks-kill-john-f-kennedy.

136 *Dear Wife*: Billy Lee Brammer to Nadine Brammer, January 15, 1960, Brammer Papers.

136 *convertible couches*: Ibid.

136 *I have decked the bed*: Ibid.

136 *Want to get this stuff*: Billy Lee Brammer to Nadine Brammer, n.d. [1960], ibid.

136 *Don't you forget*: Billy Lee Brammer to Sidney and Shelby Brammer, February 11, 1960, ibid.

137 *I know Nadine is better*: Billy Lee Brammer to Nadine Cannon, May 16, 1960, ibid.

137 *pussytrack the bedspread*: Billy Lee Brammer to Nadine Brammer, May 31, 1960, ibid.

137 COULD YOU TAKE THIS: Billy Lee Brammer to Nadine Brammer, postcard, n.d. [1960], ibid.

137–138 *weak and pallid*: Lyndon Johnson, cited in Robert A. Caro, *The Passage of Power* (New York: Knopf, 2012), 33.

138 *strange piece of ass*: Nadine Eckhardt, interview by the author, December 5, 2014.

138 *Just like the rest of the culture*: Sidney Brammer, interview by the author, December 6, 2014.

138 *even if it means going*: Sam Houston Johnson, *My Brother Lyndon* (New York: Cowles, 1970), 91–92.

138 *It is the politician's task*: Lyndon Johnson, cited in Caro, *Master of the Senate*, 57.

139 *Lyndon Johnson Será Presidente*: Caro, *Master of the Senate*, 69.

139 *The Number One Enigma*: Ibid., 71.

139 *Son, you've got to learn*: Lyndon Johnson, cited in ibid.

139 *highly-financed new-style machine*: Johnson, *My Brother Lyndon*, 103.

139 *Lyndon stayed away*: Ibid., 103–104.

140 *I dreamed that the good Lord*: Bill Adler, ed., *More Kennedy Wit* (New York: Bantam, 1965), 15.

140 *Johnson [always] ran on his record*: Harry McPherson, *A Political Education: A Washington Memoir* (Boston: Houghton Mifflin, 1988), 52.

140 *I have never seen anybody*: George Smathers, cited in Caro, *Master of the Senate*, 52.

140 *I was invited to [a] reception*: Billy Lee Brammer to Nadine Brammer, n.d. [January or February 1960], Brammer Papers.

141 *Cuba's oil grab*: Billy Lee Brammer, press release, paraphrased by Tim Clarke,

"Venezuela Target of Soviet Oil Offensive," *Houston Post*, July 20, 1960, Brammer Papers.

141 *You've never had a heart attack*: Lyndon Johnson, cited in Caro, *The Years of Lyndon Johnson: The Passage of Power* (New York: Knopf, 2012), 61.

141 *hundred dollar bills*: Ibid.

141 *Get those damn things out*: Lyndon Johnson, cited in Johnson, *My Brother Lyndon*, 96–97.

141 *got tight*: Billy Lee Brammer to Nadine Brammer, February 16, 1960, Brammer Papers.

141 *Janeway accosted Brammer*: Eckhardt interview, December 5, 2014; see also Caro, *Master of the Senate*, 82.

142 *You ask about the Johnson prospects*: Billy Lee Brammer to Nadine Brammer, May 31, 1960, Brammer Papers.

142 *we ought not to be doing the job*: Lyndon Johnson, cited in Caro, *Master of the Senate*, 89.

142 *Johnson seems to have straddled*: Billy Lee Brammer to Nadine Brammer, May 31, 1960.

142 *We don't want*: Ibid.

142 *The deal is Reuther*: Ibid.

143 *How the hell*: Lyndon Johnson, cited in Caro, *Master of the Senate*, 85.

143 *were hoping to get some mileage*: Billy Lee Brammer to Nadine Brammer, May 31, 1960.

143 *An yew know whut*: Ibid.

143 MOVE TO KENNEDY: Caro, *Master of the Senate*, 99.

143 *one has the feeling*: Norman Mailer, "Superman Comes to the Supermarket—I," in *The Time of Our Time* (New York: Random House, 1998), 345; originally published in *Esquire*, November 1960.

143 *I haven't had anything given*: Lyndon Johnson, cited in Caro, *Master of the Senate*, 106.

144 *worth a bucket of warm piss*: McPherson, *Political Education*, 179. McPherson replaces "piss" with "spit," for decorum's sake.

144 *John Kennedy obviously realized*: Johnson, *My Brother Lyndon*, 107.

144 *Most of the Texas staff*: McPherson, *Political Education*, 178.

144 *Something people always seem*: Price Daniel, cited in Jimmy Banks, *Money, Marbles, and Chalk: The Wondrous World of Texas Politics* (Austin: Texas Publishing, 1971), 96.

145 *revolution*; *I stand*: John F. Kennedy, acceptance speech, Democratic National Convention, Los Angeles, July 15, 1960, available at www.presidency.ucsb.edu/ws/index.php?pid=25966.

145 *In the cool of the afternoon*: F. Scott Fitzgerald, "Thousand and First Ship," in *The Crack-Up* (New York: New Directions, 2009), 67–68.

145 *Title . . . gives me some anxiety*: Billy Lee Brammer to Ronnie Dugger, cited

in Ronnie Dugger, "To a Novelist Dying Young," *Washington Post*, June 18, 1978, F3.

145 *Don't worry*: Dorothy de Santillana to Billy Lee Brammer, May 20, 1960, Brammer Papers.

145–146 *sharp, sensitive, comic*: Samuel D. Stewart to Billy Lee Brammer, April 12, 1960, ibid.

146 *You write such good dialogue*: Anne Barrett to Billy Lee Brammer, n.d., ibid.

146 *Way back in 1955*: Robert Benton, interview by the author, May 6, 2015.

146 *Sorry for the best laid plans*: Dorothy de Santillana to Billy Lee Brammer, October 11, 1960, Brammer Papers.

146 *We put that son of a bitch*: Bobby Kennedy, cited in Bill Minutaglio and Steven L. Davis, *Dallas 1963* (New York: Twelve, 2013), 57.

146 *Lyndon, I believe you're cracking up*: John F. Kennedy, cited in ibid., 56.

147 *They're having a little disturbance*: Minutaglio and Davis, *Dallas 1963*, 59.

147 *evening [he] won*: Ibid., 58.

147 *The prettiest bunch of women*: Bruce Alger, cited in ibid.

147 *If Khrushchev could vote*: Ibid., 59.

147 *Traitor!*: Ibid., 60.

147 *LBJ Sold Out*: Ibid., 62.

147 *Mink Coat Mob*: Sam Roberts, "Bruce Alger, 96, Dies, Tilted at a Texan," *New York Times*, May 1, 2015, A29.

147 *You ought to be glad*: Minutaglio and Davis, *Dallas 1963*, 61.

147 *Turncoat Texan*: Ibid., 62.

147 *I asked the policemen*: Lyndon Johnson, cited in Roberts, "Bruce Alger, 96, Dies."

147 *moved with excruciating slowness*: Steven L. Davis, *Texas Literary Outlaws: Six Writers in the Sixties and Beyond* (Ft. Worth, TCU Press, 2004), 87.

148 *Let's just let them do*: Lyndon Johnson, cited in Minutaglio and Davis, *Dallas 1963*, 64.

148 *with a martyr's embarrassed smile*: Davis, *Texas Literary Outlaws*, 87.

148 *It was the most triumphant*: Lawrence Wright, cited in Roberts, "Bruce Alger, 96, Dies."

148 *If he could have thought this*: Bill Moyers, cited in ibid.

148 *was decided that day*: Lawrence Wright, cited in Davis, *Texas Literary Outlaws*, 88.

148 *We lost Texas*: Richard Nixon, cited in Minutaglio and Davis, *Dallas 1963*, 66.

148 *Brammer . . . has jokingly told friends*: unidentified clipping from the *Austin-American-Statesman*, precise date unknown [circa 1960], Nadine Eckhardt Papers, Southwest Writers Collection, Texas State University, San Marcos; hereafter cited as Eckhardt Papers.

148 *We felt betrayed*: Celia Morris, *Finding Celia's Place* (College Station: Texas A&M University Press, 2000), 106.

148 *well-lubricated*: David Richards, *Once Upon a Time in Texas: A Liberal in the Lone Star State* (Austin: University of Texas Press, 2002), 20–21.

148 *now a gray flannel executive*: unidentified clipping from the *Austin American-Statesman*, date unknown, Eckhardt Papers.

149 *What a formidable amount of work*: Dorothy de Santillana to Billy Lee Brammer, May 6, 1960, Brammer Papers.

149 *depressing business*: Billy Lee Brammer to Nadine Brammer, n.d. [1960], ibid.

149 *it is much too rough and tough*: David Harris to Sam Stewart, telegram, December 29, 1960, ibid.

149 *I am sending you*: Dorothy de Santillana to Billy Lee Brammer, January 6, 1961, ibid.

149 *most barbarously large and final*: William Brammer, *The Gay Place* (Boston: Houghton Mifflin, 1961), 3.

11.

150 *being three related novels*: William Brammer, *The Gay Place* (Boston: Houghton Mifflin, 1961), title page.

150 *The country is most barbarously*: Ibid., 3.

151 *pleasant city*: Ibid., 4.

151 *migratory cotton pickers*: Ibid.

151 *flounder[ing] in his bedcovers*: Ibid., 5.

151 *You think it's gettin' better*: Ibid., 11.

151 *I think most colored people*: Ibid., 12.

151 *'windowmaker' in Hill Country German*: Al Reinert, "Billy Lee," *Texas Monthly*, February 1979, texasmonthly.com/politics/billy-lee-2.

151 *Nothin' tastes like it used to*: Brammer, *Gay Place*, 11.

151 *Goddam; Sir*: Ibid.

151 *most eligible married woman in town*: Ibid., 23.

152 *Hell of a note*: Ibid., 17.

152 *nutboy liberals*: Ibid., 39.

152 *happiest when anyone belabored him*: Ibid., 24–25.

152 *Oppose [my] goddam bill!*: Ibid., 94.

152 *half-a-loaf*: Nadine Eckhardt, interview by the author, December 5, 2014.

152 *I want unanimous consent*: Brammer, *Gay Place*, 95.

152 *like high school*: Ibid., 50.

152 *I been sucklin' my babes*: Ibid., 179.

152 *last week's illusions*: Ibid., 222.

153 *[We] were all such amateurs*: Ibid., 142.

153 *last time he'd seen real passion*: Ibid., 231.

153 *really had it*: Ibid., 241.

153 *nigger bill*: Ibid., 395.

153 *run out of gas*: Ibid., 292.
153 I *get down*: Ibid., 334.
154 *poet-politician*: Ibid., 396.
154 *Life is awfully well ordered*: Ibid., 259.
154 *up against him*: Ibid., 261.
154 *side by side trying to recapture*: Ibid., 387.
154 *hills above the city*; *old radio receiver*: Ibid., 276–277.
154 *Not so much long gone youth*: Ibid., 281–282.
154 *Most of us came into town*: Ibid., 325.
154 *old attack bomber*: Ibid., 227.
154 *Can't seem to catch his eye*: Ibid., 400–401.
155 *Love was not the natural condition*: Ibid., 337.
155 *I like the Senate*: Ibid., 313.
155 *sandhills*: Ibid., 413.
155 *I keep thinking*: Ibid.
155 *It's because we're driving*: Ibid., 414.
155 *quality, characteristic of those*: Ibid., 91.
155–156 *simulated adobe huts*: Ibid., 416.
156 *Hell of a country*: Ibid., 415.
156 *good face*; *He mentioned the possibility*: Ibid., 435.
156 *They were not quite people*: Ibid., 423.
156 *from the [disorienting] mountains*: Ibid., 433.
156 *Invited in*: Ibid., 16.
156 *Arthur Fenstemaker's transformation*: Ibid., 437.
157 *dead remains*: Ibid., 469.
157 *pale and blue*: Ibid., 526.
157 *I suppose there was probably*: Nadine Eckhardt, cited in Reinert, "Billy Lee."
157 *[w]hen I read [it]*: Nadine Eckhardt, cited in Jan Reid, "Return to *The Gay Place*," *Texas Monthly*, March 2001, texasmonthly.com/the-culture/return-to-the-gay-place.
157 *I can't believe*: Nadine Eckhardt, cited in Don Graham, introduction to *The Gay Place* (Austin: University of Texas Press, 1995), xvii.
157 *woven through it*: Reid, "Return to *The Gay Place*."
158 *Billy Lee's ghost*: Al Reinert, interview by the author, March 9, 2015.
158 *were no Texas voices*: Reinert, "Billy Lee."
158 *Brammer's book got Texas right*: William Broyles, foreword to Billy Lee Brammer, *The Gay Place* (Austin: Texas Monthly Press, 1978), i.
158 *When I read* The Gay Place: Ibid., iii.
158 *inhabit Nostalgia Ville*: Graham, introduction, xxvii.
158 *cheap*: Dobie, cited in ibid.
159 *captures hints of cultural change*: Graham, introduction, xxviii–xxix.
159 *Groups of people*: Brammer, *Gay Place*, 511.
159 *burrowing in the luxuriant folds*: Ibid., 516.

159 *genius gone to seed*: Ibid., 30.

159 *democratic politics is the country's* and all other quotations from Christopher Lehmann, "Why Americans Can't Write Political Fiction," *Washington Monthly*, October–November 2005, washingtonmonthly.com/features/2005/0510.lehmann.html.

12.

161 *Janeway's nicer*: Billy Lee Brammer to Nadine Brammer, December 1959, Billy Lee Brammer Papers, Southwest Writers Collection, Texas State University, San Marcos; hereafter cited as Brammer Papers.

161 *little cocktail party*: Ibid.

161 *which rarely spends money*: Ibid.

162 *I hope* Time: Dorothy de Santillana to Billy Lee Brammer, April 10, 1961, ibid.

162 *The last thing he wanted*: David Halberstam, cited in Jan Reid, "Return to *The Gay Place*," *Texas Monthly*, March 2001, texasmonthly.com/the-culture/return-gay-place.

162 *I wish I could resign*: Billy Lee Brammer, cited in Ronnie Dugger, "To a Novelist Dying Young," *Washington Post*, June 18, 1978, F3.

162 *Bill Brammer knows his people*: Houghton Mifflin Company, press release, July 1960, Brammer Papers.

162 *This isn't just another "gifted"*: Dorothy de Santillana to Billy Lee Brammer, February 25, 1960, ibid.

162 *Brammer has an authentic*: *New York Times Book Review*, cited in Reid, "Return to *The Gay Place*."

162 *I don't know of another work*: Gore Vidal, "Comment," *Esquire*, May 1961, 56.

162 *Mr. Brammer has crashed the literary world*: Roger Shattuck, "Politics, Its Responsibility and Thrall," *Texas Observer*, April 8, 1961, 6.

162 *By the time I'd read*: Maurice Doblier, review of *The Gay Place*, *New York Herald Tribune*, March 9, 1961, Brammer Papers.

162 *It is a conscientious work*: Ernest B. Fergurson, "Texas Political Science," *Baltimore Sun*, April 9, 1961, ibid.

162 *a first novel full of*: Lon Tinkle, "New Novel by Texan Lampoons Politics," *Dallas Morning News*, March 5, 1961, sec. 4, 9.

163 *Pre-release, press notices*: C. Richard King, untitled comment on *The Gay Place*, *Daily Texan*, February 23, 1961, 6.

163 *love duets*: Shattuck, "Politics, Its Responsibility."

163 *immensely responsive*: A. C. Spectorsky to Elizabeth McKee, February 27, 1961, Brammer Papers.

163 *From reading an early version*: Ronnie Dugger, "Observations," *Texas Observer*, November 11, 1966, 11.

163 *You put in the good Johnson*: Dugger, "To a Novelist Dying Young," F4.

163 *William; Famous Arthur*: Eckhardt interview, December 5, 2014.

163 *It is a wonder that I survived*: Billy Lee Brammer, "A Famous Arthur Returns to Dallas," *Texas Observer*, December 27, 1962, 1.

164 *When I was a kid*: Sidney Brammer, interview by the author, December 6, 2014.

164 *I don't know what bacchanalia means*: Ibid.

164 *Salinger was off someplace*: Hugh Sidey, cited in Seymour M. Hersh, *The Dark Side of Camelot* (Boston: Little, Brown, 1997), 335.

165 *He was shaking*: Ibid., 336.

165 *If this were Britain*: Robert Kennedy, cited in ibid., 335.

165 *Uncle Cornpone; Riverboat Gambler*: Eckhardt interview, December 5, 2014.

165 *Every time I [come] into*: Lyndon Johnson, cited in Robert Dallek, *Flawed Giant* (New York: Oxford University Press, 1998), 7.

165 *lightweight*; *sonny boy*: Ibid.

165 *lift him physically*: Ibid., 4.

165 *he went on an incredible*: Ibid.

165 *good many dark-haired ladies*: Billy Lee Brammer, cited in Dugger, "To a Novelist Dying Young," F3.

166 *Diana the Vague*: Eckhardt interview, December 5, 2014.

166 *there was an empty place next to me*: Diana de Vegh, cited in Sally Bedell Smith, *Grace and Power: The Private World of the Kennedy White House* (New York: Random House, 2004), 147.

166 *Hugh, this is the darnedest thing*: Ibid., 146.

166 *Power*: Ibid.

166 *The second novel*: Elizabeth McKee to Billy Lee Brammer, February 24, 1961, Brammer Papers.

166 *Your book has sold only*: Dorothy de Santillana to Billy Lee Brammer, June 20, 1961, ibid.

167 *telephoned wishing more money*: Dorothy de Santillana, report to Houghton Mifflin Company Executive Committee, June 20, 1961, ibid.

167 *He sent me a delightful picture*: Dorothy de Santillana to Elizabeth McKee, March 22, 1962, ibid.

167 *image is poor*: Ben Bradlee, cited in Hersh, *Dark Side of Camelot*, 337.

167 *revolutionaries in Cuba*: Norman Mailer, "Superman Comes to the Supermarket—I," in *The Time of Our Time* (New York: Random House, 1998), 346–347; originally published in *Esquire*, November 1960.

168 *good, sound, conventional*: Ibid., 347.

168 *the long electric night*: Ibid.

168 *was a hero America needed*: Ibid., 353.

168 *To anyone who could see*: Ibid.

168 *reveal . . . the character*: Ibid., 355.

168 *lay abed* and all other quotations from *Fustian Days*: Billy Lee Brammer, *Fustian Days* rough draft manuscript, Brammer Papers.

170 *That damn magazine*: John Kennedy, cited in Smith, *Grace and Power*, 128.

170 *file the Bible*: Ibid., 130.
170 *like a cricket*: Ibid., 129.
170 *He seduces me*: Henry Luce, cited in ibid.
170 *there must be loyalty*: Hersh, *Dark Side of Camelot*, 219.
170 *Kennedy was consumed*: Ibid., 10.
171 *I don't care if it's horse piss*: John F. Kennedy, cited in ibid., 237.
171 *You had to really work*: Diana de Vegh, cited in ibid., 31.
171 *Jack Kennedy is down in*: Billy Lee Brammer to Hazel Foshee, July 19, 1961, cited in Smith, *Grace and Power*, 146.
171 *Title for a memoir*: Billy Lee Brammer notebook, n.d. [1961], Brammer Papers.
172 *I thought he was a big joke* and all other quotations from Brammer's notebook: Ibid.
175 *girls*: Hersh, *Dark Side of Camelot*, 388.
175 *I must have had fifty friends*: Bobby Baker, cited in ibid., 389.
175 *Beneath the suntanned surface*: "Summer of Discontent," *Time*, July 7, 1961, 11.
175 *The President moved easily*: Ibid., 12.
175 *Even in the midst of briefings*: *Time*, July 21, 1961, 11.
176 *He's been in the pool* and all other quotations from "President Glooey": Billy Lee Brammer, "President Glooey," *Texas Observer*, January 10, 1963, 10–12.
176 *You know what he does*: Lyndon Johnson, cited in Smith, *Grace and Power*, 173.
176 *J. Edgar Hoover*: Ibid.
176 *he was waiting*: Frank Stanton, cited in ibid.
176 *You are dealing*: John Kennedy, cited in Dallek, *Flawed Giant*, 10.
177 *gilded impotency; that little shitass*: Smith, *Grace and Power*, 174–175.
177 *But we're over the ocean*: Dallek, *Flawed Giant*, 13.
177 *few fingerless lepers*: Ibid.
177 *The next song*: John Lennon, cited in "John Lennon Shares Identity with NPR Producer," October 8, 2010, www.npr.org/templates/story/story.php?storyId =130435561.
177 *Billy abandoned me*: Dick Schaap, "Behind the Lines: Johnson's Boswell," *New York Herald Tribune*, date unknown, Brammer Papers.

13.

199 *I've survived* and all other quotations from Katherine Anne Porter: Billy Lee Brammer (unsigned), "First Novel," *Time*, July 28, 1961, 70.
200 *Bill didn't really know*: David Halberstam, cited in Sidney Brammer, "My Old Man," *Texas Observer*, April 21, 1995, 20.
200 *It was a humid midsummer night*: *Time*, August 18, 1961, 12.
201 *I know that LBJ*: Halberstam, cited in Sidney Brammer, "My Old Man," 21.
201 *I don't think [Lyndon] ever read*: Horace Busby, cited in ibid.

201 *Nadine remained convinced*: Nadine Eckhardt, interview by the author, December 5, 2014.

201 *Houghton Mifflin and Eliot Janeway*: Elizabeth McKee to Billy Lee Brammer, August 6, 1962, Billy Lee Brammer Papers, Southwest Writers Collection, Texas State University, San Marcos; hereafter cited as Brammer Papers.

202 *across the U.S. South*: *Time*, October 13, 1961, 26.

202 *small group of Negroes*: Ibid.

202 *Negro children*: Ibid.

202 *I'd rather be dumb*: Ibid.

202 *new cars*: *Time*, November 24, 1961, 15.

202 *young white trash*: *Time*, December 8, 1961, 25.

202 *Southern Negro college students*: *Time*, January 12, 1962, 15.

202 *He was once the idol*: Ibid.

202 *predominantly white office building*: Ibid.

202 *meekly posted bond*: Ibid.

203 *There was a wistfulness in Bill*: Halberstam, cited in Sidney Brammer, "My Old Man," 22.

203 *Nadine just said one day*: Sidney Brammer, interview by the author, December 6, 2014.

204 *My experience with Billy Lee*: Nadine Eckhardt, *Duchess of Palms* (Austin: University of Texas Press, 2009), 60.

204 *I knew [Bob] had the potential*: Ibid., 59.

204 *Certain men wind up*: Ibid., 60.

204 *With both Billy Lee and Bob*: Sidney Brammer interview.

204 *We just swung back and forth*: Ibid.

204 *I adore you*: Billy Lee Brammer to Nadine Eckhardt, n.d. [1961], Nadine Eckhardt Papers, Southwest Writers Collection, Texas State University, San Marcos; hereafter cited as Eckhardt Papers.

205 *At a certain point*: Eckhardt interview, December 5, 2014.

205 *I was living with Gloria Steinem*: Robert Benton, interview by the author, May 6, 2015.

205 *Private money receded*: Gloria Steinem, cited in Daniel Brandt, "Gloria Steinem and the CIA," *Portland (OR) Free Press*, April 1997, available at www.umsl.edu/~thomaskp/pfp.htm.

205 *We all had dinner one night*: Benton interview.

206 *issues central to the festival*: Peter Flynn and Ed Winckler to Billy Lee Brammer, May 4, 1962, Brammer Papers.

206 *He was just adrift*: Benton interview.

206 *Were you batonned*: Warren Miller to Billy Lee Brammer, August 9, 1962, Brammer Papers.

206 *from the Ritz Hotel bar*: Al Reinert, "Billy Lee," *Texas Monthly*, February 1979, texasmonthly.com/politics/billy-lee-2.

206 *There are a lot of people*: Merle Miller to Billy Lee Brammer, n.d. [1962], Brammer Papers.

206 *broken-toe pills*: Ibid.

206 *looked through the medicine chest*: Ibid.

206 *falling apart*: Billy Lee Brammer to Elizabeth McKee, n.d. [1962], Brammer Papers.

207 *Broken-Down Bill*: Elizabeth McKee to Billy Lee Brammer, September 14, 1962, ibid.

207 *You are going to be*: Merle Miller to Billy Lee Brammer, May 13, 1962, ibid.

208 *I think it better*: W. B. Yeats, excerpt from "On Being Asked for a War Poem," in Billy Lee Brammer notebook, n.d. [1962], Brammer Papers.

208 *Do you know where I*: Eckhardt interview, December 5, 2014.

14.

209 *Let me tell you about groupies*: Billy Lee Brammer, notebook entry, n.d. [1963], Billy Lee Brammer Papers, Southwest Writers Collection, Texas State University, San Marcos; hereafter cited as Brammer Papers.

209 *spiritual property*: Larry McMurtry, *In a Narrow Grave: Essays on Texas* (New York: Simon & Schuster, 2010), 158.

209 *Almost everyone seemed to be*: Jay Dunston Milner, *Confessions of a Maddog: A Romp through the High-Flying Texas Music and Literary Era of the Fifties to the Seventies* (Denton: University of North Texas Press, 1998), 68–69.

209 *uncannily accurate picture*: Ibid., 66–67.

209 *Students, journalists, lobbyists*: Jan Reid, *The Improbable Rise of Redneck Rock* (New York: Da Capo, 1974), 1.

210 *Austin always seemed to embrace*: Milner, *Confessions of a Maddog*, 69.

210 *showed a generation of writers*: Bud Shrake, cited in Jan Reid, "Return to *The Gay Place*," *Texas Monthly*, March 2001, texasmonthly.com/the-culture/return-gay-place.

210 *We noticed immediately how cute*: Bud Shrake, cited in Steven L. Davis, *Texas Literary Outlaws: Six Writers in the Sixties and Beyond* (Fort Worth: TCU Press, 2004), 98.

210 *I thought that for a writer*: Ibid., 96.

210 *Ah wah, Billie Lee*: Larry L. King to Billy Lee Brammer, January 24, 1963, Brammer Papers.

210 *confused work*: Billy Lee Brammer, cited in Davis, *Texas Literary Outlaws*, 46.

210 *a rare charisma*: Milner, *Confessions of a Maddog*, 72.

211 *Innumerable women*: Ibid., 72–73.

211 *I don't think Bill ever*: Robert Benton, interview by the author, May 6, 2015.

212 *way of marking one's difference*: Barry Shank, *Dissonant Identities: The Rock 'n' roll Scene in Austin, Texas* (Hanover, NH: Wesleyan University Press, 1994), 40.

212 *Looking back on the situation*: John Clay, cited in ibid., 41.

212 *underground contingent of people*: Tary Owens, cited in ibid., 48.

212 *fertile with conflict*: Larry McMurtry, cited in Jason Mellard, *Progressive Country: How the 1970s Transformed the Texan in Popular Culture* (Austin: University of Texas Press, 2013), 10.

212 *had a great talent*: Milner, *Confessions of a Maddog*, 71.

213 *just out in the open* and other quotations from Cartwright: Gary Cartwright, cited in Davis, *Texas Literary Outlaw*, 94.

213 *mascot of debauchery*: Shelby Brammer, interview by the author, December 5, 2014.

213 *Depressing*: Billy Lee Brammer, notebook entry, n.d. [1963], Brammer Papers.

213 *Shoot fire, Willie*: Milner, *Confessions of a Maddog*, 68.

213 *imagining lurid scenarios*; *I called him*: Ibid.

214 *Women are nine-faced bitches*: Billy Lee Brammer, notebook entry, n.d. [1963], Brammer Papers.

214 *His belting style*: Cited in ibid.

214 *Hemingway doomed bitch-heroine*: Billy Lee Brammer, notebook entry, n.d. [1963], Brammer Papers.

214 *dissatisfied married women*: Ibid.

214 *too perfect*; *stepped out on him*: Billy Lee Brammer, handwritten notes, n.d., Brammer Papers.

215 *might have the presumption*: Billy Lee Brammer, notebook entry, n.d. [1963], ibid.

215 *a gang of revelers*: Milner, *Confessions of a Maddog*, 71.

215 *Shortly after midnight*: Ibid., 72.

216 *I long to talk*: Billy Lee Brammer, notebook entry, n.d. [1963], Brammer Papers.

216 *Something in him was letting go*: Ronnie Dugger, "To a Novelist Dying Young," *Washington Post*, June 13, 1978, F4.

216 *book with Love and Lust*: Ibid.

216 *Gives you a new perspective*: Ibid.

216 *caused brain damage*: Dorothy Browne, interview by the author, April 16, 2015.

216 *I choose not to choose*: Ibid.

216 *it was not dissipation*: Robert Benton, cited in Paul Cullum, "The Second Act," rough draft manuscript, Brammer Papers.

216 *It wasn't 'letting go'*: Browne interview.

216 *He never moralized*: Dorothy Browne, cited in Al Reinert, "Billy Lee," *Texas Monthly*, February 1979, texasmonthly.com/politics/billy-lee.

216 *He wanted to see where*: Sidney Brammer, interview by the author, December 6, 2014.

217 *I can see why he*: Dorothy Browne, cited in Cullum, "The Second Act."

217 *He was my graduate school*: Browne interview.
217 *Bereft of hope*: Dugger, "To a Novelist Dying Young," F4.
217 *It seemed to me that*: Larry McMurtry, cited in Reinert, "Billy Lee."
217 *We were both, at the time*: McMurtry, *In a Narrow Grave*, 158–159.
217 *local culture hero*: Ibid.
218 *I didn't know [Billy Lee] well*: Larry McMurtry to the author, January 21, 2015.
218 *He wasn't getting anything back*: Larry McMurtry, cited in Reinert, "Billy Lee."
218 *distinguished drinker* and other quotations from *Fustian Days*: Billy Lee Brammer, rough draft of *Fustian Days*, n.d., n.p., Brammer Papers.
219 *very mangled state*: Elizabeth McKee to Billy Lee Brammer, September 4, 1962, ibid.
219 *didn't leave it with*: Elizabeth McKee to Billy Lee Brammer, October 15, 1962, ibid.
219 *Your reminiscences*: James H. Silberman to Billy Lee Brammer, December 8, 1961, ibid.
219 *I am already a little*: John Arnold to Billy Lee Brammer, November 12, 1962, ibid.
219 *In case you think our enthusiasm*: Elizabeth McKee to Billy Lee Brammer, September 24, 1962, ibid.
219 *As for the drug needs*: Unnamed publisher cited in ibid.
220 *He said that sometimes*: Milner, *Confessions of a Maddog*, 70.
220 *Now they'll* really *take it out*; *too much*: Bill Brammer, cited in Al Reinert, interview with the author, April 15, 2015.
220 *When we were in high school*: Tary Owens, cited in Robert Draper, "O Janis," *Texas Monthly*, October 1992, texasmonthly.com/articles/o-janis.
220 *A key to [Janis's] personality*: David Moriarity, cited in ibid.
220 *we weren't allowed*: Tary Owens, cited in ibid.
220 *Nigger lover!*: Draper, "O Janis."
220 *We went to Mr. Kenneth Threadgill's*: Milner, *Confessions of a Maddog*, 67.
221 *persuaded to sing along*: Ibid.
221 *more and more weird*: Shank, *Dissonant Identities*, 48.
221 *little bar became a haven*; *a young regular*: Reid, *Redneck Rock*, 16.
221 *she was already neurotic*: Ibid.
222 *Allen Hamilton, chief of police*: For information on surveillance of the Ghetto, see Thorne Dreyer, "The Spies of Texas," *Texas Observer*, November 17, 2006, texasobserver.org/2343-the-spies-of-texas-newfound-files-detail-how-ut-austin-police-tracked-the-lives-of-sixties-dissidents.
222 *rumored that women could have*: Ramsey Wiggins, cited in "Ghetto History," posted at texasghetto.org/GhettoHistory.htm, accessed in 2014; the website is no longer active.
223 *Dope will get you through*: Gilbert Shelton, cited at ibid.

223 *best sentence ever to appear*: Larry McMurtry, *Literary Life* (New York: Simon & Schuster, 2009), 71.

223 *Even if one succeeds*: Dave Hickey, cited in ibid.

223 *a green paperback*: Tom Walker, "Ode to Billy Jeff," in *Signed Confessions* (Burlington, VT: Fomite, 2012), 140.

224 *with the use of many blankets*: McMurtry, *Literary Life*, 64.

224 *He was still* sort *of Establishment*: Sidney Brammer interview.

224 *Enter Enig-Man*: Ibid.

224 *Beckman brought Bill upstairs*: Browne interview.

224–225 *were all such beautiful women*: Sidney Brammer, cited in Reid, "Return to *The Gay Place*."

225 *When we walked in*: Gary Cartwright, cited in ibid.

225 *right to know how much*: Al William, "Court Backs Her," *Austin American-Statesman*, May 16, 1963, 1.

225 *on the bus*: Jan Reid, interview by the author, April 16, 2015.

225 *ran at a pretty high gear*: Ken Kesey, cited in Cullum, "The Second Act."

226 *what every American writer of importance*: "Works in Progress," *Esquire*, July 1963, Brammer Papers.

226 *He was always giving someone*: Gary Cartwright, cited in Cullum.

226 *just like his old pal Lyndon*: Cullum, "The Second Act."

226 *I think he wanted to be*: Bob Simmons, cited in ibid.

226 *first vial of blue liquid*: Paul Drummond, *Eye Mind: The Saga of Roky Erickson and the 13th Floor Elevators, the Pioneers of Psychedelic Sound* (Los Angeles: Process, 2007), 44.

226 *Close your eyes and stick out your tongue*: Bill Brammer, cited in Reinert interview.

226 *Oh yeah, he was always*: Susan Walker, interview by the author, April 15, 2015.

15.

227 *Ugliest Man on Campus*: This story is cited in many sources; see, for example, Robert Draper, "O Janis," *Texas Monthly*, October 1992, texasmonthly.com/articles/o-janis.

227 *The dusty road calls you*: Ibid.

228 *He walked onto the dance floor*: Billy Porterfield, "Texan Carried to Fame by Talent, LBJ's Power," *Austin American-Statesman*, June 9, 1989, B6.

228 *old man*: Claudette Lowe, interview by the author, April 16, 2015.

228 *But he's so interesting!*: Dorothy Browne, cited in ibid.

228 *Darthy*: Dorothy Browne, interview by the author, April 16, 2015.

228 *He was the gentlest man*: Dorothy Browne, cited in Joe Frolik, "Author Dies Money Poor, Friend Rich," *Austin American-Statesman*, February 14, 1978, A3.

228 *crook, a communist sympathizer*: Steven L. Davis, *Texas Literary Outlaws: Six Writers in the Sixties and Beyond* (Forth Worth: TCU Press, 2004), 105.

228 *We need a man on horseback*: Bill Minutaglio and Steven L. Davis, *Dallas 1963* (New York: Twelve, 2013), 108.

228 *To us, sports were too dumb*: Gary Cartwright, *The Best I Recall* (Austin: University of Texas Press, 2015), 36.

228–229 *Texas Negro athletes*: Gary Cartwright, "The Word on Integration," *Dallas Morning News*, February 12, 1963, sec. 2, 1.

229 *We've all watched*: Gary Cartwright, "Bishop Sheds its Image," *Dallas Morning News*, February 21, 1963, sec. 2, 1.

229 *Rightwing nutcases*: Cartwright, *Best I Recall*, 41.

229 *Big Circus Face*; *check scores*: Ibid., 26.

229 *living room would be full*: Gary Cartwright, interview by the author, April 24, 2015.

229 *dearest friends*: Cartwright, *Best I Recall*: 50.

230 *classy joint*: Jack Ruby, cited in Cartwright interview, April 24, 2015.

230 *makes you a positive thinker*: Jack Ruby, cited in Seth Kantor, *Who Was Jack Ruby?* (New York: Everest House, 1978), 31.

230 *smart and funny*: Cartwright, *Best I Recall*, 39.

230 *There's a 'New Frontier' joke*: Brammer repeated this joke in a letter to Nadine Brammer, July 12, 1961, Billy Lee Brammer Papers, Southwest Writers Collection, Texas State University, San Marcos; hereafter cited as Brammer Papers.

230 *That's the best little piece*: Lyndon Johnson, cited in Cartwright interview, April 24, 2015.

231 *He had received a suspended sentence*: This story is still a matter of intense speculation in Austin. One version suggests that Josefa, Wallace, and the dead man were involved in a love triangle and that the killing was motivated by jealousy. The jury convicted Wallace of murder, but the judge gave him a suspended sentence. Also, Wallace had worked as an economist at the US Department of Agriculture, an unusual background for a hired killer.

233 *I'll keep my dogs where*: Jack Ruby, cited in Gary Cartwright, interview by the author, April 25, 2015.

233 *Don't you have children?*: Jack Ruby, cited in ibid.

233 *consisted mostly of her dropping*: Cartwright, *The Best I Recall*, 43.

233 *She was a remarkable woman*: Ibid.

234 *It was a better act*: Cartwright interview, April 24, 2015.

234 *Cartwright admitted later*: Ibid.; see also Cartwright, *Best I Recall*, 19.

234 *large group of Chicago racketeers*: Kantor, *Who Was Jack Ruby?*, 20.

235 *the CIA had enlisted*: Bryan Bender and Neil Swidey, "His Brother's Keeper: Robert F. Kennedy Saw Conspiracy in JFK's Assassination," *Boston Globe*, November 24, 2013, https://www.bostonglobe.com/metro/2013/11/24/his-brother-keeper-robert-kennedy-saw-conspiracy-jfk-assassination/TmZ0nfKsB34p69LWUBgsEJ/story.html.

235 *well-dressed young matrons*: David Richards, *Once Upon a Time in Texas: A Liberal in the Lone Star State* (Austin: University of Texas Press, 2002), 32; see also Davis, *Texas Literary Outlaws*, 120–121.

236 *When Ann and I finally*: Richards, *Once Upon a Time in Texas*, 32.

236 *just how deranging the place*: Ibid.

236 *There was something very ugly*: Minutaglio and Davis, *Dallas 1963*, 251.

236 *that little shitass*: Lyndon Johnson, cited in Jess Shesol, *Mutual Contempt: Lyndon Johnson, Robert Kennedy, and the Feud that Defined a Decade* (New York: Norton, 1998), 183.

236 *nut country*: Minutaglio and Davis, *Dallas 1963*, 302.

237 *It is an era*: John F. Kennedy, cited in Ronnie Dugger, "The Last Voyage of Mr. Kennedy," *Texas Observer*, November 29, 1963, texasobserver.org/archives-last-voyage-mr-kennedy.

237 *G.I. families*: Dugger, "Last Voyage of Kennedy."

237 *Texas Belongs to the South*: Ibid.

237 *three times as much electric power*: Ibid.

237 *more Castilian*: Ibid.

237 *Cuba is a cancer*: Ibid.

237 *I hope nothing happens*: Nadine Eckhardt, cited in Gary A. Keith, *Eckhardt: There Once Was a Congressman from Texas* (Austin: University of Texas Press, 2007), 185.

237 *It's ride with Lyndon*: Davis, *Texas Literary Outlaws*, 299.

238 *That hat protects you*: Dugger, "Last Voyage of Kennedy."

238 *It would not be a very*: John F. Kennedy, cited in Minutaglio and Davis, *Dallas 1963*, 302–303.

238 *Wanted for Treason*: Davis, *Texas Literary Outlaws*, 123.

238 *Kennedy is showing*: Dugger, "Last Voyage of Kennedy."

238 *Well, I'm taking my risks*: Henry Gonzalez, cited in ibid.

238 *Thank God, Mr. President*: Stanley Marcus, *Minding the Store* (Denton: University of North Texas Press, 2001), 255.

238 *I just want you to know*: Davis, *Texas Literary Outlaws*, 123–124.

239 *Don't let that woman in*: Jack Ruby, cited in ibid.

239 *I just want to warn you*: Ibid.

239 *Kennedy looked directly at us*: Gary Cartwright, cited in ibid., 124.

239 *The president's grey eyes*: Edwin "Bud" Shrake, *Strange Peaches* (Austin: Texas Monthly Press, 1987), 260.

239 *The scene was a disaster*: Richards, *Once Upon a Time in Texas*, 33.

239 *The only reason you and I*: Chas. Batchelor to M. W. Stevenson, memorandum, November 28, 1963, available at jfk.ci.dallas.tx.us/03/0338-001.gif.

239 *that at 10:45*: Ibid.

239 *gave the name*: Ibid.

240 *Let's hurry up*: Ibid.

240 *Ronnie Dugger . . . did not recall*: Ronnie Dugger to the author, e-mail, February 23, 2015.

240 *memories of that day*: Cartwright interview, April 24, 2015.
240 *restatement to Nadine*: Nadine Eckhardt, interview by the author, December 5, 2014.
240 *a motorcycle policeman*: Dugger, "Last Voyage of Kennedy."
241 *What happened?*: Ibid.
241 *Well, Mr. President*: Nellie Connally, cited in Minutaglio and Davis, *Dallas 1963*, 312.
241 *groin muscle*: Seymour Hersh, *The Dark Side of Camelot* (Boston: Little, Brown, 1997), 12.
241 *Pieces of skull*: Shrake, *Strange Peaches*, 261.
241 *I heard three loud explosions*: Ralph Yarborough, cited in Dugger, "Last Voyage of Kennedy."
241 *Goddamn the sons of bitches!*: Doug Kiker, cited in ibid.
242 *If a city has a conscience*: Dugger, "Last Voyage of Kennedy."
242 *It wasn't a city of hate*: Gary Cartwright, "Who Was Jack Ruby?," *Texas Monthly*, November 1975, texasmonthly.com/politics/who-was-jack-ruby.
242 *Take the play away*: Jack Ruby, cited in ibid.
242 *was always at the center*: Ibid.
242 *Twice during a press conference*: Ibid.
243 *When the team was introduced*: Cartwright, *Best I Recall*, 54.
243 *Have you been watching TV?*: Bud Shrake, cited in ibid., 55.
243 *The name just slipped out*: Ibid.
243 *It just seemed like*: Jesse Curry, cited in Kantor, *Who Was Jack Ruby?*, 69.
243 *You all know me*: Jack Ruby, cited in Cartwright, "Who Was Jack Ruby?"
244 *I have been used*: Jack Ruby, cited in Kantor, *Who Was Jack Ruby?*, 10.
244 *The subtext of everything*: Gary Cartwright, cited in Davis, *Texas Literary Outlaws*, 140.
244 *I think I hit the jackpot*: Bill Brammer, cited in Cartwright, *The Best I Recall*, 56.

16.

245 *Darthy, my love*: Bill Brammer, cited in Dorothy Browne, interview by the author, April 16, 2015.
245 *seamless*: Dorothy Browne, cited in Sidney Brammer, "My Old Man," *Texas Observer*, April 21, 1995, 22.
245 *He loved to go shopping*: Dorothy Browne, cited in Ronnie Dugger, "To a Novelist Dying Young," *Washington Post*, June 18, 1978, F3.
245 *scary as shit*; *witches in* Macbeth: Browne interview.
245 *father was, as I understand*: Jay Dunston Milner, *Confessions of a Maddog: A Romp through the High-Flying Texas Music and Literary Era of the Fifties to the Seventies* (Denton: University of North Texas Press, 1998), 83.
246 *bawdy laugh*: Celia Morris, *Finding Celia's Place* (College Station: Texas A&M University Press, 2000), 117.

246 *fuckists*: Larry McMurtry, *All My Friends Are Going to Be Strangers* (New York: Simon and Schuster, 1972), 7.

246 *decided it would make a most*: Milner, *Confessions of a Maddog*, 84.

246 *I can just imagine Dorothy's*: Ibid.

247 *Billy just couldn't believe it*: Dorothy Browne, cited in Steven L. Davis, *Texas Literary Outlaws: Six Writers in the Sixties and Beyond* (Fort Worth: TCU Press, 2004), 149.

247 *upset about Fenstemaker*: Browne interview.

247 *What really hurt me*: Brammer, cited in Bruce Jackson, *Disorderly Conduct* (Urbana-Champaign: University of Illinois Press, 1992), xv.

247 *abortion services*: For a full account of Johnson's handling of the Bobby Baker scandals, see Michael Beschloss, *Reaching for Glory: Lyndon Johnson's Secret White House Tapes, 1964–1965* (New York: Simon and Schuster, 2001).

247 *Walter Jenkins*: Ibid.

247 *any reporter could be bought*: Nadine Eckhardt, interview by the author, December 5, 2014.

247 *grating*; *Was there another country*: Harry McPherson, *A Political Education: A Washington Memoir* (Boston: Houghton Mifflin, 1988), 259–260.

247 *put[ting] out these mean books*: Lyndon Johnson, cited in Beschloss, *Reaching for Glory*, 117.

248 *LBJ character . . . warmly*: "Fenstemaker for President," *Time*, August 21, 1964, copy in Billy Lee Brammer Papers, Southwest Writers Collection, Texas State University, San Marcos; hereafter cited as Brammer Papers.

248 *Sort of*: Browne interview.

248 *Few men in our history*: William Brammer, "Don't Fence Him In," *Book Week*, March 29, 1964, Brammer Papers.

249 *I thought it was boring*: Browne interview.

249 *He figured if he was going*: Ibid.

249 *Oh, I tried everything*: Dorothy Browne, cited in Dugger, "To a Novelist Dying Young," F4.

250 *All my money?*: Bob Simmons, "Bud Shrake, 77: This Texas Tall Tale Is a Literary Legend," *Rag Blog*, May 11, 2004, theragblog.com/bud-shrake-77-this-texas-tall-tale-is-a-literary-legend.

250 *Leary in a white robe*: Bud Shrake, cited in Davis, *Texas Literary Outlaws*, 147.

250 *We would sleep at his apartment*: Sidney Brammer to the author, e-mail, January 19, 2015.

250 *wanted to see, smell, feel, and do*: Nadine Eckhardt, cited in Dugger, "To a Novelist Dying Young," F4.

250 *If Bob and I had been mature*: Nadine Eckhardt, *Duchess of Palms* (Austin: University of Texas Press, 2009), 63.

250 *Bob and I were proceeding*: Ibid., 66.

251 *flower child*: Milner, *Confessions of a Maddog*, 77–78.

251 *wasn't a bunch of spaced-out*: Ibid., 76.

251 *Next to the candy dish* and all other quotations from "White Collar Pill Party": Bruce Jackson, "White Collar Pill Party," *Atlantic*, August 1966, 35–37. Brammer is not named in the piece, and the setting is fictionalized, but Dorothy Browne affirmed in an interview with the author on April 16, 2015, that the article describes a party at Brammer's apartment.

252 *You'd better research the hell*: Bill Brammer, cited in ibid., 37.

253 *We were there for a month* and all other quotations from Claudette Lowe: Claudette Lowe, interview by the author, April 16, 2015.

253 *I had written Bill a letter*: Hugh Lowe, interview by the author, April 16, 2015.

253 *A gram of dextroamphetamine*: Jackson, "White Collar Pill Party."

253 *He couldn't speak Spanish*: Claudette Lowe interview.

253 *He was a real word player*: Hugh Lowe interview.

253 *The people were dragging every*: Ibid.

254 *The high-intensity presence*: Robert Stone, *Prime Green: Remembering the Sixties* (New York: Harper Perennial, 2007), 153–154.

254 *It was impossible to tell*: Ibid., 158.

255 *Just in case you didn't*: James Silberman to Billy Lee Brammer, November 4, 1964, Brammer Papers.

255 *I'm going to be the President*: Lyndon Johnson, cited in Robert Dallek, *Flawed Giant: Lyndon Johnson and His Times, 1961–1973* (New York: Oxford University Press, 1998), 112.

255 *Whatever your views are*: Ibid., 183.

255 *a highlight*: Billy Lee Brammer, cited in William E. Leuchtenburg, *The White House Looks South: Franklin D. Roosevelt, Harry S. Truman, and Lyndon B. Johnson* (Baton Rouge: LSU Press, 2005), 322.

255 *toward some distant vision*: Richard Goodwin, cited in Dallek, *Flawed Giant*, 80.

255 *We entered the pool area*: Ibid.

256 *For a century*: Lyndon Johnson, cited in ibid., 81–82.

## 17.

257 *We were one*; *Our expectations were too high*: Robert Stone, *Prime Green: Remembering the Sixties* (New York: Harper Perennial, 2007), 228–229.

257 *a higher sensibility*: Novalis, cited in Marcus Boon, *The Road of Excess: A History of Writers on Drugs* (Cambridge, MA: Harvard University Press, 2002), 28–29.

257 *sympathetic ink*: Thomas De Quincey, cited in ibid., 40.

258 *My dear Théophile*: Fernand Boissard, cited in ibid., 134.

258 *I miss . . . football*: Billy Lee Brammer, cited in Ronnie Dugger, "To a Novelist Dying Young," *Washington Post*, June 18, 1978, F4.

258 *walked right into a speed crowd*: Chet Helms, cited in Alice Echols, *Scars of Sweet Paradise: The Life and Times of Janis Joplin* (New York: Owl, 1999), 77.

258 *We thought we were growing*: Linda Gottfried, cited in ibid.

258 *made a particular kind of art*: Diane di Prima, cited in ibid., 77–78.

258 *A lot of artists have*: Janis Joplin, cited in ibid., 78.

258 *She gave me all this propaganda*: Dave Moriaty, cited in ibid., 95.

258 *She* still *looked different*: Ibid., 111–112.

259 *will herself to be*: Ibid.

259 *The different threads of the underground*: Ben Graham, *A Gathering of Promises: The Battle for Texas's Psychedelic Music, from the 13th Floor Elevators to the Black Angels and Beyond* (Winchester, UK: Zero, 2015), 93.

259 *Close your eyes and stick out*: Bill Brammer, cited in Al Reinert, interview by the author, April 15, 2015.

259 *I still don't know Bill's*: Madeleine Villatorro, interview by the author, May 19, 2015.

259 *social swirl*: Henry Wallace to the author, e-mail, February 16, 2015.

259 *landed like an electrical pulse*: Ed Guinn, interview by the author, June 1, 2015.

260 *Billy Lee was a good*: Ibid.

260 *Billy Lee was incredible*: Tary Owens, cited in Brad Buchholz, "Tary's Tale: In the Face of Mortality, a Story of Music, Drugs and Making Things Right," *Austin American-Statesman*, March 26, 2000, available at maryannprice .com/tale.html.

260 *He was married to Dorothy*: Villatorro interview.

260 *He would do this thing*: Dorothy Browne, cited in Paul Cullum, draft of "The Second Act," 13, Billy Lee Brammer Papers, Southwest Writers Collection, Texas State University, San Marcos; hereafter cited as Brammer Papers.

260 *to live means to spend*: Honoré de Balzac, cited in Boon, *Road of Excess*, 174.

260 *I'd wake up*: Dorothy Browne, cited in Cullum, "The Second Act," 8.

260 *a kind of new nitpicking disease*: Billy Lee Brammer, cited in ibid., 8.

261 *Writing is just so murderously hard*: Billy Lee Brammer, cited in Larry L. King to Leonard Saunders, July 24, 1966, Larry L. King Papers, Southwest Writers Collection, Texas State University, San Marcos.

261 *When I was thirteen*: Sidney Brammer to the author, e-mail, January 19, 2015.

261 *If they didn't like the president*: Al Kooper, cited in Michael Corcoran, "Didja Know? Dylan and the Band Debuted in Austin 9/24/65," September 2005, available at michaelcorcoran.net/archives/894.

261 *got it*: Bob Dylan, cited in ibid.

261 *down South*: Levon Helm, cited at "Paul's Freewheelin' Bob Dylan Page," https://www.prismnet.com/~superego/dylanlists.html.

262 *It was so in-your-face*: Angus Wynne, cited in Corcoran, "Didja Know?"

262 *power of electric music*: Powell St. John, cited in Graham, *Gathering of Promises*, 67.

262 *often surly*: Jan Reid, *The Improbable Rise of Redneck Rock* (New York: Da Capo, 1977), 33.

262 *You're all just a bunch*: Sid Vicious, cited in Jerry Jeff Walker and Susan Walker, interview by the author, April 15, 2015.

263 *psychedelic rock*: Graham, *Gathering of Promises*, 84.

263 *were the natural descendants*: Paul Drummond, *Eye Mind: The Saga of Rocky Erickson and the 13th Floor Elevators, the Pioneers of Psychedelic Sound* (Los Angeles: Process Media, 2007), 9.

263 *They decided it was time*: Ed Guinn, cited in Barry Shank, *Dissonant Identities: The Rock 'n' roll Scene in Austin, Texas* (Hanover, NH: University Press of New England, 1994), 44.

264 *I felt no need*: Ibid., 45.

264 *It worked*: Ibid., 46–47.

264 *In 1955*: Harvey Gann, cited in Drummond, *Eye Mind*, 38.

264 *Jack Kerouac crowd*: Burt Gerding, cited in Thorne Dreyer, "The Spies of Texas," *Texas Observer*, November 17, 2006, texasobserver.or/2343-the-spies-of-texas-newfound-files-detail-how-ut-austin-police-tracked-the-lives-of-sixties-dissidents.

264 *Nobody gave a fuck*: Wallace to the author, February 16, 2015.

265 *Onward through the fog!*: Ibid.

265 *enemy*: Burt Gerding, cited in Dreyer, "Spies of Texas."

265 *The eyes of Texas*: Guinn interview.

265 *electrical violations*: Jerry Jeff Walker, interview by the author, April 15, 2015.

265 *always an anticommercial scene*: Jim Franklin, cited in Shank, *Dissonant Identities*, 65.

266 *I'm the first hippie pin-up*: Janis Joplin, cited in Buchholz, "Tary's Tale."

266 *There was a strong Austin*: Willie Nelson and Bud Shrake, excerpt from *Willie: An Autobiography*, in Bud Shrake, *Land of the Permanent Wave: An Edwin "Bud" Shrake Reader*, ed. Steven L. Davis (Austin: University of Texas Press, 2008), 176.

266 *Much that would be celebrated*: Graham, *Gathering of Promises*, 258–259.

266 *We went out there and played*: Bob Brown, cited in Reid, *Redneck Rock*, 40.

266 *Haight Street smelled like piss*: Ibid., 39.

266 *We found out that*: Powell St. John, cited in Graham, *Gathering of Promises*, 83.

267 *college frat boys*: Clementine Hall, cited in ibid., 79–80.

267 *From then on*: Dorothy Browne, interview by the author, April 16, 2015.

267 *Since he was always a little*: Sidney Brammer to the author, e-mail, January 19, 2015.

267 *Bill had never paid the tuition*: Nadine Eckhardt, *Duchess of Palms* (Austin: University of Texas Press, 2009), 67.

268 *I couldn't stay mad at him*: Sidney Brammer, interview by the author, December 6, 2014.

268 *cheapskate*: Ibid.

268 *remained upset about our marriage*: Eckhardt, *Duchess of Palms*, 66.

268 *Bob certainly needed my emotional support*: Ibid., 67.

269 *That certainly is cheerful news*: James Silberman to Billy Lee Brammer, February 11, 1965, Brammer Papers.

269 *letter of introduction*; *an Rx for heart medicine*; *didn't make no grabs*: Bud Shrake to Billy Lee Brammer, n.d. [1965], ibid.

269 *We trained in southern California*: Peter Gent, foreword to *North Dallas Forty*, thirtieth-anniversary ed. (Toronto: Sport Media, 2003), n.p.

269 *promised to introduce us*: Billy Lee Brammer, cited in Gary Cartwright, *The Best I Recall: A Memoir* (Austin: University of Texas Press, 2015), 63.

269 *We're tired*; *Cops treat black people*: Ibid., 64.

270 *We let the devil*: Ibid.

270 *There's a sniper*: Pamela Colloff, "96 Minutes," *Texas Monthly*, August 2006, texasmonthly.com/articles/96-minutes.

270 *imposing his will*; *What if I had exposed you*: Billy Lee Brammer to Dorothy Browne, n.d., Brammer Papers.

271 *It's one of the moves*: Browne interview.

271 *He made up this thing*: Ibid.

271 *consulting with this shrink*: Billy Lee Brammer to Dorothy Browne, postcard, n.d. [1965], Brammer Papers.

271 *Women generally look for weakness*: Billy Lee Brammer, notebook entry, n.d. [1965], Brammer Papers.

271 *Shrake scares hell*: Ibid.

271 *You may grow old*: Billy Lee Brammer, quotation from T. H. White, ibid.

272 *He did two things for us*: Guinn interview.

272 *great stacks of paper*: Bud Shrake, cited in Steven L. Davis, *Texas Literary Outlaws: Six Writers in the Sixties and Beyond* (Fort Worth: TCU Press, 2004), 190.

272 *check dated*: Nadine Eckhardt, ledger entries dated April 1967, Nadine Eckhardt Papers, Southwest Writers Collection, Texas State University, San Marcos; hereafter cited as Eckhardt Papers.

272 *has disappeared into Texas Limbo*: Davis, *Texas Literary Outlaws*, 190–191.

273 *I was head of the PR department*: Hugh Lowe, interview by the author, April 6, 2015.

273 *I came back, tail between legs*: Browne interview.

273 *I found [it to be] a most interesting*: John Lunk Kriken, oral history interview by Suzanne Riess, 30–31, Ryerson and Burnham Libraries, Art Institute of Chicago, http://digital-libraries.saic.edu/cdm/ref/collection/caohp/id/18073.

273 *most interesting group of people*: Ibid., 31–33.

273 *A really remarkable character*: John Kriken, interview by the author, February 3, 2015.

273 *The door opened and there*: Lonn Taylor, interview by the author, January 21, 2015.

274 *job was to write proposals*: Lonn Taylor, "Rambling Boy: Lionel Sosa and HemisFair," *Big Bend Now*, April 19, 2012, bigbendnow.com/2012/04/rambling-boy-lionel-sosa-and-hemisfair.

274 *regularly received packages containing*: Ibid.

274 *Pavilion de Dope Fiend*: Davis, *Texas Literary Outlaws*, 191.

274 *a bunch of us were listening*: Browne interview.

275 *Ken called*: Larry McMurtry, "Stark Gets Off the Bus," in *Spit in the Ocean #7*, ed. Ed McClanahan (New York: Penguin, 2003), 104–106, available at "The Magic Bus," cathryncasamo.com/themagicbus1.htm.

275 *every cop in Bexar County*: Browne interview.

275 *we were dropped off*: Sidney Brammer, "My Old Man," *Texas Observer*, April 21, 1995, 20.

276 *I . . . set [Brammer] up in a cottage*: John Korty to the author, e-mail, December 13, 2014.

276 *He wanted to make this movie*: Browne interview.

276 *We [my film company and I]*: Korty to the author, December 13, 2014.

276 *Korty and Billy Lee*: Dorothy Browne interview.

276 *It was really heavy-handed*: Ibid.

277 *a variety of woodwind reeds*: Kevin Opstedal, "A Totally Symbolic Location," in "Dreaming as One: Poetry, Poets and Community in Bolinas, California, 1967–1980," posted at bigbridge.org/bol-02.htm.

277 *To be right*: Kevin Opstedal, "The Bolinas Hit," in ibid., posted at bigbridge.org/bol-03.htm.

277 *Editor at Sea*: J. David Moriaty, publisher, *The Rip Off Review of Western Culture #1*, June–July 1972.

278 *The Hippie Cult*: *Saturday Evening Post* cover, September 23, 1967.

278 *My motivation*: Chet Helms, cited in Ben Fong-Torres, "Love is Just a Song We Sing but a Contract is Something Else: A Discordant History of the San Francisco Sound," *Rolling Stone*, February 26, 1976, www.rollingstone.com/music/features/love-is-just-a-song-we-sing-but-a-contract-is-something-else-a-discordant-history-of-the-san-francisco-sound-19760226.

278 *famous arthur*; *cultural jewel*: Bob Simmons to the author, e-mail, February 25, 2015.

279 *total experience theater*: Ibid.

279 *Of course, Billy Lee*: Browne interview.

279 *Bill wasn't really managing anything*: Simmons to the author, February 25, 2015.

279 *I remember how embarrassed we were*: Ibid.

280 *Often, money disappeared*: Ibid.

280 *in the heart of a*: Bob Simmons to the author, February 25, 2015.

280 *It's really amazing*: Bill Brammer, cited in ibid.

280 *his nice VW*: Simmons to the author, February 25, 2015.

281 *We want the world*: For a full account of the Doors' show at the Denver Family Dog on December 31, 1967, see the post by Jim Parker on the website The Doors: Collective Archives and Online Marketplace, mildequator.com /performancehistory/concertinfo/1967/671231.html.

281 *The Democratic Party's goal*: Bob Eckhardt, cited in Gary A. Keith, *Eckhardt: There Once Was a Congressman from Texas* (Austin: University of Texas Press, 2007), 197–198.

281 *[Voters] demand that I demean myself*: Ibid., 170.

281 *I believed in my heart*: Eckhardt, *Duchess of Palms*, 71.

282 *For God's sake*: Keith, *Eckhardt*, 34.

282 *nuts*: Eckhardt, *Duchess of Palms*, 68.

282 *Before Congress convened* and all other quotations from Nadine Eckhardt in this paragraph: Ibid., 69.

282 *legislative entrepreneur*: Keith, *Eckhardt*, 204.

282 *Too little . . . legislation*: Bob Eckhardt, cited in ibid.

282 *Congress is set up*: Eckhardt, *Duchess of Palms*, 71–72.

283 *LBJ liked to party*: Ibid., 78.

283 *He's a* bred *congressman*: Lyndon Johnson, cited in ibid., 69.

283 *You act like you like*: Ibid., 77.

283 *previous incarnation*: Eckhardt, *Duchess of Palms*, 77.

18.

284 *I want a friendly book*: Lyndon Johnson, cited in Ronnie Dugger, *The Politician: The Life and Times of Lyndon Johnson* (Old Saybrook, CT: Konecky & Konecky, 1982), 16.

284 *Don't you understand*: Doris Kearns Goodwin, *Lyndon Johnson and the American Dream* (New York: St. Martin's, 1991 [1976]), iv.

284 *I've decided to do some teaching*: Lyndon Johnson, cited in ibid., vi.

285 *Leading [me] through the White House*: Dugger, *Politician*, 21.

285 *We killed Diem*: Lyndon Johnson, cited in ibid.

285 *He takes one step*: Ibid., 21–22.

285 *blank-faced boy*; *hoisting himself*: Dugger, *Politician*, 22.

285 *We killed Diem*: Lyndon Johnson, cited in ibid.

285 *No deal*: Dugger, *Politician*, 16.

286 *I knew I wasn't*: Ibid., 23–24.

286 *I know exactly*: Lyndon Johnson, cited in ibid., 23–24.

286 *The USA will come together*: Steven L. Davis, *Texas Literary Outlaws: Six Writers in the Sixties and Beyond* (Fort Worth: TCU Press, 2004), 229.

286 *dirty hippies*: David Richards, *Once Upon a Time in Texas: A Liberal in the Lone Star State* (Austin: University of Texas Press, 2002), 128.

286 BIG FUCKIN' DEAL: Ibid., 130.

286 *I am involved in political work*: Ibid., 133–134.

287 *Of course, by the time*: Ibid., 135.

287 *The 13th Floor Elevators*: Tary Owens cited in Brad Buchholz, "Tary's Tale: In the Face of Mortality, a Story of Music, Drugs and Making Things Right," *Austin American-Statesman*, March 26, 2000, available at maryannprice.com/tale.html.

287 *We didn't feel like we*: Bob Brown, cited in Jan Reid, *The Improbable Rise of Redneck Rock* (New York: Da Capo, 1977), 44.

288 *Pathetic State of Texas Liberalism*: Richards, *Once Upon a Time in Texas*, 126.

288 *corruption of the Texas Liberals*: Ronnie Dugger, "Observation," *Texas Observer*, November 11, 1966, 11.

288 *When we got back from Colorado*: Dorothy Browne, interview by the author, April 16, 2015.

288 *earlobes [were] on fire* and all other quotations from Larry L. King anecdote: Larry L. King, "The Best Little Whorehouse in Texas," in *Of Outlaws, Con Men, Whores, Politicians, and Other Artists* (New York: Viking, 1980), 96–98. King changes the names of the people involved, but Al Reinert confirmed to the author that the events described pertain to Brammer and his friends.

288 *You know and I know*: Larry L. King to Billy Lee Brammer, September 8, 1968, Larry L. King Papers, Southwest Writers Collection, Texas State University, San Marcos.

289 *These guys who'd gotten rich*: Sidney Brammer, interview by the author, December 6, 2014.

289 *I am sure we will not*: Darrell Royal, cited in Davis, *Texas Literary Outlaws*, 208.

289 *I recognized [my bust]*: Gary Cartwright, cited in ibid., 211.

289 *Now then golly goddam*: Billy Lee Brammer, "Is There Life after Meth?," rough draft, n.d., Billy Lee Brammer Papers, Southwest Writers Collection, Texas State University, San Marcos; hereafter cited as Brammer Papers.

290 *It's possible . . . that America*: Billy Lee Brammer, "Apocalypse Now," *Texas Observer*, November 1, 1968, 8–10.

290 *The plain hairy fact is*: Billy Lee Brammer, notebook entry, n.d. [1968], Brammer Papers.

290 *Midafternoon dope*: Ibid.

290 *heightened perception*; *Anybody who has faced up*; *Suddenly I am aware* and all subsequent notebook entries: Ibid.

291 *You have to work at*: Nadine Eckhardt, cited in Myra MacPherson, *The Power Lovers: An Intimate Look at Politicians and Their Marriages* (New York: Putnam's Sons, 1975), 116.

291 *Alice B. Toklas brownies*; *some of those God-awful functions*: Ibid., 78.

291 *You sit between some little*: Ibid., 390.

291 *Congressmen make the worst Daddies*: Ibid., 393.

291 *Good, supportive wives* and all subsequent dialogue between Nadine and Bob Eckhardt, unless otherwise noted: Ibid., 392–394.

291 *the Congressman*: Nadine Eckhardt, *Duchess of Palms* (Austin: University of Texas Press, 2009), 73.

291–292 *We were moved around so much*: Sidney Brammer interview.

292 *we might have been the only*: Sidney Brammer, "My Old Man," *Texas Observer*, April 21, 1995, 22.

292 *Bill would send us posters*: Sidney Brammer to the author, e-mail, January 19, 2015.

292 *He had these reel-to-reel tapes*: Shelby Brammer, interview by the author, December 5, 2015.

292 *a box of eight-track tapes*: Willie Brammer, interview by the author, April 15, 2015.

292 *He was always offering knowledge*: Shelby Brammer interview.

292 *It seemed so sleepy*: Willie Brammer interview.

292 *Look, kids, it's the evil stepmother!*: Billy Lee Brammer, cited in Jan Reid, "Return to *The Gay Place*," *Texas Monthly*, March 2001, texasmonthly.com /the-culture/return-gay-place.

292 *Willie's little hands*: Sidney Brammer interview.

293 *When he was with you*: Shelby Brammer interview.

293 *something was wrong*: Sidney Brammer, cited in Reid, "Return to *The Gay Place*."

293 *Nadine liked brilliant, rather passive*: Sidney Brammer interview.

293 *Nadine also liked* power: Ibid.

293 *Jim Rowe*: Eckhardt, *Duchess of Palms*, 85.

293 *seemed sad and tired*: Ibid., 82.

293 *I knew the Congress as well*: Lyndon Johnson, cited in Goodwin, *Johnson and the American Dream*, 282–283.

293 *who had a rifle in one hand*: Ibid.: 283.

294 *big daddy*: Eckhardt, *Duchess of Palms*, 82.

294 *The leaders of our country*: Ibid.

294 *It is absurd to say*: Billy Lee Brammer, notebook entry, n.d. [1968], Brammer Papers.

294 *Johnson confided to Doris Kearns*: Goodwin, *Johnson and the American Dream*, 342.

295 *he loved the sound*: Ibid., viii.

295 *One day, Jay Milner*: Jay Dunston Milner, *Confessions of a Maddog: A Romp through the High-Flying Texas Music and Literary Era of the Fifties to the Seventies* (Denton: University of North Texas Press, 1998), 95.

295 *Commies were right*: Billy Lee Brammer, notebook entry, n.d. [1968], Billy Lee Brammer Papers.

295 *How in the hell can*: Lyndon Johnson, cited in Goodwin, *Johnson and the American Dream*, 332.

295 *I just don't understand*: Ibid., 333–334.

295 *Early on*: Sidney Brammer interview.

295 *You know when I first thought*: Eugene McCarthy, cited in Goodwin, *Johnson and the American Dream*, 338.

296 *The war poisons the wellsprings*; *Our commitment is to humanity*: Gary A. Keith, *Eckhardt: There Once Was a Congressman from Texas* (Austin: University of Texas Press, 2007), 219.

296 *reclaim the throne*: Goodwin, *Johnson and the American Dream*, 343.

296 *How is it possible*: Lyndon Johnson, cited in ibid., 340.

296 *This country's ultimate strength*: Ibid., 348–349.

297 *Everything we've gained*: Lyndon Johnson, cited in Robert Dallek, *Flawed Giant: Lyndon Johnson and His Times, 1961–1973* (New York: Oxford University Press, 1998), 533.

297 *You southern boys*: Celia Morris, cited in Keith, *Eckhardt*, 221.

297 *We found ourselves surrounded*: Eckhardt, *Duchess of Palms*, 80.

298 *Those people out there*: Lyndon Johnson, cited in ibid., 83.

298 *Bill and I met Arthur*: Browne interview.

298 *Ah, my god*: Billy Lee Brammer to Dorothy Browne, n.d. [1968], Brammer Papers.

299 *sick society*: Dallek, *Flawed Giant*, 548.

299 *stopped work*: Ibid.

299 *It would have been hard*: Goodwin, *Johnson and the American Dream*, 350.

299 *nation watched in horror*: Eckhardt, *Duchess of Palms*, 85.

299 *I thought, Screw this*: Sidney Brammer interview.

299 *resident intellectual*: Harry McPherson, *A Political Education: A Washington Memoir* (Boston: Houghton Mifflin, 1988), 270–271.

300 *More than any other modern*: Al Reinert, "Billy Lee," *Texas Monthly*, February 1979, texasmonthly.com/politics/billy-lee.

300 *from beginning to end*: Lyndon Johnson, cited in Goodwin, *Johnson and the American Dream*, xiii.

300 *Of course I will*: Doris Kearns, cited in ibid.

300 *Now you take care of yourself*: Lyndon Johnson, cited in ibid., xiii–xiv.

300 *Listen*: Ibid., i.

300 *no matter what I say*: Ibid., 357.

300 *would rather be doing anything else*: Ibid., xiv.

301 *Anyone out there hear America*: Billy Lee Brammer, notebook entry, n.d. [1968–1969], Brammer Papers.

## 19.

305 *I saw that he'd gotten old*: Sidney Brammer, interview by the author, December 6, 2014.

305 *wore down*: Sidney Brammer, "My Old Man," *Texas Observer*, April 21, 1995, 22.

306 *He says he has written*: Elizabeth McKee to Herman Gollob, December 29,

1970, Billy Lee Brammer Papers, Southwest Writers Collection, Texas State University, San Marcos; hereafter cited as Brammer Papers.

306 *claims he is in truth*: Bud Shrake to Larry L. King, August 1, 1969, Larry L. King Papers, Southwest Writers Collection, Texas State University, San Marcos; hereafter cited as King Papers.

306 *Some believe that Bill's greatest*: Sidney Brammer, "My Old Man," 22.

307 *The only interested people*: Jan Reid, *The Improbable Rise of Redneck Rock* (New York: Da Capo, 1974), 45.

307 *run off to Mexico*: Jay Dunston Milner, *Confessions of a Maddog: A Romp through the High-Flying Texas Music and Literary Era of the Fifties to the Seventies* (Denton: University of North Texas Press, 1998), 84–85.

307 *our Norman Mailer*: Ibid., 94.

307 *had drawing power*: Ibid., 85.

308 *It was incredible*: Dorothy Browne, interview by the author, April 16, 2015.

308 *heart medicine*; *jackoff landlord*; and all other quotations from Bill Brammer in this paragraph: Billy Lee Brammer to Dorothy Browne, August 11, 1969, Brammer Papers.

309 *nourish[ing] desperate desires*: Peter Gent, foreword to *North Dallas Forty*, thirtieth-anniversary ed. (Toronto: Sport Media, 2003), n.p.

309 *livers, kidneys, and spines*: Ibid.

309 *gave all the rookies*: Ibid.

309 *Billie seems serious*: Jay Milner to Larry L. King, August 11, 1969, King Papers.

309 *glum landscape*: Billy Lee Brammer to Dorothy Browne, August 1969, Brammer Papers.

310 *heavy cats like Janis*: Ibid.

310 *barely post-pubescent*: Ibid.

310 *a gathering place for the*: Ibid.

310 *The door was just literally open*: Sidney Brammer interview.

310 *female art major*: Gent, *North Dallas Forty*, 95.

310 *alone in the front room*: Ibid.

311 *He was wonderful*: Browne interview.

311 *[H]e'd come into class*: Dorothy Browne, cited in Ronnie Dugger, "To a Novelist Dying Young," *Washington Post*, June 18, 1978, F3.

311 *We were crammed* and all subsequent quotations from Max Woodfin: Max Woodfin, interview by the author, February 5, 2015.

312 *We exchanged cosmic resolutions*: Milner, *Confessions of a Maddog*, 87.

312 *league that never disappoints*; *everything that's wrong*: Gent, foreword to *North Dallas Forty*, n.p.

313 *In our hearts*: Milner, *Confessions of a Maddog*, 87.

313 *Billie keeps asking me*: Jay Milner to Larry L. King, January 13, 1970, King Papers.

313 *entered upon a renaissance*: Milner, *Confessions of a Maddog*, 88.

313 *bright lights*: Roy Hamric, "Authors Take Over Journalism at SMU," *Dallas Morning News*, January 5, 1970, sec. D.

313 *Teaching is the best thing*: Billy Lee Brammer, notebook entry, n.d. [1970], Brammer Papers.

314 *I don't know exactly*: Milner, *Confessions of a Maddog*, 88.

314 *A politician sensitive*: Billy Lee Brammer to Dorothy Browne, n.d. [1970], Brammer Papers.

315 *I personally know*: Milner, *Confessions of a Maddog*, 94.

315 *although he grumbled*: Ibid., 89.

315 *pretty, pleasant*: Billy Lee Brammer to Jay Milner, October 18, 1970, cited in ibid., 90.

316 *Oh. You're the ones*: Billy Lee Brammer, notebook entry, n.d. [1970], Brammer Papers.

316 *I just wanted to look good*: Janis Joplin, cited in "Goodbye, Janis Joplin," *Rolling Stone*, October 29, 1970, rollingstone.com/music/news/goodbye-janis-joplin-19701029.

316 *She seemed cheerful*: Chet Helms, cited in ibid.

316 *wonderful old gal*: Kenneth Threadgill, cited in ibid.

316 *rocky roll*: Billy Lee Brammer, notebook entry on the music of Doug Sahm, n.d. [1970], Brammer Papers.

316–317 *Bowling Green is somewhere*: Billy Lee Brammer to Jay Milner, October 18, 1970, cited in Milner, *Confessions of a Maddog*, 91.

317 *Rotter-in-Residence*: Ibid., 93.

317 *Should I put off college*: Sidney Brammer interview.

317 *You're currently living through*: Billy Lee Brammer to Sidney Brammer, October 28, 1970, Brammer Papers.

318 *straight crystal methedrine*: Al Reinert, "Billy Lee," *Texas Monthly*, February 1979, texasmonthly.com/politics/billy-lee.

318 *who the hell was showing movies*: Jay Milner to Larry L. King, February 1, 1971, King Papers.

318 *Oh my god, she's got*: Sidney Brammer interview.

318 *cool*: Ibid.

319 *busted in the company*: Larry L. King to Bud Shrake, March 29, 1971, King Papers.

319 *he was sorry*: Ibid.

319 *No one wants to see*: Jay Milner to Larry L. King, n.d. [1971], King Papers.

319 *have a garage sale*: Sidney Brammer interview.

319 *Starting senior year in college*: Billy Lee Brammer, notebook entry, n.d. [1971], Brammer Papers.

319 *Dope depends*: Ibid.

320 *those who corrupt their own bodies*: Walt Whitman, "I Sing the Body Electric" (1855), available at the Poetry Foundation website, poetryfoundation.org/poems-and-poets/poems/detail/45472.

320 *The spiritual is none*: Billy Lee Brammer, notebook entry, n.d. [1971], Brammer Papers.

320 *sing the body electric*: Whitman, "I Sing the Body Electric."

20.

321 *a curious ritual*: Doris Kearns Goodwin, *Lyndon Johnson and the American Dream* (New York: St. Martin's, 1991 [1976]), xvii.

322 *Political oratory*: Ibid., ix.

322 *I've got an instinct*: Lyndon Johnson, cited in ibid., xvi.

322 *And when she dies*: Ibid., 365.

322 *Rumors were all over Austin*: Al Reinert, "Billy Lee," *Texas Monthly*, February 1979, texasmonthly.com/politics/billy-lee.

322 *It's come to that already*: Billy Lee Brammer, notebook fragment, n.d., Billy Lee Brammer Papers, Southwest Writers Collection, Texas State University, San Marcos; hereafter cited as Brammer Papers.

322 *He collects people*: Warren Woodward, cited in Joe Phipps, *Summer Stock: Behind the Scenes with LBJ in '48* (Fort Worth: TCU Press, 1992), 335.

322 *Back in Austin*: Shelby Brammer, interview by the author, December 5, 2014.

322 *desire to become a peaceful*: Probation notice, n.d., Billy Lee Brammer Papers.

323 *the antiwar demonstrators*: Gail Caldwell, *A Strong West Wind* (New York: Random House, 2006), 62–63.

323 By God, *I wish we*: Julian Bond, cited in Jan Reid, *The Improbable Rise of Redneck Rock* (New York: Da Capo, 1974), 95.

323 *The progress has been much*: Lyndon Johnson, cited in Felicia Coates, Harriet Howle, William Broyles, Dave McNeely, and Bill Brammer, "Briar Patch," *Texas Monthly*, February 1973, texasmonthly.com/articles/briar-patch-11.

323 *had something of the air*: Ibid.

323 *It remained . . . for Mr. Johnson*: Ibid.

323 *was in a mellow mood*: Ibid.

324 *President Johnson*: Ibid.

324 *The only person*: Ibid.

324 *Hidy. Got any speed*: Bill Brammer, cited in Sidney Brammer, interview by the author, December 6, 2014.

324 *He was shooting crystal Methedrine*: Reinert, "Billy Lee."

325 *One of the more improbable figures*: David Richards, *Once Upon a Time: A Liberal in the Lone Star State* (Austin: University of Texas Press, 2002), 83.

325 *could be passed out*: Sidney Brammer, cited in Ronnie Dugger, "To a Novelist Dying Young," *Washington Post*, June 18, 1978, F5.

325 *endless love and gentle schizophrenia*: Cited in Sidney Brammer interview.

325 *That's him:* Sidney Brammer interview.

325 *Honey, please don't worry about me*: Sidney Brammer interview.

325 *Stop being an overachiever*: Sidney Brammer, "My Old Man," *Texas Observer*, April 21, 1995, 21.

325 *marvelously happy*: Nadine Eckhardt, cited in Dugger, "To a Novelist Dying Young," F4.

325 *Nothing turns one sour*: Billy Lee Brammer, notebook entry, n.d. [1972], Brammer Papers.

326 *freaked out*: Susan Walker, interview with the author, April 15, 2015.

326 *Billy was afraid*: Ibid.

326 *lovely sense of humor*; *didn't bullshit*: Shelby Brammer interview.

326 *had a cool dad*: Ibid.

326 *He* did *steal*: Ibid.

326 *forgetful*; *nicer*: Willie Eckhardt, cited in Myra MacPherson, *The Power Lovers: An Intimate Look at Politicians and Their Marriages* (New York: Putnam's Sons, 1975), 394–395.

326 *None of that*: Nadine Eckhardt, cited in ibid., 390.

327 *he didn't drink until 5 p.m.*: Nadine Eckhardt, *Duchess of Palms* (Austin: University of Texas Press, 2009), 74.

327 *How I had the time*: Ibid., 85.

327 *If Bob had not been*: Molly Ivins, cited in ibid., 89.

327 *one of the Supreme Court justices*: Susan Walker interview.

327 *I am exhausted*: Eckhardt, *Duchess of Palms*, 97.

327 *I became close friends*: Richard West to the author, e-mail, March 25, 2015.

327 *several eye-opening episodes*: Willie Eckhardt, interview by the author, April 15, 2015.

327 *Was* I *there*; *Sort of*: Susan Walker interview; Willie Eckhardt interview.

327 *convinced that my state*: "Organizational History," *Texas Monthly* Magazine Archives, Wittliff Collections, Texas State University, San Marcos, available at thewittliffcollections.txstate.edu/research/a-z/txmonthly.html.

328 *Neither Bill [Broyles] nor I*: Greg Curtis, interview by the author, April 15, 2015.

328 *Brammer was the second person*: William Broyles, foreword to Billy Lee Brammer, *The Gay Place* (Austin: Texas Monthly Press, 1978), ii.

328 *Billy Lee really* had *done*: Curtis interview.

328 *Billy was that which he'd*: Reinert, "Billy Lee."

328 *I had been a cub*: Al Reinert, interview by the author, March 9, 2015.

328 *We had a sort of bullpen*: Curtis interview.

328 *It became clear*: Ibid.

329 *for an eye appointment*: Ibid.

329 *He could sit for an hour*: Broyles, foreword to *The Gay Place*, iii.

329 *Eddie Wilson*: Willie Nelson, excerpt from *Willie: An Autobiography*, in Bud Shrake, *Land of the Permanent Wave: A Bud Shrake Reader*, ed. Steven L. Davis (Austin: University of Texas Press, 2008), 179.

330 *Bud Shrake explained*: Ben Graham, *A Gathering of Promises: The Battle for Texas's Psychedelic Music, From the 13th Floor Elevators to the Black Angels and Beyond* (Winchester, UK: Zero, 2015), 299.

330 *where the 'necks met the heads*: Jim Franklin, cited in ibid., 302.

330 *Cheap pot and cold beer*: Susan Walker interview.

330 *jangling clash*: Reid, *Redneck Rock*, 102–107.

330 *By the time Ed Guinn*: See Jason Mellard, *Progressive Country: How the 1970s Transformed the Texan in Popular Culture* (Austin: University of Texas Press, 2013), 89.

331 *We'd be out carousing around*: Jerry Jeff Walker, interview by the author, April 15, 2015.

331 *holy madness*; *fantastic threatened*: Caldwell, *Strong West Wind*, 61–62.

331 *not as strong as his*; *had never recovered*; *I was twenty years younger*: Ibid., 74.

332 *Austin knew and understood [Lyndon] Johnson*: Reid, *Redneck Rock*, 95.

332 *unexpected death of a heart attack*: Eckhardt, *Duchess of Palms*, 97.

332 *Steam rising*: Reid, *Redneck Rock*, 95–96.

332 *The weather was miserable*: Ibid., 93.

21.

333 *I conned* Texas Monthly: Al Reinert, interview by the author, March 9, 2015.

333 *I will make my home*: "Agreement to Return," September 26, 1973, Billy Lee Brammer Papers, Southwest Writers Collection, Texas State University, San Marcos; hereafter cited as Brammer Papers.

333 *I suppose I knew*: Reinert interview.

333 *By that time*: Robert Benton, interview by the author, May 6, 2015.

334 *How do you settle within*: Seymour M. Hersh, *The Dark Side of Camelot* (Boston: Little, Brown, 1997), 23.

334 *Absinthe makes the hard grow*: Billy Lee Brammer, notebook entry, n.d. [1973], Brammer Papers.

334 *Elaine's is a pile of shit*: Billy Lee Brammer to Grover Lewis, n.d. [1974], Ibid.

334 *timorous press*: Ibid.

335 *one of those roads*: Jan Reid, *The Improbable Rise of Redneck Rock* (New York: Da Capo, 1974), 311.

335 *It was miserable and great*: Billy Porterfield, cited in Dave Thomas, "The (Almost) Definitive Chronology of Willie's Fourth of July Picnics," *Austin American-Statesman*, May 21, 2012, http://www.austin360.com/entertainment/music/the-almost-definitive-chronology-willie-fourth-july-picnics/epxt0xanBfN3Rv395DbW8J.

335 *writers, lawyers, artists*; *Doing Indefinable Services*; *Everything that is not*: Steven L. Davis, *Texas Literary Outlaws: Six Writers in the Sixties and Beyond* (Fort Worth: TCU Press, 2004), 234–235.

336 *gambling, saloons*: Ibid.

336 *I was not terribly impressed*: Shelby Brammer, interview by the author, December 5, 2014.

336 *I didn't like those people*: Sidney Brammer, interview by the author, December 6, 2014.

336 *One night I dropped by*: Susan Walker, interview by the author, April 15, 2015.

337 *The thing with Orissa*: Shelby Brammer interview.

337 *Author Billy Brammer*: Winston Bode, "Capitol Talk," *Hays County Citizen*, May 15, 1975, 5.

337 *legal fiction*: Bob Eckhardt, cited in Celia Morris, *Finding Celia's Place* (College Station: Texas A&M University Press, 2000), 188.

337 *If you think I'm taking*: Ibid., 189–190.

338 *has had no Homer*: Larry McMurtry, "The Texas Moon, and Elsewhere," *Atlantic*, March 1975, 29.

338 *If I were to choose*: Ibid., 32.

338 *Billy Lee was wounded*: Jan Reid, interview by the author, April 16, 2015.

339 *Has to do with not being afraid*: Billy Lee Brammer, notebook entry, n.d. [1975], Brammer Papers.

339 *In which we trade off* and subsequent quotations regarding the Kearns project: Billy Lee Brammer, "Strategies for Pumpkin Article and Doris Kearns Material," n.d., ibid.

340 *Only then*: Billy Lee Brammer, notebook entry, n.d. [1975], ibid.

340 *who proved to be the subject*: Al Reinert, "Billy Lee," *Texas Monthly*, February 1979, texasmonthly.com/politics/billy-lee.

341 *He was such a trickster*: Nadine Eckhardt, interview by the author, December 5, 2014.

341 *His many friends*: Reinert, "Billy Lee."

341 *It was really important*: Kathy Gunnell, interview by the author, February 24, 2016.

341 *a joint memoir*: Nadine Eckhardt, *Duchess of Palms* (Austin: University of Texas Press, 2009), 101.

342 *it would take some event*: Ibid., 91.

342 *I remember it was a Sunday*: Eckhardt interview.

342 *I told him I would*: Nadine Eckhardt, cited in Ronnie Dugger, "To a Novelist Dying Young," *Washington Post*, June 18, 1978, F4.

342 *He was really like*: Ibid.

342 *What shall we work on*: Ibid.

342–343 *Insulted and angry*: Eckhardt, *Duchess of Palms*, 103.

343 *on the downward slope*: Sidney Brammer, "When Leslie Got the Call," 1, draft provided to the author by Sidney Brammer; final version published in the *Southwest Review* 94, no. 3 (Summer 2009).

343 *no other cultural apparatus*: Ibid.

344 *low-level violence*: Sidney Brammer interview.

344 *talking the libber talk*: Sidney Brammer, "When Leslie Got the Call," 19.

344 *got John laid*: Sidney Brammer interview.

344 *He was surrounded by boxes of his stuff*: Shelby Brammer interview.

344 *He would come around*: Hugh Lowe, interview by the author, April 16, 2015.

344 *table lamps*: Reinert, "Billy Lee."

345 *Billy Lee [was] a fantastic*: Michael Eisenstadt, comments posted November 22, 2007, at "Austin Ghetto List: More Fletcherizing," pairlist.net/pipermail/austin-ghetto-list/20071122/008283.html.

345 *The world we inherited*: Reid, *Redneck Rock*, 339.

345 *American taverns*: Ibid., 335.

346 *From Janis and Threadgill*: Bill Brammer, review from the *Austin Sun*, quoted on the back cover of Reid, *The Improbable Rise of Redneck Rock*.

346 *I'm sure he had dark*: Jan Reid, cited in Paul Cullum, "The Second Act," draft, 13, Brammer Papers.

346 *I was interviewing*: Michael Erard, "Writing around Politics," *Texas Observer*, December 22, 2000.

346 *His friends' refrigerators*: Reinert, "Billy Lee."

347 *I may have been his last*: Anita Howard Wukasch, "The Image of LBJ in Billy Lee Brammer's *The Gay Place*," 3–4, draft of a talk, provided to the author by Nadine Eckhardt.

347 *She will by god*: Billy Lee Brammer, notebook entry, n.d. [1977], Brammer Papers.

347 *crack whore*: Sidney Brammer interview.

347 *set free a malignance*: Billy Lee Brammer, notebook entry, n.d. [1977], Brammer Papers.

347 *He made a perfect dive*: Dorothy Browne, cited in Dugger, "To a Novelist Dying Young," F5.

347 *The part of him*: Sidney Brammer, "My Old Man," *Texas Observer*, April 21, 1995, 20.

347 *I don't know how much*: Shelby Brammer interview.

348 *Next morning*: Sidney Brammer interview.

348 *something kinda bad has happened*: Sidney Brammer, "When Leslie Got the Call," 1.

348 *several bottles of vitamin B-12*: Manley Stevens, cited in Mike Cox, "Former Aide to LBJ Dead," *Austin American-Statesman*, February 19, 1978.

348 *The intelligence of the nation*: Ezra Pound, *The Selected Letters of Ezra Pound, 1907–1941* (New York: New Directions, 1950), xix.

348 *drove around the block*: Sidney Brammer to the author, e-mail, December 14, 2014.

349 *was not [being] upfront*: Ibid.

349 *cops found him*: Ibid.

349 *In his own way*: Reinert, "Billy Lee."

349 *veteran legislators, dope dealers, musicians*: Ibid.

349 *Well, hell, Billie Lee*: Larry L. King, cited in Davis, *Texas Literary Outlaws*, 363.

349 *Billy Lee didn't look like himself*: Shelby Brammer interview.

349 *devastated look*: Sidney Brammer interview.

350 *Brammer was a gentleman*: Marge Hershey, eulogy for Billy Lee Brammer, draft copy in Brammer Papers.

350 *It was a cold and windy day*: Shelby Brammer interview.

EPILOGUE: THE GREAT SOCIETY

351 *Bestowed from birth*: Billy Lee Brammer, note, n.d. [1977], Billy Lee Brammer Papers, Southwest Writers Collection, Texas State University, San Marcos.

351 *No. 1 rule*: Grover Lewis, "Cracker Eden," in *Splendor in the Short Grass: A Grover Lewis Reader*, ed. Jan Reid and W. K. Stratton (Austin: University of Texas Press, 2005), 250.

351 *were streaked with phantasmagoric blight*: Ibid., 251.

352 *It was early in the day*: Ibid., 261–262.

# INDEX